Mail Order Moonlighting

REVISED EDITION

Cecil C. Hoge, Sr.

TEN SPEED PRESS

My Thanks

To my dear wife, Fritzi, and my fine son, Cecil,
for all their years of help.

Adele Pollack, who typed the first manuscript, and
Dolores Layden and Judith Kovach, who word
processed and edited the second edition.

Lynn Sanders and Elizabeth Obolensky, who
edited the first edition, and Barbara Obolensky,
who proofread the second.

Cover, book design and typography by
Fifth Street Design Associates, Berkeley, CA

TEN SPEED PRESS
P.O. Box 7123
Berkeley, CA 94707

Library of Congress Cataloging-in-Publication Data

Hoge, Sr., Cecil C.
    Mail Order Moonlighting

    1. Mail-order business. 2. Supplementary employment.
3. New business enterprises. I. Title.
HF5466.H572 1988   658.8'72   87-17953
ISBN 0-89815-222-4

Manufactured in the United States of America

1 2 3 4 5 — 92 91 90 89 88

61299

Contents

x

Preface

My Mail Order Moonlighting Method helps those starting in mail order to be successful at it. After nine printings, it is completely rewritten and updated.

My method remains simple and fundamental. It eliminates much of one of the greatest threats to any starting business . . . overhead. It reduces other risks as well. More than ever, opportunities for mail order moonlighters have proliferated.

Mail order moonlighting is the way many big and sound mail order businesses have started. Many of these have gone on to employ large staffs, with big plants and the latest technology. Many have now gone beyond mail order to manufacture and distribute products in conventional ways through normal channels. Those owners who have never forgotten the lessons of their moonlighting start have rarely later failed.

In doing acquisition work for others and for ourselves, I have looked at the financial statements of many, many small businesses . . . and analyzed their beginnings as well. The sound businesses usually started soundly from the beginning. Again and again I discovered that those who started part-time . . . from home . . . on a moonlighting basis . . . were even years later far sounder than many others which I investigated.

Some huge money makers in the mail order business have started this way. For years I earned a living elsewhere and moonlighted in our family business while my wife worked at it full-time. That's when our family business built the base of its present capital.

Mail order is suited to more people with more backgrounds than most activities. My method is safe, entirely practical and based on the methods of sound, conservative and successful mail order people. In the years since I wrote Mail Order Moonlighting, our family business has grown at an increasing pace.

My method is no panacea . . . just as mail order is not for everyone. My method can help you analyze whether you are suited to mail order at all . . . whether you can go it alone . . . or best combine your strength with others . . . for a real chance . . . and, if so, how to select the right partner . . . and negotiate the right deal.

I have helped others get started in mail order . . . and some I've helped have made a great deal of money. It is my hope that the Mail Order Moonlighting Method can help far more people than I could personally.

I tell it as it is in the real mail order world . . . with its difficulties as well as opportunities. I try to advise you as if you were in my office . . . and keep working with you as if you were in business with me.

Most of my alumni, after their success, have kept in touch with me. From Japan and Canada, Italy and England, Germany and Norway — friends over the U.S. and the world, those who have read Mail Order Moonlighting, have written or phoned me. And if you succeed with my method, do me a favor. Just drop me a line and tell me about it.

Your example may then help others as I hope to help you. Best of luck.

Cecil C. Hoge, Sr.
Oldfield, New York

President
Huber Hoge and Sons Advertising, Inc.
104 Arlington Avenue
St. James, N.Y. 11780
(516)724 – 8900

BOOK I

WELCOME TO MAIL ORDER

. . . the real mail
order world

Chapter 1

ROLLER COASTER

*Thrills . . . frustration . . . fun . . .
dangers . . . satisfactions of mail
order*

When you start my Mail Order Moonlighting Method – at home, in your spare time – you will probably open each envelope yourself. As you do, your tingling spine will rarely fail to excite . . . thrill . . . or *frustrate* you.

Later, however huge your business may become, you will always be impatiently waiting for the mail to reveal fate's latest cast of the mail order dice. In either case, mail order is fascinating, if sometimes un-nerving. And once in your blood, it's a business hard to leave.

The mail order roller coaster can start off as the real one does . . . slowly. As tests are successful, it can pick up speed, just as at the amusement park. But this roller coaster can *race upwards* faster and faster . . . to express train speed . . . as ad after ad pays out profitably time after time . . . until you're seemingly jet propelled.

You can get *hooked* on the intoxicating thrill of it. A successful campaign can rocket ahead so fast and so high that its upward-racing progress can seem *perpetual* . . . often just as it is about to slow. Then it can pick up speed again, this time racing *downward* at sickening speed. It can twist, curve, turn . . . up, down, all around. Your future can seem wildly, erratically different from day to day. And always, the mail order count regulates its speed.

One day the mail can come in unexpectedly heavy and fat . . . fairly bursting with nice checks for you. Another day you may see a thin, rubberbanded *sliver* of mail. When you least expect it, good counts from a test ad of a new item can make you feel like a millionaire. And when you are really counting on a certain new test ad to succeed, the mail can be so bad that you may want to give up mail order for good.

Yet now more than ever there is an art and a science to making money in mail order that can reduce the risk and greatly level out the rollercoaster effect. Now mail order can be more predictable. Now it is possible to get into mail order more safely. Now you can maintain a steadier and more continuous upward grade, as our family business has been able to do for quite a few years. My Mail Order Moonlighting Method is my effort to help you do so also . . . from the beginning.

Mail order has been good for my family and our business and way of life, and it can be for you. I have made money and lost money in mail order. I've been fortunate to have had some great mail order talents pass through my portals, first in the advertising agency of Huber Hoge and Sons (handling top mail order clients), and then also in the mail order business itself.

Some of our alumni are quite rich today as business owners. Some are highly-paid advertising executives. Some are the men and women in the big mail-order divisions of the largest companies. And some have found riches of a different kind; they own and operate smaller enterprises or activities they've nurtured with loving care that now provide them with not just a living but a way of life. They've used their mail order know-how to change and balance their life style. They live where they want and divide their time between working and other interests, as they will.

Let me help you risk less and make more in mail order and direct response. Let me pass on to you lessons I have learned in a business lifetime.

Mail order is suited to more people . . . in more fields . . . of more varied backgrounds than most activities. It's an extra leg for the career table of an executive, business beginner or professional man or woman. Mail order is an ideal man-and-wife business. It's perfect for a woman to own and operate and even raise a family at the same time. It's a perfect way to help launch a business in stores, through catalogs or in specialized fields, and it's open to anyone.

Mail order has wide scope and many benefits. Mail order can be operated anywhere . . . in the most pleasant climate and the most attractive surroundings. I know of one quite profitable mail-order business operated in the United States from Nice, France, for years. Mail order can be combined with world travel, a favorite hobby or retirement.

Mail order is often a *cash* business, important in today's world when cash is king. It's a way to *borrow* money and finance trade business. It's a way to move slow inventory at a profit. Mail order can build up income and draw peripheral trade customers.

Years ago, mail order know-how began to give us many extras. Gradually we learned how to *capitalize* on mail order to get benefits we had never fully realized existed – a method now called direct marketing.

We used mail order advertising to get a hearing from retail stores. We used the success stories of our products to persuade mail order catalogs to stock our goods.

We learned to modify our mail order ads and convert them to department store cooperative ads. We learned to apply them to an electronic counter action display, to a billing insert and to a take-one folder at a counter. We learned to use quick mail order cash to finance long-term dating orders from wholesalers. We learned to use mail order to launch and distribute store businesses that could survive long after the mail orders faded away. And it can give you extras, too.

Direct marketing know-how has helped us in our businesses . . . in selling through stores, in our packaging, in our trade catalogs and in any consumer advertising we do. We apply it to mailings to the trade and to each business letter we write. And there's scarcely a retailer, service company, wholesaler or manufacturer of any size which cannot apply the principles of mail order and direct marketing in various ways to get far more benefit from dollars spent. And whatever business you go into, you can too.

Mail order know-how is surprisingly applicable to operating any business, because mail order is like any other business.

Its main characteristic is that it is *measured* by each day's mail. Mistakes are almost *instantly* revealed. It's harder to brush errors under the carpet . . . or to pass the buck. It disciplines you to meet problems *head on and act quickly* on them.

And the same direct marketing strategies and principles convert to almost any field, any method of selling and any product. If you can succeed in mail order, it becomes an exceptional business course to succeed in almost any kind of business.

Direct marketing is so huge that you can be in it any number of ways. You may wish to build a specialized catalog in any of many fields or in a more general area. You may wish to sell only on television, entirely to doctors or only to schools . . . all by mail.

You may wish to use mail order methods *but* avoid all mail order risk. We did so for four years. We turned over the mail order sales of all our items, with our ads and artwork, to a firm that did a total sales volume of over 100 times ours. I wrote new ads myself. We took the short end of the stick, but none of the risk, and we prospered.

Whatever field of mail order you care to concentrate on, I want you to succeed, not fail. I cover as many areas as I can. I can do so because the research for this book is all my mail order life. I've put the essence of all I've learned into it.

In my life in mail order, I've helped some who had never before been in business at all and others already extremely successful in business but unfamiliar with mail order. Some of you I am writing to have a great deal of business experience. Some have none. Some are in between. However experienced or inexperienced you may be, I hope that you will find good value in my course. If anything in this book is so simple and familiar (or so advanced) that you have no need of it . . . just skip through that part.

Had someone told me in advance what I so painfully later learned, I would have been saved much grief. I want to warn you, in time, of mail order dangers. I tell it as it is. I want you to stay away from mail order if, after getting the facts, you feel that it is not for you. Because mail order can be a great business, I hope that you decide to stay in it, develop a "feel" for it and succeed in it.

That's why this book walks a tightrope between caution and encouragement. Let's start with the dangers of mail order . . . and then what it takes to surmount them.

Chapter 2

GREAT EXPECTATIONS

---

*Misconceptions . . . slaughter of the
mail order innocents . . . and
survival in the real world*

For all too many, mail order can lose money faster and more certainly than most businesses.

All that's needed is to pay too much for too standard an article without an advantage over competitors . . . then just sell it for too little . . . advertise it to the wrong people, and pay too much for the advertising for each thousand people reached. Now just say and show too little or too much or too inadequately in your advertising. Simply advertise in the wrong place, in the wrong season, too early or too late or just commit for too much inventory, too much advertising, too much overhead or too much personal draw from the business.

As in any business, there are countless ways to lose money in mail order, and most losses occur because newcomers to mail order simply assume it's more *automatic to make* money than is possible. Unfortunately, many people starting off are foolish in mail order. And a fool and his money are soon parted . . . super fast in mail order.

Don't get discouraged too fast. There's plenty of money to be made in mail order. Hang on and I'm going to make a real effort in my course to help you make your share safely. But if any friend asked me my advice about going into mail order and I did not point out these dangers and misconceptions, I would not be a friend. I'd like to warn you and then try to help you in my course to overcome such problems.

Today far more products and services can be sold profitably via mail order – but perhaps in a way not available to you. Some of the most potentially profitable mail order products, even with ample margin and perfectly made, will fail with ineffective advertising. And developing successful advertising, even with the aid of the greatest experts in the field, still involves great trial and error. I have never ceased to wonder at how regularly test ads that I expect to succeed . . . fail. And I am not alone.

To survive in mail order, every advertisement, in any form of advertising, must produce a *minimum quota* of dollars of sales. This is the

---

break-even figure. If your advertisement produces 60% . . . 70% . . . 80% . . . or even 90% of your *minimum quota*, you will lose money. A losing advertisement loses more money each time it runs. Yet I have proudly created mail order advertisements that produced 5% to 10% of the minimum quota. We made money by keeping such test costs small and making so much more on successful offers run very widely as to do well overall. But the mail order newcomer with no reason to be in mail order may never find a successful item.

Yet, if you are an able salesman or sales manager, you might get your product into retail distribution store by store . . . and make money with each sale to each store.

But in mail order, *every* advertisement has its *minimum quota*. And when you run many advertisements, you really need to roll seven almost every time, or you'll be wiped out.

The truth is that making money in mail order is not automatic. For if it were so simple as some newcomers expect . . . *and always worked* . . . we'd all be billionaires. The real mail order world is hard and tough. Yet many make fortunes in it. And many, many more find safe niches in it to build income and create capital.

The first thing to remember is that there are no simplistic solutions . . . contrary to get-rich-quick ads.

It's hard to make money and even to survive in any business today. To survive in mail order, some sort of special advantage can help. Those who do survive and prosper often find some special "edge" over others . . . made possible by their special situation.

Big mail order advertisers get bargain rates and prime positions in publications or broadcast time. That's become their "edge." An advertising agency which goes into mail order on its own, as an entrepreneur, may consider its 15% agency commission on advertising it buys as its edge. A sales representative of a publication or broadcast station may go into mail order as an entrepreneur and consider his commission on advertising in his media as an edge. Sometimes one organization, both advertising agency and sales representative, will go into mail order as an entrepreneur and consider its two commissions on advertising as a *double edge*.

A magazine publisher or a broadcaster may sell his own mail order items in his media. His advertising in his own media costs him less than the higher rate which he charges outsiders. This is his edge.

A big direct marketer may have a big list of customers who want to buy by mail. A big retailer may have a trusted name. Any huge company may have a big organization and top consultants highly skilled in direct marketing. Each has an edge.

Our edge is that we use mail order to launch store distribution products. We consistently make money on mail order alone, but our real benefit is that our extensive mail order advertising creates a demand and trade acceptance for a store distribution success.

Don't feel that *you* can't compete. As a moonlighter, you start off with the special advantage of almost no overhead. Just realize the importance of gaining your own special additional advantage. As you continue with this course, and afterwards, keep looking for that extra edge. And you will find it.

Let's examine in a little more detail how others succeed in mail order.

Chapter 3

A QUICK ZOOM CLOSE-UP

. . . of mail order's biggest success
. . . and what it can teach us in
making our own

Let's take a quick look at the operation of a firm which, year after year, decade after decade, *always* makes a profit in mail order. Let's see what makes the biggest mail order operator of all time *tick . . .* in the real mail order world. Let's take a stroll through the pages of the Sears-Roebuck catalog.

Here, *every* article *is* sold by mail order. And the items seem to be just about *anything* people might ever dream of buying. And Sears has *specialized* catalog after catalog, which gives infinitely *more choice* of endlessly more items.

And Sears sells each item without any great excitement. There's no mystery to it. Sears shows it attractively and describes it factually. So what *is* the great complication and mystery of selling *anything* by mail order? If Sears can do it, why can't we do it? Because you and I, and even General Mills or General Foods, *cannot* do in mail order *what Sears can do.*

I have just completed a book, The First Hundred Years Are the Toughest, on Montgomery Ward and Sears Roebuck . . . and on the *100 years* it took to make the Sears catalog the marketplace it is.

Next to the Bible, the Sears catalog is the #1 most popular book in the world. The Sears catalog is *only* available to people who *prove* they are Sears customers by *buying* from Sears a *minimum* determined by Sears. Sears is *trusted*; Sears is *believed* . . . as you and I cannot *hope* to be for *any product* we initially sell through mail order.

Sears is bigger than many countries in total gross product produced. Behind every Sears mail order product is its giant buying power. Sears has an *army* of buying talent all over the world. In any consumer distributor business that you and I succeed in, Sears may become our biggest customer. Sears owns its own factories for item after item. Sears can produce its catalog at lower cost per thousand copies, pull more dollars of sales from each square inch of catalog space for each thousand catalogs, pick up more related sales from each customer and sell more later to that customer. Sears can *buy* most items it's seriously interested in (or make their own) at lower cost.

Let's turn the pages. In item after item, Sears simply offers more value than you or I could ever hope to. Furthermore, in most items Sears makes itself, few companies could possibly afford *to set up* any competitive manufacturing operations without an investment so great most of us could not conceive of it. Even giant companies could find it unjustified for the potential profit.

Well, if so, who are we to try to sell *anything* by mail order?

Let's see how Sears started . . . without any catalog . . . any money . . . any mail order know-how . . . any of the advantages Sears now has . . . and without *some* advantages you and I now have.

When Richard Sears started in mail order, the dominant catalog – and first general catalog – was Montgomery Ward's. There seemed very little chance that Sears-Roebuck could catch up.

Richard Sears started by selling *one item only . . . watches*, and only one basic kind of watch with very little choice of styles and sizes. He hired Alvah Roebuck to repair the watches. Then Sears sold one additional item after another, until he spread or, it is said, rather sprawled his operation all over Chicago . . . in lofts and cellars and small offices . . . and initially *without* a catalog.

Mr. Sears, like some mail order men today, was said to be a bit of a mail order buccaneer. Not all of his items would pass the laboratory tests Sears now requires. Not all of his first advertising copy (and it was often longer then) would now clear through the Sears internal censorship for factual truth and accuracy. Mr. Sears ran ad after ad in the same issue of individual magazines, sometimes up to 60 or 70 of them.

And it was only when Sears was taken over by a partner with ethics, organizing skills and vision – Julius Rosenwald – that it began to take its present form. Rosenwald grew up in the retail business. He was in the mens' clothing manufacturing business, which had sold mens' suits to Sears-Roebuck. Rosenwald became fascinated with mail order (just as you and I have today) and the day-to-day operations of Mr. Sears.

Without Mr. Rosenwald, Mr. Sears might have had more fun, but never built a *lasting* business. Mr. Rosenwald was the orderly *builder* who made possible all that you see in the Sears catalog today.

Let's see how *we* can become a winner in mail order, even if we don't build a business as big as Sears-Roebuck – or Montgomery Ward . . . both of which were started by mail order moonlighters. Both started *without most* of the mail order *advantages* that you and I have today. Thanks to Sears-Roebuck and others, more and more people, overwhelmingly more than in their time, are *willing* to buy mail order, *willing* to send you and me *bigger* sums of money, because they feel *safer* buying mail order from *anyone* than in those early days.

There are many, many *ways* of selling mail order that never existed then, and many, many *helps and allies* for mail order people that never existed then either. Today there are innumerable mail order niches, nooks and crannies where new mail order operations can survive and prosper, do undreamed-of volume and make proportionate profits . . . all *without* head-on competition with Sears or any other giant. But it requires selectivity, judgment and a "feel" for mail order.

Chapter 4

THE KEY INGREDIENT

*... to mail order survival and
success. With it you can get rich.
Without it chances are slim.*

Mail order is a feel-your-way . . . stop . . . start . . . test . . . project
method, for people with a "feel" for it, to get rich surprisingly fast. Mail
order loses money for far more people than it ever makes money for,
simply because they don't have a "feel" for *any* business, but get
tempted into mail order as an *easy* business . . . often by shrewd
entrepreneurs or biased advisors who get rich luring the ignorant and
unbusinesslike into activities they are often unsuited for.

Mail order is a rare opportunity for those with a "feel" for it, and
not at all simple for anyone else. I call it mail order "Fingerspitzen-
gefuehl." In German this means the tips of your fingers; it refers to a
special sensitivity. For the man or woman with a "feel" for mail order,
it's a gold mine . . . the secret of mail order success. That "feel" is the
basic know-how of correct mail order principles. It's a sound sense of
correct mail order strategy. It's quite vital in today's mail order.

I have seen profitable ways of doing business, faithfully followed
almost as a religion, suddenly become unprofitable business heresy.
Techniques and tactics that had worked like clockwork began to fail
almost automatically. Profitable practices of yesterday can become
business suicide today or tomorrow. That "feel" tells you how to use
and benefit from the latest mail order tactics and techniques. It guides
you to drop those which are suddenly obsolete.

Today's swirling direct marketing world is fast moving. The tactics and techniques are complex and constantly changing, but the principles and basic strategies are extremely simple and do not change.
The latest tactics and techniques are great, but more painfully acquired, and only practical to use if you have the mail order "feel" to do
so safely. Without a firm understanding of correct principles and sound
basic strategies, trying to use the latest tactics and techniques is like
trying to steer the latest-model ship without a rudder.

With middle and large-size companies, the greatest limiting factor in their entrance into and growth in mail order is the know-how,

experience and mail order "feel" of those they select to manage their direct marketing operations. For these companies, *mail order disasters are overwhelmingly due to the shortage of executives with the background, skills and ways of thinking necessary.*

If you can master mail order and get a "feel" for it, *you have* developed a highly marketable asset. Here's one moonlighting activity that can make you substantially more valuable to your present employer (even with no present plans for mail order) when the moment of decision comes for that new mail order division.

And if you develop a "feel" for mail order, you may become the catalyst that suggests and gets your employer into mail order and direct response. Direct marketing know-how may get you a raise or a better job.

Let's discuss your suitability for mail order and the practicality of your going into business on your own.

Chapter 5

YOU AND MAIL ORDER

Psychology needed . . . and hidden
mail order assets you may have . . .

In any business, each day is a threat, every transaction a possible time bomb and every agreement a possible misunderstanding. Because mail order moves fast, failure to *see* and *act* on what is wrong can quickly get you out of business.

Analyze yourself. If too cheerful, and if you can't suspect *anything* and don't like detail, stay out of mail order or team up with a trustworthy negative type . . . and make a fortune together.

How are you at buying and selling . . . anything? Some people seem born with the trading instinct, perhaps inherited for hundreds or even thousands of years.

Others feel helpless in any transaction. To buy cheap and sell dear is the first step to maximize profit. Sheltered first at home, then at school and college, and later in a corporate cocoon, for many it's emotionally disturbing, distasteful and psychologically almost impossible to be ever vigilant on costs, overhead, commitments and risks.

If money vigilance is not suited to you, you're not suited to business operation . . . by yourself. Even so, you could still make good money in mail order. You may have some assets perfect for mail order and be able to get a partner to buttress any weaknesses.

If you are creative, with ideas for products and advertising, you can still make a fortune in mail order. But you can only do so with the right associations. You can be the creative partner with a money-sense partner by your side . . . perhaps your own spouse. You can be the creative star employee of a money-sense owner with an income based partially on the results of your own creativity.

Whatever your background, even if unbusinesslike, there may be ways to cash in on it. In a little field like manufacturing fishing lures, dentists who like to fish have designed better lures and retired on them. These lures have usually been made out of metal. Realize that every dentist has the makings of a metal sculptor. They simply sculpted lures in metal. A supplier of foam rubber upholstery to French automobile factories liked to fish and came up with a rubber minnow. An employee

---

of a Detroit plastics factory came up with hard plastic lures. Each used his background.

I've seen artists create jewelry sold by mail, music teachers create home piano courses, doctors come up with medical items to sell to hospitals, beauticians create their own cosmetics, programmers create big mail order businesses in software, actresses and demonstrators produce mail order success in videotapes, collectors profit from selling collectables by mail, sportsmen sell hunting items and so forth. Housewives often do best of all, because the items they create are usually those used in the home and therefore are most universal.

Countless people have perfect situations for mail order and are *not taking advantage of them,* simply because they've never been told the facts regarding just how to go about getting into it.

You *may* already have a unique "feel" for mail order. Your present background, company or job, your interests or hobby may have given you just the set-up you need to benefit. Your skills, your needs and the way you like to work can determine the correct answer to the item you select to sell, how you handle your advertising and your entire mail order operation.

Whatever you do for a living may give you an advantage that can be helpful in mail order.

Certain activities give a good deal of off-time: being a member of an airline crew, a school teacher with summers off, a fireman or post office worker – anyone with less than average pressure most of the time. Occasionally, a company may wish to cut certain executive jobs to several days weekly. Any of these situations may give you a particular advantage in operating a moonlighting mail order business.

Some activities give you the knowledge of a product need or exposure to *new,* intriguing products. If you're a lawyer, accountant, bookkeeper, or credit manager, you may have the ability to watch costs and risks better. If you're a buyer, technician, engineer or chemist, you may know how to find, create or improve a mail order product with better continuing quality control.

Use your background, experience, hobby or interest. Do what you're good at and like. Team up with others to *compensate* for any areas you feel weak in. There are many forms of profitable mail order marriages.

The right association may overcome your lack of experience. In our case, we may create an item, pay a royalty to someone else who creates it, buy it from a U.S. supplier, import it, go into a temporary joint venture (or permanent partnership) with someone who controls it, hire a specialized expert to run it or work for a client as the advertising agency for it. In each case we make a profit putting *our* know-how to work on it.

If you are in financial difficulties, read this carefully: "To him that hath it shall be given and from him that hath not shall be taken away that little which he seemeth to have."

In any business, desperate people usually lose money. Mail order as a straw to grab at is usually a loser. The man or woman out of a job who takes last savings out of the bank and gambles it in mail order . . . usually loses it. Those in financial trouble who resort to mail order usually lose still more.

Desperation warps judgment. In mail order, it usually means selling the wrong thing at the wrong price in the wrong place with the wrong margin. Desperation causes out-of-season, rush testing of advertising, usually too early or too late to pull profits. Desperation means rush. Rush always involves much more cost in advertising production. Desperation accepts a worse advertising position, often at too high a price for the advertising.

When you're broke is the time to get a *money partner* . . . get someone else to take the risk . . . and then operate as if you're rich. A newcomer to mail order who is not desperate and who capitalizes on past experience or know-how, whether in business, profession, hobby or interest, *does* have a *better chance*. Money makes money and starting any business with ample money is desirable.

Being financially independent of a business makes the decisions for that business far sounder in most cases. But what do we do if we're out of work . . . can't get a job . . . have used up our savings . . . are pursued by creditors . . . and desperately need to get back on our feet?

Of course, you must first get a job, even part-time. This may be difficult or even impossible. But in my experience, most unemployment problems are aggravated by ego. There is a fear of loss of status . . . a hesitation to go back a rung . . . a holding out for equivalent importance of job and money benefits. Often such poker playing pays off. But I grew up in the depression, when unemployment was high and employment often could be gained only at far lower wages than the lost job. I believe that when you're down, you are not out, that water seeks its own level, that you must take some employment, however disagreeable. Then you can only get started in mail order by using hours off the job.

You must first gamble your time to find the right mail order product . . . or with someone who has one. Being broke does not keep you from *seeing* the right mail order item. It may not prevent you from getting a sole-rights contract. Only you know fully your financial condition. Others may have more confidence in you than you realize, even if they realize your financial limitations.

You may be able to sign an option contract on a protected, patented product that is unobtainable elsewhere. You may then be able to turn the rights over to a strongly financed, big-volume mail order company.

As long as you're willing to risk your time and ability, instead of money, you'll find ways of making money without risk in mail order. Being broke does not prevent you from gaining mail order skills. You will find a way to cash in on them. If you take *no* risk of any kind and can in some way live independently of your mail order activities, you will gradually build up mail order capital. Later we'll discuss simply *selling* your product to mail order firms.

A newcomer in your business or profession would make mistakes through lack of knowledge and experience, mistakes that you, with your expertise, would not make.

People knowing nothing of mail order can do the same and compound the problem by selling an article that they know nothing about. Frequently, the same people could easily capitalize on their background and greatly improve their chances of success. They could actually use hidden mail order assets which they don't realize they have.

We pay royalties to fishermen who know *nothing* of business and care only to fish 12 months a year, if possible!

But these are *expert* fishermen who have often successfully started in a small way to sell fish lures profitably . . . *mail order* . . . before selling out to us. Their sole advantage was their unique ability to create, perfect and quality-control a superb fish lure superior to others . . . and their intimate knowledge of those who could benefit from using it . . . and how to appeal to them.

I've seen airline pilots, firemen, dentists, teachers and lithographers *each* succeed in this way with fish lures *because* they were *master fishermen . . . and knew their subject . . . and their market.*

The same is true of housewives with a flair for home sewing, creative stitchery or other hobbies. Again and again, I've seen them succeed in mail order with no previous knowledge of it. Because each developed a superior product filling a real need . . . quality-controlled its making . . . started making and shipping from her home . . . and was frugal all the way. These hobby items needed the explanation and demonstration of mail order. Often the mail order *led* to store distribution.

I know one housewife who, as a cub scout den mother, developed simple craft item instructions using leftover material around the house, often from grocery packing materials, etc. The kids were delighted and their mothers too, because it was fun, simple and almost costless. The same housewife began to sell mail order the same kind of kit and instructions in a little magazine for mothers and children. First with her husband and now also with her son, she has built a more-than-million-dollar-a-year business.

Are you an executive? In my lifetime, executives have become less independent and more dependent on their companies and bosses. Today executives feel less secure. The perils of the economy may affect your job. You may be asked (virtually ordered) to move to a location your spouse doesn't like. Your company may be acquired and personnel duplication (perhaps you) eliminated. Becoming an executive moonlighter *before* such problems occur can have benefits for you.

The largest corporations can be perfect launching pads for home businesses on the side. For some jobs, time off is substantial, vacations long and pressure low. Take your time to get started. Find or develop one item at a time. Stick to a field your business background or hobby interest gives you some expertise in. Team up with one or more partners, if each background strengthens and supplements the other and you work well together. Your first successful mail order test can give you a greater personal strength and confidence than in years.

How would you like to start a business with your spouse? A husband and-wife mail order business can be quite a marital thrill. Husbands and wives seem to complement each other in business as naturally as in home life. A woman naturally seems more cautious, more careful, more thorough, often more shrewd in buying and watching payroll and day-to-day expenses. A husband is freed by his wife to do what he is best at . . . planning . . . negotiating . . . closing deals . . . making sales . . . creating increased business. But activity can be split any way.

Sometimes the wife is designer and creator of the products and the man the business manager. Often both husband and wife can start by *each* moonlighting from their respective jobs. Then, after some success, one can work *half* time, often the one with the lower-salaried job. Then that one can go into the business full-time, and later the other can do the same.

At one period long ago, when business was very bad, I made money *outside* the business and came to our business one day every five or six weeks. My wife ran the business entirely in between, and we did very well.

If you're a working mother, even a small home mail order business can give you income and keep you with your children and maybe give you a chunk of capital as well. One woman built a ten-million-dollar business starting that way.

A mail order business is not recommended just to get out from under emotional strain. Only go into it if, after taking this course, you feel suited to it. Investigate it. Start cautiously. If you find some initial success, proceed further . . . alone or with others.

Are you retired? Many people succeed in mail order after retirement. One company, started in mail order by a retired executive, for years hired only retired people. The staff ranged in age from 67 to 94. It built sales of over two-million dollars yearly.

Some psychologists believe retirement shortens lives. Many a man or woman feels a void after retirement and longs for some business activity to participate in. And those who are retired have a wealth of experience to draw on.

If you're retired and smart, you can find a form of mail order to cash in on that experience. Take your time. Proceed at your own pace. Work as few hours a day as you're up to. You can work in the morning . . . take lunch and a nap . . . and work in the afternoon. You can match your experience with a younger, physically stronger partner and use your brains and his brawn. You can keep the entire enterprise as small as you desire or let it grow to whatever size you prefer.

Caution! Mail order *can* strip you clean. If retired, gamble in mail order what you can afford to lose. Don't risk a small retirement income.

Attention, young people! When you start work, you've got all the common sense you'll ever get. All that's added is experience. In our business, we've seen some mighty young people make a lot of mail order money fast. I've had a partner in his early twenties make $60,000. I've seen clients in their twenties make hundreds of thousands of dollars. My belief is that a man or woman can come straight from college, own his or her own mail order business and make a fortune in the first few years. I've seen it done without college, straight from high school with only two or three working years first.

The biggest danger for young people is *judgment.* I've seen them make money in their own mail order business super fast and then ruin themselves financially for life. My advice is don't wait if you feel confident..but be *cautious* and *discipline yourself.*

Young people *trust others without investigation.* Young people are optimistic . . . and can't believe potential disasters can occur. Young people find it more difficult to force themselves to thoroughly carry through.

You're strong. These are your *prolific* working years. You're enthusiastic. You're at your most creative period. Business can be more fun for you. Go to it! You can succeed in mail order with no experience . . . and *stay* successful . . . if you can be super cautious and super suspect of all eventualities.

You can even get started without a penny. If you're young, even if you're unemployed but live at home, any temporary distasteful job, from washing dishes to supermarket clerking, can actually finance your tiny first tests and get you on your way.

Today there are disagreeable jobs that most people on unemployment don't care to take. My suggestion is take *anything*, even the most menial job, but *preserve* free time. Work *four* days at something you don't like. Work every spare minute at something you like. If mail order is your cup of tea, *do it.*

Get *others* to take *all* risks . . . or work so hard you put aside $100. Hundreds and possibly thousands of mail order businesses have started with tests of $100 or less. Many have started with a classified ad. Don't be afraid to team up with others and own a *minority* of a joint venture. Just don't mortgage *all* of yourself with a lifetime partnership. We'll discuss this later.

Good luck and good hunting!

What are your chances in mail order if you have no idea how to apply past experience, no idea of a better product or service and no contact with anyone who has?

The majority of those considering mail order are in this predicament. Most fail . . . and I believe often needlessly. I believe that many, by going about it correctly, could still develop a "feel" for mail order and still succeed in it.

In our own employ, I have seen beginners completely unfamiliar with mail order – hired to be a messenger, clerk or typist – develop that "feel." Most had no suitable past experience and before being hired had no idea of a better mail order product or service and no contact with anyone who had. Yet some achieved lifetime success in mail order.

And many successful in mail order started out equally unfamiliar with it. Simple *exposure* to mail order and its opportunities, *encouragement* that success in it *was* possible, and some guidance seemed most important in my helping others to succeed in mail order.

This course is an effort to give anyone in a similar situation a similar chance. And willingness to *be exposed* to mail order potentials and pitfalls is the first necessary step. Otherwise, chances in mail order become those of a lottery ticket.

Just taking it easy . . . taking your time . . . and saturating yourself in mail order background may plant the seed of that "feel" for mail order that can make success sure.

But the safest formula for individuals has been to take a product you create and perfect yourself in a field you intimately know. Be sure it's unique and needed. Know your costs. Have ample margin. Keep your present job. Start moonlighting. Draw nothing from the business. Then let the profits accumulate. But whatever your situation, don't rush in or give up . . . too fast. The more familiar you get with mail order, the safer and *easier* you will find it.

I believe that most of you *can* develop a "feel" for mail order . . . and that my method plus your own future experience in mail order can give you that "feel" . . . *if* you give both my method and mail order a *real chance.* Let's discuss what that means and whether you are willing to do it.

Chapter 6

THE NEW PIONEERS

---

*Making a hobby of making money
. . . what it takes . . . and what it
gives*

Success will come fastest to those who apply to mail order the advantages they possess . . . develop a "feel" for it . . . and work at it.

Most people like making money and gladly work harder for more money. The border between work and fun is in your own mind. Most people work harder at a hobby and call it fun. My Mail Order Moonlighting Method makes a hobby of making money. Give it the same interest as you would to any hobby that you want to become really good at. Give it the same time and emphasis that you would to become a good cook, fisherman, dressmaker, athlete or winner at anything. Avoid emotional hang-ups, go at it simply and, with any aptitude for it, you should succeed. Mail order is suitable to more people than many hobbies and interests.

But with my Mail Order Moonlighting Method, there's a big difference. You find out if you're unsuited to it faster than in most activities. You don't have to work as long to master mail order as many other activities. Instead of becoming a slave to it, it becomes easier with time. If you start making money, you can make more of it with less effort in the future. Mail order takes very few years of above-average effort to enjoy long years of below-average strain. It's really the laziest way to live in the long run.

This is a hobby that brings greater security for you, your wife and children. Often this hobby can be mixed with another hobby. You may invent or improve ways to garden, cook, play tennis or whatever activity you know best, sell it mail order and *combine* two hobbies for a favorite super-hobby.

In any sport or hobby, as you put more time and effort into it you get better. As you research your subject, observe those more expert than you, get the experience of others up against the same problems, read what experts advise . . . you improve still more. It's the same in mail order moonlighting. You don't have to develop manual dexterity. Tedious practicing is not required in this hobby. What is needed is

---

study of what others do, analysis of your own past actions and judgment decisions regarding your future actions. The more effort you put in, the more you take out . . . in cash.

Initially, you may feel ill-suited for mail order, yet find later that you do have an innate feeling for it. A horseman has to work hard from early years to feel "part of the horse" . . . a surfer to feel "part of the wave" . . . and mail order takes time and effort to become just as natural for you.

To train yourself for mail order means training yourself to be frugal, to work, to avoid unneeded expenditures and to watch pennies accumulate to dollars. You must drive yourself to be a self-starter, *create* sales and not wait for them. You must sacrifice now for future benefits. It's the old Puritan ethic . . . sorry about that. But often it's fun . . . the fun work ethic.

If you do train yourself this way, making money is absurdly simple. We have to know enough to stay out of the business rain and cut risks when things are bad. We have to go when the "goin's good" and go all out. We've got to keep things simple and not overcomplicate them.

If this hobby makes work fun, it can't be all bad. If having fun tempts you to work more, you may work a lot less later. If what I describe is more effort than you care for, you may prefer to forget it. It becomes too dangerous a lottery.

Chapter 7

MAKING IT IN MAIL ORDER

*Sizing up your chances . . . IQ,
emotional stability and work needed
. . . overcoming fears . . . remarks on
testing*

For most, making it in mail order comes down to willingness to work sufficiently and overcoming fears of dangers. I propose to make the work fun and take out some of the fear and use the rest to make mail order safer.

The overwhelming majority of people with enough I.Q. to read this simple book have the I.Q. necessary to operate a business as simple as mail order can be. They also have enough emotional stability.

I assure you that you can have a lot of fun in mail order with my method. You don't lose money on needless overhead. I advise you on ways of starting with little or no other risks.

My "Mail Order Moonlighting" method is simple. It's safer. It makes a hobby of making money. You don't have to rush and can take your time. If you have almost no overhead, keep losses below savings from your job and develop any "feel" for mail order, success should be almost inevitable.

I am going to try to give you that "feel." But I can only help you if you follow my method.

First you apply your know-how or contacts to find or create a better mail order item. Next you develop a more effective way to present it yourself or with others. Now you develop an edge in some way over others in the mail order business. You may have this edge or associate with those that do. It may be a lower advertising rate, a specific, very responsive list to mail to, the ability to get placement of packaging enclosures, a creative skill, a product buying advantage. But in some way, you want a better chance than average. Then you apply extreme frugality in every phase of operations.

A mail order "test" is a mail order ad run to prove something. It can be run in any form of advertising. Today it's proven that more and better research will result in more scientific marketing tests, which increase chances of success. And research that only requires your time and common sense can often make a big difference. But most tests still fail. If you go into mail order with one item and a one-time test, your chances are smaller. The more tests you run, done professionally, the greater chance you will have that one test will work.

The first test is to determine whether you should proceed further with the product. It is simply the best ad you can create. Running ads in more places is called "projecting."

There are many kinds of tests to determine if a change of presentation increases orders or inquiries. Counting the mail gives the answer. We'll discuss it all in more detail later.

If one test is successful, and if professionally projected with national advertising, profits should wipe out test losses and give you a net profit overall. Some successful items have short lives. Others give income for years. Once you get your first "hit" item, you can far more easily get the next, and so on.

Once success starts to snowball, mail order is such fascinating fun that even the laziest of us enjoy the extra work that makes still more money. And some fear or lack of courage, properly used in mail order, can help *insure* success by avoiding missteps . . . in time. Incidentally, you may get that big "hit" the first test you make. It does happen. You're probably better off if you don't.

Each successful test has the thrill and excitement of a winning lottery ticket . . . but we often learn more and make more money in the end from tests that fail. Each unsuccessful test helps prepare you for later success. No lesson sinks home quite the same as your own personal post mortem of the test that has just failed.

Lessons learned from unsuccessful tests are so vital that sometimes initial success from an early-in-the-game test can greatly lessen chances of later, bigger success. Whenever there's a downward economic trend, I rejoice at starting work in 1934. The coming collapse has the cozy "gemutlich" feeling of old times "deja vu." All that I learned in those days of 25% unemployment can now become my secret weapon. And adversity in tests can help you too.

Mail order, like any other business activity, loses money when incorrectly operated. Its virtue is that you usually see immediately the losses that occur. With any "feel" for mail order, mistakes are glaringly apparent, and you can often quickly stop wrong moves. It therefore becomes easier than in other businesses to overcome weaknesses, to learn and improve, to catch an error before it's too late. And it becomes safer too.

If you're willing to go ahead, knowing the odds against you and the effort and discipline required, let's get started.

From here on in my method takes up the basic factors that determine mail order success or failure divided into: what you sell, how you sell, and how you operate your day-to-day business.

First we'll discuss what you sell . . . selecting the product. Let's get into finding that mail order item that just may make us rich.

BOOK II

THE EXPANDING UNIVERSE

*The many worlds of
today's product
selection . . . the new,
wider scope of what
you can now sell
profitably*

Chapter 1

THE FIRST MAIL ORDER
MISUNDERSTANDING

*What to sell . . . what to pay for it
. . . and what to charge for it. What
you can't profitably, legally or
practically sell*

More money is lost in mail order from poor product selection than in any other way. But the flair and "feel" for right product selection makes fortunes for mail order men and women.

The advertisements in magazines luring little people into mail order often mislead them on the ease of finding mail order items. They are the greedy leading the blind.

The impression is that everywhere articles exist . . . easy to sell by mail order, easily available from wholesalers and with ample margin between cost and selling price to sell at a fat profit after all costs.

The truth is sadly different. *Most* items sold by mail order are sold by trusted, established firms to those who trust them most – their customers. To secure a new customer is the hardest task in mail order. Offered to non-customers, most items fail. Careful selection of exactly whom to offer it to can greatly increase chances of success.

Even then, the right item must have enough profit margin to succeed. Purchasing it through a wholesaler rarely leaves adequate margin to pay for mail order advertising . . . and show a profit.

Even most manufacturers find that most of their own products are *not* suited to sell via mail order to most non-customers, even with the *full* gross profit they enjoy. And the occasional successful mail order product a manufacturer or importer may find for himself out of his line usually yields only modest profits, even when the manufacturer-mail order man has his *entire* profit to work with.

If the manufacturer makes a profit and sells to you as a mail order man, you usually can't make a profit. And if the manufacturer sells to a wholesaler and makes a profit, and the wholesaler sells to you and makes a profit, then mail order chances for you grow even dimmer.

As in other fields, some mail order is based on substantially lower profit margins.

The more standard the article, usually the less suited it is to mail order, *except* under certain conditions, one of which is a bargain price. This can only be possible when advertising costs are very low, as in a package insert in a mail order shipment. Or again, it may be possible if the merchandise is bought at an unusual bargain, as in a purchase of an odd lot from a distress sale.

Some mail order businesses perpetually seek and rely on such distress merchandise. But this, in reality, can only be achieved irregularly, and a regular flow of merchandise at known costs can be rarely achieved.

In direct mail advertising, the secret is to mail to names of people most desirous of your product or services. You may find a specific list of customer names so responsive, so above average in its response per thousand, that you can afford to pay more for an article particularly related to the list, such as a sewing article for a sewing list.

And of course, in both selling through the trade – through the wholesalers and retailers – and via mail order, there is considerable variation in needed profit margin by products and situations. You can buy from a manufacturer or even a wholesaler and make a mail order profit in specific situations.

If you develop a catalog with a variety of items, you will normally have a substantially lower selling cost than for a specific mail order item sold through most forms of advertising. You can then afford to buy smaller amounts of a variety of items from manufacturers or even wholesalers.

What can you sell by mail order? Lots and lots and lots!

On the next two pages are items sold over the years by mail order direct response methods by clients of Huber Hoge and Sons (including ourselves). In considering selling such items yourself, please realize that special factors which caused any success of these items might not hold in your case.

Each item was a special *kind* of seed, knife, comb, toy or whatever, with unique advantages over others. Profit margins were right. Cost was low enough and selling price high enough to provide enough gross profit to give hope of returning profit after advertising. Advertising presentation was painfully accomplished and above average. Buying the advertising was carefully negotiated. Timing was right. Another caution: what worked in one *form* of advertising often failed in another.

So don't rush in where mail order angels fear to tread . . . until we've spent a little more time together. Incidentally, this only represents 50 years of one advertising agency's experience and one mail order man's business lifetime. The experience of other mail order authorities indicates far more possible items, fields and areas ideal for mail order direct response methods.

But our list may give you some ideas of mail order items you'd like to consider. Here's our list!

accident insurance
adding machines
adult education
apartment rentals
aprons
art courses
art materials
art prints
auto accessories
auto insurance
auto seat
awnings
beach mattresses
beauty courses
bedspreads
Bibles
blouses
boats
book clubs
broilers
bulbs
buttons
canoes
car oil additives
car washers
children's records
children's toys
Christmas gifts
Christmas trees
cigarette lighters
cigarette-making
  machines
classic records
clothes
club plans
coffee makers
combs
cookie presses
corn poppers
correspondence
  courses
cosmetics
coverlets
cowboy suits
creamers
curlers
cushions
cutlery
defrosters

dinghies
dish cloths
dolls
dress forms
drills
drug products
electric heaters
electric paint
  peelers
electric razors
exercise equipment
fertilizer
fish lures
fishing clubs
flatware
floats
food covers
food mixers
fryers
fuel oil additives
games
garment bags
gladioli
glassware
globes
grass growth
  retardant
graters
hair vacs
harmonicas
health books
history books
home dry cleaners
homework courses
hosiery
IQ tests
indoor plants
insecticide
inspirational books
ironing sets
jewelry
jiffy whippers
juice extractors
kitchen knives
kitchen slicers
knife holders
lamps
land
language records

language aids
law books
lawn sprinklers
life insurance
life jackets
live turtles
magazine
  subscriptions
magic sets
magnolias
mechanical
  knitters
memory courses
men's shirts
mens' socks
mixing bowls
model airplanes
mops
name stamps
night driving
  glasses
paint brush
  cleaner
paint brushes
paint rollers
paint sprayers
patterns
pencil sharpeners
pencils
pens
perfume
pet care
piano courses
pianos
pillow cases
pipes
plastic banks
plastic dishes
plastic kitchen
  gadgets
pools
power saws
rafts
rat killer
razor blades
real estate
recipes
record clubs
reducing tablets

piano courses	rolling pins	tonics
pianos	roses	tools
pillow cases	rug-making	towels
pipes	saws	toy zithers
plastic banks	scarfs	train sets
plastic dishes	seats	travel books
plastic kitchen	seeds	trays
pools	sewing machines	tulips
power saws	shampoos	TV antennas
preparers	sharpeners	TV repair
rafts	sheets	TV sets
rat killer	silver polish	vacuum cleaners
razor blades	slipcovers	vegetable
real estate	staplers	vegetable
recipes	steak knives	vitamins
record clubs	steam irons	wafer molds
records	steamers	wallets
records	subscriptions	watches
reducing tablets	sun visors	water heaters
refrigeration	T-shirts	will forms
rentals	telephone	wind-up cars
retardant	thread	wool remnants
roasters	toasters	

The above is mainly in the broad consumer field.

It doesn't touch the technical field, office field, industrial field and innumerable special hobbies and interests.

In the book field alone, I once calculated that we have sold for our clients over 300 kinds of how-to instruction books. Opportunities to find the right products and services, perhaps in your present business, are everywhere. But for the conditions you as a moonlighter are liable to face, sure *losers* are even *more* prevalent.

How do you find the right mail order items? You *look* for them or stumble over them. They sometimes walk right in the door.

I have looked at over 10,000 different items over a lifetime. I've investigated seriously several thousand to find the best.

For clients and ourselves, we've tested over 1,000 items. Let's discuss what can often make the difference between losers . . . and winners . . . and particularly what may be the right item or items for *you.*

In considering the sale of anything by mail, there are certain mundane but vital factors.

First, does it *do* what it purports to do? You are legally responsible that it does. Have you personally used it? Have you tested in the simplest way what it does vs. what you have been told it does?

Is it dangerous to use? Can it be misused by a child or whomever? Can it harm or hurt anyone by *overuse?* You are responsible. Your ignorance is no legal or moral excuse. Does it carry liability insurance? Can such insurance be obtained? How much does it cost?

Is it *any good?* Is it made well? Do the parts *fit?* If shipped disassembled can anyone ever put it together? Is it made yet or are you just setting up to make it? If so, how do you know you can ever make it right? Can you get more of it? Can you get more parts for it? How much does it cost vs. its replacement cost to you? Will you go broke assembling, painting or decorating it?

Is it *practical* to sell it by mail? Is it even shippable via post office or UPS? Does it weigh too much in relation to its price? Is it too bulky? Are its dimensions too odd? Is its package *printed* in a way unacceptable to the post office? Is it too perishable to ship or too fragile? Is it dangerous or even *illegal* to ship?

All this is primary but it happens! Let's see how we can avoid it.

Chapter 2

HOW TO BE A MAIL ORDER DETECTIVE

Snooping . . . shopping . . . listening
. . . advertising . . . answering ads
. . . analyzing trends . . . developing
your own

Finding the item is the first chore in going into mail order.

And finding a new item will be all-important to you for the rest of your mail order life. Of course, the fastest, easiest and safest way to get a new item is to "steal" one. We don't, but others do it regularly.

The first step is to *study* mail order advertising. We do it to spot new trends and techniques. Every publication that carries mail order ads becomes your textbook. Next, open your mail, particularly your third-class mail – junk mail (advertising you may usually throw away) and particularly your office advertising mail. Now file every direct mail piece carefully away.

Watch the movies on TV where most mail order commercials run. Tune in when you drive . . . from radio station to radio station. Watch TV shopping network shows for items which are featured again and again.

Start answering mail order inquiry ads. As the literature comes in, file it away. Start *buying* by mail yourself.

Go through trade and technical magazines. In each, you'll find mail order items for that trade. Go through Popular Science, Popular Mechanics, Mechanix Illustrated and Science and Mechanics. See what they feature editorially and what is advertised mail order. Do the same with the airline magazines, computer magazines, handyman, gardening and other hobby and special-interest magazines. The more specialized the better – from beekeeping to collecting plates. Look through every direct response postcard publication you run across.

The more you study and analyze, the more you'll form opinions as to the type of mail order item you prefer yourself. Start attending trade shows . . . and roam from booth to booth. Go to the Premium Show in New York or Chicago. Try the Stationery Show, the Gift Show,

---

the Hardware Show, the Housewares Show, the Business Show, the Boutique Show, the Consumer Micro-Electronics Show, the Boat Show. There's even a Mail Order Show . . . whatever shows are most convenient to you.

At every show there are some provocative items exhibited by underfinanced companies that are hoping to find a promoter angel. If you're financed to do volume and want to go after it, you have a chance to negotiate a takeover of *all* distribution rights. You can start with a mail order test . . . project in mail order and right on into distribution. Question such exhibitors closely. They may already have had a successful mail order test and need only help to project it. Each conversation you have gives you more of a "feel" for mail order.

Every retail store is a "new item trade show" for you.

Particularly study off-beat, intriguing, small specialty stores . . . the ones with flair, style and character. The bigger the city, the more specialized stores can survive, but stores with personality are popping up everywhere.

Look for craft stores, fashion boutiques, hobby stores, off-beat stores like African import stores, the Kite Store in New York, art print and book stores, college campus stores of all kinds, lapidaries and gift shops. Many times the owner is also the designer and creator of some of the most intriguing items. Here again, sometimes the owner would like to do mail order but lacks finances or feels insecure. Often it's possible to acquire mail order or complete distribution rights on a royalty basis or on a joint venture basis.

The next step is to look for imports. Study Made in Europe and equivalent publications advertising products made and available in different parts of the world. You're even told when items are available on a sole-rights basis. If you can afford it . . . travel. Go to the great fairs in Hanover, Frankfurt, Milan. Go to Japan, South Korea, Taiwan, Hong Kong, Singapore and mainland China and India. Don't forget the Philippines, Brazil and Mexico. If you're in an airline-employed family, it can cost very little, or team up with someone who is. You're now a step ahead, looking at some items *before* they've been exported to the U.S. at all. Besides, you'll enjoy it.

Often a new item comes from a friend of a friend. If people know you're in mail order, and believe you're honest and competent, they'll recommend you to people they know who have new items.

It's hard to launch a new product. Small entrepreneurs trying to get traditional distribution are more and more frozen out. Small enterprises are always running out of money, often with a quite desirable product.

We try to keep at arm's length from past losses and mistakes, but to take over rights of intriguing items, either on a royalty basis or a sixty-forty ownership basis.

If the old corporation owns inventory, we offer to pay for it at cost as needed and if approved by us as acceptable. If the old corporation invested substantially in tooling, we offer to pay an extra 3% or so tool-ing royalty on our sales until their original layout of cash is returned. Of course, we do so only after we verify the reasonableness of the costs. In this way, we can help bail out money tied up but never really risk any money other than on new tests.

Once you succeed with one item, tell your suppliers, your friends, your acquaintances that you're looking for a new item. As soon as you succeed with one item, they'll be far more likely to recommend you to the owner of another. It will become easier and easier. Don't grasp at straws. Don't be in a hurry or feel that you must get a new item by a certain date.

Remainder books are those left over from an edition which the original publisher could not completely sell out through book stores and regular book wholesalers. Consider them. Go to a remainder book wholesaler or the equivalent. Browse through the remnant shelves. Find a how-to book that appeals to you. You can buy it at a bargain . . . and advertise it at full retail price. It will usually sell, or not sell, based more on your presentation than on price. If your tests are suc-cessful, you can often arrange to reprint the book on a royalty basis . . . and even to sell back some of the edition if you can't sell it at all . . . or to joint-venture the edition. Some of these books are excellent.

Best of all, develop your own item yourself or with some creative person who seems to have something better in the works. Take your time. Develop it gradually. But be proud of it. Often the slower pace of developing and perfecting your item is far safer and often less liable to be copied.

Analyzing the mail order items you see can teach you a lot. Par-ticularly watch the items that run in a publication more than once. Let us assume, as we hope, that you do not choose to "duplicate" the other fellow's apparently successful item. But you can cash in on the *trend* it indicates without hurting him at all. If it is a "nostalgia item" that's repeating, running the same ad in the same publication or even the same ad in many publications, then consider finding or creating another "nostalgia" item and so forth.

Study mail order catalogs, particularly the specialized ones. Notice the items that are featured in largest space and most prominent position . . . in successive catalogs. Learn from them in the same way. Read main editorial pages of newer, specialized shelter magazines like Colonial Homes – as well as all mail order ads in them.

Answering ads for items and businesses can often be like looking for a needle in a haystack. Yet we have bought businesses located through such classified ads. My brother acquired a six-million-dollar business locating it in just this way. We have acquired items this way as well.

But it requires great patience and an ability to quickly screen out proposals impractical for you. Many of those advertising are dreamers. Some are liars. Most are failures. The big majority can be time wasters.

Just reading the ads, day after day, takes time. We try to answer such ads with the briefest of letters, sum up our background and give our Dunn & Bradstreet credit rating. We try to screen the proposal on the telephone. We only have a personal meeting with someone who has the rare proposal that seems to make enough sense to justify it. In the meeting we try, within 10 to 20 minutes, to screen out those who slip in quite different terms and variations to their proposal as stated by telephone. If the individuals seem honorable and competent, their business or product desirable, and if their reports of test results of sales are encouraging, we try to get an option agreement to make our own tests. Generally, our tests do *not* verify theirs. Often the product turns out to be manufacturable only at far higher costs. Sometimes their mold (if they have one) turns out to be defective. Occasionally the product cannot be made at all. But it all comes out in the wash.

As for advertising for items ourselves, it can be even more frustrating. Often we are deluged by answers. Many of them seem intriguing, although we can screen out many more as obviously unsuited to us. When we advertise, no matter what limitations we put in, we often get inquiries from all kinds of people with all kinds of products. The percentage of dreamers is still higher. Just the cost of telephoning inquiries all over the country is far greater than running the ad. And answering by mail only prolongs the agony. But we have occasionally found items this way.

Run and answer ads. But expect to work long and hard to find that one good item we all need.

Chapter 3

EACH TO HIS OWN

---

*Personal judgments . . . items we
like and don't like . . . where our
best items come from . . . suiting the
item to you*

There are items that our policy will not permit us to sell . . . items that make big mail order money . . . but not for us. Because gradually, over the years, we've made certain basic policy decisions on new items. We will not sell an erotic item . . . a contraceptive or even sex information . . . the effect of which, on younger people, we are not sure. When I think of such items, I always think of my children, nieces, and nephews and the children of friends and what it may do to their future lives.

I can't look at any weapon or possibility of a product being used as a weapon without visualizing a possible crime committed with it. When I see guns, I think of President Kennedy killed with a mail order gun. When I see hunting knives, I think of teenage gang warfare with mail order knives. Items like these are the safest items to sell, but perhaps the most dangerous to buy . . . and we don't touch them.

Most other dangerous items are harder to spot. We don't sell internal medicine or remedies. In some kinds of items, we erred in our youth and have, thereafter, stayed away from them like the plague.

You will quickly develop your own "do's" and "don't's" regarding selecting items.

We avoid handcrafted items because we like to do a volume business. But if you have a "feel" for crafted items and love to travel, you can travel all over the world, as a business expense, seeking out fascinating crafted items, once you have a good, profitable business to justify it. Do you like original Mexican handwoven hammocks, ponchos from Peru, handcrafted African jewelry, handmade crafted items from Mainland China or shell necklaces from India? They can be a joy to buy and, at the height of their appeal, highly profitable to sell. They are not for us, but they could be for you.

We avoid ancient artifacts like old Roman coins. We're not archaeologists. We assume that many items of this sort sold by mail are

---

frauds. We don't want to take the chance by going into them. But if archaeology is your hobby, here's your chance to pursue it as a business expense and make money from it as a hobby.

We usually avoid fashion items because we're not fashion designers. We do not have a professional fashion-merchandise-buying background. But perhaps you have a flair for spotting fashion trends in clothes, accessories or jewelry. If so, mail order is often a perfect way to turn your private fashion hunches into big profit.

Some of my friends (and alumni) have been among the most successful entrepreneurs of records via mail order TV. They have no previous background in the record business. But for years we have sold Worlds' Greatest Books, excerpts of 50 famous sellers and popular classics, for a publishing client! Applied to records, this has been successful in many forms. They simply used know-how gained in the book mail order field to sell many millions of dollars worth of records.

You may have either a perfect professional background or a flair for selecting the mix of songs that sells best in bargain combinations. And you may have just the right professional contacts. Or you may have a flair for an off-beat record success like the sound of birds, insects, thunder, and the running water of natural springs . . . which, incidentally, sold well.

Once we helped launch a piano course with a piano teacher of many years. He had also been an arranger to a famous bandleader for years. His background helped make his course a success. With a famous pianist, a performer of delightful, light, musical-comedy music, we helped develop another piano course. We sold over 287,000 of them, first for a top publisher, and later for ourselves.

The piano is less popular now. But you may be a teacher of . . . or a devoted student of . . . or a professional performer of . . . the coming new instrument. It may become more popular than the guitar is today. And you may have just the teaching method that can be sold in big volume by mail order.

To me, publishing in all its varied forms is particularly fascinating. Whether we work as an advertising agency . . . are in partnership . . . or sole owner is far less important than just working on the creating and selling of books or courses, newsletters or publications, cassettes or videotape. It's all publishing to me.

Years ago we used to create special network radio shows on hobbies and interests. On each show the commercial was for a book. For just one field, sewing, on just one network, we created and produced programs amounting to over one-million words a year on sewing. We created such programs in field after field. We did the same on each TV network and most top TV stations. This has been a field suited to me.

From the age of seven, I have been a voracious reader. For over 20 years, our advertising agency work for large publishers kept teaching us our trade. Our adult education subsidiary succeeds because of this background. The hobby products we sell came about from our knowledge of how to sell hobby books and publications. For clients we've sold just about every kind of how-to book and fiction magazine or book club. It's simply our cup of tea.

And it may be *yours.* You may be a teacher of any subject or hobby . . . a coach or star performer in any sport . . . a writer in any such field . . . or a devoted hobbyist or amateur sportsman. You may have made a hobby of devising a better way to do anything . . . from helping your children in homework, your wife in the kitchen, your husband in his work to whatever. And you may be able to express it perfectly in a better instruction form than yet available. It may be for a brand new interest just becoming popular, whether it be hot-air ballooning or paddle tennis. If you can't, you may know someone who can, for whom you'd be the most perfect editor or business partner.

If so, do-it-yourself instruction may be your field.

Many items *we* avoid may be just right for other mail order firms.

We avoid ties, shirts, socks and shoes that are staple. But the Haband Company has built their big, successful mail order business on just these items. Old clients of ours have, too. We avoid such items because the margin is usually tight. Also, most efficient retailers everywhere offer the *widest possible* selection. But Haband has built a loyal customer list, happy with similar purchases from them, who respond well to just these items. And once you succeed in selling any item, you quickly develop buying power that improves the margins.

We usually avoid "gag" items like Beethoven sweatshirts or funny bumper stickers. To us, they're too unpredictable. But others thrive on them . . . bring out one after the other . . . and pay out on a satisfactory percentage of them. And you may have a flair for this type of item. If so, be cautious on inventory. Any such hit item might drop dead at any time.

We avoid one-time items like an item tied to a candidate in a presidential election. We confine tests to items that can sell year after year. But others make money with one-time items.

A number of years ago, the leading mail order advertising agency expert in the country was approached by an ambitious young man seeking advice. The young man wanted to sell a tape recorder for $99.95. The expert told him to save his money and forget it; an item that expensive could not be sold for cash. The young man thanked him politely and then tested an ad which succeeded in the New York Times. With more ads, he quickly sold $300,000 worth of tape recorders. Sometimes experts must live and learn.

Today we take orders by telephone for as much as $2,600 – on a credit card. But as a new moonlighter, if you ask only for checks, you'd better stick to $10 to $30 in mass media and up to $50 to $100 in media appealing to higher incomes. Very rarely do we sell an item for $5 to $9. We offer items via a choice of three of the top four credit cards. But many sell only via Visa and Mastercard, which have the lowest charges for a mail order seller.

The mail order item we like best is one that has just succeeded, but not yet projected, and we can still acquire.

But this is very rare. We like items that are fresh and ingenious but related to items that have had great past success. We like revivals that some cultural change suddenly makes ripe for a comeback.

We like universal-appeal items, but not yet broadly distributed. We like bigger-ticket items of the widest possible appeal. I once analyzed the biggest purchases which the average family buys. It starts with land and a house, then a car and nowadays a camper or a boat, then appliances of every sort, then clothes and food. Other items can be major purchases. In 1987, the New York Times cost $234 a year to have delivered. And $234 or more spent on a hobby or sport you're interested in is just the beginning.

We like many hobby items. We believe do-it-yourself has been a bit overdone. We avoid any item that has too great an investment for our bank account or in relation to future sales. We avoid religious items selling to members of a religion (from a matter of personal taste). We avoid very limited-potential items, although many mail order people make a living safely and happily, lifelong, from just one item. We'd rather have a chance at broader sales. One of the first questions my wife asks about any new item is, "How many colors and sizes does it have?" And we avoid the item if too many are required. We're trying to cut down and not add to inventory.

We avoid shopping for bargains which we can advertise at a special reduced price, but others thrive on them. Odd-lot purchases of distress merchandise usually mean real and major reductions. We don't like them because it's hard to get more. It's difficult to project in volume.

If you're small, you can do some things that you can't do later. In the book-publishing field, there is always a supply of remainders (leftovers) of editions – often of how-to books ideal for mail order. You can buy low at a distress price. You can often sell high and sometimes at full or higher retail price. The same is often true in other fields.

We only like such bargains when – as is sometimes possible – you can obtain the plates, dies or molds on a royalty or cash basis and develop a proprietary product.

Sometimes a sweeping technological change can greatly lower manufacturing costs and make possible dramatic savings, as in many consumer microelectronic products. We're usually afraid of such situations, because competition can wipe us out overnight with still lower reductions. But sometimes, rare and perfect situations come about.

Sudden popularity of a new type of product can jump manufacturing volume and slash product costs – as in computers, software, accessories . . . videotapes, compact discs and audio tapes. Records shrink in sales vs. compact discs and audio tapes, but can be offered at a great bargain which may sell by mail order for a while.

Our best mail order products have come either from research or association in something else.

Later I'll go into more detail on research. But it's impossible to research anything without stimulating some ideas for something associated or quite unrelated. At least this is so for my grasshopper mind. And most contacts for items we sell came about from introductions for quite different purposes.

Researching the background to help sell a how-to book will come up with a fascinating do-it-yourself product in that field. Often the author will discuss in the book ideas for improved products for that interest. In publishing, any subject briefly described in any fairly encyclopedic coverage may seem worthy of a book itself. Researching any new product can sometimes uncover a needed accessory which can be a business in itself.

We imported and sold pocket adding machines because a representative for a cosmetics business we operated brought around his uncle. We sold dress forms for home sewers for 23 years because a young Dutch importer, from whom we bought four-million bulbs, met a movie starlet who had invented a dress form and introduced her to us. We are in the inflatable boat business because a young Frenchman, who first approached us with a pair of glasses to better see fish underwater, became our good friend and partner later.

We're in exercise equipment because my son, Cecil, while in Paris on business, bought an exercise device in a drug store. He used it, liked it and acquired the rights for it to be marketed in the U.S. – and now in Canada.

As you research first your own background and contacts, and then start actively researching possible mail order projects and selling your first items, one thing will lead to another.

Try to base the selection of the item you choose or develop on your special background and know-how. It gives you a big advantage. Use that special engineering, sales or creative experience. The more you do this, the sounder your mail order business will be.

Chapter 4

SURPRISE HITS

The unexpected ... fun gag items
... ugly ducklings ... trend items
... revivals ... future item portents

This is the story of a fun gag item that started a one-hundred-million-dollar business. Once upon a time, there was an ambitious young man who longed to get rich in mail order. His first job was to write a column reviewing mail order items in a national magazine. All sorts of mail order items came across his desk. His job was to select from the intriguing items and describe them in his column. He noticed that fun gag items often did well, and he came up with one of his own. He announced it to the world in a one-inch ad in Esquire magazine. The first ad made him over $3,000, and he ran it in many more magazines.

I personally would not have selected this item or any type of fun gag item. Success would have seemed too wildly improbable. But this man (later my good friend and personal client) has an uncanny knack for selecting the right mail order item at the right time. And that, combined with many other talents and incredibly hard work, catapulted him to almost unbelievable mail order success . . . living in palaces, surrounded by luxury, finally culminating in the selling out of a business of over one-hundred-million dollars yearly . . . a business he acquired with mail order profits and made a success of with mail order direct response methods.

I mention it because he developed a "feel" for mail order success in directions I personally do not have. And each mail order man develops his own "feel" and touch, often uniquely personal.

And let us hope you will too.

Here's the story of a mail order ugly duckling. Some years ago one of the world's largest publishers gave up on selling an inexpensive art course. Sales had been running about $75 a month *at retail*. The publisher turned over the rights and the plates for $250 to the artist-author.

The creative head of Huber Hoge and Sons, our family-owned advertising agency, met the author in Doylestown, Pennsylvania, where the author had an art instruction class. It turned out that the artist-author had since had some success on a TV test, demonstrating the course and shipping it himself. It further turned out that the publisher was a client of ours.

We asked the publisher to take back the publishing rights and let us take a try at selling the course. We felt we knew the way to project widely the success the artist-author had on his own test.

The publisher and author signed a new contract. The publisher was Doubleday. The author was Jon Gnagy. We sold a Jon Gnagy course to one out of every 14 TV set owners in the U.S. Arthur Brown, the art materials firm, launched a Jon Gnagy art-materials line and became our client. The Jon Gnagy art-materials business became a public company on its own, with nationwide store distribution for its products.

TV presentation and Jon Gnagy's performing talent made the difference between a product gathering dust on a counter and undreamed-of mail order and direct response store distribution success.

Moral: You may find mail order success from a store distribution or even present mail order failure . . . with proper mail order "feel" and know-how.

How would you like to ride a mail order success on a national wave? Cashing in on a trend is the way to make money in any business . . . and certainly in mail order.

Timing is all-important . . . to sell an item or service at the very peak or just before that peak of its being desired. Many trends seem apparent only years later. Then you may realize that you made money in a certain item because you got into it when the trend was ripe. Your objective should be to spot one in time.

Every enormously popular activity creates an entire train of associated accessory opportunities. The enormous rush to the suburbs of city dwellers created a hunger for products and services to beautify and improve their new houses. Mail order helped fill the gap with plants, fertilizers, painting applicators, decorative items and an ever-increasing number of home improvement products.

The former population explosion of the age group that moved through nursery school to college and into jobs like army ants created an entire array of mail order opportunities, from remedial homework courses to aids for getting a better job. The trend towards far greater leisure time has produced opportunities for every type of hobby, sport and special-interest equipment and instruction.

And with every new, lurching swing of popular activity, there will be huge new mail order opportunities, often *reviving* mail order items long in moth balls. So keep your eye on the next trend and cash in on it in mail order. Some mail order items seem eternal, others transitory and some cyclic. Consider revivals.

A former creative head of Huber Hoge and Sons was a student of mail order and advertising in all its aspects. He located an advertisement run successfully before 1900 for a book on how to make money in real estate. It was short, simple and effective. A Huber Hoge and Sons client was currently publishing a book on how to make money in real estate. Our creative director transposed a word or two out of the old ad to bring it up to date and applicable, and he ran it for our client. The old ad sold the new book quite successfully, apparently pulling as well as it had before 1900.

On the other hand, for another publisher client we re-ran one of the great mail order ads of all time (in another form of advertising) . . . the "Which fork should I use for chicken salad?" ad of the 1920's . . . for the same Lillian Eichler Book of Etiquette brought up to date. The old magic had died. In fact, no ad we came up with pulled by mail order for any etiquette books we tried. People were no longer socially insecure in this way.

A recession makes some depression mail order items revive successfully, particularly economic survival books of various kinds. Cable TV revived some of the mail order items of early TV, which in turn revived long-dormant demonstration items of all kinds. We used to drive to Atlantic City. pick up demonstrators and drive them back to film studios or TV stations. The same demonstration that worked in Atlantic City usually worked on TV.

This is the story of a portent of a quarter-billion dollars of mail order sales from outer space . . . many years before it happened. A number of years ago, in a few months time, our family-owned company, Harrison-Hoge Industries, Inc., sold over one-million dollars of pocket adding machines.

The machine was the ADDIATOR, made in West Germany, a superb, meticulously made but extremely simple stylus-into-slots machine. You simply pulled down the stylus to get the solution in the answer window.

What opened my eyes was its absolutely universal appeal. We could run a page in Time or in Woman's Day, run on radio or TV . . . day or night . . . equally successfully. We obviously sold to housewives, students, salesmen, shopkeepers, whatever. I realized that it indicated a hunger for an adding machine far away from the offices. I felt that someday an electric office model would be low enough priced to get this market.

This was the market that was ready and waiting when the first chip calculator (a by-product of the space industry) was advertised in small ads in the Wall Street Journal, the New York Times and magazines. The ads, as they got bigger, had an uncanny resemblance to our ADDIATOR ads of years before, but asked about 25 times as much for the product.

The rest is history. The mail order introduction of chip calculators burst like a comet on the distribution scene, outmoded every previous method of selling calculators, created an undreamed of giant industry . . . leading to huge markets overseas and even an improved U.S. balance of payments. It happened so fast that few people got in on it. I didn't.

So let's keep our eyes open for the next mail order bonanza.

Chapter 5

ITEM DECISIONS

Right items for the medium . . .
luxuries vs necessities . . .
personalized . . . demonstration . . .
seasonal . . . Christmas items

Each medium of advertising creates its own associated offers. TV, radio, the Wall Street Journal, credit card magazines have each had powerful mail order side effects. And so does every important medium of advertising.

Years ago, top-hit bargain combinations in batches of 16 current hits, 24 current hits and so forth first began to succeed on "Top 40" radio stations and then to boom on "dance party" teen TV shows. Old movies proved the perfect vehicle for *old time* nostalgia record hit combinations.

The Wall Street Journal's incredible mass circulation among businessmen made every type of business aid and executive luxury sold to businessmen suddenly capable of surprising mail order success. The credit card magazines – Signature, Carte Blanche and Travel and Leisure – opened up still higher-ticket merchandise of the same type. Jewelry selling for $100 to $200 . . . executive training courses . . . lavish wallets . . . language records and innumerable other executive items, particularly those that could be charged to business and used personally, became suddenly far simpler to sell.

At our suggestion, a client of ours once bought 15 minutes on network radio before and after the Metropolitan Opera. Week after week, we played records of next week's opera and advertised and sold tens of thousands of Stories of the Great Operas, edited by Milton Cross, who regularly announced the Metropolitan Opera programs.

We call them "related offers" because, in a sense, the entire medium becomes a vehicle for the offer, greatly multiplying the effectiveness of the advertising and often making the purchase of the advertising an extreme mail order bargain. And with every new media success, there's new opportunity for you to tie in with mail order items.

Let's consider luxury items vs. necessities. Your choice will be largely determined by your operation and by the general economic situation at the time.

In the late depression, when I started out, a dollar taken from a wallet for a purchase could give the owner a traumatic shock. He or she might resent being sold. Only some overwhelming benefit could justify the awful wrench of parting with that dollar. We had to concentrate on necessities in those days.

I knew one publisher who specialized in taking "blotting paper" editions – sets of lots of volumes of thick paper pages and small numbers of pages – and compressing them with the same number of words into bulging, one-volume editions at a bargain price. He did well in the worst of the depression . . . and badly when business conditions improved . . . and the market for "blotting paper" editions revived.

For quite a few years, the trend has been to luxuries. I know a wine and liquor importer who has become rich since the depression with a simple formula. He sells only the most expensive wine, champagne or liquor. If a liquor store or restaurant lists a competitive brand at a higher price, he doesn't want to sell to them anymore. He has found his market of successful, prosperous executives and coupon-clipping retired people and widows who are insecure about wine and liquor selection. They can afford the best. They are happy to solve their selection problem by choosing the most expensive wine or liquor on the list.

In mail order, even the lowest-cost items have usually been far from necessities. Mass circulations for those with above-average incomes, like the Wall Street Journal, made higher-priced luxuries more easily saleable. The credit card revolution made it far easier still. But each time economic conditions look bad, I get out my list of depression mail order hits. Luxury items may continue. Some mail order firms may have an affinity for selling them. Yet I feel that for some years the public will again be far more selective and more determined to get real *value* and benefit from articles they buy by mail.

Fads and fun items are the most speculative of all. They tend to lose their appeal as suddenly as they originally gained it. They may become even more speculative if unemployment continues high and incomes continue to buy less than formerly. The future trends will probably be more and more to value, as far as luxuries are concerned, and with more emphasis on basic necessities.

Personalized products are often ideal for mail order, but many fail anyway. While some retailers offer personalization of some items, most retailers do not. Most personalized items are not generally available via stores. Yet the vast majority of personalized items *can be* handled via mail order. Often someone who has purchased a personalized product likes the idea of personalization, and he or she will gladly buy more personalized items from the same mail order company.

Many manufacturers have items ideal for personalization. Many retailers are set up for personalization. Yet many of them have never *explored* mail order operations based on their present capabilities. Some businesses are entirely based on personalization, and are far more suited to mail order than to store distribution. Coats of arms, birth signs, place mats, greeting cards, pens and pencils, clothes markers, name plates, book matches, mail boxes, address number signs – the numbers and kinds of personalized items are endless.

We have sold TV repair instructions individualized for the TV set you own. We know of birthday records with the name of your child played on the record. The computer hath wrought many personalized wonders, from I.Q. tests to individualized story books with the name of your child all through the book. The percentage of personalized products that sells well via mail order is higher than for other items. But the percentage of nightmares in fulfillment is higher, too. We have dropped some personalized offers as impractical *for us* to fulfill. Often a percentage of orders *cannot* be fulfilled.

When personalization was based on stocking a variety of alternatives, we often found no way to automate the picking of items. Labor cost was often out of line. Frequently, too much space and too much inventory were required, and some inventory loss was hard to avoid.

Go into an intriguing personalized product . . . if your "test" advertising succeeds, if you've made some sort of time-studies of labor time of fulfillment and you still feel you can make money.

The typical mail order item is a demonstration item. It's an item that, seen by itself, does not convey what it can do. And packaging and ordinary display alone rarely do the job. It's a product that can do something better or has an entirely new use, but that has got to be seen *in action* to be appreciated and believed.

Without display, it often gathers dust in a retail store. But with a demonstrator, it becomes a lead item. To project *personal* demonstration *in stores nationwide* is more complex than we have up to now been capable of. But sometimes the identical demonstration can simply be shortened, streamlined, videotaped for TV and run with a mail order offer in huge and profitable volume on stations nationwide. It's ideal on a TV shopping network. It's perfect for a video kiosk in any traffic area which can show a videotaped demonstration and take credit card orders.

Sometimes a successful demonstration can be converted into a newspaper or magazine ad. It often can be successfully done with step-by-step picture sequences in direct mail brochures. We've successfully demonstrated with an automated electrical display.

Demonstration items can be in any field. They're frequent in housewares, hardware, toys, games, hobbies, sports, and in industrial, technical and business office products and for accessories for almost anything from cars to appliances. Demonstration items run up against resistance from many of the giant retailers. Such retailers can only handle so many demonstration items. Life is simpler for many in the organizations without them. But demonstration items are the most sought-after items and best opportunities for mail order people.

Seasonal items are sometimes neglected somewhat by retailers and can be a mail order opportunity. They also can be more *dangerous* in mail order than more year-round products. They require advance planning far ahead of the season. They usually require more gamble in inventory than year-round products. If you test a new seasonal product and get a hit, it's often too late to get an adequate supply for all you can sell that season. Therefore, it's tempting to stock up ahead of season, perhaps before your product is adequately tested. We've made money with seasonal products, but we find the testing and projecting frustrating.

Testing and projecting a non-seasonal item is considerably safer. There's less likelihood and less of a problem in "carrying over" unsold inventory. Go into seasonal items, but with extra caution.

Christmas items can make big profits, but can be dangerous.

Some Christmas items are hard to sell the rest of the year. Carrying them over can tie up money. If people buy a Christmas item, they want to get it in ample time to mail it themselves and have it delivered before Christmas. If advertised in December, it should be offered for delivery by second-day air. Otherwise it will arrive too late and cause angry, disappointed customers. This is vital in December magazines; otherwise run no later than the big holiday advertising issues in November, either delivered to subscribers or on the newsstands.

I have known a mail order man to take as many as 10 pages of Christmas items at a maximum discount price in the peak gift issue of November in the one magazine he found best. Sometimes he and his art and production man worked *all night* to prepare it. But selling cost was usually lower and profit per dollar higher for that one issue than otherwise during the year, so the effort was usually well worth it.

Often a new item which must be explained and demonstrated is best pioneered at other times of the year. It is not yet a *demand* Christmas item. As we advertise more in our normal season, the desire for the product grows. The concept of giving it for Christmas becomes acceptable. Finally, the Christmas season can become its peak selling period.

A new item that has swept the country for the previous year or so becomes the best Christmas item of all. Many successful mail order items can become Christmas items. Many sell poorly at Christmas.

Many successful Christmas items in stores lose money as mail order single items sold in print or on TV. Other items which are not as successful in stores at Christmas will prove ideal TV-demonstrable Christmas items. Some Christmas items are excellent in mail order catalogs but poor as single items sold by mail order outside the catalog.

Children's Christmas items, such as toys and games and children's hobbies, are bought in stores in the worst of times, when the scrimping is more in adult presents. Jewelry, both for men and women, will sell far better at Christmas than otherwise. But we have been in the toy manufacturing business and found it difficult to sell most of the toys we made as mail order items. We've been in the costume jewelry manufacturing business and found most of the jewelry items difficult to sell through mail order at Christmas or at any other time.

Because we successfully sold the toys through major catalogs, we did not compete with a catalog of our own. We had one successful jewelry mail order item, but did not secure enough other unique jewelry items to justify a catalog. In a trusted catalog, many items will sell profitably which will not sell profitably outside the catalog. Only some of the most successful items within the catalog will sell at a profit through ads and commercials elsewhere. Neither our toys nor secondary jewelry items were successful enough to do so.

Don't advertise by mail order a toy or game sold very widely before Christmas at substantially lower prices in the discount stores. If you do, you will probably lose money with your mail order ad. You're best off with an item not sold in stores.

We rarely sell games. The old favorites are sold widely and discounted. New games are difficult to predict, "fad" items that may or may not catch on. Often they're hard to explain as to purpose or rules. But some games seem so instantly simple and clear, and yet different and unique, that they may be ideal for a gift.

Executive gifts, luxury gifts and hobby gifts are often ideal. A Christmas item that is low in price, as well as strong in appeal, has maximum chance. New toys, instantly desirable when demonstrated, are perfect to sell before Christmas on TV. We have sold huge volumes of toys by TV before Christmas.

We avoid Christmas items for mail order that cost less than $10 and those that cost much more than $100. We avoid them if they seem hard to explain or demonstrate. We avoid items that might break in shipping. In jewelry, we also prefer items from $10 to $50. We seek an item that has already succeeded as a Christmas item, yet is not at all widely available.

Every year Christmas items are tested successfully – too late to project that year. It may be in a fall issue of one magazine or in just one mail order catalog. It may be in just one store catalog or as a cooperative ad (in which the manufacturer contributes part or all of the advertising cost) for just one specialized store. It may be advertised on just a few TV stations.

The test results can be a source of invaluable information. If it's your item, keep it quiet. Your chances of making a killing during the next Christmas season are largely based on your secrecy during the long months in between. If you find someone who has had such success, and you can acquire the item on a sensible basis, do so. Every year, there are tiny entrepreneurs who, with their last dollars, find some Christmas success.

Such items have to be re-tested the following year before projecting. Conditions can change radically in the meantime. It may have been seen and copied at a far lower price, or copied and radically improved ... making your item obsolete. You may have been lied to about results.

I'll discuss this more in our section on testing.

Chapter 6

FINDING ITEMS TO SELL
ITEMS

---

*Keeping eyes and ears open for
items as giveaways, self-liquidators
and partial self-liquidators*

When you find your first item, you may want to look for a giveaway, another item to give with the item that you will sell. The right giveaway can increase tremendously your item's chances of success.

The perfect giveaway for us is an item we have just *heavily* advertised through mail order and that is *related* to the item we are selling. It is *low enough in cost* so as not to significantly reduce the gross profit margin of the item we are selling. It is light enough and compact enough, preferably *flat*, to slip into the item package without significantly added postage. It will please and not disappoint. The ideal giveaway of any type should lend itself to demonstration. A giveaway that carries a trusted, famous brand name can extend its prestige to the product being sold. It should be instantly desirable when illustrated and require very few words of explanation. Its use should be clear and apparent. All this is not always feasible. Most items are impractical giveaways – and the wrong item can *decrease* your sales.

It can *cheapen* the appearance of your advertising and lower the reader's opinion of your product. Its advantages may not be sufficiently clear. It can take precious advertising space or time away from your product that will lose more orders than it adds. A merchandise giveaway packed with a book can require a higher postage rate than the far cheaper book-rate postage and cost more in added postage than the giveaway costs itself. It can break or damage your product in the mail or harm it in some other way, as for example a chemical staining your product. It can cost too much and require more extra orders than it secures.

To find the right one and avoid the wrong one, you have to be a giveaway detective, just as you need to be an item detective. You can be both at the same time. Fortunately, giveaways with just some of these desired qualifications are sometimes extremely successful.

We try to combine two successful items related to each other. Sometimes a giveaway fits a product ideally and greatly increases sales. We have sold water-soluble fertilizer and plants with great success, mailing advertising of one to the just-secured mail order customers of the other. When we took a successful offer of three different color roses growing on one plant and gave it free with a sale of water-soluble fertilizer, we had a hit.

For years all over the world, sewing machine companies gave away our Perfect Fit ADJUST-O-MATIC dress form with their sewing machine. The dress form, by making custom-fit dressmaking possible, increased the benefits of the sewing machine. It also added a substantial-value known gift. By running a great deal of advertising for years, we established price value as well as desirability of the form.

An excellent giveaway is frequently an instruction book or booklet in a related field, which can make or save many times the product's cost. Sometimes an accessory giveaway can increase the use value of your product. Sometimes a remainder item, preferably related, has previously sold at a substantial price and is a perfect bargain giveaway.

We often succeed with a giveaway with just some of our preferred qualifications. An unrelated item, for instance, is often great. When new automated equipment first brought ballpoint pens down to a small fraction of their former price, successful bargain offers of 20 pens, 40 refills, etc., began to be made. We had sold close to one-million dollars worth of ADDIATORS through mail order, but results then dropped badly to below the break-even point. By combining a pretested offer of ballpoint refills with another pretested offer of ballpoint pens, and offering both free with an ADDIATOR, we got a new hit that did almost another one-million dollars at good profit.

Instead of a giveaway, you may look for a self-liquidator – an extra item that you offer at cost including mailing. You give a bigger bargain in return for the customer purchasing your item. The saving you offer is often far more dramatic than the value of a pure giveaway. When first introduced, self-liquidator prices were low. For years, the average self-liquidator price asked has constantly risen. Products offering self-liquidators have broadened from staples to luxuries and items in between. As it has become more difficult to give dramatic savings in either self-liquidators or giveaways, partial self-liquidators – offered for enough to cover part of their cost in the mail – have come in, making it possible to go into more desirable items.

Self-liquidators are widely used in mail order and very effective. Selecting a self-liquidator, or partial self-liquidator, has the same requirements as selecting a giveaway, but you can spend more per item. It's easier to select a mail order hit, or one that's just begun to drop off at its original, higher price.

Each is only effective if it produces enough extra sales to justify itself. In each case, ability to slip it into the package containing the item can greatly lessen, or even almost eliminate, extra shipping cost and enable you to give more value to the purchaser.

Among giveaways, self-liquidators and partial self-liquidators, you have a wide spectrum to consider. While you look for items, keep your eyes and ears open for all these as well.

ITEM CONCLUSIONS

*Item morals . . . doing what you
want . . . keeping things simple . . .
keeping up the perpetual search*

American as apple pie to "knock-off" – copy or steal – an item.

Certainly it's safer to go into an item someone else has originated than testing something brand new yourself. We do not like others to copy us and would vigorously sue them if our product is patented, as it usually is. We do not copy others for this reason. But it's a matter of choice and personal belief. Of course, many products are so generic that the item you might be considering copying can hardly be original.

There *are* drawbacks to copying. You may be stealing a failure. You may be copying something that has scraped the cream off the top, and you will get the skimmed milk. In any case, you're at best sharing the business . . . and as the Johnny-come-lately. Generally, those who believe in copying will copy *frequently*. They will happily accept a smaller share of other people's successes, time after time, and virtually eliminate testing loss. Those who mainly originate may hit a far bigger jackpot and become entrenched first for a far more permanent business, which is particularly important if they go on to trade distribution. So take your choice.

A mail order business can be what *you* want it to be – far more than any other business.

You can *select* the item or items which you care to sell – and later shift into any other item or items almost at will. Mail order men who make big money, most safely, usually choose to make the simpler of two choices.

Large and bulky products require 10,000 square feet to do several hundred thousands of dollars in sales. Small, light and compact items can do several million dollars from the same 10,000 square feet.

Some items require getting inquiries and closing the sale by direct mail. Others can be closed in a one-step sale. Some items are complex to make. Others are extremely easy.

My wife (and associate) asks, "Is it smelly? Is it noisy? Is it dirty?" in regard to making anything. A "yes" answer gets a "no" vote. We try to select the simpler, easier, more pleasant products that require the least financing in relation to sales. And you can keep things simple, too.

The search for new mail order items never ends.

Every business and every item has a birth, life and death. But a business can have an indefinite number of item lives. Business growth is based on adding successive life-span curves of new products to old. Therefore, a successful business has at all times more new-growth, rising curves (or a bigger single one) than declining curves of dying products.

In mail order the birth, life and death of an item is often telescoped. Usually, the greater the intensity of the mail order campaign, the more different forms of advertising used, the bigger the advertisements and the more frequently run, the more competition is attracted and the shorter is the overall product life. That's why the more successful a direct marketer is, the more keenly he or she feels the necessity of having another hit in the oven, preferably several, to replace the present hit or hits as it or they inevitably, and ultimately, decline.

Every mail order man or woman gradually forms his or her own criteria as to the kind of mail order item sought after, feeling an affinity for some kinds of items and repelled by others. The items rejected, almost by reflex action, are a multitude. The right item decision becomes the "sixth sense" of the mail order operator. And you will get this "feel" for mail order items too.

Next we'll take up selling the product.

BOOK III

MAIL ORDER
PERSUASION

*Developing skills in
creating ... testing ...
buying ... getting full
value from
publication, broadcast
and direct mail
advertising*

Chapter 1

THE CATAPULT

---

*Understanding . . . respecting . . .
harnessing advertising's power to
propel you where you want to go . . .
a brief personal history*

Advertising, effectively used, has again and again catapulted tiny mail order firms to big success.

Your success, and survival, in mail order will be greatly determined by your ability to get more effective advertising and more value from each advertising dollar, from others or yourself. In mail order, it's usually the only way to grow.

The French statesman Clemenceau said war was too important to leave to the generals. And in mail order, you may feel advertising is too important to leave solely to outside advertising specialists. Many successful mail order operators feel that to leave advertising entirely to others while risking your money is playing blind-man's-bluff. Whether you wish to get more value from your advertising agency or become your own advertising agency, it's important to develop your own mail order advertising skills. No advertising agency or free-lance writer can be perpetually available for every creative task remotely connected with your advertising. This is particularly so for a mail order moonlighter. Besides, it's a rare thrill to make people do what you want . . . by your own proposal, your words or your demonstration.

An actor gets applause as his ego bath. A salesman feels a surging sense of personal power each time he makes that sale. But to see the actual mail of hundreds, thousands, and in time, tens of thousands or even hundreds of thousands of people who never intended to perform the action *you* caused them to take – can be a supremely rewarding power thrill.

It's a great satisfaction to be able to check thoroughly into each advertising buy before you risk your money.

Any operator of a mail order business *can* develop a "feel" for making each advertising message more effective and each advertising purchase safer. The first step is to understand the *power* of mail order advertising and the tremendous variations in effectiveness of the dol-

---

lars and effort that you put into it. Yet few do.

A salesman of a nationally advertised product realizes that the advertising is an effective help to him, but often wonders *how* effective it is, and is apt to credit product success largely to personal sales ability.

A production man may consider advertising effective, yet feel that it cannot be measured and that the real secret of sales is simply to make the product better and more efficiently . . . at lower cost. And if unfamiliar with business or advertising, you may wonder whether advertising works at all.

My observation is that advertising is underappreciated by most small *non-mail order* businesses . . . is less effectively used by them . . . and less value than possible is obtained by them for each advertising dollar spent. The cost per thousand readers of mass publications used by large advertisers is often a fraction of the cost per thousand readers of small publications used by small advertisers. Few very small advertisers are knowledgeable in the media selection open to them and are influenced by salesmen, often for the *wrong* publication for them. Even medium-size advertisers rarely get the use of top advertising creative talent – and if they do, rarely get the attention and time required. Large advertisers have a near monopoly of top advertising talent employed by large advertising agencies.

Some small-town radio stations compete for a tiny share of the overall radio audience and are sometimes overpriced. Printing costs for small advertisers are often several times per thousand those for large runs used by large advertisers. A surprising percentage of advertising and promotion dollars of smaller advertisers goes into the kinds of advertising the largest advertisers feel they cannot afford, from ads in banquet programs to advertising novelties. Much of the advertising of smaller non-mail order advertisers is wasted, largely because it cannot be measured and because the operators of smaller businesses have often never been told some of the advertising facts of life that are commonplace to the largest advertisers.

Many who go into mail order expect mail order advertising to produce profitable results almost automatically. I have seen many small (and some big) mail order firms fail to get off the ground simply because of poor use of advertising. They did not have enough knowledge of, or respect for, the potential power of each advertising dollar spent. They did not harness that power fully enough.

Often it's simply a matter of quick and careless creating and buying of advertising. This can be true of some advertising agencies as well as of mail order firms. The strategy behind the advertising must be sound. Only careful, thorough, dogged research can make this possible. A sound plan must come before action. It must be based on objective analysis, not on personal preference alone.

Advertising buys can be *sold* to the client, rather than scientifically bought for the client – they can be justified instead of analyzed.

A copywriter or art director can be previously trained to please, to "sell" creative work whether good or bad – often work that is written too fast or created too carelessly. We must each learn to be a mail order perfectionist – regarding what we do and what others do for us.

There are superb mail order advertising agencies and consultants. My method emphasizes the enormous contribution of these talented professionals. In former days, some of the most talented mail order agencies invested their efforts for talented but underfinanced clients – putting in great professional efforts for small tests of new accounts.

But today the most successful direct marketing agencies are owned by the biggest general advertising agencies. The first step after acquisition is for the general agency to send in its comptroller and to fix quite large minimum fees to take on any new accounts. This tends to create a near monopoly of the best direct marketing advertising talent for big direct marketing advertisers.

You may well find an able advertising associate or small agency. The reality is that, as a mail order moonlighter, you may not get such top talent interested in handling your advertising. We'll discuss this later. But there's no reason not to be able to master mail order advertising yourself. The ad either works or it doesn't. Effective copywriters and art directors are those who create profitable ads. Effective buyers of advertising are those who consistently select additional further media similar to that profitably used in a successful test. This is called a projection. To project to more and more media and not lose is a necessity for continued success. The results tell all. Much of the art of creating or buying advertising that makes money is the thoroughness of the effort put in. In my course, I'll try to give you the basic understanding and "feel" for it.

If you're in mail order, whatever your previous background may be, mastering mail order advertising can mean a great deal to you.

If you're a top advertising professional, just *improving* your creative skills can jump your income. If you're a businessman who must rely on employees, consultants or advertising agencies, acquiring your own skills can help you get far more out of your creative people, avoid mail order losses from weak advertising, and perhaps get the satisfaction of a mail order *hit* created entirely by yourself. If you are a younger executive or just starting your business career, by developing creative skills you're gaining a highly marketable asset.

If you're a salesman, a skill in writing advertising copy enables you to translate your salesmanship into print or broadcast media, a far easier step than starting from scratch. And if you're an inventor or creator of the product, you're able to take all that know-how cooped up inside of you and convert it into money-making advertising ability.

I was born into advertising. My father started an advertising agency, Huber Hoge, Inc., in 1920. As my brothers and I grew up, we lived advertising . . . ate it and drank it . . . and slept and woke up talking it.

Today, over six-and-a-half decades after my father founded Huber Hoge, Inc., of our little group of companies we're proudest of Huber Hoge and Sons Advertising, Inc. We keep it small and we are choosy about clients.

My father, Huber Hoge, was an old-timer in advertising. For years, he had been with one of the several blue-chip advertising agencies of the day and had worked with some of the largest companies and highest-quality products.

I remember as a child going to the Advertising Club in New York at 35th Street and Park Avenue, where he was a founder. As I grew up, I sensed from others that he was a dean of the advertising field. And later, being part of Huber Hoge and Sons was a family thrill.

At first my older brother John, and then I, became fascinated with mail order. As we gathered expertise at Huber Hoge and Sons, we became fortunate enough to work with the finest blue-chip mail order advertisers.

We became specialists in broadcast advertising for direct response, first in radio and then TV. Later we went heavily into magazine, newspaper and direct mail advertising for mail order.

I took no courses in advertising. Mine was on-the-job training, as yours may be, too. First I learned to analyze, select and negotiate advertising buys. Then I learned to create advertising.

At first, I was a catalyst bringing together talented people, urging them on with encouragement, teasing them with incentives. Then I provided them with research – more and more of it. Gradually, my experts taught me. Step by step, I began to write myself . . . first in one form of advertising, then in another . . . first for the simplest advertising and, finally, the most complex.

As my mail order copy stars taught me more and more, I trained younger writers with the know-how passed on to me. And as each of them developed, each taught me more. Still today, as we develop new talent, I learn from them.

As much as we had learned working as an advertising agency for others, our thinking about mail order advertising began to change when we began to test our own products and apply our mail order know-how to making money on our own items.

We began to spend our own money . . . make our own profits . . . and take our own losses. And quickly, we *really* began to understand advertising for direct response to a fuller potential than we ever had before.

We built the business we wanted . . . created the way of life we desired . . . and obtained it from mail order know-how.

Chapter 2

THE BEGINNINGS OF
INSPIRATION

*Creating a product or company
name . . . logotype . . . instructions
. . . a classified ad . . . an editorial
story on your product*

What is it? Who are these people selling it? That's the reaction of
those reading your ad.

The right name for your company can increase the number of orders you receive every time you advertise. The wrong name can
decrease these orders. And the right or wrong name of your product
can do the same. Yet mail order names are sometimes selected with little thought. Often the product sold seems inappropriate to the seller's
name.

The right name for a catalog creates an instant image. The Banana
Republic . . . The Sharper Image . . . Victoria's Secret – all in San Fran-
cisco – project the exotic, the unusual, some mystery and considerable
mystique. This is vital because the right concept for a catalog is far
more important than a single successful opening item. The ideal is
both.

A logotype is an artist's rendition of your company or product
name, hand-lettered or in special type, often combining the name with
a symbol.

If the product name is in no way indicative of the product field, it
takes extra words and valuable space in your advertising just to make
clear what you are selling and to identify your product name and company name with it. If you ever plan to launch your product into store
distribution, this identification becomes overwhelmingly important. It's
the only way for you to get the business and not a competitor.

So let's discuss selecting names for your company, division or
product. The right name can come to you in the night.

Anyone can think of it, from your five-year-old daughter to
Grandpa. You may stumble on it by sheer accident. Any friend or pas-
serby may give it to you. Users of the product under its old name may

become so fond of it they give it a pet name – that is perfect. But we think it can best come from working on the advertising. The research alone can come up with endless name possibilities. We usually start creating advertising before we finalize the name selection. During this period, we give the product a working name for use in preliminary copy. Then, out of all our research notes and all our drafts of working copy, we pick possible names.

Now we list all the names from every source that seem at all worth considering. Sometimes we have several writers working on the project, each with his own list. Everyone in our office and factory is demonstrated the product and asked to submit a name. Sometimes we get a blend of two names, each originally on a different list.

We own a dress form for home sewers whose name we selected this way. On one list was the name Perfect Fit. On another list, the name Adjust-O-Matic. We chose the name Perfect-Fit ADJUST-O-MATIC. And that is the way our logotype for this product name appears today.

Sometimes the right name comes to you quickly. Sometimes it takes a little agonizing over . . . for days and weeks. Sometimes you later come up with so clearly superior a name that it becomes worth changing.

When you select a company or catalog name, it better be good, because you hope to live with it a long time. And it better be appropriate for activities your business will conduct later, as well as those it conducts now.

Decades ago, companies were often content to make one product line, and their company name indicated their product line. But then, gradually, things would happen. General Electric bought the Hotpoint Stove Company . . . making Hotpoint Electric stoves. Years later, the new hot item of the Hotpoint division of General Electric was a refrigerator. General Electric had to spend millions of dollars to persuade people that a company famous for hot things was good at making cold things. General Electric felt Hotpoint was a trusted name and that, since both products were electrical, it would be better to use the hot name for cold things. I would prefer to avoid inappropriate image association.

Your company name (as our parent company name) may have no special connotation for a specific type of product. It may be based on your location. Ours was. Or it may be based on your family name. Ours is partially. But the reason for name selection may change.

From the standpoint of order and simplicity, it only seems logical to have one umbrella name for all activities. But the variety of products we sell is sufficiently odd so that it seems inappropriate to advertise wildly different products under the same company name. So, gradually over the years, we have tended to create divisions with names appropriate to one product line.

My advice is to try to think ahead of the possible future contingencies that may occur before you finalize your product name. I would recommend a product name that clearly indicates what you sell and, if possible, starts the selling process. Our product, "The Stomach Eliminator," is a rower-type device particularly designed to eliminate fatty stomach bulges as part of an exercise and diet plan. I would recommend that you not select your company name on geographical location or your family name. If you keep getting partners, you may end up sounding like a law firm.

Later we'll discuss procedures for clearing the name.

A trademark is a U.S.-registered name and logotype. The first creative step for your copywriter or writers (or yourself) is to come up with the name you want to live with. The first creative step for your art director (or artist) is to come up with the perfect logotype for your product and company. It is the clothes your company and product name wear. Your logotype will largely determine the effect your business card, stationery, billhead, packaging and name of product or company will create in any form of advertising or even trade show. A major company will spend thousands of dollars simply to develop the perfect logotype.

We watch pennies. And possibly you should too. But we can try our very utmost to get the most effective logotype our money will buy. Today is a time of innovative and imaginative company names . . . from the smallest retail shop . . . and tiniest mail order firm. Their very names and logotypes call forth images of uniqueness, flair and style, and enhanced desirability. In mail order, it simply means more orders from every ad, even acceptance of a higher price as reasonable.

So suffer a little as you change that name and as you pay the art bill for your logotype. And even then, don't hesitate to change the name and logotype later if your changing situation warrants it.

After selecting a name for your product and company, your next job may be to write "idiot-proof" instructions.

Most mail order items are shipped disassembled. Many are do-it-yourself kits. And customers who can't put your items together will return them to you, particularly if they're not cheap . . . and sometimes not pay you at all if you sell on credit. Instructions that are simple and easy to follow are often the hardest to write.

Inventors are in love with their products, find them ridiculously easy for anyone to assemble and feel they require scarcely any instruction at all. Scientists have their own language, incomprehensible to us as mortals. Salesmen are optimistically vague in instructions they write. Translated instructions are ideal material for TV comedians. And writing instructions, if you've never done it before, is enough to drive you out of the business.

It takes a cool head and a disciplined mind to attack the problem. It requires guinea pigs you're not related to and don't know, who've never used the product before, to read your instructions, look at your instruction diagrams and pictures and actually put the thing together.

If you go about writing directions in a thorough, organized way it will be done correctly and save time, work and money in the end. You cut returns, eliminate correspondence with confused customers and save the work of having to re-write a careless first attempt.

Let's assume that you have your product and find that you can ship it disassembled with a saving in labor and in postage, but that you have no instructions for the user to put it together. Let's get started.

Find someone who has never before seen the product, but who is a logical potential user. Get the product inventor, owner or other proper person (perhaps yourself) to demonstrate to him or her how to put the product together . . . from opening the package to final assembly . . . and how to use it.

Have someone use a camera to take one picture after another of each phase of the demonstration. Include close-ups of important hand and arm movements, an exploded picture of all parts side by side on a table or on the floor, close-ups of picking up of parts and connecting one part to another, step by step to completion, and with any product use pictures.

Make sure that the specific name of each component part is given by the demonstrator. Check that the demonstration is clear to the prospective user. Bring a tape recorder and tape the entire demonstration, including the user's questions and the demonstrator's answers. Ask the user to open another package, assemble and use it, with the demonstrator watching. If the user makes errors, have the demonstrator explain and correct them. Tape this as well. Take more pictures. The use of a camcorder is even better.

Transcribe the tapes on your word processor. Step by step, write and type a description of each visual action as seen in the demonstration but not heard on the tape. Arrange the pictures into a sequence of steps in the order as demonstrated. Pick the best picture to demonstrate each step.

If you own a Macintosh and MacPrint, MacDraw and PageMaker software, you can do all I'll next describe far more easily and quickly on computer. Otherwise, here are instructions my sixteen-year-old son (and nine-year computer veteran) considers quite obsolete.

Paste a big sheet of paper down on a big drawing board. Place each selected picture in proper sequence in a column on the far right of the sheet. Start with the exploded parts picture and end with a picture of the completed article. Scissor out appropriate words, taken off the tape, to describe each step of this demonstration in print. Paste them down to the left of each matching picture. Start with the naming of each component part opposite the exploded parts picture. Give yourself ample room on the sheet for pictures and a description of each step. Scissor out the appropriate descriptive words of the visual demonstration and paste them opposite the matching picture and underneath the demonstration words. Use several pages if necessary.

Read and reread. Begin to edit into understandable instructions.

Try different breakdowns into step sequence. Reduce the number of pictures. Select the best to illustrate each step. In editing, make each step crystal clear as to what you are asking the user to do. Specify the use of left or right hand, thumb, index or whatever finger. Give each instruction in exact detail. Make sure that the name used for each component is as simple and self-explanatory as possible. If not, rename it – hopefully improving it. Always refer to any one part with the same name and not an alternate name. Keep all words simple. Try to write to about a sixth grade level. Keep re-editing. Cut or expand copy as needed for each step. Sharpen . . . simplify . . . and clarify until satisfied. Excerpt words and phrases that can be used as captions underneath or with arrows to important parts of pictures.

If you now feel that instructions and pictures are completely understandable to anyone who has never seen the product before, photocopy six sets. Find six logical prospective users, each of whom has never seen the product. Give each a package of your product with your instructions inside the package. Ask each to assemble and use the product. Watch each attempt to do so. If misunderstandings of instructions occur, get help from your demonstrator. Re-edit and try out your instructions on more virgin users.

If you are a lucky Macintosh owner, you can now try some desktop publishing. If you are even luckier and own a laser printer as well, you can come up with near-professional reproduction proofs to supply a printer. But you need not at first spend the money to print them.

If the directions are proven, photo-offset enough copies for your first test. If you don't own a Macintosh and followed my primitive directions, don't worry about lack of professional finish. Do worry about clarity. Clear instructions reduce returns. More professionally finished package inserts pull more re-orders, but can come later. Your problem initially is understanding, not prestige.

Once your ad is successful, you can consider more professional photographs, drawings, diagrams, typography and higher-grade paper. Only spend money to upgrade the effect as more volume justifies. You are very unlikely to have extra refund requests from photo-offset, typewritten instructions with simple photographs, except for quite luxurious products. If so, you may consider working with your art director from the start, but your initial costs will be far higher. I recommend waiting in either case until the ad pays out.

Only a big volume of shipments justifies the added investment. If so, consider with your art director whether drawings will be superior to photographs and whether one or more diagrams can help clarify. Your art director can sketch out appropriate diagrams and equivalent drawings for each picture and undoubtedly greatly improve the styling with his layout. Each added professional touch improves and costs more money. Your situation will determine your decision. You can compromise and upgrade as you reprint, a little at a time.

And even after your labor (it's happened to us after seven executives successively refined and improved one set of instructions), you'll be told that you've got a great product, if anybody could be told how to use it. But, patience. Instructions can and must be written and illustrated in a simple, understandable way.

How would you like to write a simple classified ad? Just reading classified ads can be quite an education. And writing classified ads and testing them can be a cheap and sound introduction to effective advertising.

Each classified ad that may only cost a few dollars, by either succeeding or failing is *teaching*, and at pretty low cost. Even in national magazines, the cost of one classified ad is very low. It takes a longer than-average ad, in a two-million circulation magazine, to cost $200 to $250. And one such ad has often started a profitable business that has lasted for a lifetime.

Look at your Sunday newspaper. Read help-wanted and situation-wanted ads. Read real estate ads for sale and rental of apartments, offices, factories, houses, land. Note that in these classifications there's a marketplace. Buyers are *seeking* sellers and vice versa. *Attention-getting* devices are less important than how desirable and believable the ad makes the real estate. In times of few apartment vacancies, just the fact that *any* apartment is available that has anywhere near the qualifications you seek is *news*. In such times, the ads tend to be tiny, often the minimum of two lines, or whatever required. Because one ad, in one paper, one day, will usually rent the apartment, *frugality* is important. Why take three lines to rent an apartment when two lines would do just as well?

Perhaps only 10 to 12 words are allowed. The phone number is usually counted as two words. This leaves eight or ten words. The answer, in such cases, is abbreviation. The apartment seekers have to work at it; soon they can guess, fairly accurately, what the ad is trying to say. The copy need only be factual and understandable. Clarity is important.

Now let's assume that you own a house, but have just been given a new job in another part of the country. Mortgages are hard to get and expensive. Real estate taxes are going up in your area. Houses are not moving. You must sell, or at least rent, your home *quickly* or you'll be saddled with the *double* expense of *two* homes.

The right ad may get you a handsome profit. The wrong ad, or even just an average one, may cause a capital loss. You've dressed up your home in its Sunday best, touched it up with a little painting, cleaned it top to bottom and manicured the grounds with a little raking, weeding and planting. It looks better than it has in years.

Research the *advantages* of your house and grounds. Recognize its *disadvantages* to help you in realistic pricing. Brokers will tell you what equivalent houses, with equivalent acreage and grounds, in equivalent areas, are now actually getting. Pick the broker who, more than any other in your area, is identified with sale or rent of the nicest properties of your type. Consider one of the big national brokers now taking over the real estate business. But if their local office doesn't want to run an ad at your expense, go to a local broker. Run an ad under his or her name advertising your property. The broker's suggested copy may be better, but *write* yours first. *You* have most at stake. Study the broker's ads for other desirable properties. Ask which one pulled most inquiries serious enough to produce a sale, *despite* the market.

This ad can be your model.

Follow its style. Substitute your property's strong points for the strong points advertised. Note the adjectives. Come up with your own which honestly describe the best features of your home. As you write, you'll think of more points. Your ad will become longer. Keep writing. Let it grow. Let your headline grow out of your most effective selling point. Compare your headline to that of your model. Try alternative headlines.

If your price is a bargain, feature it. If not, make them read your ad and, hopefully, become interested. Give the price near the end. If above market, but worth it, say why. Leaving the price out will draw many more inquiries, and probably most will be unable to pay your price. If time is urgent, it's best to include price.

Study the way your model ad is organized and spaced, how long each sentence and each paragraph is. Note the amount of white space in margins, above and below the ad copy and between paragraphs. Set up yours accordingly. End with the name of the broker and his address and phone number.

Start to cut your copy – not paragraphs or sentences, but single words. Consider abbreviations, but *carefully*. As you cut, if you think of more good selling points, put them in. As you cut, copy, phrases and sentences can become jerky and harder to read. Revise words so the ad reads smoothly. It's *work*, but it's worth it. Now read the ad from beginning to end. Is it confusing? Are some points in the wrong order? Do some adjectives seem too flowery or even inappropriate?

Change the order, correct, delete or add adjectives. Keep working on it. Remember, every word must work. Cut out the *lazy* words. Put in warm words in place of cold ones, live words in place of dead ones. Put the love you have for each part of the house, and each advantage, into the ad. Think of its special advantages for a special situation . . . as a doctor's house . . . for a family with very young children . . . for one that loves gardening . . . or swimming or whatever. Try to bring out advantages so vividly that your house becomes appetizing, even in a dead market.

Show your ad to your wife, husband, best friend, someone who's practical and realistic. Find out if you've left something important out, made inaccurate statements, oversold or undersold your property in some way. The advice may be good or bad. Make up your own mind and act accordingly. Now look at your real estate broker's ad. Your broker's ad may be better because real estate is the broker's business.

But your ad may be better because you know your house better, have more at stake, and have put more time and work into the ad. Very likely, each will have some strong points. If so, now take stronger points and better adjectives from your broker's ad and revise your own accordingly – or if your broker's ad is better, vice versa.

Rewrite the ad in the first person, as if you were the broker and had just discovered an unusual value was on the market and were reporting something of more-than-average desirability and highly recommended by someone who is an authority. Now cut your revised ad one more time. If you're happy with it, run it – and good luck. If it doesn't pull, you'd better consider reducing your price.

This is not a course on real estate. You may be better off selling without a broker. I have suggested running under the broker's name to get the added recommendation power into the ad.

Why put so much time and effort into such a simple task as writing a tiny classified ad? What I am asking you to do will take you a matter of hours for a day or two. It costs you not one cent more to do it. It can make you thousands of dollars. Do you know of a faster, easier way to make so much?

Writing another kind of classified ad is a similar problem.

If you need to hire someone when jobs are short and the job you offer is desired, it's the same as renting a scarce apartment. Your ad can be short. You can abbreviate freely. If the labor market is tight and your job is harder to fill, work harder on the copy. It can be a little longer.

Assume that you own a school which trains beginners to work with a micro-computer, file and work with microfilm, work with a word processor or master another new automated office skill. Your ad is listed under "Instruction." A subheading states the kind of courses you teach.

You can't increase the number of people reading the section. They are only some of those reading the paper. You're getting people looking for instruction. Readers are unfamiliar with your field and may be considering instruction in another field. They may never even read your ad unless attracted to it. You must explain the opportunities which your course opens up as well as what it is.

You have to find out the present employer market for graduates with these skills . . . if employers expect to need such employees soon . . . what employers pay or expect to pay for such skills . . . and whether they prefer to train present employees or hire already trained employees. Your research may come from employees, manufacturers of the new equipment, employment agencies, those newly employed in such fields or your own experience.

Keep your eyes and ears open for necessary facts. There may be *news* on any of the varied fields which you are teaching in your Sunday paper, on TV, in the latest issue of the leading trade magazine in the field, on radio, in the Wall Street Journal or whatever.

You should only be in business if your research has shown a real need at attractive pay for those you train. Be sure that your facts are accurate before you use them in copy. If so, you need to tell this story in your ad. Sell the results of taking your course as well as the course. It's news to most people. Be the reporter gathering the facts, and the editor selecting the most important ones to feature.

You're selling the hope of earning more . . . of being a desired employee . . . of bypassing far more senior employees . . . of being relied on, perhaps, by a boss who doesn't fully understand the new equipment himself. You may be selling the chance for a higher-status job . . . for a more glamorous job . . . of working more with the boss . . . of joining an exciting company and meeting more interesting people . . . of traveling to exotic places.

You rarely need some unusual attention-getting device. You attract by dramatizing in your headline and subhead the news of exciting opportunities in the field. Follow with one or more lines specifying the new kinds of jobs open at what pay. Capsulize your description of your instruction. Ask for action featuring phone, address and name. Model your ad after a successful ad for other kinds of courses. Keep editing, modifying and improving until convinced you've got your story across. Work and rework every word of your ad, as suggested for selling a house.

I'm asking you to work this hard on such a little ad because it can launch your business. You're competing with other education ads. I want yours to be the best and *you* to win. You want to have the *best* school and the *best* ad. If it works, you can run it more times, in more papers, perhaps for some time . . . with no more effort. Good luck!

The sheer number of tiny and unusual businesses, and their variety, whose products are sold through small classified ads never ceases to amaze me.

Just looking through the classified sections of Grit, The National Enquirer, The Village Voice or any underground paper is an eye opener. Sometimes the classified ad asks for money, usually only several dollars. More often, it asks for an inquiry to which literature or a specialized catalog is mailed. Often the specific items are extremely specialized, such as live night crawlers offered in the classified columns of the outdoor magazines.

In Grit, some of the same classified ads have run continuously, and presumably successfully, for decades. In each magazine carrying a substantial mail order classified section, the variety of unusual businesses and items creates readership. People read the section because they are intrigued by the unexpected. Each little ad is a different news dispatch. Few of them can attract attention as effectively with any device as they can with the very uniqueness of the item and the business. The art of attracting attention is based on capsulizing the uniqueness in the headline and provocatively describing it in the opening line or so.

These sections are marketplaces of the unusual. Trying to make an ordinary product or service appear unusual will rarely work. Your job as a writer is to be a reporter of the unusual. Your first task is to find it. If you start an unusual, provocative business, just telling a friend about it will excite and attract interest. And just doing the same thing in print with least work will create a provocative mail order ad.

Odd, specialized businesses have a special appeal, and far more so in a highly specialized magazine in the same field. Here the classified mail order section is the marketplace largely shopped in by those most predisposed to respond to your provocative ad.

The shortest ads usually pull inquiries. The ones that ask for actual orders are only a little longer. The longest-running ads are often the shortest. The shortest ads get about the same readership as longer ones.

Capsulize your story. Make it as short as possible. Keep your headline to one, two or three provocative words. Often simply capitalizing the first word or so is the headline. Boil down your name and address to a one or two-word name, town, state initials and zip code. Between headline and address, use the least number of words, perhaps seven to twelve, to tell your story. Pick them carefully and edit them painfully. Model your ad after the other longest-running ads. Try it and good luck.

Your next aggravating job may be to write a publicity release for one of your items to send in to editorial columns of magazines and special newspaper sections.

At your library, look through the editorial pages of whichever magazines and newspaper sections you wish to send your release to. Read carefully each editorial story describing a new product in each magazine you look at. Editors are human. The easier you make it for them, the better your chances. Write your release to the exact size of the average description of a new product or service.

Write a description of your product in editorial style. If you already have a longer ad, painstaking cutting will usually produce a better write-up than starting from scratch. Don't take a section or paragraph from a longer ad. Take the headline, main subhead, small subheads and key words in the copy story and close and put them in proper sequence with proper connecting words. It's probably still long. Cut and rework until satisfied.

If you have no longer ad, model your write-up after an actual editorial story. Research your product enough to fill in equivalent facts. Work on colorful words. Make your opening words provocative. Creating a write-up is great training for writing mail order copy for an actual ad.

Rewrite it until you feel it's perfect. It costs you only time to labor over the writing, and each improvement may bring more orders. Now study the photographs or pictures used with each write-up. You can even take your own picture of your product if you can't afford a commercial photographer. Or try to talk the most superb amateur photographer friend you have into taking it as a favor. When you get it developed, get an artist friend to retouch it and crop it.

Very likely, you'll have to do it all yourself. Don't attempt to retouch a photograph, but do attempt to crop it. Just make a photocopy. Then scissor out the really striking part of the picture from the rest. Use your common sense. Use only this part of the photograph. When you know it's right, put a piece of tissue over the actual photograph. With a red crayon trace out the borders of the good part of the photography. Your object is to make that picture jump right off the page and, like a magnet, draw eyes to your description.

How effectively you write and illustrate your story may help it become accepted and greatly determine how many orders it pulls, if the editor leaves in order information.

If you start without money, a free editorial can create your first capital without risk. If you buy a test ad and get a free write-up, how effectively you create it can determine whether you make a profit or loss from your ad risk. And it's perfect training for writing a display ad in editorial style.

But before we discuss writing any display ads, let's go into the research that can make any display ad, broadcast commercial or direct mail piece far easier to write, and more effective.

Chapter 3

90% PERSPIRATION

Research . . . asking . . . reading . . .
digging . . . pulling nails . . . the
extra question that created a
million-dollar business

"Did you ever see a robin step up behind another robin . . . and kick its legs from underneath it?"

This opening line of a radio commercial helped the commercial sell thousands of Audubon bird books. The line was not in the Audubon bird book. One of our greatest young copywriters (long since one of our most prolific alumni) found it while doing research on birds in the public library. The Audubon bird book was, of course, primarily a bird recognition book. But presumably, a reader of the book who became a bird watcher might well see such a phenomenon.

If you are buying a product simply for a catalog or some special mail order sales purpose in limited volume, a great deal of such research is not necessary. But if you plan to create and build a business on the product, if you're out to create a "solo" piece in direct mail – on one product rather than a catalog on a number of products – or a page ad or a TV commercial or program, then it is worth it. If you have an exclusive, are a sole-rights importer, or make or plan to make a product yourself, research is even more necessary. It may avoid or win a future law suit. It may cause you to go into the product far more cautiously – or drop it entirely. It may uncover a possibly dangerous association. It may correct a label error or revise wholly inadequate instructions.

We like to think that while other companies may have greater resources, far bigger staffs and many other advantages over us, we will always be determined to *dig* a little deeper than others in researching any product, service or field. Because all it takes is time and work. And we know that no copy can do a product justice until adequate research has been done. Respect for any product demands research. I'm not talking about elaborate research by huge agencies and top research companies. For our small business, we cannot afford the cost of such research. But we can go to the library. We can phone for days or weeks to get research answers.

I've often taken over 100 pages of notes to help write *one ad.* When I'm finished, I feel like blotting paper, but writing for me has been a difficult, acquired art that I actually learned from my own top writers. I learned research from them also. I have long secretly felt it was my only strength I could count on over other writers. I could *outwork* them in research . . . and you can too.

It not only pays off in far better copy, but the best ideas I've gotten have come from research on something else. Research has many byproduct advantages. It gives us *new* products, entirely fresh approaches to products we were not researching and forever unexpected insights that have helped build our business.

If you never wrote a word of advertising in your life, research may open the door. If you've written copy for years with little or no research, the first research you really work at can open your eyes to what it can do for your copy. Sometimes you will find all the research material you need already done. Sometimes you will get it very quickly from one of several sources. It may not be at all as time-consuming or as tedious as what I'm about to describe. But let's discuss how we go about it.

The first source of research on a product is the man you got the product from. Perhaps you bought a company that made it. Perhaps you took over a product from a manufacturer and are having it made elsewhere or making it yourself. Perhaps you are importing it. Perhaps you're taking it over from an inventor who has been making it in his garage. In each case, there should be a good deal of information just waiting for you. And it could be invaluable in the preparation of any mail order advertising.

Some people who make a product are quite inarticulate about it and give you very little information. Others give you *misinformation,* inaccurate, vague or deliberately misleading, or even untrue information. Many times, at a European or American trade show, I've talked to the owners of an item and have been told that the item is patented, unique and unlike any other . . . only to walk down the next aisle and see *a duplicate* competitive item. But there are many product owners who *can* give you *exactly* what you need. An inventor who has struggled for years to develop a product usually has a considerable story to tell about it. A salesman, particularly a salesman-demonstrator or salesman-instructor, may have gradually created or perfected a very detailed presentation on the product.

Those who have information often have no idea which of it can be useful to you. Getting necessary information from those who know can be like pulling nails. It starts with determining what you're trying to find out.

Research is too important for skimming through. Research *before* you take over an item can quickly warn you of drawbacks or competition that make it undesirable for you to take it on. Without *thorough* research, there's little chance of effective mail order advertising.

We usually make a detailed questionnaire before we talk to

anyone. Question by question, we take notes of the answers. Many answers seem to lead to nothing, but suddenly a breakthrough clue may come up. Years after you have a product, research can often pull out new facts you never were aware of and open the door to a completely fresh and entirely different advertising approach.

What reason is there for the product to exist at all? What are its competitors? In what way or ways is it any better than competitive products? Is it *faster . . . cheaper . . . longer-lasting . . . lighter . . . stronger?* What is it made of? How does this compare with competitors? Why does it use each material it consists of? Is there anything unique or patented or exclusive about each material? What about component parts? How does each differ from the equivalent part in a competitive product? If the product is unique and has no competition, how was the same function performed before?

And how much faster is the function performed with the new product than before? Does it save trouble over the old way? If so, how? Is it safer? Is it easier? Does it require any *skill* to use? If so, how long does it take an average person to use it? Is it easier to use than the competition? What is the history of the product? What was the reason to invent it? Was there a problem that bothered or upset the inventor and caused him to develop it? What is the history of the field? Which is the biggest competitor? What is the history of this company?

What do users say about the product? How do they compare it with others? Can they save money using it? Can they use it in any way to *make* money? Is it a convenience? Is it decorative? Is it fun to use? Is using it good therapy for worries or problems? Is it practical for children? Is it safe for them? Is it easy to put together? How long does it take to do so? Has it won any awards? How long does it *last* before wearing out? How does this compare with competitors? How many colors and sizes does it have in comparison with competition? Is it adjustable, and if so, more or less than competition?

What testimonials exist for the product? What publicity is there on it? Are there any shopping column write-ups, any major stories, and if so, are photocopies available? Has it been featured on TV or radio shows, and if so, are there tapes available? Is it patented? If so, can we have a photocopy of the patent? Or do they object to our writing Washington or abroad for a photocopy?

What documentation is there for any product claims? Have time-study tests been made comparing the product in use with competition? Has any university, hospital or government authority tested it? If so, are the results available? Were there any unusual obstacles in inventing, developing or perfecting the product? If so, how were they overcome?

Once, while doing this sort of research for a fish lure, I pieced together an interesting story from the exporter and inventor.

The inventor was a science teacher, a skin diver and an avid fisherman. He would go under the surface near an area fishermen were casting in. He would observe, underwater, exactly what happened to each lure and natural bait and how fish reacted to it. Then he would come out of the water and make research notes. From his research, he determined that minnows were the most effective in getting strikes once the fish came near. In lengthy letters in French to me, he told how he sculpted a rubber minnow out of a piece of an old tire and gave me much detail on its effectiveness. We sold over two-million of these lures and told the story countless times in mail order advertising. We then purchased the world rights and manufactured it here.

More research provided the way to get store distribution. The previous importer, whose business we later purchased, had failed with this particular lure before we succeeded with it. But often a failure has within it the seeds of success, if dogged research can dig it out. I asked the previous importer whether the firm had ever successfully sold the lure by mail. The answer was no. Had it been successfully sold by a catalog customer? The answer was still no. Had a retailer ever run an ad successfully for it? Another no. I went on and on with still more no's. Finally I asked whether an unusual display had ever been used successfully. The answer was yes. A store had put in a transparent tank (powered by an electric motor) with the lure pulled through the water demonstrating its action. The store sold over 150 lures in a week. And then what happened? Nothing! The former importer took back the display. Did you ever use it again? No! Where was the display now? In their cellar. Could we borrow it? Why, of course!

Within two weeks, we took space in a public outdoor show and did over $1,800 in a week with the original display, which had cost $150. Within months, we were duplicating the expensive glass tank and motor with a plastic tank and simple motor for $25 and doing business through key retailers. Within a year, we were making a much smaller, even simpler tank and motor, assembling it ourselves by the thousands and selling lures all over America as though there were no tomorrow.

Yet it all came from asking that one last, extra research question.

Research, effectively done, can help us assist our advertising agency, free-lance copywriter or ourselves to write far more effective advertising. Research can be the majority of the creative work. It can vastly speed the entire process of *learning* how to write effective advertising. Selecting research facts . . . assembling, classifying, rearranging and editing them . . . goes a long way to getting ads to write themselves.

Naturally, we seek and collect every piece of previous advertising, every booklet, every transcribed radio or TV commercial, every sales letter, all instructions . . . anything we can get.

If we're dealing with an importer, we try to get all material in English, but ask for photocopies of any other advertising or publicity in the original language. We get on the phone, or visit personally, and talk to distributors, wholesalers, dealers and salesmen and ask each question on our questionnaire. Answers often contradict one another. If so, we dig until we come to our own conclusions as to just what the correct answer is. The best research of this kind is talking to the actual consumer-user.

An actual user who likes the product may have used it in ways never even contemplated by the inventor and found that it's perfect for the purpose. Just why a user likes a product can provide selling points the copywriter might never think of.

Call each trade paper in the field the product is in. You can do it discreetly, not even mentioning your own product. Get the name of each competitor and any information on each the trade paper can pass along. Get copies of past articles on the field and previous companies in it. If a giant company does a big business in the field, check Fortune, Forbes, Business Week and the Wall Street Journal. Find out if major stories have appeared on the product, field or any product or company in it, and get a photocopy of every piece of advertising and promotional literature and all instructions for assembly and use of any competitive product.

My father studied industries this way, one at a time. He built an ever-growing file on each individual major competitor, kept it up and added to it for years, until finally he knew more about individual products than many executives in the company making them. He got advertising accounts by *knowing the product* far more thoroughly than the majority of his most inspired competitors.

Make a list of libraries that may have material that can help you. The trade association should have a good one and, perhaps, one or more of the trade papers. A big-city, public main library and its more specialized business or industrial branch will head your list. In many counties, one or more libraries will specialize in business books and have far more business magazines. A good university library can be a gold mine, particularly one for a business college or for the business school of a university.

If a hobby or sport, magazines on the subject should be followed up. The periodical department of your public library may have many years of every copy of virtually all such publications. Check to see if there is a library that specializes in the subject. If you feel unsure of yourself in library research, just explain your problem to the librarian and get suggestions on how to look up books on your subject. Before starting, check the *general* reference works usually out on the shelves.

Start with the Encyclopedia Britannica. The latest edition is divided into the macromedia – longer articles on subjects of great interest – and micromedia – short summary articles on other items. Each article lists sources. An extensive macromedia article on jewelry will quote many sources on the history of jewelry, jewelry in mythology, jewelry making, etc. The articles are well written and can be photocopied for you by the library. The sources quoted are the best. Look for *specialized* encyclopedias closer to your subject. Big libraries have many of them. And one of them is almost certain to provide more information and more sources for you.

The libraries will keep you busy for a while.

Now begin work on your notes. There are personal computer software programs ideal for assembling and filing your notes on a Macintosh or other computer or word processor. But if you have no computer, do as I did for decades. Write down notes as thoughts pop into your head or as you research anything. If you're like me, you'll now have a lot of them, disconnected and repetitive. The notes are therefore rather useless until you arrange them in order. I usually get a number of yellow legal-size pads. I take about six or so pads to rearrange my notes. Each pad I give a heading to. On one I mark at the top of the first page "Product Premise," and here I include notes on the main justification for the product. Another I mark "Development Story," regarding its history. Another I mark "Ease and Speed" (of operation and/or assembly). Another I mark "Other Specific Product Advantages." One I mark "General Advantages" and another "Miscellaneous," and so forth.

Next I get the same number of manila folders. With scissors, I cut each page of my original notes into clippings logical for each of these headings. There should be no clippings left on each page after distributing. I put all clippings on one subject together and put them into one manila folder. I copy all my notes from each of my folders onto one pad. I still have disconnected notes, but under the proper heading. I rewrite my notes on each pad, attempting to give the revision a logical beginning, middle and end. The first effort is an improvement, but still quite disconnected. I see obvious duplications and red-pencil them out. Each time I revise the pad of notes, it has more lucidity and continuity. I develop my original phrases into sentences. It's hard, tedious, headache work. But as I work, I'm becoming saturated with the subject.

I originally set up this method of research to aid my copywriters. They were expensive when on my payroll regularly. Free-lancers were of little use because they had no time to learn our product or business. But given enough effective research, a top writer became a bargain and a freelancer far more practical to use. Having difficulty getting others to research so intensively, I started doing it myself. Effective research can be 80% to 90% of the time, effort and capability of creating great mail order advertising.

I would summarize my research in a lengthy memorandum of 10 to 20 pages. This meant combining my product premise notes, which gave the main justification for the product, with the development story, the advantages and any documentation and testimonials.

To aid my writers, I tried to do this in an orderly way, with first things first. I tried to keep the memorandum from rambling too much and kept cutting and simplifying it. Then I made a discovery.

It was not a big step to write entire ads myself. *I* began to master the writing of mail order direct mail, magazine and newspaper advertising as I never had before. I had always written complete radio and TV commercials and programs, but now found that my research greatly improved this ability as well.

You can do the same. Simply research your product as I have described and take notes. This may seem tedious, but it's surprising how much easier it makes everything else.

Should a mail order moonlighter run his first advertising in direct mail, on radio, in newspapers, on TV or in magazines?

Most mail order moonlighters start in magazines or newspapers. What you will begin with will depend on your product and situation. You will be able to see more for yourself as we take up the characteristics, advantages and disadvantages of different kinds of advertising.

Whatever form of advertising you start with, you can try other forms later as well. Sometimes, if you fail in one form, you will still succeed in advertising in another. Let's examine some different approaches in advertising and some differences between mail order and other advertising. Then we'll take up creating each leading form of advertising.

Chapter 4

EMOTION IN PERSUASION

*Why they buy . . . psychology in
salesmanship . . . different
environments for mail order
advertising*

What *persuades* people?

What causes sweeping popularity of anything? What causes mail orders to pour in for the wildly-desired item of the moment?

We don't know. Far from having power over people, the mail order man's only chance is to find out what people really want at the moment . . . give it to them . . . and stay away from all else.

Whatever persuades a percentage of people to do something when an advertising test is run usually persuades roughly the same percentage of people to do it when the same advertising is exposed to other similar groups. This will happen surprisingly regularly – in different areas, even in different countries. It will happen for a period of time and then stop as inexplicably as it started.

The mail order man can no more force his prospective customers to buy than King Canute. could command the waves. The mail order man can only observe the tide and go with it. Mail order persuasion can only take place when conditions are right.

We have learned a little about what makes it a bit easier to persuade. Let's go into it. As you glance through the next few pages, don't get too concerned if it seems at all complex. The background will be useful to you in applying the quite simple mail order copywriting method we will then take up.

Often emotion makes people buy. They then seek a logical excuse for buying, for spouse and self. Advertising gives a one-two punch . . . emotion to cause desire . . . and rationalization to provide the excuse.

We think we act logically, and try to, but our actions are often caused by instincts and compulsions we are unaware of. Elections are won and soap sold by appeals to emotion. Let's consider emotion as used in selling. But when we use it, let's be fair. There is a line that integrity dare not cross.

Sex in advertising helps sell anything. In advertising, sex pulls, but it can corrupt your children. Use it with care. Love is still sex, but less raw. Everyone wants affection and warmth.

We all want to survive, but some of us are more worried about it than others. Appeal to survival sells super-locks, insurance, atomic shelters, a year's supply of frozen food, anti-ideologies, the manly art of self defense, guns, automatic switch-on lights when you're not home and Adolph Hitler. Appeal to the survival drive can sell relatively harmlessly or be emotional dynamite. Handle with care.

The sweetest music ever heard is the sound of your own name. Anyone unappreciated suffers inside. We all need praise, a pat on the back and a build-up. "With these pieces of ribbon I'll build an empire," said Napoleon (according to legend) as he founded the Legion of Honor. In my book, Mail Order Know-How, I describe how Joe Segel founded and built The Franklin Mint on just this premise. Entire industries are based on building other people's egos. Every salesman knows that ego building helps sales. And much advertising gets in on the good work too.

Power! People want it. The need for power has helped catapult the automobile industry to its present size. Every driver is a knight in armor. Big cars give a heady sense of power. The word POWER sells, when used from POWER STEERING to POWER LEARNING. The most humble member of any aggressor nation feels a shared sense of aggressive power – another form of dirty emotional pool. If you appeal to the drive for power, take it easy.

Appeals to retain youth and health, to gain longevity and immortality are part of the urge to survive. People never stop seeking some new way to stay young, look younger, get and keep health and live longer. In this irreligious age, they seek a religion . . . new or old . . . that promises immortality. Cosmetics, tonics, inspirational books and endless products offer help. Before you do, remember that these are the greatest fields of quackery.

Rationalizing emotional appeals in advertising has gone a bit far. Men are offered feminizing cosmetics under wild animal names in commercials delivered by famous athletes, so that a man can feel masculine as he goes feminine. Women are offered prepared, warm-up, drop-in-the-pan food with one or two tiny steps still left for the housewife so that she can still feel creative in the kitchen. People want to feel that longed-for luxuries are necessities. They like to cater to themselves while feeling that they're sacrificing for others, and the new easier way gives them the feeling that they're pioneering the old hard way. They often respond to advertising accordingly. Anyone who sells and advertises can corrupt or improve readers, listeners or viewers, making them a little worse or even a little better. Be kind to them.

A cow is calm and placid, but not very creative. As we rise above our animal origins, we become a bit more neurotic and more subject to psychological manipulation. Fear . . . anxiety . . . suspicion . . . envy . . . greed . . . desire . . . keep working on us. We seek escape, flight, to run away. We desperately need companionship, stability, roots, our safer yesterday and the nostalgia of old remembered times. We long for the familiar and become frightened of the new. We're troubled by too much change, too fast. We don't want to be left out. We want reassurance that all's right with our world. No wonder advertising, like Pavlov's bell, seems to be able to make the consumer dog froth at the mouth, hungrily expecting the food he longs for. But as explained, this is only partially so.

Psychologists say that very little veneer covers primitive reactions in man or woman today. Each product, service and institution can become a symbol, sending a message to our subconscious antenna . . . attracting us or driving us away, appealing to some inner urge and flashing "stop" or "go" to instincts and emotions or long-buried fears or desires.

Fortunately, mail order advertising is not just a push-button human reaction machine constantly working on emotions, as does advertising for some nationally store-distributed products. Mail order advertising is simpler, more straight-forward and less devious than much non-mail order advertising I have seen or heard.

For one reason, there is usually a good deal of news in a mail order ad. It is announcing something, telling a story of change and improvement. Often the mail order ad is for a new product with new advantages performing a unique new function. Mail order products that are duplicates of widely distributed and advertised trade products often do not succeed. Those mail order products that do succeed often have product differences that are more real and less trivial than many distribution products.

Mobil Oil and Texaco are quite similar, as are endless numbers of advertised trade-distributed products. Coca Cola is great, but hardly news. To tell the Coca Cola product story in depth would drive away readers, listeners and viewers. Changing the story with a new product formula didn't work. Only featuring "Classic Coke" satisfied users. Going for the psychological soft underbelly is particularly tempting for the product that no longer has news value.

There can be plenty of psychology in mail order advertising. But the main thrust is usually news, fundamental and factual, about the product itself, along with persuasive demonstration and instruction. A lot of the effectiveness of a mail order ad is your proposal . . . your guarantee . . . your request and incentive for immediate action . . . and above all, your credibility.

One of the earliest books on advertising divided all products into three stages: the pioneering, the competitive, and the retentive. This division is still true of mail order products, as well as those sold in any other way. The advertising for the mail order pioneer is most similar to the pioneer distribution product. Mail order can be the best way to pioneer a product for later store distribution success. The mail order competitive product varies more from its store distribution brother, and the mail order product in the retentive stage varies most of all.

The pioneer product is a *different* product, whose very use and satisfactions are unknown to most people. Yogurt, wet suits, photocopy machines and any new dance, game or hobby started in the pioneer stage. So did microwave ovens, compact disc players and Apple computers. Advertising for the pioneer product tells the entire story of the desirability of the *activity*, as well as the product itself.

Advertising a competitive-stage product is usually a race to feature specific advantages of the latest models that make them more desirable – before competitors catch up or even surpass these advantages. Cars and sewing machines, cameras and TV sets, boats and golf carts and most products advertised are largely or partially in the competitive stage. The demonstrator type of selling is often ideal for both pioneer and competitive products. Mail order is often the ideal way to win a competitive stage race before competitors are even in wide national distribution.

A book club is in the retentive stage, but stays competitive with its latest offer and giveaway. Advertising of the club's operation is short, but on giveaway and offers it is longer.

It is in continuity where most mail order advertising parts company with advertising of most products distributed in other ways. Intensively distributed products are usually advertised *far more continuously*, with higher intensity than even major mail order "hits" in full projection. The single-item mail order advertiser soon learns that the first ad pulls best, the second substantially less, the third far off that and so forth – for most items.

There are exceptions – products that ride a megatrend of popularity. For us this has been true of the "Stomach Eliminator," an exercise product that succeeds with the fitness trend. We have run the Stomach Eliminator time after time in many magazines, every other week in one case – and every several days in one national newspaper. But this is rare. Results usually fade off fast. Usually only a new giveaway, new offer or entirely new copy approach revives the pattern. A dramatic price reduction usually picks up results, but dies soon after.

Only a rare mail order concept, like a book club, is regularly capable of *continuous* full-page advertising, really a series of individual ads for specific giveaways and offers, each with a typical mail order life pattern. While the life span of distribution products is far shorter now that intensity of promotion is increased, a *campaign* of ads or commercials even built around a single theme can still rotate different advantages. The reader, listener or viewer is expected to absorb a little here and a little there, with a constant drip, drip, drip effect. It's ideal for products with simple or nominal advantages.

Much mail order is perpetually in the pioneering and competitive stages. It's far more necessary to tell the entire story each time. For a small mail order advertiser (like ourselves), each time each ad or commercial is run, more readers, listeners or viewers are *unfamiliar* with our product than are *familiar* with it. If we were to tell a little of our story each time, it would be in the hope that prospective buyers would take notes each time and assemble the entire story themselves. Before then, they would never know enough about the product to make a buying decision. Yet often a mail order product *is* news. Often the giveaway is news. And usually a mail order ad or commercial has its best chance of success simply by reporting the full news story.

For a number of decades, advertising has been called "salesman-ship in print." But what kind of salesmanship should be used? My father taught that advertising broke down into two main types. One was a hard-sell, onetime approach. The other was friendly and cheer-ful, a greeting with some news of a new product, a special price. It did not wear out its welcome and built a repeat business. Later I discovered subdivisions of these types.

The pitchman draws his people in as an entertainer. He amuses, puzzles or intrigues the onlooker. His opening line often gives no hint of what he's leading into. He gradually secures nodding agreement from bystanders to some of what he is saying, perhaps with a knock pitch that they do not know is related to his future "sell." Then he comes to the "turn" into the heart of his selling message, the point when his audience will drift away or stay and perhaps buy. He gradually builds up credibility. He demonstrates the proof of what he's saying with the product. He can still lose more of his audience than he can sell. He picks up speed. He offers the incentive to stay and buy now, not later. He establishes a rhythm of excitement – a shortage psychology. He causes those on the outside of the group to feel that they may be *too late to get theirs*. They push in.

Take out the brashness, cheapness, and misrepresentation, and there's still a lot to learn for anyone creating an advertisement. I've ad-mired a certain jewelry designer in action. The way he dresses, his ac-cent, his entire approach is as much a setting for each piece of his jewelry as the red velvet he removes with such care when he unveils his latest work. Simply by unwrapping the package, picking up the lowest-priced piece of costume jewelry, holding it with reverence as though it were infinitely precious and extraordinarily delicate, he adds untold desirability. For luxury merchandise of every description, his equivalent can be found. This, too, can be translated into advertising.

As home appliances and business and industrial equipment were invented and improved, the salesman trained to demonstrate came into his own. He looks assured simply approaching his product. He often can adapt to a wide variety of products. He can pick up a new kind of fishing reel or electric mini-calculator, put it through its tricks like a circus dog, and never be awkward.

Without effective demonstration and salesmanship, the cash register might never have gotten off the ground. The troops of IBM might never have started their march to world domination, and product after product might have died aborning. Demonstration salesmanship can be translated into any form of advertising. The instructor-salesman is a teacher-missionary. He or she is spreading the word . . . enthusing . . . teaching . . . making it easy, fun and fast to learn how to get in on it.

The home sewing industry was created by home sewing teachers. Entire magazines are based on instruction in specific hobby fields. On public TV, Julia Child made French cooking so easy and such fun with her wonderful accompanying chatter of instruction that innumerable viewers bought her books. Every new game that sweeps the country is sped on its way by instructor-missionary men and women.

Jon Gnagy, for whose art course and products we were advertising agency, looked on TV as though he had stepped from the Paris left bank. But he *talked* as he was, a midwestern farm boy, in the most reassuring, friendly and folksy manner possible. He instructed as he sketched – at an easy pace, with not the slightest rush. He demonstrated as he taught – starting with triangles, squares, circles and cubes, sketched out so roughly it was obvious any ten-year-old child (or adult) could do the same. Erasing line segments, he would turn them into houses, seascapes, fruit or whatever. At each step, each viewer felt he or she could easily do the same. At the end of the show, when Jon Gnagy put a frame around the finished drawing, each viewer was sure he or she could do as well.

Salesmanship takes many forms. Consider the used car salesman, direct descendant of the age-old horse trader. Observe those apostles of health who warn of the dangers of all we normally eat and drink and offer us relief at a price. A salesman can be a father figure, a fashion reporter, an irrepressible clown, an underdog, a sex symbol, a folksy countryman or any combination thereof. A salesman can be a psychologist, a strategist or a great tactician. And salesmanship in advertising can be just as varied. Each different environment creates a different atmosphere which greatly affects selling any product. Walk through the Galleria in Milan . . . along Fifth Avenue, New York . . . up North Michigan Avenue in Chicago . . . on Wilshire Boulevard in Los Angeles . . . or almost anywhere in Paris. You become part of a pageant in the well-dressed crowds, the succession of stunning display windows, the heady atmosphere of fashion and wealth. Everything is affecting you. You are being prepared to pay more for anything you're shopping for than you originally and innocently anticipated.

The same salesmanship takes place in any expensive and popular night club. The flashing lighting, the constant to-and-fro movement of people, waiters, bus boys and cigarette girls, the drink-up music, the dancing bodies – all blend, confuse and prepare you for a higher and higher bill which you become more and more tolerant of. A luxury ad in a luxury publication can have a similar effect.

Each type of publication, broadcast program, catalog or retail store offers its own selling environment and tries to create its own atmosphere. One of today's top department store merchants says an exciting sale should be like a party, the store like a theater. Let's consider how its selling environment affects a department store ad and different selling environments for mail order ads.

A department store show window *displays* goods in a setting. A few words and a price are the only copy. A department store ad for merchandise is much the same. The familiar art style and layout, the famous logotype of its name and the surrounding merchandise it also advertises provide the setting. Its newspaper ad is a show window in print. That brief, graceful message will often sell out all stock of an item in the store and force reorders. It has for us. But when we ran the exact words and picture in our mail order ad for the same product in another newspaper, it has often failed miserably.

It's always a surprise to our beginning creative people. They always start with the firm belief that advertising should be short and brief; long wordy ads can only insult the intelligence. They see many short and simple advertisements, some for mail order, that seem to succeed. If others can succeed with brief copy, why can't we, they ask. The answer is we can, if we can *duplicate* the original conditions – all of them. To duplicate the department store ad conditions, we must find a marketplace similar to the one the store has created – one that has taken some of them 100 years to develop.

Department stores pay substantially less than national advertisers for the same size ads. Department stores and other retailers usually have *franchise* advertising positions. The same store often has the same page number day after day, week after week, month in, month out, over long years. As they build up their advertising schedule to run more pages per day, their ads run again and again in the old familiar positions. This creates the marketplace that people love to turn to. Each store has a solid core of loyalists buying the paper for no reason other than to *shop*. Surveys show department store ads get as much or more readership from women as most front-page stories. These women are *looking* for the store ad, seeking something offered by that store to select. It's often part of their life, something to do, their truest pleasure. These women are not looking in the same paper for *my* mail order ad or *yours*.

The training of department store customers to *telephone* their orders in took decades to accomplish. The building of huge numbers of charge account customers, who now find it so easy to telephone their orders in, also took decades. These department store customers are nowhere near equally ready to telephone their orders to you or me. It's their *habit* to order from the department store's brief description and illustration of an item. It's their *habit* to *resist* buying the same way from an unfamiliar mail order advertiser. And remember, the manufacturers and importers have already done much to make that simple, easy sale possible. National advertising is creating retail demand.

Only a minority of all the products in a department store are advertised individually by the store. The rest are sold as a result of the constant traffic of customers coming into the store, usually attracted by the advertising for specific items. The effectiveness of the store's advertising is based on an interplay of the national advertising of the manufacturer, editorial stories in the newspapers, features in the magazines, current popular trends, interviews or stories on TV or radio, tie-ins with famous personalities or a combination of these factors.

Go-get-it national advertising drives buyers to stores. Retailer we have-it advertising pulls them in. The national advertising has to do the major convincing; the dealer advertising simply tells where it's available and for how much.

But mail order advertising usually combines both functions. It often has to introduce both an unknown product and an unknown company to a far more doubting-Thomas reader, viewer or listener. It usually takes more convincing. To convince, we must provide reasons to buy our product. To find those convincing reasons, we must uncover every research fact that could possibly influence a buying decision in our favor. A successful mail order ad may involve offering an item that's hard to get elsewhere, a major price break, a new competitive item with a lower price, or obvious extra product advantage.

Yet direct marketing as a whole has each year been creating more of an overall marketplace for direct response than ever before, and one that is far more comparable to department store advertising. Fortune 500 companies which direct market capitalize on trust in their integrity. L. L. Bean gets instant recognition and trust from readers of its ads. All mail order benefits from this growing trust.

Today we use less copy, more pictures. We often use two-step with very small space and then send a detailed catalog. But still, the nearest equivalent in mail order to a department store advertising marketplace is created by a publication, broadcaster, catalog or co-op mailing. Few are as old, established or have as many advantages as a department store marketplace. But often such a mail order marketplace has been successfully established for many years. Special advertising rates in it are often substantially lower than *outside* the mail order marketplace section in the same medium. There are limited numbers of such marketplaces, but more are being established all the time.

An ad in such a marketplace is far more comparable to a department store ad than one run elsewhere. It needs more sell and explanation than the department store ad, but far less than a mail order ad outside such a marketplace. It is the simplest, easiest mail order ad to write, takes the least time to write and gives brief copy its best chance. Writing it is just a small step beyond making up a shopping column write-up. If you've done your research as suggested, it's easier yet.

Many small and successful mail order firms only run small ads in mail order marketplaces. It limits the size of the business, but escapes much of the headaches of creating larger ads.

The classified section of a newspaper is such a marketplace. Habits are deeply ingrained to look in this section to find a job or an employee, or to sell a house, car or appliance. The shortest ad may produce an avalanche of inquiries. But run the same ad in another newspaper not carrying such a section, and you may not get a single call.

The classified display section of newspapers for antiques, travel, real estate, boats or whatever is sometimes such a marketplace where small ads and brief copy pull. But many papers have only a smattering of such ads and have not yet created an effective marketplace. The same ad run with them simply dies.

Specialized home and garden magazines have built up remarkable mail order shopping marketplaces, often with 200 or 300 ads in an issue. Mail order offers of records and tapes have run so frequently for years on the same TV stations (usually in the same movie programs) that TV has created a mail order marketplace for records. Many trade, technical, hobby and special-interest publications or co-op mailings in such fields provide mail order marketplaces for appropriate specialized products and services.

Co-op mailings, with many circulars for different products in the same envelope, have become such marketplaces. Packages of loose return postcards with advertising for a different product on each, or the same principle with postcards bound into a direct response publication, have begun to create new mail order marketplaces in many fields. In each case, the habit of mail order shopping is being built up, and brief copy often works.

Readers of advertising in a mail order marketplace are mail order shoppers. They may be "window shoppers," casually looking. They may be looking for a specific item or advertiser. But wherever attention is caught, each will read an ad more carefully. Many buy regularly by mail order. If so, they are predisposed to buy by mail order in the future if they find an item desirable enough.

In any mail order marketplace, your advertisement competes for interest with other mail order advertisements. Yet every other advertisement helps yours by contributing to the creation of a marketplace. Note the editorial stories of new products and services, often with individual pictures. Your ad is also competing with each of these. Yet these help even more by contributing editorial credibility to the mail order marketplace.

Of the many mail order ads in such a marketplace, some fail, some break even and some only succeed because of other benefits to the advertiser that you may not receive. Often a catalog house is willing to break even or even lose money on such small ads, simply to get new names to mail to regularly in the future. Some firms feel that the ad helps their store sales as well. Some may have far lower advertising cost because of a frequency or big-volume contract. Judged only on sales of the item offered, and based on the advertising rate you will pay, *most* may be failing.

This means that you need the most unique product that you can find and the best ad that you can create. If your ad is to succeed, it should be seen and believed, more so than the other ads and write-ups on the page. Year after year, people start out as you are doing and *pay out.* You can, too, if your ad, as well as product, is *better* than most others.

In your newspaper, certain stories seem new and intriguing. Others seem stale and boring. Your first glance forms this opinion. A quick glance at an editorial story and picture and headline on a new product does the same. Each such story is news. The picture in it is a news picture. And so is each ad and its illustration. Some editorial stories and ads hardly get your attention. Their story seems to be merely a rehash about some product that's been around for years. The most dramatic attention-getting device does not help. Some are genuine, fresh news of an entirely new product or real product improvement. And some are really exciting news. If your ad is news of something better, the reader is *looking* for it. If your message seems reasonably believable, the reader is predisposed to buy. If your product is not interesting news to enough people reading your ad, it will probably fail.

If your ad is in a standard-size newspaper like the New York Times, and not in a mail order marketplace, it looks small and forlorn against its readership competition of news stories, department store ads and other types of ads. Readership studies show that national ads average a readership far below that of the department store ads and news stories. And you are one of the smallest and least known of these general national advertisers. Usually your product is not known, your company is not known and the reader is not considering a mail order purchase. Nobody is looking for you. And often mail order results from such ads are next to nothing.

On a tabloid size page, your ad is nowhere near as lost. But in bulging, fat, big-city tabloids your ad seems to drown in a sea of department store ads and little news. On a magazine page, your ad is less lost, but is usually relegated to a position far back, where overall magazine readership is lower.

Occasionally, the position of your small ad is surprisingly good, at the very top of the page on the right-hand side, next to the carryover of a high-interest, number-one news story, right on top of a high-readership department store ad, or next to a *related* magazine article in the field of your product. But this is a lottery ticket usually beyond your control. Results are often poor and erratic.

Very small ads have usually proven profitable in very special circumstances. Normally, it has been because something about the ad has *grabbed* the attention of the hurried, wandering eye of the reader, usually because of the *offer* or *product itself.* Few people are not drawn to a bargain, anywhere, any time. A tiny ad for a big bargain, even with a modest headline, draws readership like a magnet.

The warts-remedy-style product, with an ad using the one word, WARTS, as a headline, can appeal to the urgent need of a small minority and with a small whisper of an ad draw as though with a shout. But few mail order products are feasible for such ads. Most need more explanation than a small ad can give.

It's hard to achieve *belief* with a few words and an unknown name and address. The most provocative attention-getting headlines may attain abnormally high readership, yet solve neither of these problems. Generally, smallest-space mail order inquiry ads have a better chance than smallest-space mail order complete sale ads.

Sometimes small ads have worked *outside* the mail order marketplaces when combined with a catalog offer. In such cases, the small ads have rotated items and gradually familiarized readers with the name. Sometimes an extra position rate has been paid in newspapers to get a forward position and keep it week after week for different items.

There are major differences in creating a small mail order ad outside vs. inside a mail order marketplace. The ad must fight far harder for attention. It must struggle more to convert a glance into readership. It must convince, despite a more casual interest. It must persuade a person far less inclined to act to do so. This is often too big a job for a small ad.

Often the small ad that works in the mail order marketplace will fail miserably in the harsher environment outside. Its product claims must have quite self-evident advantages. Its offer must be particularly risk-free to the doubting Thomases. If so, it still must *leap off the page and pop right at you* to gain necessary readership. This means the headline and illustration have a far more difficult job to do.

For many years, bigger ads usually had a higher *percentage* of success outside the mail order marketplace and were more *stable* in projection – for a one-step sale. They also produced far more volume and, hopefully, overall profit. The volume of new names built lists far faster. The volume of shipments provided a vehicle for related-product inserts. The result was more income from mailing your own list, renting your own list and package inserts. Bigger ads were time-consuming to write, but per dollar of profit potential, they were the easiest and fastest way to make money in mail order space advertising.

From one inch to half-column to one-third, one-half, two-thirds to full-page, we formerly found the full-page *safer* for broad-appeal products. It was a more adequate test of the pulling power of such products. Still, many successful mail order businesses started with a small mail order ad.

For two-step advertising it has always been a different story. An inch was traditionally the lowest-cost ad per inquiry and per sale. The reason to use bigger-size ads was to secure bigger volume, but at a higher percentage selling cost. The inch ads pulled best when columns were wider. A three-inch column was often available and was usually at least two-and-a-half inches.

Conditions are now different. The cost per thousand of full-page ads has gone up far faster than retail prices and gross profits of items offered by mail order. Meanwhile there is less need of very long copy. People have less time, more money and greater willingness to buy a wider variety of goods by mail. We now find the square third the most efficient one-step ad in most mail order situations – where this size is not overpriced. For many higher-priced items we still need a page ad. This is particularly true for clubs, such as the Book of the Month Club, or for continuity programs, such as a Time-Life book series offer.

Meanwhile, as the column width of inch ads has shrunk – making an inch ad 40% smaller on average, we need a somewhat larger inquiry ad for best results – although we still use inches profitably to pull inquiries.

But even if you need a big ad, you may only have money for a small one. Even if an inadequate test, it may be the only one that you can afford. But if your ad for a broad appeal item shows *life* in a small ad, it's usually deserving of testing in larger space.

The bigger the ad you write, the more you avail yourself of all the research you have done. With larger space you can tell more and more of the *full* story of your product. You can demonstrate better in fuller form its uses and advantages. From research on, a great deal of copywriting is in *choice* of what to say. In bigger ads the choice is easier, because you can select *more*.

Usually I start by writing a full-page ad and then smaller ads. The simplest way to learn how to make more effective smaller ads is to learn how to create bigger ads. We find that we create far better smaller ads *after* we have completed a successful *full-page* ad for the same item. Sometimes, with each reduction to a smaller size, the cutting and editing required make each word left work harder.

Therefore, let's discuss creating a full-page ad and then work backwards to smaller ads. But before we can create and complete any ad, we must construct the offer we wish to make.

Chapter 5

INCREASING AND SPEEDING MAIL ORDER DESIRE

*Offer components . . . price . . . terms
. . . giveaways . . . add-ons . . .
cash-ups . . . credit cards . . .
telephone . . . guarantees*

Claude Hopkins, author of Scientific Advertising, used to say that the right offer should be so attractive that only a lunatic would say "no."

If you want to persuade anyone to do anything, it's best to think out every possible inducement. You want to make it as attractive as possible to do what you request, and to the fullest extent. Before you say a word, you need to plan out your proposal and make it hard to resist. And it is the same in creating a mail order ad.

You have your product and have done your research. Before you write a word, you need to construct your offer to your prospective mail order customer. You are constantly torn between making your proposal *more* attractive (and possibly less profitable to you) or making it more profitable to you (and possibly less attractive). But you must decide. Until you do so, you cannot complete your ad. And how you decide may greatly affect how you create it.

The offer that you make in your first test ad is simply the one you "feel" has the best chance of success and is still safe to make. This opening offer may be varied in future tests. Much of the money made in mail order comes from a later test of a variation from the original offer. Never stop trying to make your offer more tempting, while still safe.

What *should* you charge for what you are selling? Too high a price may kill orders. Too low a price may lose money. The *right* price may be the difference between mail order success and failure. One thing is sure. The Good Lord did not figure out the price of anything sold. A human being did, and the price can be *wrong or right.*

The psychology of price constantly surprises me. In the depression, low price was all-important and may be again. But the right price varies by product as well as by the economic condition.

In every price range, some items seem more trustworthy at a somewhat higher price and more dubious at a lower price. Other items, particularly those bought by housewives, seem to them to be outrageously overpriced if higher than some arbitrary figure in their minds. Some items are "blind items," which a prospective buyer has difficulty in identifying as to what price is reasonable. But determining the right price to sell your product at can be quite important to your mail order success.

Has the price of your product recently been reduced? Or could you reduce it and still sell it profitably? An offer is often made more attractive by a price reduction. The more real it is and seems, the more it should be so. Often it can extend the life of a product for years. Sometimes it can even bring a dead product back to life.

The worse the economic condition is, the more vital a price reduction appeal is. In the best of times, price reductions are less effective. For some products we have never reduced the price. For others we have waited years to do so. And for others we have been able to give reductions early in the game. Decide for yourself before you write an ad whether to sell the product at regular or reduced price and, if so, for how great a reduction.

The terms on which you sell your product are a component part of your offer. Usually the more favorable terms you give, the more orders you will get. Asking for a check only often takes the most convincing. Selling C.O.D. is rarely done now in print but is still often used on TV for telephone ordering. It gets orders from those *without* a bank account or credit card. Sears-Roebuck passed Montgomery Ward in sales by a tremendous push with C.O.D. The words "send no money . . . just pay the postman" may have first made big-scale mail order possible.

Much later, selling via credit card – often charged by telephone revolutionized mail order. For the first time, it made possible the selling of far higher-priced items, up to hundreds of dollars and more. Those who had the capital and organization to sell on credit, charged directly to their company, usually did even better. And those who were strongly enough financed and well enough organized to sell on time payments charged directly often did best of all.

From a persuasion standpoint, you want to offer the most favorable terms. From a practical standpoint, you must be safe and keep things simple enough to be able to control what you do. As a moonlighter, you will probably start selling for all cash. Many successful mail order people never sell in any other way. For TV, you may consider C.O.D. or you may skip it as too much paperwork and trouble. You may, from the start, sell via credit cards. You may never bill any mail order customer directly – or if you decide to do so, you may only bill on a thirty-day basis and never sell on time payments.

First, you will probably make a sensible compromise between the most liberal terms that might get the most orders and the most cautious terms. You will have to consider which terms are easiest logistically for you to handle.

A very important part of your offer can be stating that you will accept telephone orders. These can be C.O.D., via credit card or charged direct. But most important is the use of the telephone in taking credit card orders. Credit cards, WATS lines and computerized credit checking of individual phone orders by the credit card companies have been a mail order powerhouse combination for higher-ticket items. The net effect is that the same cost advertising sells a higher-cost item than formerly possible and gets more orders faster than formerly possible. You ship faster, you can finance your advertising more easily, and you have a happier customer. Small mail order companies can grow now far bigger far faster than formerly possible. Your willingness to accept telephone orders can sharply increase total orders. We usually feature the telephone in our offers and advertising.

Another component part of your offer can be a giveaway, an extra gift item to add value. The right giveaway, alone, can be the difference between profit and loss in the very first test of an item. If an item pays off initially without a giveaway and results from the ad later drop below the break-even point, sometimes the right giveaway can make the ad profitable again and give it an entirely *new* lease on life.

Sometimes a surprising switch in the offer of a giveaway can create an unexpected bonanza of increased business. One of our alumni ran a test selling harmonicas, with instructions as a giveaway. Results were unprofitable, and he almost decided to give up the project. Instead, he converted the instructions into a more detailed *harmonica instruction course*, sold the course and gave away the harmonicas. The new offer was a great success, and he sold hundreds of thousands of harmonica courses.

A self-liquidator, an extra item offered for its actual cost including mailing, or a partial self-liquidator, offered for part of its cost including mailing, may be preferable. Either may offer a greater bargain. Whether a giveaway, self-liquidator or partial liquidator, the effect is that the total cost of merchandise and shipping is a higher percentage of the money you take in, and the percentage of gross profit is smaller. It may produce enough extra orders to be worthwhile.

In our family business, we often test an offer without a giveaway, self-liquidator or partial liquidator. Sometimes we add one later. Offering one can often greatly increase orders. Some mail order people scarcely make a mail order offer without one. I feel that each case should be judged individually and hope that your completion of this course will help give you the "feel" to do so.

Another component part of your offer can be an add-on. This is a request for an extra and usually related purchase. An add-on can be simply offering two or more of the same items, usually at a saving, or a set of several items at a saving otherwise individually offered at full price in the advertising. It can be a larger package. An add-on can be a deluxe edition of a book or deluxe version of an item. It can be a closely related and easily explained item, as a fishing rod with a fishing reel.

An add-on is included in an offer not to make it more attractive, but to make it more profitable. For us, an add-on of two of the items for a saving, a set for a saving, a larger size or deluxe model at modest extra cost, almost always pulls quite well; usually up to 20% more and occasionally even more. We often run our first ad without an add-on and test later whether it's more advantageous to use one.

Another component part of your offer may be a cash-up. A cash-up is an incentive offered to send in full payment now, as an alternative to buying on credit on one payment or on extended time payments. It is not used to get more orders, but simply to bring in more cash. A short-term subscription to Time Magazine may be offered on credit – with a free adding machine when paid for.

Often the incentive is such a specific giveaway, only given for full cash payment. If there is already a giveaway for prompt action, a cash-up can be an additional giveaway for full cash payment. Often it is simply an offer by the seller to prepay shipping costs to the buyer, but only for full cash payment. Sometimes it's an actual reduction in price for full cash payment. Simply making the full cash option the first option, and the credit option the alternative, can make full cash payment more the expected choice, and can increase the cash payment percentage.

A cash-up usually pulls a smaller percentage when used for higher priced items than for lower-priced items. When customers are offered billing through credit cards, more will accept a cash-up alternative than when they are offered direct billing. This is because most people realize that if they purchase through credit cards, and pay after 25 days from the date of purchase, they will start paying interest.

We often do not use a cash-up to start but do so later, after testing.

A most important component of your offer is your guarantee. But for the mail order firm that is not yet famous and is offering one or more items in one advertisement, direct mail piece or broadcast commercial, it is particularly important. Each prospective purchaser fears being disappointed or even being taken advantage of. Each worries as to whether the mail order ad claims are true. Most people still prefer not to buy by mail order. For each customer who buys, other readers of your advertising will determine to wait until a trusted retailer carries the product.

The use of a C.O.D. offer can create huge volume on TV – or an enormous percentage of refusals. To sell this way is like being hooked on a drug. The way to kick the habit is to convert C.O.D. customers to credit card customers. To do this, we offered guaranteed three-day delivery after receipt of order – for an extra fee. Such an order could only be placed by telephone. We used Federal Express, which does not ship C.O.D. Only a credit card order could secure this service. It dramatically decreased the percentage of C.O.D. orders and increased total orders. We believe that two-day air deliveries such as this are still another mail order revolution.

Only by removing all risk on the part of your prospective customer can you overcome the reluctance to deal with a stranger and buy an unknown product. Either your product works or it doesn't. Either it is a value for the price or it isn't. Either your advertising claims are accurate or exaggerated. Mail order products are returned if they disappoint. Satisfied customers keep their purchases. If your product is shoddy or overpriced, you should drop it. If your advertising is untruthful, you should correct it. If not, you usually have nothing to fear from the strongest guarantee for lower-priced products.

When mail order began, the very idea of sending money to an unknown person seemed to most to be too great a risk to consider. It was assumed that no product would ever come. Today, infinitely more people will send money, in larger and larger amounts per item, to an unknown mail order firm. As trust is built up, occasionally surprising confidence will be shown. I have known of a customer sending a letter asking a mail order firm to select certain items at their discretion, giving authority to ship and even enclosing a signed blank check. But more people are still afraid. And removing that fear is largely the job of the guarantee. In our business, we endeavor to make a clear, unequivocal guarantee and act on it promptly and without question.

We always offer a free trial. This is standard in mail order and expected by the customer, and by any governmental agency or consumer group to whom a dissatisfied customer might appeal. Any publication or broadcast station you advertise with expects that you will give a dissatisfied customer buying from the advertisement complete satisfaction! The Post Office and the Better Business Bureau expect it. The result is that, for all practical purposes, you must give replacement merchandise, or if not desired, a refund to any customer requesting it.

In lower-priced items of good quality and value, honestly represented in advertising and sold for cash, the percentage of returns will usually be minimal. Even if you strongly emphasize a money back guarantee or if the price of the item is low, returns are usually very low. It is obvious that, if sales go up 20%, a percentage of returns of up to 10% *would be profitable. Yet it is usually under 3%*, and for us usually a fraction of 1%.

For such items, we have found that the length of the trial period makes no significant difference. Whether the trial period offered is five days, a week, 10 days, 30 days or six months, returns are about the same percentage. The inertia of the average person is all on your side. Who wants to take the trouble to put something in a box, wrap it up, address it, get to the post office, buy stamps and mail it just to get back a very small amount of money? Yet we find that a longer trial period in the offer *increases* orders!

One component part of your offer is any limitation on supply of the item or on the length of time that the offer is available. If your offer expires on a certain date, it becomes an added reason for acting before that date. If your product or price is not available through retail stores or anywhere but through you, that is a reason for action. If there's a limit to the quantity of the items that you have in inventory and you cannot get more at anywhere near the price, this is also a reason for action. Even if you simply don't know when, if ever, you can repeat the offer in this publication, this is a reason for the prospective buyer to buy now. Get the facts, tell the truth and include any such legitimate limitation in your offer.

It's surprising how much easier your entire job of creating an ad becomes once you determine exactly the offer you wish to make. But price, terms, giveaway, guarantee and any other offer components must be decided *before* you write your ad. Throughout my course, we will further discuss the advantages and disadvantages of specific offer components and how to obtain the greatest advantage from each.

In your first tiny classified and display ads, you will only excerpt from your research a few essential words, and simplify your offer to suit the number of words available. In your largest ads, you will find that your main news story is surprisingly pre-planned and organized by your research. Even creating the elements of your ad will be greatly based on the component parts of your offer.

Each step greatly helps the next. Let's start creating ads.

Chapter 6

THE ELEMENTS

---

*. . . of bigger ads . . . headline
complex . . . boxes . . . captions . . .
lead story . . . presenting offer
components . . . coupons*

If we could say in one sentence how a product would benefit the user, that would be enough except for two reasons. Many do not believe advertising they see or hear. And of those who do believe and plan to buy or inquire, only a minority do. Otherwise, only the price and name and address of the seller would have to be added. Long copy, most pictures, demonstrations, testimonials, documentation of claims, are simply to get believability and action. A short message about an unknown product by an unknown seller can usually not achieve this. When a mail order ad fails for a good product with apparently effective copy, it may not be believed. The reader may have been afraid to buy it by mail and didn't trust or believe the mail order seller.

A survey of college students revealed that 94% did not believe TV commercials they watched. Readers, listeners and viewers take all advertising with a grain of salt. They believe less of the advertising, accepting some points and rejecting others. Yet people regretfully disbelieve. To attain believability in a skeptical age, the first step is to tell the truth, in letter and spirit, in what you say, your qualifications and the average person's understanding of them. One legally safe, weasel-worded paragraph that does not conform to the spirit of truth can make your entire advertising lose belief. Extreme claims are like hypodermic needle-injected drugs, plunged deeper and deeper to attain the same effect. More extreme claims by more advertisers cause more disbelief. Legitimate claims can be overdramatized.

The purpose of a mail order ad, in any form, is usually to cause the reader, viewer or listener to order or inquire. Mail order persuasion means to cause action at once. Yet research shows that three times as many people who read, view or listen to a mail order ad, mailing or commercial intend to buy or inquire than actually do. Tests prove that the more inducement you give in your advertising, the better chance you usually have of getting action on your proposal. The right incen-

---

tive and repeated reminder to act now can cause more people who intend to buy to do so.

Attaining believability and causing immediate action takes more words, but not overlong selling copy. You want to get across certain selling points, first things first, in the order of importance. The only purpose of each selling point and word is to get the desired belief and action. There's a limit to the importance of any product. Its story may fascinate you, bore anyone else and drive away otherwise interested readers. Everyone knows the salesman who makes the sale in the first two minutes and loses it in the next 10 – not knowing when to stop. Such overselling can be like trying to kill flies with sledge hammers.

Some odd and unusual research facts about your product may not be important news to readers. You are not writing an essay, but primary news to readers. There's no room for the majority of your research. Your job is selection of the most important news facts. Shorter and simpler, more believable ads, with more pictures and fewer words, usually win out against overcrowded black masses of overselling words. But such shorter, simpler ads can best be written after mastering the creation of longer ones. Let's analyze what goes into these longer ads. If it seems complex, don't worry, I'm going to give you an easier way to create complex ads. Then we'll go into creating simpler ones.

Once a competitor hired a fairly expensive copywriter. For weeks, the writer was given just one job, to read and re-read each ad which our advertising agency, Huber Hoge and Sons, had recently written. Only then was the writer given a copy assignment.

After research, the first step to writing successful mail order ads is to study successful mail order ads selling similar products in a similar price range. Collect full-page mail order ads run widely and frequently for broad-appeal products in mass media where the product and company name is new to most readers. This requires a good deal of convincing and long copy. Let's observe one such full-page ad.

Draw a semi-circle from the middle of the headline through the main and subsidiary subheads, further through the main copy blocks down into the coupon. This is the main readership path. Note carefully how these ads are constructed to avoid losing readership of the impatient, while providing answers for the most picayune objections of slow moving, cautious doubters.

The most necessary, vital facts are in the headline, the main subheads, subordinate subheads and subheads that interrupt copy. For a prospective buyer who doesn't want to read long ads and can make up his or her mind fast, the readership path becomes a speedway to the coupon. Some buy just this way, scarcely reading the detailed copy in the ad. Those who want a fuller story can follow the same readership path and read the full main copy story, but skip the supporting evidence. Many buy this way. The interested but still dubious can read thoroughly every scintilla of evidence before making their decision. Notice how frequently the copy asks for action right through the ad.

Notice certain similarities in most full-page mail order ads. The headline is rarely pure attention getting. It is normally a sweeping product claim. Sometimes it is both. The main subhead usually follows up with subsidiary claims or immediately starts citing proof. Usually there is a prominent box on top citing documentation of claims. Often the main picture is upper right. Normally the coupon is bottom right. The main copy block usually starts upper left, under the main and subsidiary subheads. Often there is more detailed proof in a box at lower left. Sometimes, for book ads, it is a detailed catalog of contents.

The type size can vary considerably. Even in a crowded ad, the opening lines of the main copy can be in bigger, more readable type. Sometimes it can drop in size after several paragraphs and toward the close drop in size again. Pictures subordinate to the main picture can often be graduated down to quite small size. Captions can be in type so small that in the main body copy it would discourage reading. In boxes citing evidence that proves claims, copy can be smaller than the main copy story. Reading these portions of the ad is optional. This is the extra evidence for doubting Thomases. A catalog of claims may contain just one so urgently interesting to a specific reader that it clinches the sale. It's worth including more claims or contents, but in small type.

How do you start creating a big ad?

For the simplest or most complex ad, your first problem is to get anyone to even notice your advertising, then to read it and finally to order or inquire. Many creative people start with an idea for a picture and headline, then the main subhead and then the lead to the copy story, main copy block and supporting elements. Sometimes the picture idea stimulates the headline. Sometimes the headline idea calls up the picture concept. I start with research and build from it a main story concept. Then I come up with subhead ideas from the copy and last of all the ideas for headline, picture and main subheads. You will find, by trial and error, the method best for you.

In a traditional full-page mail order ad, there was little white space. Headline, subheads, picture and copy crowded in. Much of the strength and sometimes the clincher came from supporting evidence carefully prepared and strategically placed throughout the ad. A full-page mail order ad was usually jammed with a complex combination of painstakingly put together elements, each designed to do a specific persuasion job.

Today space is so expensive and people read so hurriedly that smaller ads and shorter copy are used with a bigger percentage of picture and more white space. To sell a concept, the effect of layout and even typography is all-important. A page itself is smaller, and the ad is narrower. The strategy of the traditional big-space ad is followed, but copy is capsulized. It is necessary to accomplish all that the traditional ad did, but faster. The art of simplicity, clarity and summation becomes all-important. Belief and desire to act must come quickly.

My son Cecil is superb at all of this. Stan Rapp, chairman of the board of one of the greatest direct marketing agencies, Rapp & Collins, says that Cecil's ad for our Stomach Eliminator follows every copy rule Stan and his partner and copy chief, Tom Collins, insist on.

Cecil researches even more thoroughly than I do. He lives our products. He works out with the Stomach Eliminator daily. He uses each of our boats and accessories under varying conditions. He absorbs what each product does and its advantages by contact with users, design experts and beginners, all with a kind of osmosis.

When he comes to the ad, he thinks in pictures and headlines. He uses pads with blue ruled lines of graph paper consisting of 1,452 tiny squares. With the aid of these squares, he makes a copywriter's layout, reasonably accurate as to proportion of space he uses for headlines, subheads and illustrations. He writes his copy in quite small letters along his ruled lines. His favorite size is the square kind. His ads are never jammed, always have elegance, have striking pictures – usually only one – and are quite persuasive. They are successful, while low key, and repeat successfully more than most mail order ads do.

If his ad succeeds, he continually experiments to make it better. One way is to test a small version or a big version. He goes up to a half-page, then two-thirds and finally a page, adding elements as he does. He goes down to a quarter-page, a fifth or even a sixth. The best ad wins.

For any size, one-step ad copy starts and ends with your offer. You want them to buy something or write in for information. The more you wish them to do, the more convincing is usually needed. A sale takes more convincing than an inquiry, a request for cash payment usually takes more than just to charge, and a request for a higher cash or charge payment usually takes still more.

An inquiry can usually be secured with briefest copy. A qualified inquiry usually requires more copy, not so much to pre-sell as to discourage curiosity seekers. More copy will often prepare inquiries and pre-sell them sufficiently to cause a higher percentage of closings, either by follow-up literature or by salesmen.

Writing a big ad is a big job. It becomes much simpler when subdivided into little jobs. Each ad section is a little job we call an element. We build an ad element by element.

Let's discuss the elements of which many full-page ads are constructed. Some will simply present component parts of your offer. Just clarifying your offer helps write each such element. Some component parts will be repeated and emphasized in different elements of your ad.

Most copywriters consider the most important ad element to be the headline complex: headline, main subheads and overline (if any). Many times, mail order defeat in a test has been turned to victory by a change in headline. Books could be written solely on the art of creating headlines. Newspapers have been propelled to huge circulations by the skill of their headline writers. The best copy in the world can't work if it isn't read, and often it is the headline that turns glancing into reading or gets any glance at all.

Some copywriters devote as much time and effort to creating the headline complex as they do for all other parts of the ad combined. Some never start to write the rest of the ad until they write the main headline complex. I occasionally start with a working headline complex and then write the remainder of the ad. But usually I come up with a better headline complex later.

Often a headline complex has a headline and a smaller line above, called an overline. Sometimes a headline has no overline. Often it has one or more smaller lines underneath called the main subhead. Sometimes there's no main subhead or overline. A headline can be one word or a number of lines. It can use an accompanying picture to prove or dramatize what it is saying. It can be subordinate to and introduce the main picture.

Sometimes a headline is used entirely to arouse curiosity, sometimes just to signal a special group and sometimes to make just one vital, overall claim. Sometimes the headline will be small in relation to the size of the ad. Other times it will dominate an ad with 30% or more of the total space of an ad. Some mail order men find that the more dominant the headline is, the greater the chances are of success.

Often in a big mail order ad, overline, headline and main subhead capsulize the entire story of the ad, give the main premise, fan out to subsidiary benefits, feature claim documentation and sometimes signal to kinds of users who can benefit. But there are many headline approaches.

Cub reporters are taught that "Dog Bites Man" is not a major headline, but "Man Bites Dog" is. Our headline, "Frog Murders Bass," aroused curiosity, signalled bass fishermen, promised what each wanted to do . . . and sold 123,000 kicking frog fish lures for us.

To sell a dress form for home sewers, we combined its most powerful appeal, custom fit, with its guarantee. The headline "Custom Fit Guaranteed . . . or no cost" sold over 210,000 dress forms for us. Such combinations of claim and offer are often used. People love a winner . . . and a bargain. Best of all they love quality and a bargain. Our Italian manufacturer found a way to improve dramatically the strength and length of life of our Sea Eagle inflatable boats. The headline of our most successful ad . . . "The Quality Alternative to High-Cost Inflatable Boats" helped us sell 42,000 Sea Eagle boats.

A winning headline can come from endless research, one phrase in a testimonial letter or from constant reworking and editing of body copy. Often it's worth working for.

Sometimes a "signal box" will be another element. It will list and call the attention of special groups to whom the ad is directed.

In traditional, big-space mail order ads, a frequent element was a box featuring product claims. If it contained under six strong product claims, such a box was often put up towards the top, sometimes next to the "signal box," and both became almost a part of the main headline complex. If there were many encyclopedic product claims, a bigger box was often used and placed further down in the ad, sometimes at lower left. This became a "contents box" for book publishers.

The biggest element in your ad is usually your main copy story. Often you find the basis for it in your premise and product development research notes. It's often a summary of key points from your other ad elements. Its opening words are meant to pull the reader down further into the story. Often this is done with a summary of your headline complex.

Step by step, your main copy story must get across your main selling points, always tempting the reader on to read more. Its interest should pick up smoothly and continuously. From the opening words, each sentence and paragraph, one by one, should be building rhythm and pace. Today the entire process is shorter and faster.

Think of yourself as part lawyer, part salesman, part reporter and part editor. As a lawyer, you draw from your research more and more evidence until you build an irresistible case for your client – your product. As a salesman, you draw on this evidence to build a sales story to demonstrate your product in use, tempt with end benefits, surprise with competitive comparison and come up with *an offer no sane person would logically refuse.* As a reporter, you tell a crisp, dramatic news story of product development and benefit. As an editor and rewrite man, you sum up in a fraction of former reading time the entire story.

Usually you break up your news story with subheads. Each is a miniature headline of what is to follow. We try to keep subheads to several words each and one line each. But some subheads of several lines are very effective.

Words should be simple and sentences and paragraphs short. We try to precede and follow a subhead with an even shorter paragraph, sometimes only one sentence long. White space above and below each subhead, margin on either side and these short paragraphs before and after can create an open and easier-reading look.

The main copy story usually mentions price and terms only if an advantage. It rarely mentions an add-on or cash-up. In such cases, a box or the coupon can do the job. The main story usually repeats and emphasizes any advantageous offer component, any giveaway or variation, any time or product supply limitation and any desirable guarantee.

So far, we've discussed copy only as though the picture were an afterthought. Yet the picture or pictures often govern the entire ad, as any art director will tell you. From your very first look at your product, your mind is open and alert to any intriguing picture ideas. Pictures in your ads become picture elements. It may simply be a striking way to make your product look stunningly beautiful. It may be an exciting picture proof shot, dramatically proving an otherwise hard to believe claim. It may be a step-by-step demonstration picture sequence. It may be an exploded shot showing all component parts. It may be two before-and-after shots. It may be a photograph, line drawing or wash illustration with shading and contrast.

Each step of your research brings up picture ideas. As you write and rewrite copy, you come up with more picture ideas. Some are practical; some are not. Your patent may have pictures of the product in use and of the results of using it. A salesman's presentation will often have intriguing picture ideas. Engineers' drawings and blueprints sometimes give more. For fertilizer, we've used time-lapse photography sequences of treated vs. untreated identical plants. For dance instruction, we've used high speed, stroboscopic, stop-motion shots showing the dance step in action pictures.

Make several lists of your picture ideas. Classify them under "A," "B" and "C." The "A" list should be the most practical, most immediately available, least expensive as well as effective. The "B" and "C" lists may seem more speculative as to whether they will work. They may require more time than preferable. They may be more expensive than you'd like. We'll consider them all when it comes time to make your layout and put your ad together.

You've worked hard to create a persuasive offer. Let's discuss how best to present in your advertising the component parts of that offer.

Some component parts go into ad elements. Some become ad elements. Some do both jobs. Let's start by presenting, most advantageously, the price component of your offer. If it's a bargain, document it by price comparison with competitive products. If it's a price reduction, compare the new with the former price. If your price is higher than competition, try to justify it with greater savings from use, lower costs of use, longer years of use or however the facts prove.

If price is not an advantage, you will not mention price until the coupon, and there will be no price copy element. If your offer has real price advantages, state them in a clear and orderly manner. The stronger your price story is, the more you can emphasize and dramatize its facts. It becomes a copy block, perhaps several paragraphs. Your job is to construct each element as tightly as possible, with no unnecessary word, each in the right order and each right for the job.

When the reader becomes interested in price and glances at this small piece of evidence, the spotlight is suddenly on it. You want it to be a little gem. It's the same with each element throughout your ad.

The terms may become another element. If you sell for all cash or C.O.D., you will probably only say so in the coupon. If you sell via credit cards, you may wish to emphasize it. If you offer a choice of cash or credit cards (or cash or direct billing), you may prefer not to emphasize either form of charge billing. If you sell a luxury product, you may feel that emphasis on credit will cheapen the ad. In any of these cases, you may still prefer no terms element. Advertising credit for higher-price items often sells items far less saleable for cash only. More advertising emphasis of available credit often gets more orders.

When advertising offers to charge via credit cards and to take orders by telephone, orders can climb further. Your phone number in the ad will get calls. If you say that you will take phone orders collect, you get more. If you feature the 800 toll-free number to the customer, you get a lot more. The customer is sometimes embarrassed by and does not want the trouble of the collect call. He prefers dialing 800 plus your number.

If you use a WATS 800 number, emphasize that in your advertising. Your advertising should make clear that the customer pays nothing for the call and can order by telephone merely by giving his or her credit card number. On a large-ticket item which we have in ample stock, we can usually ship in 24 hours. If you can, say so. This alone can increase orders. If you use a twenty-four-hour, seven-day-a-week phone answering service, state prominently in your ad that you can accept orders on a twenty-four-hour basis.

Whatever you do say about terms must be crystal clear. Misunderstood terms can reduce orders. Contradictory terms can sharply reduce orders. Either can lose you money.

Featuring a giveaway, self-liquidator or partial liquidator in your ad is another element. If you sell anything, you know how important any special offer is as a conversational door opener or to close your sale. In your mail order ad, it's news. It attracts attention more than most attention-attracting devices. Present it dramatically, in conformance with the character, style and taste of your business. Do so in as exciting or as discreet a manner as that of your product.

Sometimes the giveaway presentation can add to the impact of product copy. For an elaborate set of kitchenware, an additional set of four or five pieces of far less expensive but related items can add to the image of an overflowing cornucopia of product value. Inexpensive plasticware can be an added gift, for instance, with an elaborate set of china. The same principal can apply to a tool set, sewing kit, fishing tackle combination, etc.

An effective giveaway is usually emphasized. Sometimes its copy and illustration is the most important segment of your ad. Often it can be in a prominent box, in the headline or pictured dominating the ad and repeated in the body copy, the close and the coupon.

Warning! To use the word FREE in your advertising concerning your giveaway, you must state an offer to buyers of your product to keep the giveaway even if returning the product. You must state this clearly and prominently, close to the word "FREE." You can check your Better Business Bureau or the Federal Trade Commission for the latest FTC rulings on this.

Another ad element is the guarantee. The more convincing it takes to get an order, the more important a guarantee can become. For less-known or unknown products, it's even more important.

A guarantee paragraph can increase orders, a guarantee display box or certificate even more so. Spelling it out, emphasizing it and repeating it can turn more readers into buyers. Its effective use can start in your headline, subhead or overline, be in a prominent box on top, go through the opening, build in the body copy, peak in the closing paragraphs and culminate in the coupon. Often the guarantee box or certificate is directly above or next to the coupon.

Some mail order people worry whether too great an emphasis on guarantee and return privilege will increase returns. We find that far more is gained in emphasizing the guarantee of lower-priced items than is lost in extra returns. It can cause a problem only for a shoddy product. For more expensive items, too strong a guarantee emphasis can attract the something-for-nothing set. For direct time payments, overselling the guarantee can sell people who really cannot afford the product.

We are more cautious in guarantee emphasis for bigger-ticket items. We are more so for sales via credit cards than for cash. For sales via direct billing, we are still more quiet. If on direct time payment, we give least emphasis. For luxury and fashion items, we handle the guarantee more discreetly. The more prestigious your approach is, the lower key will be the style of your guarantee, but it will still be important. The emphasis will vary with the tone of your business and style of your product. However strong or discreet the handling of your guarantee is, make it simple and clear to the average person. State its limitations and length of trial period.

Another ad element may be a group of testimonials by users praising your product. A good product gets testimonial letters. It's often possible to get a legal release with permission to quote them. Their words and phrases will often be better, more colorful and more believable advertising than you could ever write. You'll often get new copy points, and sometimes new uses for your product.

A user may compare favorably and specifically your product with others. He or she may say how much more it saved or made money in a real situation, how much faster it did the job, how much more it produced, how much longer its use life was, how much more trouble free, exactly how it was more convenient, more practical or more versatile. Warning! An enthusiastic user can write in a testimonial that your product can do things that your product cannot do. To use such quotes is fraud, as it would be to make the same claim elsewhere in your copy. It then becomes subject to prosecution by the Post Office Fraud Department and by the FTC, among other government agencies. Use judgment in using quotes.

Testimonial letters can be gold mines of true claims. But sometimes a testimonial letter rambles. Irrelevant words, sentences and paragraphs straggle in between wonderful quotes. Usually space limits the use of testimonials. Using too much of one lengthy letter can keep you from using other highly desirable ones. More individual testimonials covering more situations can be more convincing.

Carefully extracting most-favorable and to-the-point quotes

leaves room to use other quotes and makes the overall effect more powerful. Careful selection can feature different advantages. We often take a longer quote from the most coherent, favorable letter with very short excerpts from quite a few others. We use the full name for a larger quote and initials for short ones. Often we'll then quote a half-dozen one or two-word quotes, preceding them with "Other users report."

Testimonials pull orders in a paragraph, more in a copy block, and more with a series of pictures. Pictures of users photographed with or using the product are most effective. Testimonials can be so powerful as to cause the entire ad, from headline and main illustration through the main copy story, to be built around them.

Testimonials from name personalities can be particularly important. Paid testimonials from sport and entertainment personalities are under criticism by government agencies. But in some form, celebrity testimonials will continue. Personalities are people. They eat, sleep and use products.

I know a man who started a modest business with one product which was bought by the most famous broadcast personality of the time for his own use. This personality liked it, gave a strong testimonial with full permission to use it – for no payment – and then invested $250,000 in the business – which prospered.

A big-name personality in show business or sports can fear becoming obsolete and dream of a related business that he can play a part in and retire to. If he likes your product, you may be able to make him a partner or give him a royalty to advertise your product. If so, surely he can say he likes and uses your product.

Personalities are known to people who don't know you or your product. If the personality recommends your product and asks that the reader try it, perhaps even giving your offer guarantee, usually more orders come in the mail. And the more the recommendation of the personality is featured in your ad, the more the results can improve.

Let's hope that you get associated with the right personality and present his testimonial to maximum advantage in your ad. Again, it can be a paragraph, a box, or the personality can write and sign your entire ad.

Another element may be any documentation you may have on your product claims. A form of this is association with other firms stronger than yourself. If your product uses a component or material with a famous trade name or made by a famous company, feature it in your advertising. Such a component or material may play an important part in the effectiveness of your product. Tests made by the famous company laboratories may be able to prove this dramatically. Your own research may uncover it. Or you may be able to suggest and arrange such tests and get permission to feature the results in your advertising, preferably showing the logotype of their brand name.

Our Sea Eagle boats are the official inflatable boats of the Boy Scouts. They have been on the front cover of four Boy Scout magazines.

They have been used by expeditions all over the world, featured in leading magazines and on a two-hour documentary on ABC TV sponsored by Mutual of Omaha. All this has been ammunition for our catalog and ads.

Your product's use by prestige companies may be important if you can simply get permission to use their names. A big-name company may tell you why it uses your product and how it finds your product superior – and do so with a testimonial letter along with permission to quote it. If you do so in an ad, you attain far more credibility. Your product may have been used and competitively tested by the U.S. Government, the armed forces, a university, hospital or institution or by any organization famous, unbiased and in a position to know the merits and defects of any product it uses or tests. If so, and if you can get permission to quote their reaction to or tests of your product, this helps gain credibility.

Perhaps you can demonstrate what your product can do for such an organization and get permission to publicize results. Perhaps a famous publication has tested your product and published an article with pictures about such tests. Perhaps you can interest an appropriate publication in researching your product and in doing a story on its merits. In any case, quotes (with permission) from an article on your product vastly increase believability of your advertising.

Your inventor may have been associated with great institutions, the government or giant companies. If so, featuring this in your advertising helps achieve trust in him and thus in your product.

An add-on is usually not brought up until the prospective purchaser is at the point of ordering. Sometimes it's only mentioned in the coupon, sometimes also in a small box next to the coupon, and sometimes it's emphasized more. A cash-up is rarely featured in an ad or mentioned until the coupon.

Don't forget yourself and the concept of your business. People like to deal with people. Small people like small business. If you can establish a personality, flavor and atmosphere by your name, concept and what you are trying to do, you will get more orders. And getting across that concept also becomes an element in your ad.

The final element in your ad is your coupon. A coupon is your only contract between the buyer and you. It is also easier for the buyer to use than to write an order without it. A coupon should be simple, clear and large enough for easy filling in. A cramped coupon can discourage orders.

Most mail order people feel a coupon in a full-page ad should be in the lower outside corner, and strongly favor a right-hand page with a right-hand coupon. But we have had success with coupons on top of the ad or even in the "gutter," the inside bottom of the page. The coupon size and location, considered mandatory, varies among mail order people.

A coupon cannot be confusing, but it can more easily contain alternative options than can mailing instructions without a coupon. A coupon is more essential for a sale than an inquiry, although also favored for bigger inquiry ads.

For lower-price items, it has been more and more customary to add postage charges, plus an internal handling fee for mail order shipping for each order, cash or credit. A simple added phrase in a coupon can explain this. In recent years, it has been mandatory to collect any sales tax due from residents of the state from which you ship or to pay the sales tax and absorb it. It may soon be mandatory nationally.

A coupon should lead off with the guarantee. It usually emphasizes the privilege of reserving the item for inspection and trial, with final buying decision to be made only after trial. The concept of the cash payment is often treated as a deposit, which only becomes a purchase if you do not return the item before the trial period ends.

A company name inappropriate to the product sometimes pulls fewer orders than one more appropriate. An address like Fifth Avenue in New York often pulls more orders than a box number. Any address in a cosmopolitan city (for fashion, jewelry, etc.) often pulls more than an address in a small village. A more appropriate area (Vermont for maple syrup) will often pull more for any product.

We'll discuss later the correct keying of coupons so that you can know the response to each of your ads and how to test different kinds of coupon offers.

If you're like me, when you first complete each of your elements, each will need editing. Now comes the time to turn confusion into clarity. Writing and cutting, putting more in and trimming down, this is the first step in editing.

My first sentences are long and wandering. But overlong sentences can be divided into two, three or more. My first paragraphs are also too long, but each paragraph can be subdivided as well. My first product news facts come out of sequence. The disorder of my mind comes tumbling out in the disorder of my wording. I murder grammar and crucify the King's English. I'm foggy about commas and confused about proper sentence construction. But somehow it all gets straightened out by simply redoing it, by writing it and reading it and rewriting what doesn't seem to come across. I keep changing the order of sentences and even paragraphs. I lengthen a sentence that doesn't seem clear and cut every word I can.

In copy (and later in layout), something works or it doesn't. Trial and error, writing first one way and then another, often indicates what works and what doesn't. I cut my sentences down and down. I make my paragraphs shorter and shorter. Between interrupting subheads, I try to open with a one-sentence paragraph. I try to close with almost as short a paragraph. I try to keep paragraphs to three, four or five sentences. When I'm finished cutting and capsulizing, I read and reread the final version. Often I find sentences turned to gibberish by overcutting. Now I must put back some of what I took out. It's a slow back-

and-forth process. But it costs no more rent and causes no more overhead for me to work and rework each ad until it becomes the best effort I am capable of. And one such ad, properly written, can often pay rent and overhead for some time to come.

Now let's look at several specific kinds of big ads. To introduce a new product in a new field, the ad must explain the entire field as well as the product. The reader doesn't understand what it is or does. Your ad must show the need, create desire and close the sale. It may require the instructor type of selling. Sometimes there's romance, tradition and nostalgia to be dramatized by pictures and words. The product may have exciting new use applications to show and describe. Instruction picture sequences may be able to make using it seem easy and quick. The component parts may need to be pictured.

The headline and subheads may be able to capsulize the new popularity, the ease and speed and the many applications of your project. The contents boxes may be able to catalog "use" projects. The copy may tell of the development of the product and the use benefits it makes possible. It may close with savings the product makes possible and the no-risk examination privilege. Quotes from leading magazines and newspapers or famous personalities may document the new wave of interest. Testimonials may tell how easy and quick the product is to work with, how much fun the projects are and how much each finished project can give you in satisfaction and savings.

A format quite natural to the introduction of a new product is an editorial ad. For years, the Reader's Digest ran occasional stories on new miracle products in which the development of the product over obstacles was presented dramatically. Often the magazine sections of the Sunday papers will run a story on the leaping popularity of a new hobby or even on new developments in a particular field. Often a national magazine will run such a story. Occasionally we've had our own products mentioned in such stories. The growing popularity of any field of activity is news, as is the development of any product (particularly over difficulties) which does something of popular interest better, faster or easier. The public wants to read such stories, or publications would not run them. An advertisement modeled after such a story has a good chance of added readership and added credibility. Both are increased by adhering as closely as possible to the editorial format of the publication in which the ad appears. Even when the word "advertisement" is printed at the top (as required by some publications), results are often increased by this format.

The development of the electronic chip calculator had everything to make it news. Today's scientist is our romanticized culture hero. The field of microelectronics is all that Buck Rogers prophesied decades ago. The background of a product first developed as part of the space program is fascinating. As variation after variation of the chip calculator was developed, *each* was an exciting news story.

One mail order firm catapulted to big success by running nothing but editorial-style ads on different new, specialized chip calculators. At such a time, with such a basic product, the hunger of the public for more and more information on any product variation seems insatiable. For decades, the automobile industry had such an aura about it. Every new car was an exciting news story. Each new model of a car was news. Just unveiling it was news.

There was a time when one of today's most everyday products, the ballpoint pen, was dramatic news. Today a full-page editorial ad on a ballpoint pen would have all the appeal of a story on the safety pin. Make sure your product is exciting news before you try an editorial ad.

Some kinds of mail order products are best sold with ads quite unlike distribution product ads, and other kinds with ads far more similar to them. The more of a luxury a product is, the less difference there is between mail order advertising and advertising of the same product in retail stores. The more style and fashion-oriented the product is, the more this is so.

A hard sell would make it undesirable. An encyclopaedic list of advantages would bore. Style and atmosphere make it wanted, despite its price. The feeling of the advertising conveyed by art, layout and typography can be more important than the words, whether the product is sold mail order or via stores.

A technical or industrial product filling a specific need requires clarity and technical accuracy of description. Emotional appeals are usually out of place and may hinder rather than help sales. What the product is and does can be important news to the audience reached. The difference between advertising by mail order and the *introductory* advertising of the same industrial or technical product distributed elsewhere is often not great.

Often the entire ad can be built around one overwhelmingly important element. Sometimes the entire ad is constructed to indicate a tremendous bargain. If a single item, one big, beautiful, dramatic picture will sometimes dominate the ad. The product will be glorified and shown to maximum advantage. The low price for the expensive-looking product will probably be right in the headline. The opening copy will start off with the price story. The copy story and boxes will cite proof of *why it is possible*. The close will be an appeal to see and judge the value for yourself, *at no risk*.

If it is a set of items at a bargain, the picture can be a cornucopia shot with the items arranged so profusely it can seem scarcely possible that *so many* items could be available for the price. Next to the coupon can be the shot of the *extra giveaway*, another set of less expensive items but still further emphasizing the overall generosity of the offer. The main copy story will start off with the summary of what you get, often repeating in only slightly expanded form the headline and subheads. The copy will move on to each item included, citing in detail the virtues of each. The cumulative effect of listing the items and the uses and advantages of each builds constantly. The cataloging box lists each with still more descriptive detail. The prospective buyer can read a little or a lot, fill out the coupon at once or brood over it for weeks.

Price reduction ads pull. Rarely does a retailer's advertisement for any item at full price pull anywhere near as well as a price reduction ad. In mail order, a special, limited-time, reduced price offer often has a similar effect. A publisher offering a new book mail order at a prepublication price, dramatically lower for ordering before publication date, has traditionally done well.

More dramatic price reductions pull better. A price reduction ad pulls best when the product has been heavily advertised at the older, higher price already presented as a bargain.

For each who bought at the old price there have been others tempted, but feeling they could not afford the product at the time. Now the price reduction opens the door to selling this already almost-sold market. Many millions may have seen the product advertised. They have never read the ad through or even seriously considered buying. Drawn by the price reduction, many *will now* read the ad.

The price reduction goes right into the headline. *The reason why* goes in the subhead. A prominent box on the upper right may show the old price X'd out with the new low price and the saving in big, bold type underneath. The copy opens with the price reduction, goes on to the reason why, and closes with the value made possible by the reduction, all at no risk.

Some product claim copy has to go to make room for the price reduction copy. As in any cutting, it's necessary to fight for every word. It usually proves possible to streamline the entire ad, speed it up, make the copy better than ever and include the price reduction story. Price reduction in a new ad is often best used in the close and in a box near the coupon. It's an extra argument to buy now, but effective only after the reader becomes almost sold by the copy.

A price reduction ad for a "blind item," which the purchaser can't easily tell the value of, is far less effective than for an item which has an established price. Some mail order firms consistently run one campaign to introduce an item at full price and then run a follow-up at a dramatically lower price. Some publishers run a title, like a damp towel, through a succession of price reduction ringers, each at a lower price level.

As you collect more ads, you will notice different kinds we have not taken up due to lack of space. We will later discuss the creating of smaller ads. Right now, we want to decide how to *finish* an ad based on what we have learned to date. The process of completing a big ad is like putting together a puzzle or a prefab house with sections you've already constructed.

The greatest difficulty in creating initial big-space ads consists of decisions. How much in space and words should you devote to each element? Which of countless approaches should you use? How big should picture and headlines be? How do you fit it together? And how much will fit in at all?

    Here's the way some of my greatest copywriters have disposed of these problems, and how you can, too.

Chapter 7

PUTTING IT ALL TOGETHER

---

*"Easiest, simplest, fastest, most
effective way" to start writing
complete mail order ads
. . . however complex*

Once one of our star copywriters brought in his latest masterpiece. As soon as the ad was read in the office, the praise began. It was at once considered the best ad that he had ever written. I started to read it. I saw at once *why* it was such a great ad and looked over at my star. He looked back and began to smile.

His ad was an overwhelmingly successful paraphrase, great because it was modeled after one of the greatest ads of all time. His product was Lythrum, a plant just propagated in a Canadian Government horticultural test station. His ad was modeled after the great classic ad for Canada Dry Ginger Ale, written by James Mathes a number of decades before.

The Canada Dry ad started with the line, "Down from Canada came tales of a sparkling new beverage." The Lythrum ad started with the line, "Down from Canada came tales of a new horticultural discovery." Line for line and word for word, the appropriate copy for the Lythrum story was substituted for the great Canada Dry copy. The rhythm, the pace, the poetry feeling was kept intact. Our writer had written the ad originally as a lark for the sheer fun of it. But it sold Lythrum with great success.

Paraphrasing is the quickest way to write ads. It teaches beginning writers faster than any other way. Paraphrasing can be of ads for products in fields remote from yours, in no way affected by your paraphrase of their success.

One Huber Hoge writer later became a competitor and developed a talent for paraphrasing that was uncanny. Our writers would take several months to create a brand new, successful ad for a new product. Our alumnus could paraphrase it in one day for a totally different product. When our writers would get upset and complain, I would ad-

---

vise them to master the technique of paraphrasing their own ads themselves. No one was hurt by such paraphrasing. I am not amused when
a competitor copies our product and our ad. I am not at all disturbed
by paraphrasing our ad for a product in a quite different field.

I could only smile when I saw how ingeniously our alumnus
paraphrased our automobile oil additive ad into his orchid ad or our
fertilizer soil conditioner ad – "Turns hard-baked clay into soft loamy
soil" – into his cosmetic ad – "Turns dry, baked-out skin into soft,
youthful complexion."

What will science think of next?

Let's do what they did. Let's select one full-page ad from the file
of ads collected and paraphrase it element by element, paragraph by
paragraph, sentence by sentence, and word by word. Let's use a layout
plan for the ad modeled exactly on the simple ad. Let's adapt our ad to
the successful model ad in every way. For your first full-page ad, it is
particularly helpful to be guided by a model ad.

And you will find many of them. Clip them, classify them, file them
and study them. Observe differences and similarities. Some are
crowded with type. Some have far more pictures. A few are
predominantly one or more big pictures and shorter-than-average
copy. From your collection of full-page ads, pick one as your model.

The model ad can be on a completely unrelated product, but
should be related in style and purpose. Take a luxury product ad as
model for your luxury product ad, a price reduction ad, a product introduction ad, an industrial, technical or whatever ad that is most
similar to yours in what it is trying to do. Take a *successful* mail order
ad that runs widely and repeats its insertions. Use your research notes.

The first thing you'll realize is that no matter how big your ad,
you'll never be able to use all the research material you've gathered.
Usually you still must select, no matter how much you boil down and
streamline your product story. Just starting on your paraphrasing
gives you ideas for more research that results in still more material.

Select a working headline to start. As you work and rework your
full-page ad, you'll develop more and more headline candidates for later
consideration. Select a working subhead and subsidiary subheads.
From your research, begin to make a list of subhead possibilities to interrupt the main copy story.

Count the words in the main copy story of your model ad. You'll
quickly discover that the number of words allowed for the main copy
story is not nearly as many as you might have expected. Before you
start paraphrasing the main copy story, look over the other component
parts of your model ad. Any enlargement in your ad of your *equivalent*
element will *reduce* available copy elsewhere.

Look at your working headline. If it takes two lines instead of one
in your model, you will have to reduce the ad elsewhere. Try to reduce
your working headline to approximately the same number of characters per line and number of lines as in your model ad. Perhaps you can

save characters in the headline versus your model, even reduce from two lines to one.

Look at the picture or pictures in your model ad. Does your product for some reason *require* more or bigger pictures? Do you have the picture possibilities to use *as much* space effectively? If so, the rest of the ad will have to be adjusted accordingly. Look over each caption. Can you paraphrase your captions to the approximate number of type characters as those of the model ad?

Look at the boxes in the model ad with testimonials or other documentation and with cataloging of contents or listing of product claims. Do you have equivalent testimonials, documentation and contents or claims? If not, how will your paraphrase vary from the model? Look at the guarantee box, if any, and the coupon. If you paraphrase either, modify it to your offer. It can be done quickly, and it will either fit in the same size guarantee box and coupon as your model or require larger space or occasionally *less* space.

Assume that your other elements, outside of the main copy story, can be paraphrased in about the same overall space as in your model. If your coupon is a bit larger or smaller, adjust the number of words allowable for your main copy story accordingly.

Now just paraphrase the main copy story, word for word throughout. Keep the same number of subheads as your model with approximately the same number of words in each subhead, the same amount of white space above and below, the same margins on either side.

You want your ad to have the same rhythm and pace as your model. This means that each sentence must have about the same number of words and each word must have about the same number of characters. If you substitute a longer word for a shorter word, delete an extra small word and balance out the syllables. This keeps the rhythm.

Build sentence by sentence, paragraph by paragraph. The more you have saturated yourself with your research notes, the faster the right substitute words come to mind. Keep editing, sharpening, smoothing. Read your ad to yourself for rhythm and pace. If you make one sentence or paragraph longer than your model, make the next shorter.

Reread what you have written yourself. Does it have the rhythm and feel of your model? If so, the rest will follow. If you're mentally fatigued and blocked, go back to reworking your research notes. Go at your own pace. The right words will start coming. Thomas Mann wrote a page a day, but a perfect page. If in doubt, write alternate words, sentences, paragraphs.

The opinions of others may be helpful, but most will not understand what your ad *should* be, why you follow that style and write to that length. You, yourself, must be the judge. Does each word, sentence and paragraph leave you more anxious to read the next? Do they build interest, desire and belief? Does the rhythm and pace have an excitement and electricity? Are the news facts *new* or *stale?* How does *your* story compare with similar *actual editorial news stories?* Would your ad cause *you* to keep reading *and buy* if you had no association with the ad or product? After you've completed only your first *third* of the main copy story, you will know the answer. If it "works," keep going, however slow your progress, and your entire copy story will "work" as well.

If the first third doesn't "work," keep rewriting it until it does. Once you've written the main copy story, completing the rest of your ad becomes a certainty. Think of each other element as a separate ad which you want to write equally perfectly, however long it takes. It may come far more quickly than you expect, and completely to your satisfaction. Reread your research notes. What *important* points are not covered in your main story? How can you best work *each* in?

Take it easy. Do an easy element first. Write your *guarantee*. Here the equivalent guarantee of your model is most easily paraphrased. What in *your* offer of a return privilege *varies* from that of your model? What about servicing, the length of your free examination period, your policy on factory defects and all other points of your guarantee? Adjust accordingly.

Does your model ad document its claims? Look again at your research notes for equivalent documentation. If the U.S. Government uses the product in your model ad, who uses yours? If a celebrity recommends the product in your model ad, what star personality recommends yours? If General Motors supplies the key component in the product of your model ad, what giant corporation supplies the key component in *your* product?

The more you've done your research homework, the faster your paraphrased ad writes itself. Primarily what you need to do is to select the most appropriate news facts for the blanks in your paraphrasing. The actual words and phrases that have most color and excitement will come straight from your research notes. You're putting together a jigsaw puzzle. And you can take plenty of time to do it, because it can make your fortune.

Now let's get to product claims. Here again, your research has done almost all the work for you. You want to include all you can. But priority goes to the most important, and not all can get in. You may vary more from your model. You want to keep total words to the same approximate number. But perhaps your copy can be tighter and briefer, use three words instead of five, or two in place of three. You may be able to get in *more* than your model. Adjust accordingly.

Does your model ad have demonstration picture proof? Your research should come up with the right equivalent. Does your model ad have testimonials? If your research hasn't uncovered any, interview users and ask for product opinions. Where favorable, get testimonials and signed releases. What about the other picture elements in your model ad? Does your research give you picture idea equivalents, either photographs or drawings of any kind? Now take a further look through your entire notes. Are there any important points you still haven't covered anywhere in your ad? Can one or more of them be worked into picture captions? Each may get more readership than the average line of your main copy story.

Now put your entire ad together. Read it. Compare it from beginning to end with your model. Sleep on it. Modify it or let it stand, and prepare to meet your art director.

Before you do, make a "copywriter's layout" of your own. Many copywriters (perhaps most) will make a "copywriter's layout" as soon as they come up with first headline and picture ideas. We have used the layout of the model ad. Now we need to make our own layout showing each adaptation we have made.

Now you must make what may be your most important creative decision, your choice of picture or pictures. Study the layout of your model ad. Select from your "A" list the picture or pictures that seem to do the most equivalent job.

Get a ruler. Measure your model ad. Rule out a space 50% larger, but in the same proportions, on a 14" X 17" pad of layout tissue paper. You can get it from any art store. Measure the exact height and width of the headline of your model ad. Do the same for the subheads, then for the illustration, next for each paragraph of body copy and coupon. Measure the space between paragraphs, above and below subheads and margins on each side of headline, subheads, illustrations and body copy. Now rule out the equivalent space, but make it 50% wider and 50% deeper for each section within the layout space you've ruled out. It will be easier to work with this space 50% larger than your model ad. It can be reduced back later.

Roughly sketch in, however crudely, your indication of the picture or pictures to be used. If this is too difficult or time-consuming, simply write in the space you've ruled out for the picture what the picture or pictures will be.

Now, letter by letter, pencil in your headline. You've already ruled out the bottom line and top line of each letter. It's simple to pencil out the letter fully from bottom line to top line. Use upper or lower-case letters exactly as your model ad does. Carefully write in your substitute wording, line by line, throughout.

For each line of copy in your main news story, make a double line. With these double lines, indicate the number of lines of actual copy and any indenting at beginning and close of each paragraph. If you have paraphrased a paragraph pretty exactly as to number of words and characters, the paragraph length and structure should be the same as your model. If you have lengthened one paragraph and shortened another, roughly indicate so by the number, length and indentation of the double lines you show for each paragraph.

Keep proportionately the same white space between paragraphs and also between columns of copy. Pencil in your new subheads in place of those of your model. Allow the same proportionate margin above and below.

Rule out in proportion each element which you have adapted from your model. If your paraphrased copy is shorter or longer, reduce or enlarge in proportion. Pencil in subheads. Rule out double lines to indicate copy. Do the same with your coupon. In brief, indicate in proportion the equivalent of each element in your model ad, *but* reduced or enlarged in proportion to your copy adaptation.

Execution of any ad *can* be far from the great expectations of your copy and "copywriter's layout." Fighting to insure that the final effect equals or surpasses your expectations is an unending battle.

Before we discuss that battle in detail, let's get back to creating smaller ads. Doing so will help prepare you to learn the simplest, fastest, easiest and most economical ways of finishing ads as they actually appear in print. The first step is to build a big collection of every size of smaller mail order ads from an inch up.

Compare the ads that come from mail order marketplaces with those that run outside such sections. Notice that specialized products run in *related* specialized publications often use briefer copy.

Let's consider writing a small ad for another item. If for a specific magazine, study ads in it closest in size to the ad you are about to write. Study carefully a number of issues. Note the ads that *repeat* most frequently.

Study how many words each uses in its headline, how much white space above and below it and in the adjoining margins. Study the picture or pictures each uses, their location and their space allowance in relation to copy. Notice the body copy. Count the total words of copy in each ad. Count the words in each line of copy, the words in the average sentence, the number of sentences in the paragraph. Note where parts of sentences are used and where abbreviations are used. Notice the size of the type in headline, subhead, and paragraphs. How many words are in each subhead? Select a model ad to paraphrase. After creating a page ad, it will seem far easier.

Now paraphrase the model ad. Make your headline the same number of words. Substitute for any subhead your own subhead of the same number of words. Count the number of characters of headline and subhead. Keep your substitute headline and subhead each within several characters of the original, as well as cutting to the same number of words each.

Does it have one or more pictures? Plan to use an equivalent picture or pictures in the same spot or spots. Paragraph by paragraph, line by line and word by word, count the characters and substitute your own paraphrased words. Include equivalents for any subheads or captions.

You may have to simplify your offer for a small ad. The offer in your model ad may differ from the kind of offer you are making. If so, look for another same-size model ad *just for the offer wording.* When you find it, paraphrase your offer, word for word, as close to it as you can. Use this copy block instead of paraphrasing the offer copy of your original model ad. Notice if the model ad has a coupon. A one-third-page or larger ad is seldom without it. Smaller ads sometimes have one and sometimes don't. Smallest ads down to an inch seldom do.

If your model ad has a coupon, paraphrase the coupon wording to your product or to that of the alternate model ad just mentioned, using your price and terms. If there is no coupon, paraphrase the appropriate mail-in instructions as close to word for word as possible. If necessary, paraphrase a more appropriate alternate coupon. Be sure to remember to include any shipping and handling charge and tax in your state that you do not wish to absorb. Be sure your ad states your address correctly, with a proper mailing key. We'll give keying instructions later. The entire job is far less complex and far simpler than creating your full-page ad.

Research writes your ad to a surprising degree. Actual writing starts with *selecting* from the wealth of news items uncovered by your research, those with most interest to most people. If you have done a thorough research job and have a very small shopping column ad, you can only *capsulize* the *news facts* that your research has uncovered. This gives even more of a *news feeling* to your ad.

Each *news fact* must be boiled down to an ever briefer form. What is the single most universally interesting news fact about your product? What is the second, the third, etc.? Your headline often comes from the most exciting news that your research uncovers about your product. Your headline is a capsule of your number one news fact. It may be one word or several lines. Only by selecting a working headline can you get started. Only by writing down *enough alternatives*, one after the other, can you make the best headline choice.

From a list you will have prepared of various alternative headlines and subheads, you must make the final best choice you can. Your experience with your big-ad headlines will be a great help.

You must give *priorities* of importance to each *news fact* you boil down. Just arranging your news facts in this *news priority* order causes your ad to take form. Editing is trial and error. Word by word, sentence by sentence, paragraph by paragraph is the only way. Sometimes the revision comes in a rush, sometimes with painful slowness. Generally, the more thorough the research and the more saturated and impregnated you are with news facts about your product, the faster your news story rewriting builds. But it's far easier than in your bigger, more complex ad.

When you have completed paraphrasing the copy of your model ad, paraphrase its layout. Do so exactly as instructed for a page ad. This time it will be far simpler. Make your copywriter's layout 50% larger on the layout pad, just as you did before. Follow the layout of your model ad as carefully as possible, but indicate any variations you have made, just as you did on your page ad. Keep the same spacings between paragraphs, same margins on either side, same indentation, and allow the same space for pictures as your model ad.

After you have written successful ads, you will begin using your own past successful ads as models for future ads. You will make more and more of a study of successful mail order offers and ads. You will adapt much from them, but in your own way. Once you've written and produced your first full-page "hit," you'll have quite a different viewpoint on smaller space ads. My son Cecil starts by writing the smallest ad he feels will succeed.

I prefer to write my full-page ad *first*, even if I don't produce and run it first. To write my full-page ad, I am forced to saturate myself with my product story so thoroughly that smaller-space ads come faster and easier. They become tighter and more effective.

The art of first cutting and then capsulizing to get down to smallest space is a discipline to acquire. But the result is superior to the first effort at writing a smaller ad *before* the full-page ad. I have found that writing a nine-line and picture editorial shopping column ad for an item is far improved after writing a page ad. Even in a one, two or three-inch ad, the essence of the full-page ad can strengthen it greatly.

Often a picture element developed for a full-page ad creates a dramatic impact for a smaller ad. Often the heart of the headline of the full page ad becomes a magnet headline for the smaller-space ad. Subheads supply meaty copy for small ads. Captions, even without pictures, are sometimes good copy phrases for smaller ads.

I like to start with a page, then write a half-page, a column and a half-column. By the time I've finished the small ads, I've often found improvements for the full-page ad, too. The smaller the advertisement is, the shorter and more to the point must be the ad copy. I keep cutting and capsulizing. I keep searching for key copy words to excerpt.

In a very small ad, I may only have a paragraph or two of copy. My sentences sometimes become phrases. My connecting words become fewer. My sentences may drop a noun and start with a predicate. Each word must work. None must be lazy. Each must be specific. Often my smallest ad is scarcely more than the headline and subheads of my largest ad.

I then write my smaller ads *two* ways. One is a version of my full page ad cut down to however small my small ad is. For the other, I select a model smaller ad and paraphrase by excerpting from my full-page paraphrased copy. Either way creates a better ad for me than starting from scratch. Then I often merge and combine into one far better ad.

The more research I do and the more I paraphrase, the more I also originate entire ads. Often you'll go back to original research for more appropriate word choices. You may conclude that your smallest version is totally inadequate. And originating your own copy can come fast as soon as you master paraphrasing of ads. It's still a matter of doing more research than others, studying with care the advertising of successful mail order products and applying what you wish to your own ads.

Try writing, without a specific model, a tiny classified ad of several lines. Create a very small ad, without a model, entirely in your own words. Try larger ads. Work up to a Time Magazine-size page ad. Originate each time. Then cut and capsulize to smaller ads again.

Done in this simple progression, creating your own original advertising won't seem hard. In giving my suggestions at each step, I may have seemed to make too much of writing a simple classified ad or any other first creative task. However, it has only been to emphasize how much easier writing more complex ads can later be when you have mastered writing simpler ones.

Let's now take up producing finished ads.

Chapter 8

PRODUCING FINISHED ADS

*... without ... or with an art
director ... ad production problems
... "translating" into size variations
safely*

By now, you may know the exact cost of running your test ad in a publication. You're probably not familiar with its possible production costs. These preparation costs often start with the use of an art director, an artist who makes "layouts" by roughly sketching out your intended ad. If you are small, an art director usually can help you as a production manager to carry through the execution of the ad. Or you may place your advertising through an advertising agency with an art director and art and production department. If so, you will turn over to their specialists the problems of completing your ad. You may work directly with a free-lance art director or art studio. You may work with an advertising consultant. All this we will discuss later in more detail.

Total costs of ad production can be quite a shock. You may have no choice but to do everything in the simplest way. You may try to avoid the use of an art director and most other professional costs of preparing an ad. If so, don't be too concerned. Many moonlighters have started with almost no preparation cost for their first test ad. Many firms have started out successfully in mail order without the perfect advertising agency or formed their own. Many firms without an agency have operated without an art director or expensive preparation costs.

This is most feasible for simpler, smaller ads. A very small ad with no illustration has the very least production cost and best chance of coming out closest to the effect anticipated. Paraphrasing a simple, small ad with or without a picture gives you a good chance to work without an art director. The more precisely you paraphrase, the more this is so. Your model ad provides the layout and guide in setting type. You can make a simple paste-up of a photostat of the picture, headline, subheads, body type and mailing instructions or coupon with your logotype. The less crowded your model ad is, the better chance your ad has of coming out correctly without an art director.

The best way to create ads without an art director is with the Macintosh and Pagemaker, MacDraw, MacPaint and other appropriate software or with another personal computer or word processor and suitable software.

The paraphrasing of a page ad is the best way to get a "feel" for writing ads of any size. But your first test will probably be a small ad you have paraphrased. It is safer to try without an art director and, perhaps, without an expensive typographer. The smaller and simpler your ad, the easier and safer it is to create with your personal computer or word processor.

For your first page ad, and particularly a complex one, I recommend that you work with an art director. As you make money in mail order and create more big ads, your art director will become more and more your right arm. His creative contributions will pay his way at each step. The more you get into the preparation of your ads, learn about production methods and do the work yourself, the more you will save in preparation costs. You will also achieve better results. In some kinds of ads, you will become more independent. In others, you will not feel safe without using an art director.

A professional typographer for major advertising agencies may have software for a very wide variety of typefaces. An art director can create a mood for an ad by selection of just the right type as much as by layout. A small print shop may offer only a few choices of type. A personal computer can obtain software for some variety, but it is still limited. A newspaper usually has little choice of type.

The easiest way to get the best-looking small ads without an art director is to set your own on your own personal computer or word processor. As you successfully set smaller ads, it's just a step to go on to larger ones. Many moonlighters go right on to full-page ads. The more editorial the style, the easier this is to do.

Moonlighters with little or no money and no computer or word processor can deal directly with the publication production manager instead of an art director. The smaller and simpler your ad is, the more feasible this becomes. Saving money by doing without an art director and a good typographer can sometimes limit the desired effect, take longer and require more effort and know-how on your part. The smaller and simpler your ad is, the more feasible this becomes.

Newspapers usually set type without charge, but charge for photo engravings or linecut plates. Magazines usually charge for typesetting. If you can't afford an art director, you usually can't afford a good typographer. If you sell a luxury product, a fashion product or a prestige product of any kind, it's dangerous not to use a good typographer. Newspaper-set type, while often adequate, is seldom elegant.

Each way to save money on typesetting has limitations. A small local newspaper is often a very low-cost typesetting source, but the choice of type faces is very limited.

Certain shops with simpler IBM-computerized typesetting machines cost considerably less than full-scale typography. Most of these shops also have quite a limited choice of type faces, but variety of choice is growing. The effect is usually more finished than the newspaper setting job, but substantially less than that of a top typographer. The simpler typeset cost is usually far less than the regular typographer and more than the small newspaper typesetting job.

One solution is to use the expensive typographer for headlines and subheads and the simplest typesetting for body type. There is also available headline and subhead phototype in a variety of sizes on adhesive-backed paper. These can be pasted down letter by letter. The more you learn about production, the more money you can save.

Just as you can choose simple products to go into, you can confine yourself to the simplest kinds of ads. I know one very successful mail order man who only sells a product for which he can create a very simple ad with the smallest possible production cost. He avoids complicated ads because preparation costs can go up with each slight additional bit of complexity in an ad.

Paraphrasing your page ad simplifies layout and production problems and saves preparation cost. The more closely you have kept to the exact number of words, syllables and characters of your model ad, section by section, the simpler should be your art director's job. Show the model ad, cite its success and explain the success of other paraphrased ads. If mail order experienced, your art director will instantly agree to follow it.

If limited financially, you may use the art director solely to follow the paraphrased layout exactly. This will save his time and your money. If your art director *improves* your ad, he will need extra time. This will cost you more money but might increase results sharply. As you succeed and create other ads, it should pay to get even more time from him.

Layout work is only part of the cost of making an ad. It costs just as much to set type for bad copy as for good. Sometimes it costs even more, because bad copy is often needlessly overlong. It costs as much to reproduce a bad picture as a good one. The paste-up cost is the same for a bad or a good ad.

If you've worked to *write* copy as suggested, you have painfully gone through many partial rewrites to perfect each paragraph. The art director's equivalent of a partial rewrite is an overlay. It would be fruitless to have endless rewriting by a copywriter and no revision of a layout. Yet this often occurs. Usually this is because an art director is given the problem of meeting a near-impossible production deadline. Often the high hourly cost of the art director makes the cost of layout after layout seem prohibitive.

This is not so. By laying a tissue overlay on the first layout and sketching in an alternative layout of part of the ad, a dramatic improvement can sometimes be achieved in *three minutes*. The more your art director understands what you are trying to achieve, the better prepared he is to make such quick, creative contributions. The cost of properly *orienting* your art director *before* the layout is an hour or so of billing time. If you total the cost of making the ad, including typography, engraving, paste-up, photostats, messenger pick-up and incidentals, you can usually get ample overlays and even additional layouts for only 20% to 30% more total cost.

Your art director must be convinced of the advantages of overlays and be willing to make them. Without this additional overlay and layout time, your ad becomes more of a lottery ticket. With overlays you can improve your ad together, step by step. He must help you in this way to marry words to layout and pictures, or you must perform the function yourself.

As you work more with your art director, it may become advisable to get together earlier with him in planning and creating your newest ad. My suggested method of writing your full-page ad assumes that you are just starting on your own as a copywriter and would waste more of your art director's time and your money consulting before you finished your ad. Until you finish your ad, you might not be properly prepared. I'm assuming that you've not yet gained a close rapport with your art director. Usually it comes *after* you've worked together on ad after ad. When you first approach him, if your ad is finished to this degree, you may get more consideration as a professional and more cooperation.

Have your art director read your copy and glance through your research notes and list of picture ideas. He may see picture possibilities which you have overlooked. *His* layout may soon *transform* your ad. If you can afford it, ask him to make two layouts. He can follow *your* version fairly faithfully, but make his own entirely *his* way. In his version, he can use more space for pictures, less for words, change the ad in emphasis on headline and subheads, *enlarge* some words, make others smaller, whatever he feels best.

The more professionally you have done your work, the more he will respect it and faithfully carry it out. However closely he follows your copywriter's layout, he will add little touches which one by one will improve your ad. Keep an open mind to each layout change he suggests. Each time, encourage him to do it two ways, first your original way, then with an overlay, his way. You may find that you prefer his when you see it. If each seems equally effective, *favor his*. As soon as he realizes that you're giving serious consideration to his ideas and that you're not always adamant about your own, more of his ideas will begin to flow. The ideal is to stick to your guns concerning your layout until you see it fully laid out, while encouraging overlay after overlay of his alternatives and a complete layout of his own.

When he completes the two versions, take them home to study carefully. Your own version faithfully carried out may surprise you. If your paraphrase contained more copy than the model, it may look cruder and cheaper than expected. It may not seem as clear. His version may be superior. If your version is an exact paraphrase, it usually will "work." His version, as a whole, may be impractical. But it will give you ideas. It will usually contain elements you never thought of, but which "work" exceedingly well. Sometimes fitting elements of his ad into yours, or vice-versa, improves it. *Consider* other ways of improving your ad.

Try your own overlays. Crystalize your thoughts on possible layout revisions. Look again at other ads. Keep studying both versions of layout and copy. Your art director may contribute a change of emphasis that quite alters and improves the effect of your ad.

If you like your version best, stick to it. It is expensive to test two page ads different enough to require resetting type throughout. If each version seems to have a strong chance, consider testing both. Consider whether either version can be strengthened by using parts of the other. Consider any overlay ideas for each.

Seeing the layouts may stimulate rethinking on copy. Any worthwhile ideas can be worked into an alternative copy section to be considered. Read the ad as it was and with your substitute insert section. Select the version which "feels" most right. Hopefully, your art director has also looked over both versions and has some suggested overlays completed. If so, give consideration to his creative contributions. Otherwise his suggestions may quickly dry up. Don't compromise simply for public relations. Make your own final command decision.

Rework any copy section or changes that the final layout requires. New picture ideas will require new captions. Any layout idea that devotes more space to any ad element will require revising the layout and appropriate copy block. Supply your art director with final complete copy. Include all copy revisions requested by him to conform with your final layout.

Now he (or when you're bigger, your production manager) specifies type for every word from headline to coupon. He calculates whether your entire copy will fit, and if not, how much needs cutting. If you've done a good job of paraphrasing, the principal cuts required will come from agreed layout changes. Cut your copy as your art director or production manager requests. Typesetting can now be ordered.

Now the type proofs come back. For full-page ads with simple formats and short copy, the problem is simple. But for a big, crowded ad, complex and tight, you can still expect a surprise or two. Handwritten corrections (if your handwriting is like mine) can cause typographical errors. Any misspellings will be faithfully reproduced. If your art director failed to calculate or miscalculated his typography arithmetic, the effect will be glaring and costly. If done reasonably correctly, there will still be minor corrections. There may be "widows" – one word of the last line of a paragraph carried over as the only word of the next line. Cutting just one word from the preceding line is the equivalent of cutting an entire line of type elsewhere.

Some corrections you can make from the typographer's proofs.

You may find more errors when your art director makes the "paste-up" of your ad. All type will be pasted down. Photostats already made to correct size of each piece of artwork, whether drawing or photograph, will be pasted into position. Take your first real look at your ad. If you have paraphrased your model ad closely and followed your art director's instructions for copy changes required, you should be happy. This assumes that you have a competent art director.

Let's take up the selection of the right art director and the most effective way to work with him or her. Being aware of problems and disasters that may occur, you can often avoid them.

You may avoid much costly grief by going into partnership with an advertising specialist. A top art director, copywriter or production manager might consider becoming your partner and contributing professional work.

If you can afford it, you may prefer to hire the best specialists. On the right fee basis, you may secure an advertising agency more suitable for you. You may hire a top mail order advertising consultant. You may hire a really outstanding mail order advertising art director. You can leave to others many of the problems of art and production. However, you will feel better knowing more about what you are paying for. Going first-class *can* pay off faster. But in mail order advertising, it can cost you at every turn.

You may not be able to afford an advertising agency or consultant or get the one you need. If so, use an art director as needed and at lowest possible cost. If you decide to select one, get a recommendation from a successful mail order firm or a friend in the advertising agency business. Check the nearest substantial department store. They can't have cheap-looking art, yet they buy everything at fairly rock-bottom prices. The store's advertising manager may give you several good leads. Look for commercial artists' situation-wanted ads. You might run a classified ad addressed to art directors, art studios and artists. Look under "commercial art studios" in the yellow pages.

There are untrained and trained art directors, hacks and "pros," inexperienced, tired, old, fresh, those full of vitality and knowledgeable ones. Art studios can be "factories" or quality outfits. If you start with little or no money, you're fortunate to get anyone competent. But have confidence in yourself. Find good talent and sell yourself as a prospective growing client.

An art director in a larger advertising agency makes layouts only and does not work on finishes. An art director in a small agency or freelancing outside often does both. Some art directors are thoroughly trained in graphics, including a considerable knowledge of typography, engraving, printing and various processes involved. That's the experience you need.

Later you will prefer your art director to do no finishes and just work with you creatively. At first, you can't afford that. You want him to help you get the best ad at lowest production price. You pay him for his services, partially in the fees for "finishes" he does for you and partially for layouts.

If you could find a young man or woman starting out, already thoroughly, professionally trained, yet willing to bet on you as a future client, that would be ideal. But most learn "on the job." Beginners often are the blind leading the blind. Their work is often slow. When hours are added up, only the appearance of your ad is cheap. Decisions they make on your behalf may give you nightmares, delay you and cost you far more than any savings you may think you're getting.

Seasoned "hacks" give you mediocre to poor work. But there are many excellent art directors, artists and art studios. Art studios are where beginners turn into professionals. Beginners supervised by professionals work far faster, and mistakes are caught by superiors.

Check other clients of the art director you are considering. Look over samples of his work. Select the best art director you can get. Only trial and error can determine if the chemistry will be right and whether he or she turns out as you hoped.

Cost per hour is not as vital as it would seem, especially after you get your first success. It's better to do without an art director than select a cheap but poor one. Location is important. An art director needs to be in a large enough city to have a one-hour photostat service, overnight typographer and engraver nearby and, preferably, messenger service to his door. The less you know about production procedures, the more vital it is that your art and production manager be technically well informed and up to date on the broadest variety of production problems. If you have no production manager and no production background, it's vital that your art director be technically capable of being your production manager.

The art director, properly selected and worked with, can give expression to your copy and layout or help to create an ad quite different than you visualized and far more effective.

If your art director is an old hand at creating and producing mail order ads, you'll get your ad laid out quickly and professionally. The better your art director is, usually the higher his or her hourly cost will be. If your art director has no mail order experience, this is not necessarily bad. You may get a still fresher, more interesting layout. The ideal is that your art director have a selling sense as well as an art and layout sense. Your art director should be a good creative partner to you, translate your ideas into layout and create his own. He should be able to give and take. If he has a professional knowledge of production processes, he can recommend the one most practical for execution of an ad. He should have a sense of frugality in production costs.

Because an art director's time is expensive, there is a tendency to rush in, race through an explanation of the problem and race out. Often the art director is busy at another job and cannot start on your project until later. Anything that you've told him verbally may never have been clearly understood and later largely forgotten. The layout he comes back with may reflect this. The art director may want to get away from *you* and work by himself, then show you what he's done and sell it to you.

Try to protect the art director's time and your own. Remember, the meter is always running. Every anecdote you tell is costing *you* what may be a stiff hourly fee. The hourly fee, however high, is usually quite reasonable for actual board work – making layouts and executing ads. Organized preparation for board work can only make it more effective. Before you meet your art director, assemble everything needed. Keep it in one neat package. Don't get charged for fumbling through your own briefcase. Make notes beforehand of exactly what you want to go over with him. If you waste an art director's creative time, your creative costs will quickly go sky high.

Every product has a different picture potential. Some are ugly and some are stunning. A great photograph can create desire for some but have less effect for others. Each product has the possibility of being shown to advantage in some special way. For some, full color is magic. For others, black and white is superior. For some, a single picture, a before-and-after shot or a use sequence, can indisputably prove product claims. Picture research requires detective work. The more picture research you do, the more tools you bring your art director.

Often a copywriter comes up with a picture idea that might be great. Sometimes his lack of knowledge of art and photography result in his having a vague and fuzzy concept of how his picture idea will look. The art director, with far more professional knowledge, is more capable of visualizing whether such a picture idea can "work." He's often apt to be far more prolific with picture ideas. His will be, on the average, far more practical.

Artists and copywriters are natural adversaries. Artists firmly believe that a picture is worth a thousand words. To some artists, copy is primarily a design block to be balanced with other design features. To such artists, the ad is a poster. As artists, they may not think in business or in sales terms. Most artists feel that most copy is too long and that a copywriter's layout does not give sufficient picture emphasis, leaves insufficient white space, gives an unnecessarily cramped and crowded effect and cheapens the effect of the ad and the product. Yet this different viewpoint can *help* you to get the best from your art director.

Some copywriters are picture people who think like and work well with art directors. They conceive a picture idea or grab one from the art director and build their ad from it. Usually they are headline people, too. With the right picture and headline idea, they work out their ad. Sometimes art directors develop a talent at writing or directing writers as well.

But generally, copywriters are word people. They want pictures to attract attention, to prove, demonstrate, emphasize or otherwise increase the effectiveness of their words. *A stubborn attitude on the part of both art director and copywriter can stalemate their joint effort.* A dominating copywriter deprives the art director of contributing his true talent. The reverse is also true.

A *compromise* in which each yields some points can sometimes be a case of too many cooks spoiling the broth. But being adversaries can improve the creative product, provided each respects and tries to be receptive to the other's viewpoint.

Assuming that your art director is professional and a perfectionist, you should gradually find a way to work together effectively. As your art director grasps more of what you are trying to achieve, he can contribute more. It is important that you both *believe* in what you are jointly trying to do. He may be professional but think you're not. He may feel that you're merely *torturing* the ad, spending time and money uselessly, making the ad *less effective* at the same time you think you're improving it. And he could be right.

When starting to write, *feel* your way. If your art director is an old veteran of mail order layouts, let him be the *senior* of your team. Even if not, *respect* his opinion. One thing the new copywriter learns, but sometimes slowly, is that *emphasis* requires *contrast. Everything* can't be big. At first, you want to get across too much at one time. In the New York commercial art studios, there is the old phrase, "*smash* with class," to sum up the apparent meaning of the client's instructions. There is eternal conflict between the smash of a "buckeye" layout, with accent on everything, and the class of good taste which is, in turn, *restraint* in color shading, design blocks, type faces, art and logotype.

So be reasonable, at least at first. As you go through the creative process ad by ad, you'll gradually find *conviction* and *assurance*. You're becoming a pro, and as you do, you'll become more senior in your creative team.

It's a pleasure to watch a top art director and an equally good copywriter work together as a team at the board. They've been through the wars together. Each knows the other's way of working. The art director almost intuitively knows the effect the writer wants him to achieve, just by reading the copy. The writer can visualize in his mind what the artist is going to do as the first rough sketch starts on the board. Each is relaxed and can joke with the other. Each can disagree without offending the other. The art director first indulgently does the layout the copywriter's way. Then, in a quick movement, he tears off a tissue from the pad, puts down his overlay and, with a few deft motions, shows his first recommended change. The copywriter smiles and admits it's better. They've made their first change.

I've seen two stars together for hours, the copywriter's chair pulled up close, but the copywriter usually standing, looking over the art director's shoulder. Not many words are necessary. The copywriter will say, "Let's try an overlay where you hit the headline harder." The art director has his overlay in scarcely a minute. Or the art director will suggest, "Let's put in a before-and-after picture back here." Again, the overlay is done in minutes. Each wants the ad to be the best they've done together. Sometimes they'll disagree. And sometimes I've gotten them over it by suggesting that we test each of the two alternative approaches. The overlay usually settles the argument. Before the overlay, it was just an idea. After the overlay, they usually jointly agree that the change should or should not be made.

Your object is to develop that kind of relationship with your art director. If he is not mail order oriented, explain very briefly how scientifically it measures results. He may be intrigued. Get across that the two of you are a team and how your work together can greatly affect results. Consider offering a bonus over and above the art director's regular fees if your joint efforts create a "hit."

Art directors are human. They're often under pressure. If you come to an art director with a deadline, his eye may be half on the clock. If you come to him without a deadline, he's apt to push your assignment gratefully aside while he goes back to other rush assignments. It's important to come to an understanding. You have to gamble board work time. He has to reserve board work hours. If you've labored mightily to get your ad this far, it's not right to rush it through the layout phase. The overlays should determine when the layout is right.

This ad may be your main project at the time and one on which you are prepared to concentrate. He may be under pressure from other directions and simply be thrown from the layout problems of your ad to those of others. He may be so battered by all the layout problems he has contended with that he can't think of any of them in off hours.

Art directors can sometimes be tired and careless. I have known art directors who, when jammed up (often the case), would order type and specify it, but omit the necessary calculations to know beforehand whether the type will fit. Sometimes, too, an error is made in calculating the number of words that can fit in a given space. The result often is overset. Your ad looks great, except that, as you read it, you find it ends *partway through your copy.* The rest is neatly set in type on the art director's paste-up next to your ad. Now you can only make corrections at the expense of resetting, probably your entire body copy, and possibly even subheads and heads. It can all be your fault, giving too tight a deadline, rushing in too late and interrupting other jobs, fighting too hard for all your copy when your art director is just too weary to explain the inevitable result. It may be your art director's fault for being careless or lazy or not meeting the reality of the situation early enough. It may be a case of insufficient production knowledge of all concerned, the blind leading the blind.

Then the art director gently says, "Cut 10% of your copy." It may be 20%, even 30% or more. But often after type is set the situation can still be saved without completely resetting the copy. Headlines can be smaller. So can pictures. Captions can be shortened and smaller type used. Subheads can be cut from three lines to two or even one and made smaller. Body type can start with the original size called for and drop a size later on. Copy can be cut and often improved in the cutting.

But it calls for give and take between art director and copywriter. It takes more overlays on the layout pad to get the visual effect. A look will often help make the decision of further cuts or smaller type. The earlier it takes place, the easier, more effective and less costly the solution is.

When you get your proofs back, everything may fit but look far more jammed than you expected. It may cause the ad to seem difficult to read. You may have pushed your art director into accepting more copy than he would have recommended. Often your art director is torn. His art training rebels at a jammed ad. But he also feels very much aware that crowded, jammed ads have often succeeded in mail order. He doesn't want to be personally responsible for your ad's failure by insisting too strongly on your adhering to his standards, particularly before he gets to know you and work regularly with you.

Your art director has visualized accurately how the paste-up will look. But seeing the paste-up of your first full-page ad, you are probably somewhat surprised. Let us assume that the copy sent to the typographer was clean and correctly spelled. Let's also assume that the type calculating was correct and there is no overset. But now your ad looks more crowded. Yet the more of a quality product you are selling, the more of a *quality effect* you desire. Your art director may not have realized how important this is to you. Now you need his help to keep the selling effect of your ad and get more of a quality effect as well – even at this late date.

Look at your headline and main subsidiary subheads. Here's your biggest change possibility and the *least costly* per square inch to make. Each word of type usually costs the same to reset – big or small. You want to "open up" your ad and give *more* emphasis to the headline itself. Write out alternate shorter headlines. Often the effect of your headline can be dramatically *enhanced* by a last-minute change.

Do the same with your main subhead and main subsidiary subhead. Preferably, just simplify and shorten your present one. Try for *shorter* lines and *wider* margins. Ask your art director to pencil in an overlay to get the effect. If it looks hopeful, he can reset an alternative version. He may even be able to get most of the words from extra proofs of present type. Then the alternate can be pasted up as an overlay.

You quickly see which "works" best. Often such a change quite transforms your ad at trifling resetting and art expense. You may even be able to make your main headline, if shortened, *bigger* and still "open up" your ad.

Look at your subheads interrupting copy. Each three or two-line subhead that you cut to *one* line saves at least one or two lines of copy. How much more depends on how much bigger than your body type your interrupting subhead type is. Try to cut even one line from several words to one or two. If you do, you create air . . . white space . . . in bigger margins on either side. Often your interrupting subheads are improved by the cutting.

Desk-top typography can speed the entire process. You can cut and change copy at home. The ideal combination is art director, copywriter and professional, computerized typesetting in-house. The entire process goes very fast. The more ads produced the faster, the more the expense of doing this can be amortized.

You and your art director may be pleased with your headline, subheads and type, but you may be disappointed with your picture effect. The pictures you have substituted for those in your model ad may not be equally effective. And only when you saw the photostats of your art in your pasteup could you fully realize the difference.

If your picture is bad and if your art director is a hack, he may try to sell you on how good it is. If he's a perfectionist, he will insist on whatever steps are necessary to save the situation. He may be normally a very conscientious craftsman, but right now very tired or with his mind on other, urgent, past-deadline work. I've seen copywriter and art director work virtually all night to get out ads when both have been physically exhausted. Again and again, I've seen one last extra change "save" the ad.

It may simply be "cropping" the picture, "blowing it up" a little larger plus retouching highlights, or a last-minute substitution of one piece of art for another. It may require reshooting one or more photographs. It may be substituting a drawing for a photograph or paying for a new substitute drawing by a specialized artist. The less your experience, the more dependent you are on your art director to achieve the finished effect you seek. You'll either get on each other's nerves or be an effective team determined to get a final ad you're jointly proud of.

Most problems in the execution of an ad come from rush . . . and the use of the wrong specialist for part of the job . . . or one not properly oriented. A taxi driver has to contend with people in a rush, often too late in starting to ever reach where they're going in time. To survive, a taxi driver has to be a philosopher. He may turn, twist, dodge and race in traffic to help you reach your impossible goal. *But to keep his sanity, he must keep himself removed from your emotional trauma about your situation.*

Production people have to have a somewhat similar approach to life. They are inclined to be sympathetic but philosophical. Some are hacks, some perfectionists and some in between. But they deal with clients who give them all manner of problems. Their customers batter down their prices, push them to difficult deadlines, misunderstand their technical limitations and are often incoherent in explaining requirements. The more you learn about production processes, the more you'll understand what your specialists are talking about, the limitations they work under and what you can expect from them.

Just one poorly selected or oriented specialist can spoil your entire ad. Your production process may be wrong for the medium you are using. A photograph that will look effective in a magazine may look like *mud* in a newspaper. The artist or photographer selected may be superb in his or her field, but quite unsuited to the assignment. You may strive to achieve a Tiffany effect and use an engraver great for discount stores, get cheap work for a cheap price and destroy your ad.

You will need to assemble specialists for the job who each take pride in contributing to the final effect. It takes time, recruiting effort, trial and error in selection and accidental luck. It takes fair treatment, ample time for a given job, thorough but not long-winded explanation and, often, incentive. But you will assemble your winning enlarged team, if you're determined to do it.

Chapter 9

TRANSLATING A "HIT"

Various size ads needed . . .
improvements . . . risks of changes
in newspapers and magazines . . .
switching to color

If you have a "hit," it's exhilarating, but also worrisome. You want to make all the money that your successful test has made possible.

An axiom of mail order is that you should never change any element of any successful mail order advertisement in any future advertising schedule, except for new tests of variations. This means every word, picture, layout element or slightest variation in offer. And it is true of every direct response method used by non-mail order people.

Some changes are slight. Some are major. All are important. Simply running the identical magazine ad in a newspaper is a change that might not work, even if run exactly the same way.

Many of the biggest mail order money makers I know will avoid like the plague *any* change in a "hit" ad without a split-run test. Of course, they *can't* always avoid it. Occasionally they are forced to make a minor change without testing. Most feel that even the deletion of two or three words from the original coupon (for a smaller coupon) can imperil the success of the changed ad.

Your main picture photograph may look great on the glossy paper of a magazine and lose detail completely on newsprint. The smallest type of your body copy may be quite readable on the glossy paper of a magazine and become fuzzy and far harder to read on newsprint.

In a newspaper, black headlines become grayer. Newspaper regulations often require greying out of more than a minimum allowed blackness. Drawings often need to be substituted for photographs. Retouching becomes more important. Poor engraving will lose more detail than is good for the ad. A greater perfection of production detail is needed at each point.

You want to avoid risk. You prefer to run your original ad without change. But if attractive media opportunities open up, some may require changes in your ad. Each change *is* a risk. Try to make *minimum* changes with *maximum* care. Try to avoid too many deadlines, too fast.

Make haste slowly . . . with "meticulous speed."

Not all magazines have the same page size, although 7" x 10" pages are becoming more standard. If smaller, you have a copy cutting job to do. Any perceptible cutting may change the effectiveness of your original ad. The ideal would be to make a small test of each such modification before running a major space purchase. I'll explain later why this is not always feasible.

Each substantial change is a "translation" of your original ad into a different form. You want to make the safest "translations" at the lowest production cost into other needed size variations.

Work as hard on each modification as on the original ad. Have your art director make overlay after overlay of various possible rearrangements. For some size variations, you may find a way to run your original copy intact. You may improve your ad, increase the power of your headline, subheads and main headline.

Any cutting or adapting needs to be done with extreme care. Usually the main body copy can be cut only slightly. However, it often can be set in part or in full in a smaller type face. The headline copy sometimes can be shortened somewhat. You may be able to shorten and further simplify main subheads. The main picture element needs to be kept. Sometimes it can be reduced. Sometimes a secondary picture can be dropped. The coupon can often be shortened somewhat. The copy of supporting boxes can be cut most. Sometimes a supporting box can be eliminated.

In reducing from a Time Magazine-size page to a TV Guide-size page, such surgery can be considerable and affect results greatly. Expanding from a Time-size page to a TV Guide-size double page is quite a different layout problem with quite different dimensions. You and your art director may see how to *improve* the layout effect dramatically. You may find it a *more difficult* layout problem. It will depend on how suitable your headline, main subheads and main illustrations are to a double spread, and on your and his ingenuity to modify and adapt them.

You may have *another* picture ideal for *horizontal* cropping that is far more effective. Or your pictures may not "work" as well in a horizontal layout. After revision, your double page may be considerably modified from your original page. It should incorporate your entire original copy. Try alternate layouts. You may surpass the effects of the original Time-size page.

In a Parade-size Sunday newspaper magazine section, your Time-size ad can often run as a three-column, ten-inch-high "junior page" with no changes required. You may want to run a vertical half-page (slightly smaller, higher and narrower). You may consider a vertical two-thirds, a three-fifths page, a four-fifths page or a full page. Each change of dimension can give a different layout effect and be both a problem and an opportunity.

It's a very simple change from a three-column, ten-inch ad to the almost two-and-one-half inches more space per column required by a three-fifths-page ad. The same copy can obviously be used. The art director can slightly enlarge and rearrange headlines and main and main subsidiary subheads. Or with no resetting, simply putting more space between lines, he may be able to open up the main copy block. This creates more white space between interrupting subheads. He may be able to recrop the illustration a little more vertically. At little expense, he'll probably achieve a better effect with the same basic layout and identical copy. It's also quite safe.

The half-page is narrower and about the same number of square inches. If not, you may have some copy cutting required. Do it with care, and your cuts should not affect results too much. If you go to four columns, you attain a more open ad. If you go to five columns, your tight 7" x 10" ad can be greatly improved simply by rescaling and rearranging the layout. The proportion of headline to copy and illustration to copy can be somewhat bigger. Their size can actually be larger. You can go to a slightly larger type face in your main copy story and perhaps put in more space between lines. You may be able to add more white space above and below your interrupting subheads. Or you can, of course, put in more copy.

But why not stick with the exact copy of your "hit" ad and simply get the added power and quality effect of the larger page? Each change is a risk.

We often will convert a successful Time Magazine full-page ad to a somewhat larger newspaper ad to make it easier to read the small type. Often a *different* photograph with less detail to lose does better in newspapers.

Turning your copy and layout concept into a professional and finished advertisement is seldom simple or easy. In four-color, it's more difficult, complex, speculative and far more expensive. We try to be cautious with color. Sometimes we start plans for four-color advertising, but limit our gamble to color photography only. We may start with color photography by staff members, just to feel out color possibilities.

The next gamble is to have a top color photographer take on the assignment. If you are not an art director and do not have professional knowledge of color photography, selecting the photographer can be speculative. A poor art director can select a poor photographer.

The *right* photographers and artists, each for his or her specialty, *can*, one by one, become trusted members of your enlarged creative team. If you start with the *right* art director, it's far easier. If you're working with the *right* advertising agency, the team may already be there.

Often the more superb a photographer is, the more *specialized* he is. Some specialize in black and white, some in color, some in studio shots, some in outdoor photography, and some in special areas of *these* kinds of photography. But the biggest difference is between poor, mediocre and superb photographers.

Amateurs and mediocre beginning professionals, even if they charge nothing or very little, can be worse than the most expensive. The pressure for low-cost photography makes hacks worse. They become picture factories. You get your low price. They devote little time. The result is usually disappointing.

The cost of the best in anything is always a staggering surprise. Superb color photographers are often expensive. But there is always the dream of finding not-yet-recognized, superb talent. Just running any color photograph in any national publication, in an ad that does it credit . . . and gives him or her credit . . . can start off a new star. To get superb work at low cost, you're helping launch a career. If not qualified, the color picture may be bad. You may get little for your money.

A *top* photographer can be more cooperative than you expect. Expensively equipped studios can have a high overhead. Occasionally, to start off a promising client, and at a time *between* two big assignments, a top photographer will go substantially below his or her normal price. If your job is fairly simple, it may be fitted in *after* another job is finished in otherwise unused hours. Sometimes a top outside photographer will have an assignment with all travel expenses paid by a big client in just the place *perfect* for your shots. And sometimes he'll fit you in for a far more nominal fee.

If you can explain your situation frankly . . . and if the photographer *likes* you . . . and does not feel that you're taking advantage of him, he may go along with a lower price. Remember, you can always afford to add an incentive bonus for *extra* payment if your ad pays out. If it does, keep your word. Your photographer may be pleased and surprised and willing to gamble again.

The *right* color photograph makes *right* color reproduction possible. It does not *insure* it. The quality of the paper printed on, the printing process and the quality of the color plate or color separations all affect color reproduction considerably.

A bad color photograph will look bad anyway. A good color photograph will, under certain circumstances, look far worse than you expected. The first question is whether color retouching is required. For some photographs in some situations, color retouching *is* required. This can be more expensive than you ever expected. Time and money are important factors.

Color separations and color engravings take time and craftsmanship. More time and more craftsmanship cost more money. If you try to make a magazine closing date with inadequate time available, craftsmanship is not possible at any price. If you try to cut costs, there are those who are eager to serve you. They can sell you either color separations or color engravings for less by subtracting more time and craftsmanship than the price reduction warrants. Cruder, more primitive color *processes* also cost less. But superb color reproduction worthy of superb color photography is an art. Poor color can harm the effectiveness of your ad and often be *worse* than black and white.

Color processes are constantly improving. Different processes on different paper surfaces still vary in quality. Color on newsprint is not the same as on glossy paper. For certain purposes, color on newsprint is highly effective. For others, it is very disappointing.

Color is more complex than black and white. More can go wrong. This is true for reproducing other forms of color art as well as color photography. It takes an artist more time and costs more. The artist may be unsuited to the assignment. It's harder to be frugal and use color. Using less than four colors is less expensive. It can be effective, but attempting to achieve the effect of four-color with three-color or a two-color reproduction can be a big letdown.

An art director usually can visualize the final effect . . . before proceeding. You may have more difficulty. Less than perfect color reproduction and less than four-color reproduction can still stop the eye and often increase readership. Sometimes it can also cheapen your product and make it look less attractive than black and white. If you change your mind in black and white, tear your ad apart and start over; it's expensive, but in color, the expense of such changes can be a small catastrophe.

Color can be overwhelmingly effective. It can glorify your product. It can give more picture detail. It can be the difference between mail order profit and loss. But until you have considerable confidence in the judgment of your advertising agency, art director or yourself, be *careful* with it.

We've started discussing creating advertising by taking up newspaper or magazine advertising . . . quite arbitrarily. You may find your first "hit" in any form of mail order advertising: publications, TV, direct mail, radio or in variations or hybrids of mail order advertising.

Any successful test in any form of mail order advertising has a chance to succeed in another form. A product may be more suited to one form of advertising. A product that succeeds in one form of advertising may fail in another. To succeed in *one* form is an accomplishment. To succeed in *all* forms is a near miracle. It is possible today to "translate" mail order success into more forms of mail order advertising than formerly.

Newspapers and magazines with free-standing inserts and other hybrids become a direct mail medium and can use a variation of a successful direct mail piece. Direct mail co-op mailings with postcards offer the equivalent of small space in magazines or newspapers and can often run the identical copy. Radio, TV and even newspapers are sometimes successfully used as a *support* medium for an enormous direct mail campaign.

"Translating" a successful ad into another form of advertising is far easier than creating an advertisement or commercial from scratch for an entirely different product. Many years ago, Huber Hoge and Sons specialized in radio and TV advertising. Sometimes we would be given successful newspaper, magazine or direct mail advertising to "translate" into broadcast commercials. We were spared the research. And from your first successful test for any item in any form of advertising, your creative job will be much simpler in any other form. We must try to "translate" it into each other feasible form of mail order advertising. Let's first take up direct mail advertising.

Chapter 10

DIRECT MAIL

Package enclosures ... insert ...
loose postcards ... bound postcard
publications ... multiple mailings
... samples ... solos

Direct mail advertising is any advertising which you receive in the mail.

Direct mail is the infantry of mail order ... the queen of battle. Direct mail has sold most mail order merchandise for years. Of all forms of mail order, direct mail is more complex, more swiftly and constantly changing and more confusing to the newcomer.

In recent years, direct mail has become more expensive. Costs have gone up more per thousand than for a page of advertising in many leading magazines. It never stops. One staggering postage increase follows another. Paper prices shoot up when business is good and rarely go down when business is bad. Printing keeps costing more. Costs in the mail zoom up when response from the mail drops down. Yet profitable use of direct mail has soared. Moonlighters can sometimes still start with little investment and make money.

Here's why it's still so profitable. Credit cards, computers and telephones changed the mail order world – most of all in direct mail. They and automation created a direct mail revolution.

Credit cards took away risk and financed credit for medium-size and smaller companies. Computers and telephone credit checking gave mail order credit managers a scientific right arm. Computerized list selection gave safer names to mail to. Individual credit checks were made faster and at lower cost. Automation slashed mailing labor cost.

Bigger companies began to sell mail order using direct mail, including many Fortune 500 companies. But entirely new ways of using direct mail made it profitable for small mail order moonlighters, too.

Direct mail began to proliferate and to create new hybrid media. The flexibility and forms of direct mail have become as varied as the most innovative mind. It is the medium of the unexpected.

Newspapers, general magazines, radio and television are shotguns. Direct mail is, more than specialized magazines, the rifle. The

---

computer has revolutionized aiming that rifle. You can reach whom you want with less waste duplication.

Creating direct mail advertising usually requires more time and work than other forms of advertising, but is less frustrating. It has fewer limitations and is more versatile. You can use more of your research, tell far more of your product and giveaway stories, in more detail, and put in more of your customers' own words. You can show more documentation of use and laboratory tests, show more before and after, and use pictures to better dramatize and glorify your product and giveaway.

You can select paper texture most perfect to reproduce desired color effect. In huge mailings, the ratio of cost of color to black and white has become *more* favorable. You can do many unusual things. You can send a sample of a textile material, include a recorded message from a celebrity or put in a perfume. You can vary direct mail in more ways. A laser letter can be personalized to a degree and at a low cost unimaginable years ago. You can often be more personal in style.

The computer helps you do more and more. It compiles, keys and credit checks lists. It eliminates duplication and nixies (names of people who have moved with no forwarding addresses). It corrects addresses from old to new. The computer selects names from lists, types labels, bills statements and types collection letters. It welcomes new club members and expels others. It helps rent and manage lists.

The computer keeps track of customers for recency, dollar volume of purchases and classification of purchases. It personalizes letters with mention after mention of the recipient's name in the letter. It intertwines in a personal storybook the first names of your child and friends along with the story. The computer will even judge contests and score aptitude tests and then send inquiries the results.

Direct mail is ever different. A lush color piece can come electronically sealed into a transparent plastic film or envelope. A personalized letter can adhere to a super-size, brightly colored postcard, doing the job a color broadside usually does inside an envelope. When business mail comes in every brightly colored variation, a new winner will come in a brown, unmarked envelope. Or in place of elaborate selling material to business firms, another "hit" will come in the form of a several-page interoffice memorandum on plain blue paper backing without a single illustration.

A direct mail kit can include a coin, a stamp or other gift to bribe you to open and read it. It can be addressed in simulated longhand . . . by machine. It can be printed in and mailed from Rome, Italy, or anywhere in the world. It can come in an engraved envelope as if an invitation from a member of the nobility of any country. It can be a simulated telegram. It can come third-class with stamps affixed by machine to look like first-class. Patented envelopes turn into letters. Patented postcards tear out from letters.

Its post office cancellation mark can be that of an odd and obscure small village like North Pole, Alaska. It can be a first-class, personalized letter. It can come as a simulated newspaper, newsletter or magazine. It can be a collection of postcards or one oversized double card with a tear-off return order card.

In countless ways, the outside envelope can tease and tempt you to open it. It can seem to be enclosed with a bill or a check. It can offer a free gift, announce a contest or promise a saving. And inside the envelope, the variety is even greater, as we will soon describe. But nothing has aided direct mail to overcome leaping costs more effectively than its constantly increasing ability to sell higher-cost items.

The trend to higher-price items for direct mail has been underway for decades. People became accustomed to buying more expensive mail order items by direct mail. The average price of items sold by direct mail has gone up and up (even subtracting inflationary factors). As incomes have gone up, people have grown accustomed to buying more expensive products and services by mail order.

Direct mail can present such products in more detail, color and variety. Direct mail can aim at lists of higher-income people specifically interested in the need the product supplies and who have bought higher price mail order products from others.

The rewards of success in direct mail have increased enormously over the years. A number of factors have made it possible to mail less and sell more. Targeting the right offer to more exactly the right names has become far more of a science. Computerized elimination of duplicate names has cut waste in mailing. New technology has kept printing cost increases below general inflation. The habit of responding to direct mail has increased. So has the willingness to buy far more expensive items and a far greater variety of items and services offered by mail. But there are still plenty of limitations.

Most successful direct mail is to customers already satisfied with products previously sold to them by the firm making the offer. Most successes are for products and services with higher prices and profit margins than for most products sold through print or TV. Few moonlighters have the right product or service at the right price for direct mail success to cold names – those who have never heard of the moonlighter. A big percentage of mail order tests by moonlighters for direct mail still fail – often unnecessarily.

The standard full-color mailing piece of yesterday, with broadside, letter, return card, return envelope and giveaway flyer, all in an outside envelope, has become the big-time "solo" piece. The economics of using it in color often require a million mailing. Smaller tests, at two or three times the cost or more per piece in the mail, usually lose or, at best, break even. Only the million mailing projection can bail out the "successful" test. The advantage is to the giants and against the moonlighter. Some mailing pieces are so elaborate and lush as to bewilder a mail order moonlighter.

How can a mail order newcomer possibly compete with these and endless other offers of the giants? How many can give huge prizes in a contest? How many can print enormous pieces in rich color? How many can give six swatches of material? Who can send an actual record in the mail? Or who can guarantee to buy back a coin collection in five years at the identical price? What mail order newcomer can proceed in the huge volume required for such operations? Who can afford the expense even of the top direct mail creative talent required? And how can you possibly paraphrase for your own products such incredibly complex and super-lengthy mailing kits? It seems like competing with loaded dice. More and more, direct mail has become the domain of the mail order giants. Yet more and more direct mail nooks and crannies keep coming up . . . ideal for moonlighters to get started in and prosper in at low cost . . . and risk, as we will shortly discuss.

In the wonderful world of the handful of super-giant mailers, many factors tilt in their favor. List costs per thousand often drop substantially for a full list rental. Giant mailers develop giant lists and can then swap them. List rental costs then drop to that of mailing their own lists. These lists may include hundreds of thousands of specialized names suitable to mailing a specific new offer. For the first million mailing that web-press color usually requires, the list rental cost may be low indeed.

New computer efficiencies of list compilation and revision are best used for biggest, most frequently mailed lists. These are the lists owned and swapped by this same small club of giant mailers. In this magic world, the offers themselves are swapped. Each successful offer of a giant mailer can be "syndicated" and offered to other members of the informal giant mailer's club in a manner quite lucrative to each party.

One giant can buy the merchandise from the other and mail the other's offer to his list. Often a giant mailer develops a warmer, more clubby feeling with his own customers than with any outside "cold" list. By substituting a warmer, more informal letter on his letterhead, recommending the offer and leaving all other elements the same, results from the same list can often double or triple.

Thus it is more profitable for one giant to sell merchandise to another than to rent the other's list. Using a letter and recommendation from each giant to his own list makes a "cold" list hot. It is also, by the same alchemy, more profitable for the other giant to *buy* merchandise and make a profit selling to his list than simply to rent his list. This combination of factors often makes mailings safer and more profitable for those in the "club" than those knocking on the door.

In the old days, a small mail order firm could do its direct mail to a surprising degree all on its own. Its own employees could type labels on addressograph or equivalent plates. It could buy simple printing equipment and print and mail on the premises. It could maintain its own lists and rent or swap names directly. Now a mail order moonlighter can be baffled even by the zip code separation job the post office requires for third-class bulk mail. Personnel cost has soared so high as to make handling your own direct mail prohibitive in labor cost.

Only automated equipment can offset these costs. A small, new mail order firm cannot amortize such equipment's cost. The small firm has the same problem with computerization. New ways of putting names on computer become obsolete because still newer ways are always being developed. The answer is to use outside specialized services. But to get started safely, feel safe entrusting yourself to others and decide *whom* to turn to is not easy. Yet you can. Become more familiar with what others do. Observe the giants and gain their assistance.

For those who know how, it's easier than ever to use direct mail profitably. It's possible to project success so much farther that more test failures can be washed out and still make a handsome profit overall. It has also become, by necessity, simpler. Just as full-page space increased costs have forced greater use of smaller ads, the increased costs of elaborate direct mail have forced the use of stripped-down, simpler pieces. And busier people have had less time to read the huge pieces formerly mailed in bigger quantity – and are more willing to buy from a simpler presentation.

Moonlighters can quickly use sophisticated services. In my book, Mail Order Know How, I tell the story of a mail order moonlighter couple, Roger and Carolyn Tyndall, and of their consultant-partner Dick Benson, one of the greatest brains in direct marketing. Their partnership got up close to ten-million dollars a year with one employee, with the Tyndalls still moonlighting and all using direct mail to outside names.

Smallest moonlighters can profitably use direct mail, often helped by the giants, who have no realization that they are helping. We can learn their secrets from them. Gradually, as we do, we realize that giants are not impregnable; they are not perfect, nor do they hold all the cards for mail order success. Small fry do have a chance. Just let them start helping you.

How would you like the biggest, richest and most successful mailers to give you direct mail seminars at no cost? How would you like them to teach you their latest improvements in technique almost as fast as they develop them? How would you like to learn from them and never stop learning from them how to make far more money for yourself?

All you need to do is *read the mail.* Simply get on more and more lists. Get more and more friends to forward to you their direct mail. Then read it, compare it and analyze it. Almost every direct mail piece you receive teaches something. As varied as direct mail pieces are, all have much in common.

The copy tries never to get in the way of the quick decider, yet tries to overcome every objection of the slow decider or of those in between. The envelope yearns to be opened. The broadside wants to be seen and glanced through, and the letter wants to be read. The order card, often assisted by return envelope, begs to be checked, initialed or signed and dropped in the mail.

The giveaway is even more essential in direct mail than in any other form of advertising. A giveaway featured on the envelope often is the most effective way to get it opened. A broadside (brochure) featuring it at the top gets looked through. A letter starting with news of a giveaway has a good chance of being read throughout. It even helps to get an order card read thoroughly.

More than in any other form of advertising, the giveaway gets more readership of the selling message throughout. As a mail order product becomes more familiar and accepted, a giveaway can be profitably featured more often. In some cases, the giveaway can take the spotlight away from the product. Even in a full page, you could never have enough space to tell as exciting a story about the giveaway or do it such justice.

In newspapers and magazines, an editorial ad often has a better chance because readers think it is an article. A direct mail piece often has a better chance of being opened if it appears to be something more welcome in the mail.

The envelope is the opening battle. Will it be thrown away unopened, or will it be opened and glanced at? One reason to select a plain brown envelope for a business "solo" mailing kit is economy. More important is its similarity to vital business correspondence. It might be from your lawyer or accountant. It might be an interoffice memorandum. It has a plain but important look with no word on the envelope front or back. The first glance when it is opened may determine whether it will survive to be read or perish in the waste basket.

That glance must be converted into reading more, or the battle is still lost. Sometimes just revealing part of the picture of the giveaway as the envelope is opened tempts you to look underneath. Often the most prominent words you read are "FREE" or "FREE TRIAL." It doesn't seem too dangerous to read on. Each direct mail kit from a giant is teaching you how the "giants club" operates.

As soon as you create your own direct mail piece, reading the direct mail pieces of others will have far more meaning. You'll watch out particularly for duplications, where you receive the same piece two, three or more times. You'll find in some cases they are split-run tests with some seemingly minor element in the piece different from another.

Recently I noticed two seemingly identical direct mail pieces from one company. One was a computer-personalized letter with my name and address mentioned several times on the first page. The other was an obvious form letter with no more personalization than the name and address seen through the address window.

It's exciting to discover the split-run tests of others. Keep watching for them. You become the judge of the contest. Sometimes you can even ask the company which won. Some say nothing. Some are friendly and helpful to mail order newcomers, not competitive. But either way, you keep on learning. Over a period of time, you often can discover the winner. It's the *survival* piece.

Little things about each direct mail piece you receive begin to interest you. You begin getting a "feel" for direct mail. Some mailers keep using some identical techniques in their mailing pieces. Some prominently feature telephoning orders in, yet others don't. You wonder why, if one giant finds it works, another giant makes a similar offer and leaves it out. Some mailers use their own numbers and others an 800 toll-free number. Some solicit calls in office hours and others 24 hours, seven days a week. One business publishing firm always gives its address, telephone number, TWX and Telex. You may order or inquire in any of *four ways.*

Not all the giant mailers get all the benefit they could from their direct mail. Our experience indicates that featuring the telephone substantially increases orders, that the 800 toll-free number outpulls an offer to phone your own number collect, and that accepting phone orders 24 hours a day, seven days a week, outpulls limiting order handling to office hours. Many giants continue the somewhat less profitable way.

You're motivated more than most employees of the giants. You watch latest trends more intently. Your interest spurs you to come up with ideas for profitable changes. Being small, you often have tighter control, can watch tests more closely and implement changes faster.

Notice that, for higher-priced products, copy is often longer and the mailing kit more elaborate . . . and note the reverse. As postage, paper and printing goes up, so does the price of merchandise offered by direct mail. Notice how tax services often mention the per-issue cost without mentioning total cost, and state inconspicuously that they will bill the full amount in 15 days.

Notice that when you buy anything by mail from any company, you begin to get direct mail on other offers from that company and from other companies, too. Years ago, giant companies began to discover they had a fortune in their mailing lists. Banks began to loan big money on them. I know one businessman who skyrocketed to success in a series of acquisitions originally fueled by one loan on his mailing list.

How do you get into the "giants club"? The answer is simple. Become a giant.

The fastest way to do so is to start in a very small way. The best way to start is the simplest. Direct mail is a huge field. You can drown in an ocean of decisions as to how to get started. You can spend a small fortune in production bills and get a result that can greatly disappoint you. You can lose a lot of money getting started the wrong way. That's why I start discussing not "solos," but package inserts, billing inserts, loose postcards, bound postcards and the simpler ways of getting started in multiple mailings.

The next step is to become a small ally of the giants. Play the mouse to their elephant in a mutual aid society. Every executive of a giant wants to be a hero, but not a dead one. Each test you get under your belt makes you more of a potential meal ticket for one of them. Even a microscopic test success has meaning and deserves a greater confirming test. Let a giant project your successful test.

Some talented entrepreneurs confine all their risk-taking to creating an effective direct mail kit and proving that it's profitable on a very small scale. From then on, they are "syndicators," offering the right to the giants to use the mailing kit and buy merchandise from them. An important step to becoming a giant is associating with them. If your offer works, you become a supplier to them. You can go on your own later.

The next step is to work harder than the employees of the giants. If you do, water can seek its own level. If you search harder than the employees of the giants, you may find or originate a better offer faster. If you do more research, you may come up with more exciting facts. If you are more of a perfectionist, you will create better copy and layout and produce more effective finished advertising. All this comes more out of your heart and your head than your pocketbook.

You can overcome advantages of big mailers by developing better offers and better direct mail pieces than they do. A giant is a giant employer. The work is done by employees, who are usually specialists. Often they're great in their specialty and lost out of it. No employee can obtain as great a personal reward as a far smaller entrepreneur off on his own. You have an incentive no employee will ever have. If you're a partner in an advertising agency, you can usually make more money than important employees of your biggest client. Even as a moonlighter, you're an entrepreneur. He or she isn't.

Innovation can seem more dangerous to the career of the company's top employee than playing it safe. The bigger the giant in any field is, the safer the employees of that giant like to play. The giant is slower, more ponderous and subject to internal politics. Many genuinely exciting offers never get off the ground. The giants have great muscles and can be muscle-bound. They have all the tools, yet often do not use them. A giant publisher can occasionally forget it owns plates to a very saleable book. And the same is true in other fields. The giant tends to make offers similar to those other giants make, although some never copy. The giant tends to paraphrase the techniques of others *without* introducing freshness and individuality, although some are most distinctive. The giant tends to have higher overhead, although some are extremely frugal. The giant tends to pay more for specialists, services, advertising production and a host of other costs, just as a Cadillac buyer may pay Cadillac prices for every repair and part thereafter. Yet some giants have tight control of such costs.

We can compete with the giants if we always remember we are not giants. We can get into direct mail gradually. We can benefit from the latest direct mail techniques. We can understand the latest changes and their effects. Let's get back to fundamentals. We simply want to create the most effective direct mail advertising possible and send it to the most suitable list, at the right time and at lowest possible cost in the mail.

We want to get into direct mail with the least risk. We want to benefit most from the customers we gain. We want to take out the confusing gobblydegook of the experts, benefit most from new method advantages and do it all in the fastest, simplest way. We want to make money from direct mail advertising and avoid disasters due to misuse of new methods. We want to get away from complicated words and foggy terminology and cut through to hard facts. It's not as complicated as it's made out to be. Let's try to simplify it.

A computer is a very fast filing clerk. It files more things in more ways. It pulls them out of the file faster. It can group them very fast. It can check the files very fast, look for something and report back fast. It segregates names faster and better. It aims your direct mail rifle more accurately. Some of what it does is better and cheaper than done without it. It does some things not feasible before. Some things it does can benefit some firms and not others. In direct mail, for smaller users, it can be used outside through a specialized service. A microcomputer in your location can be invaluable.

The complicated or slang words describing new computer abilities translate into simple words. "Merge-Purge" (and dozens of name variations) simply means taking out duplications. "Hot-line" names mean recent names. And so it goes. A moonlighter can understand new techniques and can find a niche to succeed in.

Start by saving and filing your own direct mail research – every piece of direct mail you receive. Save everything in the envelope. If you have a credit club card, a charge card, a bank card, save every mailing and every billing insert. If you buy anything by mail, save each package insert.

If you're in business, you'll get far more direct mail advertising. Junk mail can mean money in the bank to you now. Keep it all. When you get a fat package of postcards, keep the entire package. When you get any multiple mailings with different literature from different manufacturers, keep it, too. Get your friends to keep theirs for you. Write in for literature from companies offering it, particularly for products similar to yours. Particularly look for and keep in one file a series of mailings.

Keep separate files for single package inserts, multiple package inserts, single billing inserts and multiple billing inserts. Do the same for single inquiry follow-up mailing pieces, series of follow-up mailing pieces, "solo" mailing pieces not inquired for, multiple mailing pieces not inquired for and so forth. Have still more people collect for you. Each is on certain mailing lists the others are not. Not only will your collection grow faster, but you will begin to get duplicates of the same mailing pieces. The more duplicates of one mailing list you get, the more lists the offer has been mailed to. If you get duplicates of one offer for a period of time, it is probably a successful offer.

Let's consider several kinds of direct mail which are the easiest to create and have the lowest initial testing cost.

The enormous growth of direct mail has created new forms. Billing inserts and package inserts have always been the safest, cheapest, and most lucrative per-dollar way to sell anything mail order. Now they are used in a far bigger way. Multiple billing inserts and multiple package inserts make extremely low-cost tests with maximum chance of success feasible. Co-op multiple mailings give surprising volume, yet can be tested at very small cost. Computer-personalized letters for appropriate offers can be profitably used in runs of 25,000 or even less and tested with virtually no production cost. Simple "solos" can pull without color. In black and white, the problem is far simpler. Fifty-thousand to 250,000 mailings usually get close to maximum economy per thousand.

What should your first direct mail test be? Let's assume you are successfully selling one mail order item in newspapers and magazines. You are mailing packages every day. Total volume is beginning to mount cumulatively to quite a few thousand. You hope to sell over 20,000 in the entire year. Let's consider starting with a package insert in your own shipments.

You want the most practical package insert for your situation. The extra business is quite profitable if the cost per insert is quite low. But volume is limited. Total gross profit is limited. It can only grow if you ship more of the original item. This is speculative. For any mail order item, sales may stop at any time. You may sell less through the year than expected.

Your time is limited. You work hard and have much to do. You can afford very little advertising production expense and time for the limited profit potential. But you don't want to neglect the opportunity. The ideal is to have an ad for a second successful mail order item. Just photo-offset the ad with a typewritten coupon change. Even if the ad is break-even or a slight loser, if the item is related you should have a package insert winner.

If your package is big enough, insert your full ad reprinted on one side. Keep the other side blank. Any waste of paper in a tiny test is not worth rearranging your ad on half the paper size on both sides. A small, quite light package may require reprinting on tissue-thin paper. We have done so quite successfully with a New York Times-size full-page ad reprinted on one side and folded several times (by the printer).

For a tiny package, you may find it necessary to print half your ad on one side and half on the other. This is the first big difference between publication and direct mail advertising. Here's how to try it for a Time Magazine-size, full-page ad set in three columns. Cut a photocopy of it horizontally in half. Underneath the headline, main subheads and top illustrations and boxes, cut out the second and third columns of body copy of the top half. Switch with the entire first and second columns of the bottom half. Paste the new front combination on one piece of blank paper and the new back combination on another. When you read this, it may seem complicated. But when you do it, you'll find it quite simple.

Now comes the finer scissors work. The front will have too much and the back too little. The ad will, however, read consecutively from front to back. Make more photocopies of the new front and back combinations. Scissor out all overcopy at the bottom of the second column of the new front combination. Cut out the third column at the top of the body copy and pull it down to make room for the overcopy of the second column. This means much more overcopy at the bottom of the third column. Scissor it all out. Done with a word processor, it's far faster, simpler and better.

The new rear combination will not have enough copy to fill the first and second columns. Cut out the copy in the second column and pull down to the bottom of the column. Cut enough from the bottom of the first column to fill the empty space at the top of the second column. Cut out all copy left in the first column and pull to the bottom of the column. The overcopy of the new front combination should fit perfectly in the space now open at the top of the first column. The new front and back combinations should each be exactly half the ad space and together should contain every word and read consecutively. It's taken no rewriting and cost no money. Just photo offset. Further changes might greatly improve it but can come later. For your first package insert test, I suggest only one. At the right bottom of the new front combination, type in parentheses the word "(over)."

If you don't have a mail order ad but do have a second item, proceed as if creating a publication ad. Find a model ad for a product of similar quality selling to similar people. Paraphrase exactly as previously shown. But write a *quickie* mail order ad. Cannibalize any trade or consumer advertising or literature for your product to get type and illustrations for reproduction. Use as much as possible. Fill in with typewritten copy. Make a copywriter's layout. Get someone neat (perhaps yourself) to cut up the literature and paste in position on white paper. Make your own typewritten coupon. Put in a department number as a key. If higher-priced, offer it with a credit card option. Keep it on one side unless small package size requires putting half on each of a half-size piece. If you have no other items to include, put in a re-order insert for the original merchandise. Put in an offer of a savings incentive for customers to buy bigger sizes or multiples of your item. An insert reorder can average 50% more than the original order received for the item. Your insert can be two or three mimeographed paragraphs or a simple letter. Either way, include a coupon. If you do it all on a personal computer, it will be much easier.

If your package is still too small, you'll have to take an existing small ad or write a still smaller ad. If the item you're shipping is larger, you can add a "Dear Friend and Customer" letter. Write your letter as though to one single customer for the order.

Your logotype is important now. Your stationery should make a good impression. Don't use cheap-looking stationery, especially with a quality product. Use *appropriate* stationery. If you advertised the product you're shipping under a name different from your company name, print stationery to conform to the name used.

People feel friendly after buying a product they look forward to using. If you talked to each personally, you could talk in a friendly, personal and simple manner. Do so in your letter. Try to get across the personality of your company in your letter. Explain the extra pride you take in finding or developing your product or products. If your business is in a small town, capitalize on it. People expect more frankness, honesty and integrity from others they do business with in small towns. But be yourself. Don't be folksy if you're not, or extroverted if you're an introvert.

Write in the style you usually write in. Read your own letter carefully. Make sure it includes the points you want to get across. Be sure it has an introduction, body and conclusion. Keep sentences and paragraphs short and to the point. Start with a very short opening paragraph to key interest. End the same way to hold your point. A rewrite or two should straighten it out. Keep it fairly short.

Include in your letter the story of how you located the item for which you're enclosing literature. Write how unusual you feel it is and your own experience using it. Cover in the letter the most important advantages you've already covered in your photo offset sheet. If you have an appropriate model letter, paraphrase it. If not, do the best you can. Ask for the order. Give a reason why you are making the offer. Offer an incentive with your P.S.

For both insert and letter, try to combine extreme frugality in preparation cost with effective presentation. Spending money on art, engravings, color separations or expensive typography can take away all potential profits and leave a deficit. With little or no preparation cost, package inserts are great. With excessive cost, they're sometimes not. Photo offset in one color as few as 1,000 and start inserting.

When those first orders come in, you begin to realize the surprising profit potential you have been missing up to then. For a printing bill of $58, you might make $240. For a printing bill of $520, you might make $4,650, and so forth. It could be far less or even more.

Just a mimeographed form for re-orders only can do this. For a trifling extra cost, you have gotten a tasty extra profit benefit. There's nothing in mail order that you can do that can give you so attractive a ratio of profit earned to money risked.

Let's hope you are surprised at the success of one of your package inserts. You feel you could do more with it. What should you do next?

What you need now is a package insert to suit the packages of other firms. If successful for others, projection volume could be big.

You can now produce your insert somewhat more professionally. But before going ahead, consider the *next* step, which might be billing inserts. The same insert might work in packages and in bills. Let's presume that you are selling entirely for cash or through credit cards and do not send out bills to your customers; but others do, so which of them will enclose your insert?

For your first test, keep closely to your successful package insert copy. The cost per thousand for another mail order firm to insert your advertising is often the same for a somewhat smaller or larger piece. If you sell your product to another firm which inserts your advertising, a more effective piece benefits both. If a more effective piece requires larger copy and more illustration, this is preferable.

Whatever size is required, stick closely to your proven package insert copy. If you don't have a successful package insert, but do have a successful publication ad close to the same square-inch space, use it. In either case, reset your copy after layout and type specification by your art director. It will look better, be more acceptable to other mail order companies and, hopefully, pull better.

Project as a package insert and test as a billing insert. Let's hope it succeeds both ways. You can keep projecting to bigger volume in package inserts, and you will also have a "hit" to project in billing inserts. If you succeed with smaller inserts, you can experiment with larger inserts which may produce more sales. Only do so at minimum production cost, preferably in black and white.

When you project package inserts and billing inserts in bigger runs, you can consider color. Most big users of inserts arrange for one web-press printer to print a number of different inserts of the same standard size on one big sheet. By printing only one on a side in some cases and three or six on a side in others, smaller runs can be printed along with bigger ones. And all can be printed in color. While quality is not perfect, it can be quite good, and the cost per thousand of a color insert can be quite modest vs. printing an insert in color by itself for a small run.

If you have color material already, the production and test expense may not be too great. The first step is to have color photographs and transparencies of good color quality. The next is to have color separations of the right size. Even if the size is wrong, the separation can be reduced or enlarged at not too great an expense.

As in magazines or newspapers, cost per thousand will still be far lower on bigger runs. Inserts printed on a web press in 500,000 lots will sometimes be closer to the cost of black and white inserts than the cost of color to black and white in some magazines.

If a new offer, it's also worth considering translating into still other forms of advertising. If you have not yet tested magazine or newspaper advertising, let's translate the successful package and billing insert. If a small insert, test a small ad of approximately the same square-inch space. Although the dimensions can vary, only translate a bigger insert in a space ad with caution – in an ideally suited magazine, at an inexpensive cost per thousand readers and with very modest preparation cost.

Loose postcards! Who would have expected it? A package containing 50 or so postcards is mailed third-class. People open it, glance through the cards, pick out one or more, fill it in and drop it in the mail.

Wonder of wonders! This is profitable in many cases for individual advertisers. Each card has advertising and often a coupon on one side and return address on the other. Usually these packages of "direct response cards" are mailed to a specialized list, and most often by a trade magazine.

It's one of the easiest, simplest, fastest and least expensive ways to get started in direct mail. It's one of the hybrids, part direct mail and part publication. A half-column ad in a Time-size magazine can be reset to fit comfortably on one side of the postcard. If you have a successful half-column ad, it's a simple and often safe "translation."

If you have no successful half-column ad, simply paraphrase from the most appropriate model card. One package of loose cards can give you plenty to choose from.

It's worth spending time with a layout pad to prepare alternative copywriter's layouts. It's not too risky to prepare without your art director. In style, it's closer to the shopping column editorial. The printer can set type.

People seem to enjoy getting these collections of little postcards and thumbing through them. The mailing becomes a marketplace. The more specialized the list is and the advertisers are, the more this is apt to be so.

It's called a direct response publication and is sold like a trade publication, often by the same space salesmen. Each postcard is news. The more real, bonafide news your product is, the better chance of profitable response it has.

The more technical and professional the list mailed is, the more factual and businesslike should be the copy treatment. The return card is particularly productive for inquiry advertising. We have also been successful in completing the sale with it.

I would recommend testing a successful half-column magazine ad as is, only giving more space to the photograph. If you have no small-space copy, follow the copywriting and layout method as though for a half-column ad. If you then succeed with your original postcard mailing, it's easy to translate it into a half-column ad in an appropriate publication.

Before you test loose postcards, you may already have a successful full-column magazine ad in a publication reaching a similar circulation. Or if you don't, you may find that when you write copy you require twice as much copy as you can fit onto the advertising side of the postcard. In either case we have sometimes successfully run our advertising on both sides of the card. However, you do not always gain more with larger copy than you lose giving up the return card.

Do not leave off a coupon in any case. With advertising on both sides and a coupon on the reverse side, the reader must drop the card in an envelope, address the envelope and mail it. With the return postcard, the sender need only mail the completed card.

In preparing copy for both sides, either use successful copy for one column or write as though a one-third-page ad. Put the words "turn over" at the lower right bottom of the front side. It helps to use some picture element back as well as front. It's wise to give near headline value to a subhead at the top of the reverse side. This attracts readers who passed over the front side.

A postcard can be read horizontally or vertically. Most cards in a loose postcard package are set up vertically. This is about the right size to fit in a vertical half-column ad. But some cards are set up horizontally. This means that your vertically cropped picture, which may be at the top of your half-column ad, will probably go to the right of your advertising half of the postcard. Your copy will probably go on the left and have wider but fewer lines and therefore require resetting.

Your headline, set horizontally on the postcard, will be changed in effect. A three-line headline becomes two, and a two-line headline often becomes one. You *need* a coupon on the card and may have had none in your half-column ad. Making room for one may require cutting copy. If you use advertising on both sides of the card, you may have room for a little more copy even than in your one-column ad. Your coupon will be on the back side only. You'll have a little extra space on the front side. If you have a *successful* one-column ad, rather than adding copy use *more* space for headline or picture or both.

Loose postcard packages are usually black and white on light cardboard stock. Black and white photographs will usually have better reproduction than newspapers and worse than magazines. This growing form of advertising is ideal for the specialized product appealing to a specialized list.

From the success of loose postcards grew the first bound postcard publication.

We have sometimes used bound postcard publications even more successfully than loose postcards. They are often more flexible. Often they are printed in color, with a four-color front cover.

The postcards are printed horizontally three to a page with perforated lines around them. Each can easily be torn out and mailed. But more alternatives are available. Most bound postcard publications have several non-perforated pages in a shopping column format. These are used with a "bingo" card, on which the prospective customer circles items he or she would like information on, for inquiries only. This works well for specialized equipment when mailed to the same kind of specialized list. The number of words varies. A picture to illustrate your product or service usually runs alongside the copy.

With a bound postcard publication, you can also effectively use a double card or triple card.

A double card on both sides can often carry the full copy of a Time-size page. The layout has to be changed and copy reset. It requires more picture element emphasis, so there should be pictures on front and *back*. The subhead going across the top of the back of a double card is even *more* of a headline.

Use your successful page ad with the fewest possible changes. If you do not have a successful page ad, follow my instructions for writing one. With your art director, simply modify to the requirements of front and back as described. A double-panel credit card billing insert can be used almost as is.

We have used the double postcard successfully. But a triple postcard is sometimes more successful. In this case, the front side of all three postcards usually will take 80% of the copy from a Time-size full page. Sometimes the entire copy should fit with very little change, if any. It will need to be rescaled to somewhat different proportions and about 10% smaller. If you have to cut, follow my instructions for cutting a space ad. Fight for every word, but yield to your art director if he feels some cutting is necessary. Probably it will not be. Use the postcard on the bottom rear as a return card. This will leave you two half-cards to fill. We recommend using them for one or two other items with one coupon.

You may have copy and layout ideal for a triple card on both sides. This could be a successful "solo" piece with a horizontal broadside that is approximately the same size. You may be using a newspaper free-standing insert that can be reduced to the triple-card size. A successful full-page magazine section in the Family Weekly and Parade-size should fit nicely when rearranged for both sides of your triple card. If the postcard publication is printed in color, it will usually be on a web press. Its color reproduction on cardboard stock will be better than newspapers, but not as good as the magazine section of a newspaper. It can usually use the same color separations to reproduce from.

If you have no proven ads near this size, prepare copy as though for a Parade-size page with this exception: get particular help from your art director in laying out the back as well as the front. If possible, put in more picture elements. Keep the back page from having an all-type appearance. Make the subhead on top of the back page still more of a headline.

Another alternative is to create an ad and coupon for one half-card only, with no return card on the back. We have done so successfully. Another is to feature one or more items on *each* side, with a coupon for all items on *one* side only. Generally, the lower the price of the item, the less the space size you should consider. Even a *half*-card may be too much for too low-cost an item. It is possible to feature three or more lower-priced items on each *half*-card. The ideal is a low-cost item which can be ordered in larger quantities. Add-ons in the coupon for multiple orders, bigger sizes or deluxe models can be very important to overall success.

For each alternative, adapt your successful magazine ad from the nearest equivalent size. Or write copy from scratch as suggested in the instructions for writing such a size ad.

Constantly rising postage has caused multiple mailings to be used more and more. Multiple mailings are far more flexible than bound postcard publications or loose cards. They usually include inserts of various sizes. The very diversity of sizes and types of inserts in one envelope makes it more interesting for the recipient to go through. Insert material can range from the equivalent of a single-panel credit card insert to the main broadside of a "solo" piece. Each can be in black and white, or in black and white and one or two colors. Or it can be in full four-color reproduction. You supply the printed piece to the company organizing the mailing. You usually pay just as much for your share of inserting, addressing, mailing and list rental, regardless of the size of your insert or whether it is in black and white or full color.

Whether you have separations and complete mechanicals in their size can best determine which size you use. If you have production material, full color in larger-space mailing inserts will only cost more for running costs of printing. If you have used color successfully in billing inserts, it won't be such a big step to use it in a multiple mailing. Your art director should be able to guide you to do so most frugally. The volume potential in projection can be huge. If cost of inserting and mailing is no higher for the larger piece, it becomes tempting to go ahead with one. You can do so in steps, starting with a less complex piece. You can use the largest package or billing insert you have as your first multiple mailing insert. If you pay out with present smaller material in a multiple mailing insert, consider creating a still larger one.

Go through your collection of solo mailing kits. Look for a broadside that seems an ideal model. Study your most successful inserts and ads. Reread your research. List all your picture and copy box ideas. Start to paraphrase your model broadside using all your advertising and research. Take your time. Meet with your art director. Show him a number of broadside models and be sure he agrees that you have selected the best model. Go over your picture, headline complex and layout ideas with him. He may have a big improvement for you and help you crystalize your layout and thus your writing plan. Don't take too much of his time yet. It can be expensive and premature. Include a coupon in your broadside regardless of your model. Discuss how to lay out the rear page of the broadside. Consider paraphrasing different elements from different broadsides and combining them.

Don't be too worried if you can only afford a black and white brochure or color in type, borders and backgrounds only and not full-color art. Often in a multiple mailing, black and white is contrast to one lush color piece after another. Often flash color has great emphasis.

Construct your broadside in segments. Take one step at a time. Take days and weeks. Try each day to make it a little better. Try to see your art director next when you have completed copy and made your copywriter's layout. It will be less costly, more helpful and speed his job. Follow through as though for a page ad, but expect more problems because it's a bigger job. Have more overlays made. Rewrite more. Perfect and test.

If your broadside works, the next step may be to include a letter as well. In some insert negotiations, you may not have to pay more to insert and mail your letter. Your sole extra cost might be to prepare and print your letter.

Go through your library of solo's again and pick out a model letter to paraphrase. Select a size letter that will fit comfortably with your broadside and be acceptable to the insert program that you are considering.

Notice how your model indents, spaces between paragraphs, changes paragraph construction and how wide its margins are on each side of paragraphs. Notice how your model underlines, uses capital letters and alternates colors. (You can try the color another time.) Notice the color and texture of the stationery and how the logotype and signatures are used and how any pictures are used.

You'll find your model letter far easier to paraphrase than your broadside and far easier than paraphrasing a page ad. Be thorough. Keep improving it. Take your time. Come back to it from time to time. Now test your double insert, broadside with letter.

You now have an arsenal of direct mail weapons. Most kinds of inserts in a multiple mailing are simply variations of some other kind of insert or advertisement you know how to prepare, and so are many kinds of inserts in magazines and catalogs. Some of your same pieces can be used in different ways. The same insert can be used as a package insert, billing insert or in a direct response publication. You can translate a Parade-size page ad, Time-size page ad, a half, third or sixth-page ad into direct mail or vice versa. You have a size range from one side of a postcard to a big brochure and letter for multiple mailings.

You can make your original test in the form of advertising where you can start at least cost and risk. You can translate any success in any form one by one into other forms, often with only minor modifications.

You have learned a lot that you can apply in many ways. You can now see that much of what is made out to be quite complicated can be quite simple. Yet the direct mail projection of these forms of advertising is *huge*. You have already created by far the hardest parts of the "solo" kit. To try for the biggest time projection in mail order, all you need to do is finish one.

The "solo" kit has the biggest jackpot in direct mail to win and the biggest chance of losing. In the good old days of low postage and cheap paper and printing, the "solo" was far more the standard. Today, in its more lavish form, the "solo" reaps richer rewards than ever dreamed of, but for a smaller and smaller proportion of the largest mailers. It's not often for moonlighters.

The "solo" kit in its more elaborate form traditionally contained, in a four-color outside envelope, a lush four-color inside broadside, a two to four-page letter in various colors, a return envelope and a return card. Often there was also a smaller broadside on the giveaway offer. Sometimes there was a lavish color booklet demonstrating the product in use, cataloging more advantages or giving more documentation by experts and testimonials by users. Sometimes there were even more insert pieces. But more and more, even for giant mailers, cost limitations usually keep the "solo" kit to the first five basic pieces mentioned above.

The rich "solo" kit needs a lot going for it. It's lush four-color is usually hopelessly overpriced per thousand, except on a web press with a million run minimum. At this volume, every cost but postage nosedives. Envelopes sometimes drop half or more in cost, and the main color broadside even more. The most automated mailing house in the country is 10 minutes away. At this volume, its charges to insert, affix labels and mail are lower than it cost us many years ago inside our plant. But here's how to create a simpler kind of solo more practical in small volume for moonlighters.

If you've already paid out in multiple mailings with a broadside and letter, now get the most perfect model outside envelope and inside order card. You can paraphrase accordingly.

You've completed a simple "solo" kit. You've avoided the most difficult and costly problems. Your additional production cost is trifling. You've stayed away from color or already proved that it is profitable in multiple mailings. Your broadside and letter are smaller and simpler than in most "solos." If you're already projecting your broadside and letter for multiple mailings, you can print extra copies for your "solo" test at lower cost per thousand than otherwise. You can test a return envelope later.

But keep collecting simple mailing kits from smart companies. Look for least color and smallest pieces. If you get various friends to collect their mail for you, look for the simplest pieces that more friends receive from the same mailer. Among book publishers, Prentice-Hall is an ideal model for least-cost mailing pieces.

Collect direct mail kits for products and services which appeal to the kind of customers you seek. Collect the envelopes you feel must tempt the recipient to open them. Collect opening paragraphs which seem most certain to get the reader to go for the next paragraph. Collect best order cards.

Look also for mailing pieces which offer products and services at comparable prices to yours. Notice how a publisher like McGraw-Hill will have a quite simple, short piece on one book and then descriptions of about 50 words each on 10 or 12 more books at about the same price. The effort is for lower cost in the mail and for a multiple order to a higher average amount and greater gross profit for each order.

To many businessmen, the daily office mail is most important. They look in the mail for orders, bills, important letters and opportunities to save or make money. They know that such opportunities can come in third-class mail as well as first-class. A wise secretary watches out for her boss when she opens the mail. She is paid to screen out time-wasting people and junk mail and to get to her boss people or mail he really should see personally. Simple, businesslike-looking mail often gets opened and read by secretary and boss when more lavish but less to the point mail gets thrown out.

If you do not have a broadside and letter, but do have a basic offer that you feel is suited to direct mail, try creating this simplest of "solo" kits. It's ideal to use in mailings to professionals, technical specialists and, best of all, businessmen. Select a model successful kit in black and white with simplest layout and illustration. If it has a plain brown envelope with no copy or printing front or back, choose and do the same. From this and other models, select the most appropriate return order card as a model and paraphrase it word for word, as far as your offer allows. It's just a little more complex than paraphrasing the coupon in your ad. If your offer has a giveaway, look for a fairly simple flyer on a giveaway as part of one of your model mailing pieces. Paraphrase it as clearly as possible. Paraphrase your model's broadside letter and return envelope, if any.

In your paraphrasing, take one small segment at a time. For that segment, substitute your copy word for word. It may take a long time on one paragraph. The next may come right away. Don't get discouraged with a slow start. You'll pick up speed later. If you're translating an already successful ad, it will come far faster. If you're already saturated with research for that ad, your direct mail paraphrase may almost write itself. Take it easy, go at your own pace. But finish it professionally and test it. Giant mailers often paraphrase closely their own successful mailing kits for their next mailing. To do so, many actually build their new product and offer as a paraphrase of the old. Shorter, simpler direct mail kits that fit your product can often be paraphrased just as publication ads can be. For a larger, more specialized and complex direct mail kit, there is less chance to paraphrase it effectively throughout.

You are more likely to find the perfect model for *one segment* of your direct mail kit here and the ideal model for another segment there. Paraphrasing parts of model mailing kits and putting your paraphrases together is more practical, faster and safer.

The right model coupons, guarantees and envelopes are easily paraphrased. Broadsides (brochures) and letters are more specialized and individually suited to specific offers, as is lengthy giveaway copy and involved giveaway layout for very specialized giveaways. This simply means digging deeper for the right models. Find the right one for each. As soon as any successful development in direct mail is tested, it is often paraphrased by the same company and by others. The surest road to direct mail success is this combination paraphrasing of successful mailing kits.

Your first combination paraphrase will be your hardest. It will force you to think, dig deep into research and seek models. It will improve your writing structure when originating. Your sentences and paragraphs will become shorter and crisper. Searching for equivalent "color" words will help you paint product advantages more appealingly. Searching for equivalent picture ideas will develop an art and layout sense. Following the model forces a discipline on you. It tightens your layout arrangement and puts it in order.

If you paraphrase a good part of one direct mail piece, patch in paraphrases of parts of other direct mail pieces and begin to fill in with entirely new portions of your own, you're beginning to originate. The paraphrasing you do will bring out ideas of your own. Constant revision of the craftsmanship of each effective piece makes it work harder. You can recognize the research it took to write each piece. Digging deeper for your own research, more rewriting and editing is the answer. If an offer seems irresistible, make yours more enticing. When you see a near perfect giveaway, check to see if you have *any* giveaway or if you can improve it or its presentation.

When you read an almost irresistible guarantee, strengthen your own. Can you match the credit terms that tempt you? When you see others give a reward for quick action, *plus* a "cash up" incentive for quick or full payment now, check whether you can. If others take telephone orders and feature credit cards, do you? Should you use the 800 toll-free number?

Are you using the rich color words of others? Are you asking for the order soon enough and often enough? Do *your* words, sentences and paragraphs tempt the reader to go on to the next? How does your layout, quality of art and caliber of copy reproduction, choice of paper, kind of envelope compare? Each point of analysis leads to a question about your own work. And each question forces an answer that becomes an absorbing lesson.

The broadside and letter must be read and believed. The order card must seem tempting, riskless and urgent to attain immediate action. Broadside and letter should complement one another and be independently sales effective.

Introduce more and more of your own innovations into your direct mail. Gradually, you will need to rely less and less on paraphrasing any model. Your approaches will be more varied, fresh and original.

You'll consider a bigger kit. If you buy a larger ad, your cost goes up proportionally. If you enlarge your direct mail piece, your cost rarely goes up in proportion. More space used in black and white is less expensive than less space used in four-color. Pictures can cost more than words if they involve expensive photography, art and production. Greater complexity can cost far more money than space does.

When you develop a quite original direct mail hit, you'll start paraphrasing your creative mail order success. You'll want to project proven success into more products. Once you learn how to sell profitably a certain way, you'll probably go into another product ideally suited to the same technique.

The more you originate your own broadsides and brochures, the more dependent you will be on your art director. The right art director can greatly help you keep costs down while greatly increasing the creative effectiveness of a direct mail piece. The wrong art director can escalate your direct mail costs and slow final completion to the point of disaster. A direct mail piece can be made ever more complex and ever more expensive. It needs creative discipline to keep costs in line. Your art director needs to be a thorough professional in production, or you need a production manager as well. Your art and/or production manager needs to have a business head, and you do, too. So originate broadsides, brochures, booklets and entire direct mail pieces cautiously. Start simply. Be frugal.

If your art director is guiding you and can't estimate in advance the probable cost, your bill may surprise you. Direct mail can cost you anything. Originating can *multiply* the cost. If your art director is a "taxi driver," solely concerned with his hourly rate and philosophic about your costs, beware! If he's ignorant of production costs or hasn't a business bone in his body and you're unfamiliar with direct mail costs, stop before you start. With the right art director and/or production man, you can watch costs *and* be creative.

When you complete your first paraphrased direct mail piece, you'll know far more about direct mail than before. After you work with your art director on your first piece, hopefully you'll work better together on the second.

As in space ads, the creative secret of getting full benefit from your art director is getting more and more overlays after first layouts. As suggested for space ads, make your own copywriter's layouts and overlays, too. Doing so helps you understand what your art director is up against and helps him work more effectively.

Your art director may transform any idea of yours into something quite different and dramatically improve it. Your art director may come up with picture ideas far better than your own. Little by little, step by step and quite naturally, you'll become a creative team originating more and paraphrasing less from others.

Confidence comes fast with success. Confidence gives creative sureness that speeds completion of new projects and proliferates success. The endless variations of the direct mail format will no longer bewilder, but become so many keys to more success. You'll develop a reflex "feel" as to which format is best suited for which product and offer.

As you develop a strong creative team of art director, copywriters, photographers, artists, retouchers, printers and production people, projects will go faster and the finished job will become more predictable. You'll feel at home in any type of direct mail. You'll write and lay out with your art director a giant postcard, tabloid newspaper or specialized small catalog. In each case, you'll start with paraphrasing and gradually originate more and more yourself. You'll come up with quite original concepts of entire direct mail pieces unlike any others.

You will be a direct mail professional combining innovation with a thorough knowledge of what works in different situations. You will successfully compete with and probably profitably work with the giant mailers. Best of luck!

Chapter 11

SPECIALIZED MAIL
ORDER SALES

The mail order two-step . . . inquiry
getting and closing . . . telephone
selling . . . specialized catalogs

Many moonlighters have started in business with a tiny classified or small display ad to secure inquiries. Often they have profitably converted inquiries into sales with a single, simple direct mail follow-up. Sometimes they have profitably converted inquiries to sales with a telephone call.

Inquiry and conversion advertising has *two* steps: the advertising that gets the inquiry, and the advertising that completes the sale. Often a tiny ad at little expense is all that's necessary to secure inquiries. The direct mail follow-up material used by moonlighters is often simple, too. The same paraphrasing method can be used for both ad and follow-up material. Sometimes the ad and follow-up together can be simpler to paraphrase from than a one-step full-page ad for a lower-priced item.

Usually, creating advertising to get the inquiry and to close it is more complicated than creating a one-step ad. It is also more rewarding. The same small ad will often pull inquiries profitably again and again, sometimes for years. The same follow-up literature which converts a certain percentage of inquiries into sales will, under similar conditions, often do so indefinitely. The combination will often pull for a longer period and for bigger sales volume overall than a page ad campaign asking for full payment. You could be creating a business for years, or for a lifetime.

Let's take up the kind of inquiry and conversion advertising most practical for moonlighters. It's a small, simple inquiry ad and simple, black and white, one-time follow-up kit. If profitable, we can go on to bigger ads and more complicated direct mail follow-up kits. Done in the simplest way, inquiries can be quickly converted to sales, bringing in money and making operation practical for a moonlighter.

Inquiry and conversion advertising can sometimes be practical

---

for moonlighters and sometimes not. It can be used to *signal* and later sell those interested in an intriguing field such as science, toys, basket weaving, fly fishing or whatever. In such cases, the follow-up is often a specialized catalog. Sometimes, for an exotic subject, such a catalog has been typed out, photo offset without any pictures and mailed out. Or the photo offsetter has been provided with homemade photograph illustrations. If the field and subject matter are intensely interesting, simple, primitive literature can pay out as a start. Here you must have a catalog of the rare and unusual. Your research for desirable and unusual items in a fascinating field should dig up colorful background facts on each. Your catalogs should be fun to read. Often the primitive simplicity of your crude catalog can give it a personality. Many successful moonlighters have started in this way. Knowing your field can make all the difference.

Inquiry and conversion advertising can sell an item that's harder to sell in one step. It can sell a more expensive item, and often a specialized one. Only a small percentage of the mass circulation of a magazine might consider buying it. A big ad would be costly and wasteful. A little ad at small expense can signal those interested and get inquiries. Follow-up direct mail can convert inquiries into sales. Sometimes such direct mail kits can be simple. Those inquiring for professional, technical or business equipment, for instance, desire detailed, factual descriptions more than lush, expensive art, color and typography. Simple black and white material can often be used.

Presenting your product's case more effectively rather than more lavishly can be most important. This kind of presentation can be quite practical for a moonlighter. Often an imported item has been successfully sold by the inquiry and conversion method. You may only need to translate highly professional follow-up material into English. Photos, art, even color transparencies may be available from the exporter at no cost. Literature may even be available in English. Sometimes a tiny ad with such proven follow-up material available has rapidly catapulted a moonlighter to a substantial business.

Inquiry and conversion advertising is also used to recruit others to help sell your product, product line or service. It may be on a commission basis or to act as agents, franchise dealers, distributors or in any way to buy your product, product line or service for resale. This kind of business has often been practical for a salesman moonlighter with a flair for sales management. There's one simple requirement. You must have case histories of those who have made enough money reselling the product to interest others to do so. Once anyone starts making exciting money reselling your product, telling others the facts is all that is needed. You will need to collect inquiry ads with an offer similar to yours, recruiting help in selling. You'll need to collect follow-up literature to inquiries. You'll find it simple to paraphrase. Again, simple black and white advertising is often all that is needed. Fewer moonlighters have succeeded this way because items easy and profitable to resell are hard to come by. Advertising which misstates such resale earnings is fraud and leads only to grief from the government.

An effective salesman or sales manager can sometimes come up with a successful sales technique, often a demonstration technique, that he can teach another salesman. For a moonlighter, this can build a sound business if the technique described can be passed along by mail. Advertising for a business selling products mail order for resale requires *three steps*: getting the inquiry, converting the inquiry, and providing sales help and tools to the dealer or agent. Sometimes none of these steps need be complex or elaborate. Each can be paraphrased and each can come naturally to a good salesman or enthusiastic inventor or promoter. Often big businesses of this type have been started by moonlighters in the worst economic periods. When jobs are hard to get, more people want to sell something at their own risk.

Inquiry and conversion mail order businesses can be too complex for most moonlighters to consider. Sometimes a series of up to five direct mail follow-ups is required to convert inquiries into sales. Sometimes such literature is lavish, complex and expensive. Sometimes further complicated steps to benefit from inquiry and customer names become necessary to obtain overall profit. If so, more capital and logistical organization can become necessary than is possible for most moonlighters. The direct mail kits that convert an inquiry into a large sale can be more complex than many direct mail kits that complete a smaller sale. Let's stick to the kind of inquiry and conversion businesses that are simple and more practical for moonlighters, at least to start.

You want to start with an item that requires just one simple black and white follow-up. If it is profitable and inquiry volume builds, you can develop a more complex follow-up. If this works, a second follow-up can be tried. The original cost of getting the inquiry has been covered by the success of the first follow-up. Results from the second follow-up can fall off somewhat and still be successful. Several additional follow-ups may each show a profit and improve overall conversions.

For a muscle-development piece of apparatus, a single follow-up mailing has pulled an average of 17% conversion to sales. An entire series of five follow-ups for the same offer has brought the conversion rate up to 39% of inquiries. Be cautious. Expand your follow-ups carefully. Test each. Crawl before you walk. Walk before you run.

Gradually, you can consider, create and test more ambitious and complex direct mail follow-up kits. You may even go into more lavish color pieces. Just take one simple step at a time and pay for each step out of the profits of previous steps. To print and mail a single direct mail kit needed to follow up an inquiry usually costs a small minority of the advertising cost to get the inquiry. To create a more convincing direct mail kit, it can be profitable to spend more per kit than if mailed to cold names. Four-color direct mail kits, printed in smaller runs than practical for cold name mailings, can be profitable used as follow-ups.

A double-purpose direct mail kit can be created. It can justify its production costs by its use as a follow-up for inquiries. It can be tested on cold names as well. If this is profitable, it can be printed in the big runs usually required for cold name mailings and used for both purposes quite profitably.

But *start* an inquiry and conversion business that is simple. This requires a small ad, a single follow-up and black and white only.

How do you find this kind of inquiry and conversion situation? It's simple. Clip and file small inquiry ads for simple moonlighter-type businesses. To get a file of follow-up literature, send in inquiries. In future years, when *you're* successful in your inquiry and conversion business, you may spot inquiries from would-be moonlighters; if so, remember and understand.

When you send in an inquiry, key your name and address. You can then recognize any follow-up to your inquiry. We'll explain how later. Make up a simple form. Fill in the date that you mailed in your inquiry. Fill in the date that your inquiry is received. Fill in whether the reply is by first-class, third-class, or bulk rate third-class. Enter the weight of the envelope and cost of postage of the mailing kit reply. If there are further follow-ups, enter each in the same manner.

File all follow-ups received with your form in one folder. You will know the frequency of any follow-up series and the number of direct mail kits in the series. You will know the price of the item, terms, giveaway, additional ordering incentive or any price reduction later offered. You will be able to estimate probable printing, direct mail processing and postage costs.

Enter offers from the company advertising the original items on one form. On a different form, you can enter offers from probable renters of your name. File away specialized catalogs, special sales or even co-op programs sent to your keyed name.

Keep separate folders for specific inquiry and conversion offers. You can keep two groups of folders. One can be for simpler, one-time follow-up offers. One can be for more lavish literature with a more complex series of follow-up direct mail kits. You need only concern yourself with the first group to start.

Try to find ideal models to paraphrase. Try to start with a paraphrase of both inquiry and follow-up for the same item. It may be more practical to select advertising for one product as a model for your inquiry ad and follow-up advertising for another product as a model for your follow-up direct mail.

Avoid any model with advertising obviously based on misrepresentation. Consider only legitimate models. Try to avoid an unsuccessful model. Select one which has run widely and continuously for years. Paraphrase as previously instructed. Be a perfectionist. It will allow you to revise both ad and follow-up with improved effectiveness.

Selling with the inquiry and conversion method is constantly becoming more difficult for some kinds of items and easier and more profitable for others. Changing conditions make the obtaining of inquiries for and follow-up of many lower-priced items less profitable. It makes getting and converting inquiries for some higher-priced items more profitable.

For many items formerly too expensive to sell in one step, inquiry and conversion advertising is now too cumbersome. It's also too expensive and is no longer necessary. The same item can now be sold through credit cards in one step. At the same time, entire new categories of items have become profitable to sell with inquiry advertising. These items are *more* expensive than formerly possible to sell via inquiry advertising. The average price of merchandise which can be profitably closed by direct mail follow-up has been going up. Even in somewhat worse economic times, there is a greater willingness to buy more expensive *classifications* of items by mail, classifications formerly only bought in a store. Credit cards have helped. More confidence and trust in mail order has also helped.

Inquiry ads and direct mail conversion kits have special creative requirements.

Advertising must produce inquiries at low enough cost and convert inquiries into sales in high enough percentages to be profitable *after* all costs of product, ad, follow-up material, postage and processing.

The object is always to get advertising cost per inquiry *down*, volume of inquiries *up*, and to *improve* the percentage of conversions. Without inquiries, you cannot convert to sales. With poor quality inquiries, your conversions can drop precipitously. Desirable inquiries are genuinely *interested* inquiries. The higher the price of the item is, the harder it is to convert the sale and the more important it is to get an interested inquiry.

The wrong method of sharply lowering inquiry cost and greatly increasing inquiry volume may cause a *sharp drop* in the percentage of inquiries converted to sales. Even getting inquiry costs at one-half or one-third of your former cost can be *unprofitable* . . . if conversions come in at a sharply lower percentage.

How you create your inquiry ad greatly affects inquiry costs, volume and quality. How you create your follow-up material greatly affects the percentage of inquiries converted into sales. Inquiries can be obtained with shorter copy than can orders. Often short copy produces genuinely interested inquiries converting to a higher percentage of sales than inquiries from longer, hard-sell copy. But short copy often includes fewer qualifications and less pre-selling as well as possibly less overselling. Low pressure, long copy sometimes can produce more qualified inquiries with a higher percentage of conversion than shorter copy . . . and sometimes produce lower-cost inquiries in greater volume.

You can get more inquiries with more dramatic product claims and more urgency. Featured offers pull more than not. Any device that makes it easier and lazier to mail back an inquiry pulls more.

New ways are constantly being developed to obtain inquiries in bigger volume and at lower cost, as are new ways to improve percentages of conversions into sales. New ways to obtain still further benefits from the use of inquiry and customer names are being developed just as fast. The art of getting and closing inquiries is getting so complex it has become a big business for big companies. There are mail order advertising agencies and consultants who specialize almost entirely in inquiry and conversion advertising.

You may start very simply as regards both your ad and your follow-up. But as soon as you succeed, you will want to advance to even more productive methods. Don't attempt to learn everything at once. But keep up with changing techniques. Keep answering more ads . . . and filing different follow-up techniques.

Let's discuss ways to get more inquiries and how each affects conversions.

If you use direct mail to *get* inquiries, a return postcard or envelope which can be dropped in the mail without postage will pull more. Postage is paid by the advertiser. An enclosed postcard will have the original address label affixed to it so that the label can be seen through the window envelope of the original direct mail kit. The recipient often needs only to check a box on the return card and drop it without postage in the mail. Inquiry response can soar. But prank and crank mail increase, too. Usually you are better off with a lot lower inquiry cost and a little lower conversion rate. But sometimes it's vice versa. Careful testing and entering of test results is necessary.

A patented device which makes it easier for a recipient of a letter to *pull out* a return postcard increases inquiries. A perforated double postcard in direct mail makes it easy for the recipient to rip off the second post card and drop it in the mail without postage. Usually inquiry quality holds up fairly well. But this device must be tested for each offer to make sure that it does not cut conversion.

The telephone is the most *immediate* way to get an inquiry. The featuring of the telephone in advertising can sharply increase inquiry volume and cut inquiry cost. Persuasive urgency, combined with a toll-free telephone privilege, can jump inquiry volume. But inquiry quality can be *lowered*. Telephone inquiries need to be tested before going all out. The telephone can be invaluable as an aid to getting more inquiries that do close satisfactorily . . . particularly when a WATS line toll-free 800 number is featured.

As explained previously, a WATS line is merely a method of getting a reduced cost per call and the use of the 800 number in return for a specified monthly guarantee. A small guarantee gets a small saving. A big guarantee buys the calls wholesale. You must get a big volume of telephone inquiries continuously to justify using it. If you don't use the WATS line sufficiently, you lose money on the deal. If you go into it cautiously, by stages, you won't. The telephone company you deal with can give you full details.

The 800 WATS line number preceding your own can be featured in your advertising and answered 24 hours a day by you or your staff – or, when your line is busy or doesn't answer, by the telephone answering service. You can indoctrinate the personnel of the answering service as well as your own staff, and perhaps better because they are inquiry answering professionals.

Properly used, the telephone can sometimes make inquiry ads, commercials and mailing pieces pay out when they would otherwise fail. The telephone can create business that would not otherwise occur. It can *secure* inquiries and become its own inquiry advertising. Specially trained operators can telephone compiled lists of prospective buyers and warm up their interest. Then follow-up direct mail kits can be forwarded.

The telephone operator can take an inquiry and convert it to a sale at the same time. The same operator can get credit card numbers to check, and even check them with the credit card company in minutes. The same operator can take a direct billing order from a big company and even take credit references.

The telephone can do most of what any follow-up literature can do, plus a lot more. It can do almost all that a salesman's personal follow-up call can do. With WATS lines, using a telephone can compete cost-wise with elaborate mailing piece costs and at a fraction of a salesman's personal call cost.

In print or on broadcast, a star personality can ask readers, listeners or viewers to call in. A recorded message from a star personality can give the effect of personal response from the star to the telephone inquiry. It can be introduced and followed up by the telephone salesman or woman. This has been done with great success. If you can ever have an association with a name personality, it could benefit you.

The telephone can be used particularly effectively for an add-on offer. The add-on may not even be mentioned in the ad, but be offered on the telephone as an alternate privilege.

I know one businessman who has done over one-million dollars in sales over a number of years with *no* advertising cost by a combination of free publicity and telephone follow-up. He has personally secured substantial publicity for some of his products in a number of magazines. The stories describe some of his items with price, name and address. When orders come in, he phones each on his WATS line and jumps the average order from a little over $30 to a little over $70.

The telephone can help you to get more value from inquiries for higher-price items. Your coupon can specify a blank for telephone number. A special-rate WATS line can be used to follow up inquiries.

The 800 WATS number can be used effectively to call back big-ticket customers and offer other big-ticket items to them. A skilled telephone salesperson can build up a rapport with such customers and develop a clientele who appreciate news of a new, intriguing product or service or a special reduction, perhaps first available to them.

The telephone can be invaluable to get more and convert more inquiries. Emphasis on replying by telephone can increase response to any advertising. But every time that you do *anything* that lowers inquiry cost, a recheck of inquiry quality is advisable.

Each technique or device to produce more inquiries can also cut the percentage of inquiries converted to sales. "Bingo card" numbers are listed in magazines, with each number representing a booklet obtainable merely by circling the numbers. A bound-in return postcard is often included with the numbers. The reader can circle various numbers and drop the card in the mail without postage. Sometimes a huge volume of near worthless inquiries is produced. Insert cards are bound into a magazine next to an ad. They can triple inquiries and worsen the percentage of conversion.

Any device that tremendously increases inquiries runs the risk of decimating the percentage of conversions. Usually a way can be found to use the device effectively, but proper controls must be set up.

From one issue of a mass circulation publication, "bingo cards" produced respectively for three different free literature offers 26,000 inquiries, 21,500 inquiries and 16,300 inquiries. For a fourth offer requesting 60 cents for a booklet, the same bingo card produced 201 inquiries. There was no advertising cost for any of the inquiries; but for the free inquiries, conversions were so negligible that follow-up cost alone was prohibitive. The inquiries enclosing 60 cents converted to sales satisfactorily.

Bingo cards producing huge volumes of worthless inquiries can be unprofitable, whatever the advertising cost or at no advertising cost. Yet bingo cards, properly and selectively used in publications where qualified prospective buyers have been accustomed to them, have helped to build inquiry and conversion item businesses.

Bind-in cards, despite stratospheric cost, have produced a torrent of inquiries at substantially lower cost per inquiry. The percentage of inquiries converted to sales has dropped, too. The net advertising cost per converted sale has often still been profitable with huge additional volume.

Take-one cards in buses, trains and subways have sometimes produced a deluge of inquiries and a desert of conversions. But used in certain areas for certain products and services, they have produced low-cost inquiries that did convert in satisfactory percentages.

There are countless ways of producing inquiries. Book matches, laundry cards and time tables have produced inquiries at low cost which have converted satisfactorily. Literature is passed out in the street, slipped into cars, left on doorsteps, given out in public places. And sometimes it works. New methods are being devised as you read this page. Each can be considered, but used only after being carefully tested.

Offering anything free pulls inquiries, but the wrong free offer or the right one presented wrongly can reduce or destroy inquiry quality. The more *related* a booklet you offer is to your product, the better the quality of your inquiry will be. It may also cut the number of inquiries sharply. The more general the audience is, the more important it is to *charge something* for the booklet, but not always. The same booklet can be offered free, for 10 cents, for 25 cents, for 50 cents, for $1.00 or whatever. Each increase usually raises the advertising cost of obtaining inquiries by cutting inquiry volume, but improves the conversion percentage. Inquiries sent in for unrelated free gifts and followed up by direct mail may convert no better than if the same direct mail was sent to cold names. The higher the price of the item, the harder it is to convert the sale by direct mail and the more important it is to get an *interested* inquiry.

Changes in offer and copy can modify inquiry cost and percentage of conversion inquiries in many ways.

The more *related* a booklet offered is to the product, the better will be the quality of your inquiry. The more your copy dramatizes product advantages, while soft-pedaling costs of product, costs of product operation and product limitations, the lower your inquiry cost will be, but also the smaller the percentage of closure.

If a product is complex and slow to assemble, spelling this out may discourage inquiries. Glossing over it may hurt conversions, if your follow-up literature *does* explain this. If neither your inquiry advertising nor follow-up literature indicates these points sufficiently, *returns* may be higher than expected.

Sometimes a copy approach can lower inquiry cost, jump inquiry volume and improve the percentage of conversions simultaneously. Sometimes a full-page ad can tell more of the product story, more dramatically and with more conviction. The headline complex may have more excitement and the body copy and proof boxes more credibility than smaller ads. Before receiving follow-up literature, the inquiry is partially *pre-sold.*

Emphasis on an offer can vary considerably. It can be buried or featured. A few words of tiny, agate type buried in the bottom of the copy can whisper the offer. Or blazing headlines, big illustrations jumping off the top of the page and copy carried through from the opening to the close can *shout* it. Or the offer can be modulated to anything in between. The same variation of emphasis can occur in radio, television, direct mail, magazines, newspapers or any media.

From pianissimo to fortissimo, you can "play" your offer like a concert musician for whatever purpose you determine. The quiet, buried offer will only be seen by someone who has read the copy through and perhaps been qualified by it. The headlined offer will reach far more people, often with dramatically lower inquiry cost and far greater volume of inquiries. The whispered offer attracts the genuinely interested offer for better conversions. We prefer to use the emphasized offer to get inquiries in volume at minimum cost per inquiry.

In the same way, the offer itself can be varied in *desirability for instant action.* You can be the mail order cook and vary your recipe . . . putting in more sugar . . . or cutting it down to a minimum. You can offer a booklet alone, or with something else. You can usually mail a booklet and an item for $5, but offer booklet and item for $2. You can offer the booklet FREE, with a $4 value for $1. Or as mentioned earlier, you can charge for the booklet alone, knowing that at each increased level you get fewer replies, but presumably more qualified ones.

Your situation can determine your decision. If you're in mail order alone, you may go for the jugular. As you begin to sell the trade more, you may wish to be discreet about the emphasis on mail order. You may vary your approach by the media. You may want all the inquiries you can get from the New York Times, but want to screen the quality of inquiries in a more mass publication or on radio or TV.

You can vary offer emphasis and desirability as you wish. If you advertise your lowest-priced model only, such as "from $39.99" for an item people expect to pay $100 for, you will get inquiries at low cost. But if your average model sells for well over $100, and your lowest-price model is not practical for the average person, then when your literature and price list arrives, conversions may be poor. If you give your full price list range in your advertising, you may sharply reduce your inquiries and increase inquiry cost accordingly, but conversion percentage may be far higher.

Increasing the believability of your inquiry ad produces more inquiries and can *improve* the percentage of inquiries converted to sales. A picture of real people using your product with their testimonials strongly featured can do so. Photography, art and often color can increase desirability and inquiries. What is needed is a constant "feel" for changing inquiry cost and the changing quality of higher or lower-cost inquiries. Ways of getting leads are always wearing out. The quality of inquiries can vary because of media, geographical area, copy, offer, competition or general economic conditions.

You can also increase the volume of inquiries at will. With printed literature, it is possible to follow up a torrent of inquiries or a rivulet. And any new way of producing a torrent of inquiries, in time, often dries up to a rivulet. It is often immaterial where the inquiries are geographically. They can be followed up just as easily. And within a range varying for each product, the quality of the inquiry can vary as described above.

It's a matter of starting and stopping, turning off and on, slowing down and speeding up. Simplistic, standard solutions are not flexible enough. What works now fails tomorrow, and vice versa. But you're at the controls and can turn the proper dials to adapt to changing conditions if you have a "feel" for it.

The president of one of the world's largest mail order advertising agencies has stated that the day of starting a big, successful catalog business on a bootstrap is over. He has said that the future of mail order would be largely with Fortune 500 and other big companies. This may be so. But as moonlighters, we are interested in nook and cranny catalogs in fields obscure and small and perhaps even seasonal enough to hold no interest for the giants. We can find one big enough to give a moonlighter a good living. And we might find a small, brand new field just about to skyrocket into giant growth. We might get in on the ground floor with a specialized catalog for that field.

Every new hobby, interest and activity has the possibility of a specialized, profitable catalog. The first creative task for such a catalog is the conception of it. As a moonlighter, you are limited in money, time and logistical organization. You can only start a catalog in the simplest way, as many, many successful catalogs have been started before you.

Send for and file unique catalogs in special fields. File separately the very simplest and most intriguing . . . those on plainest paper with simplest type and most homemade illustration (or with the least or none). Most amateurish catalogs fail. But you are looking for those that are fresh and original with a real personality. You are looking for one to paraphrase for quite a different field, not to copy. It's your creative job to come up with an exciting new field and concept in which your catalog has an original reason for being.

Desktop catalog publishing, made possible for any moonlighter by ever lower-cost personal computers and word processing ad layout and typography software, is a more and more imaginative enterprise. If your concept is innovative, if you can project yourself in print as a warm, friendly personality, if you can select the unusual and describe it in an intriguing manner, then you very likely can create a desktop catalog that will pull profitably when mailed.

It may take you considerable time to come up with the right concept. It may depend on your background or that of a partner. You want to marry your concept to a paraphrase of the right model catalog. Let's hope it's in a quite different field. You want to be sure that you are paraphrasing a successful catalog. Investigate it. Get a Dunn and Bradstreet rating on the company. Speak to space salesmen from publications that sell the company advertising. Phone the company; explain that you are starting a catalog that is in no way competitive and only seek advice. Very likely, you'll get frank answers to questions and can get an idea if the catalog is successful.

Once you have concept and model, you will need to research your potential item possibilities for your catalog. The freshness of your item copy will depend on the freshness of the items you can secure.

The dice are loaded against small ventures as regards printing cost, mailing cost, advertising cost, list cost, merchandise cost. Your concept, your field, your execution must be so superior as to overcome these disadvantages. You can't compete on the giants' own ground. But if you realize your limitations, you do have a chance. In field after field, a fresh concept for a highly specialized catalog can succeed.

Retail distribution has limited choice of most kinds of items. Someone intensely interested in jigsaw puzzles, fishing flies, books, tape recordings or endless other specialties has difficulty finding a wide enough selection. Specialized catalogs keep coming into existence to fill such needs. Some prosper.

Try to create a specialized catalog in a field where you already have a successful specialized item. Then you can start your catalog as many other successful catalogs have been started – as an enclosure with an item. You want a successful item in the field and in the price range of the items you expect to include in your catalog. It is only worthwhile to consider the catalog when you are selling your single item by the tens of thousands. The mortality rate in catalogs is very high. The soaring costs of postage, paper and printing discourage catalog experts. But building a simple, specialized catalog as a package insert can sometimes overcome those difficulties.

Once you get one specialized mail order item that sells, you're in a position to build a specialized catalog. You start with an insert in your mail order package and feature the items you have that are most related to the first successful magazine items. Your first one-page black and white insert, if successful, can quickly become a several-page folder. The next step is mailing your inserts to your customer list. Soon you're expanding to mailing to outside names and to other companies' customers for items as related as possible to those you are selling. Your catalog is growing fatter now, and more frequent, from Christmas catalog to spring and summer as well. Later, if tests prove out, you can convert to color. You may never need to.

Catalogs may become quite unlike anything now visualized, whether on microfiche, TV recording, photocopy produced at home by telephone or by facsimile reproduction from your TV set. Some new forms of catalogs may be far beyond the ability of a moonlighter to participate in. As a moonlighter, you want to get started safely and get in on the ground floor of the simplest new catalog development.

The telephone can be used particularly effectively with catalogs. The phone orders can be solicited by advertising in the catalogs themselves. Specialized catalogs can be mailed cold to compiled lists and then followed up on the WATS line.

The more successful your first steps into the catalog field are, the more potential expansion possibilities you have and, very likely, the more help you will need to attain those objectives.

If the field is quite small and projection quite limited, your choices and problems will be fewer. If the field is growing rapidly and you're successful to start, you may have the chance to build a good-sized business. A catalog can grow very rapidly. At this point, professional creative help can pay off for you. The right advertising agency or consultant with plenty of catalog experience can open your eyes to one step after another to increase your catalog profits and volume.

Let's hope you need such help. Now let's go into radio mail order.

Chapter 12

PULLING MONEY FROM THE AIR

Radio mail order . . . writing
commercials backwards . . .
avoiding "print" words . . . radio
commas, headlines and coupons . . .
time compression

Radio is splintered. FM now has 60% of the audience. AM has 40%. There are stations in profusion everywhere, even 100 in the New York City area. FM station signals go less far. On crowded dials reception suffers. Yet radio has prospered sufficiently that most radio stations bar the 120-second direct response commercials commonly accepted on TV. Instead the maximum is 60 seconds.

Despite all difficulties, radio is a surprisingly effective direct response medium – but usually to pull phone inquiries. It is often used as part of a triple play. The radio commercial asks for phone inquiries to an 800 number. A specially trained telephone "communicator" answers and converts a percentage of those phoning in for appointments, whether at an office, demonstration center or the caller's home or office. A percentage of those who make appointments keep them. Of those who do, a percentage purchase the article or service offered.

A one-step straight mail order commercial on radio is only rarely successful. Then it's usually for a trusted name with a very hard to resist offer, and on open billing . . . such as a short-term subscription for the Wall Street Journal.

A radio commercial can be simpler and easier to write than any other mail order advertising. It is not difficult to write even if you've never written any other advertising. I wrote radio commercials for years which sold profitably millions of dollars worth of products through mail order before I wrote for TV, publication or direct mail advertising. But it is not as easy as formerly to pay out profitably on radio for a mail order item.

Radio was yesterday's TV, eagerly and closely listened to. Radio today is less intensively listened to and is more often background to other activities, such as getting dressed, eating breakfast, driving a car, cooking, homework or whatever. Today the radio is more often on while not attentively listened to.

Today's mail order commercial needs to get attention, be listened to and understood throughout to obtain action. Just to achieve comprehension requires extreme clarity. Your radio commercial must get across verbally what you're selling, your offer and price and where to write or telephone to get it.

In military instruction, the difficulty of getting across clearly to anyone the simplest verbal message is always emphasized. And each time you stop your car to ask driving directions you realize this. You may not be prepared with pen and pad to write them down. If you're like me, you may only remember the first part of the instructions and forget the rest almost immediately. To get the instructions straight, you usually need to have them *repeated* to you. Even if directions are repeated, if at all complex they're still hard to grasp. A very hurried repetition helps little, if at all.

In publication or in direct mail advertising, the reader has the option to pass over, glance at, read casually or read thoroughly. If interested, the reader can act at once or tear out and keep the printed message for future study, consideration and action.

Let's suppose your own mother is listening eagerly to a mail order radio commercial you have written. With loving attention, she may never understand what you are saying. Many people are more attuned to absorb information through the eye than through the ear. A radio commercial happens quickly. You rarely are prepared with pen and paper. Suddenly it's over, and the listener may not have even clearly understood the mailing or phoning instructions.

That's why complex forms of radio commercials are usually impractical for mail order. That's why complex, choice mail order offers are usually unsuccessful in radio. And it's why commercials shorter than one minute rarely work on radio for mail order.

Have you ever taken advantage of the one-minute rate for long distance telephoning? To keep within 60 seconds on one telephone conversation can be a frenetic experience. Even if you're calling to say "Happy Birthday," one minute seems short. If you're calling someone you don't know on business, just identifying yourself, your company and your product takes precious time.

Listen to radio mail order commercials when you hear them. Sometimes, for a while, the same commercial is run on the same station at the same time each day. If you hear a mail order commercial and own a tape recorder, tune in the next day and tape the commercial. You can even telephone the station and ask for the exact time the commercial will be on next. Keep listening to and taping more radio mail order commercials. Play them back a sentence or so at a time and write them down. In five minutes or so, you can write down an entire one-minute commercial. You'll soon assemble a number of radio commercials both on tape and written out. Selecting a model and paraphrasing is simpler in radio than in any other form of advertising.

Notice which mail order commercials use dramatization, music or sound effects for background or even use more than one voice. Notice which are less than one minute. Most will be *without* dramatization, *without* music or sound effect background and use *one* voice. Almost all will be one minute or more. And if less, they will ask for inquiries and not orders.

Now listen carefully to the offer and mailing instruction portion of the commercial. Hear how often the product name, the price and the address *or* telephone number is repeated. Now time this portion. You'll find that instructions for mailing or telephoning in a free offer usually take 15 seconds or so. If not rushed, they are clear and understandable. This usually includes one repetition. If the instructions are to send in money, they take several seconds more. If there is a choice of size, color or price model, more time is needed. Any choice of telephone or mailing in an offer requires more seconds. If, for more clarity, you slow directions at all, you add more seconds. A third repetition is still longer.

You quickly realize that the mailing instructions are the minimum part needed for the commercial. Time them and subtract the number of seconds used from the commercial length allowed. You now have the number of seconds left to introduce what you are selling and describe it. You must also convince the listener to take action. You at once understand that a minute commercial is the least possible to do the job. It is simple to convince a new writer of this by asking the writer to write the commercial *backwards* – that is, to write the mailing instructions first, then time and subtract from total time allowed.

In publication advertising, if you want to make the ad *smaller* without cutting copy, you can make the size of type smaller. In radio, you can only make the announcer speak faster. Faster spoken directions are sometimes *harder* to understand. A voice that speaks faster tends to speak louder. A commercial with rushed, almost shouted instructions is not just hard to understand, it is high pressure. It psychologically causes listener resistance and tends to *reduce* the number of orders or inquiries produced. Loud, fast instructions are not friendly. Bear in mind that your commercial is just part of a clutter of various commercials that *no one* has a burning desire to hear.

For this reason, it is wise to keep your commercial simple. Your offer should be one way with no choice. It is wise to ask for mail only *or* telephone only. It is wise to *slow* down for mailing or phone instructions and to repeat product name, price and address or phone number *three* times if possible.

This will probably take at least 20 seconds and leave almost 40 seconds of a minute commercial for your actual selling job. This means 80 slower to 100 faster spoken words. To convince anyone of anything in this time with this number of words is difficult. Every word of *your* commercial must do its share. An unneeded word or even a lazy word sabotages the money the commercial is costing you.

The simpler the approach of your commercial, the better chance it has. It should be warm and friendly. You can't talk in stilted language. Don't use "print" words more natural to read than to speak in conversation. They are not simple enough. You want to talk as neighbor to neighbor. Read aloud the commercial you are paraphrasing. Try to substitute equally natural spoken words.

I try to write a radio commercial to one individual listener as I would talk to one person on the telephone. Listen to announcers on country music stations and black announcers on black music stations. Announcers often write excellent commercials because they are writing naturally – the way they talk on the air. They have naturalness, a colloquial quality, friendly talk, warm phrases and a rapport and informality with their audience that's hard to match.

Capsulize your entire product story naturally, even if longer than the commercial time allowed. Then cut to the required size. Don't cut sentences. Cut words as though each was your right arm. But don't cut as you would an ad or direct mail piece. Don't cut out the word "and" and substitute a comma. There are no commas on radio. A comma is an instruction to an announcer to take a breath, and a breath takes as long as the word "and." In radio you can't cut connecting words as easily as in print. You don't want to be too abrupt.

Word-process your commercial, all in caps, with lines triple spaced, with wide margins on either side and with no punctuation. This makes it easy for your announcer to read and easier for you to think of it as spoken.

It is wise to simplify your offer and mailing instructions to the utmost. It's easiest to start in radio by translating an already successful ad or direct mail piece. Generally, a mail order commercial should open in a natural manner, warm and friendly and not too fast. The pace can then pick up very gradually. When asking for action and giving mailing instructions, the pace should begin to slow. When name of product, price and address are mentioned, your selling voice should slow still more enough to be extremely clear.

Keep listening to your model commercial. When you write your commercial, read it aloud to yourself. Tape yourself reading it. Study it as you listen for pace, rhythm and clarity. If you have a friend with a good speaking voice, tape him or her reading it. Avoid a high voice or a nasal voice. Try to get someone with warmth in his or her voice to read it for you. It will help edit copy.

Be careful to write the clearest instructions you can. Then make this test: telephone a friend or acquaintance who has never heard of your product. Start by asking him to listen carefully to your instructions and then to telephone you back and repeat them to you. If he or she can't get your instructions straight, what casual listener can?

Once you realize the job your radio commercial has to do, it's easier to write. You'll find you're not as limited as you might fear. There are announcers who can talk faster without sounding louder. They can increase their speaking pace almost imperceptibly without raising their voices. Listeners can clearly understand almost three times the pace that a human voice normally speaks at. There is now a science of word compression by which a spoken voice can be retaped at a faster pace. It is possible to take each breath and pause out and retape at a faster yet even rate. The result is more words per minute, clearly understood and without a feeling of high pressure.

Voice, music and sound effects, background and dramatization can sometimes be the equivalent of art and layout. The right mood music and voice accent for a travel commercial can be the equivalent of a rich color page.

A taped testimonial from an actual user can be highly effective. A taping of a famous personality recommending a product can be even more effective. On stations where a station personality has a strong following, a strong, first-person recommendation by the personality will be especially powerful. An interjecting voice can be effective in citing documentation.

As in other mail order advertising, it's wise to stay with a tested commercial message. If your commercial runs frequently, alternating openings gives freshness for those who have already heard the commercial but not acted on it. But work on each opening. Each is the equivalent of a headline and subhead. A *worse* opening will *cut* orders or inquiries. Work to make *each* alternate opening *more* and not *less* effective.

Radio will work for some mail order offers. You will find it surprisingly easy to grasp what is needed and write as required. I only mention any creative writing at all in my method in case you like it, take to it and are good at it. The rule is still to do what you like and are good at and associate with others for what you are not. You can forget radio, get a competent advertising agency or find a partner who has mastered it.

Good luck and enjoy it.

Chapter 13

THE MAIL ORDER GOLD MINE

---

*TV frustration . . . fortunes to make
. . . easy commercials to write,
nightmares to produce . . . safest TV
paraphrases*

A TV commercial can be the most effective of all mail order messages. It can be so powerful that it not only sells the product profitably mail order in huge volume, but creates store demand as well. If you have proprietary rights to your product, this may give you a lifelong business. A TV commercial has everything in its favor. It has sight, sound, and motion. A closeup of your product can take up the entire screen. It can demonstrate your product in use. It can do all this in full color (to over half the viewers). TV demands viewer commitment. Many leave the room when a commercial comes on, but many more keep watching and listening.

A TV message can be pictorially dramatized in many ways. A zoom lens can leap to a closeup. Pictures can pop on the screen, fade out . . . and be successively replaced by one after another. Pictures can jump one by one into a quarter of the screen to create a montage effect. Key words of commercials can be supered on the screen on pictures already there. The announcer can talk right into the living room. He or she can occupy the entire screen or part of it . . . with supporting pictures and printed words.

Mailing or phone instructions can be shown in print on screen and spoken by off-screen voice as well. Double reinforcement helps make the instructions, price, address and phone number clearer, faster.

But of all forms of advertising, TV can be more frustrating, more difficult . . . and more disappointing when you compare the commercial as you see it on the TV screen with what you attempted to do and expected it would be. This is simply because there are more ways to be disappointed and more kinds of mistakes that can be made.

It's easy to write into a TV commercial the effects you see each

---

night achieved by sophisticated commercials. It's hard to achieve those effects *professionally* . . . particularly for very little money. But TV mail order can be so powerful, so profitable, so huge in volume that you want to participate. And if you have secured the rights to an item perfect for TV, you should.

Don't attempt to do TV *alone* . . . if you have no money or are not good at it. Associate with someone else who is. Limit your objectives. You have the product. You can ship it or have it shipped. Find someone to gamble the TV advertising for you. The most obvious candidates are those already successfully selling mail order on TV. They're making money. You haven't started. Usually they *need* new items to test. You may have one you believe will sell on TV. Often they have a successful background as professionals in TV broadcasting. You can make money from them . . . and *learn* from them. The simplest plan for them will be for you to sell them your product or take a royalty on it. They may be willing to buy it and also pay you per unit to pack and ship it. If they prefer a royalty and you are already paying a royalty, you add your royalty on top. This may or may not be acceptable.

You must be willing to make less if you associate with someone who takes over your risk. You may be able to make a deal giving up TV mail order sales only . . . for a specific period . . . and only if a certain minimum income is produced for you. You earn less but learn more while risking nothing. And if you're starting moonlighting with little or no money, you have very little choice. Once you make some money and gain some TV know-how from your association, you can try your next item on your own.

The next alternative is to get others to take the risk on making the TV commercial while you take the risk on buying TV time. The risks in *testing* a TV commercial can be small. The risks in making one can be big. Many try to eliminate risk in buying TV advertising by trying to get PI's (no-risk advertising) and paying so much per order received. We'll discuss this later. But the real risk in TV mail order advertising is the risk in making the TV commercial. It's far better to take the small risk of testing it on one or more stations and, if successful, buy cautiously thereafter. But first get someone, or several people, to take the risk of making the TV commercial.

Any professional wants to get the highest fee possible for his or her work. But many capable professionals at some time in their careers gamble their professional abilities for a share in something. Many a lawyer or law firm owns stock in corporations in return for work done.

However, let's now assume that you can afford to take your own risk of making a TV commercial. A TV commercial can be extremely complex or far simpler. No matter how much money you have, the best way to master making TV commercials is to start simply. If you can produce a simple commercial that works, you can go on to a more complex one. And if you start moonlighting with little money, you can only afford to go on TV in the simplest way. So let's not get into sophisticated production. Let's discuss the simpler kinds of TV commercials most practical for you to start with.

Some of the simplest and most effective TV commercials are demonstrations. Many were successful for years before going on TV. They might have been in stores, at fairs, on the boardwalk or house-to-house. A demonstration on TV can be *more* effective than in a store because closeups occupying the entire screen can show more clearly what is happening. The demonstration is cut to the essence, usually about one minute and 35 to 40 seconds, leaving 20 to 25 seconds for the mail and phone directions.

A demonstration TV commercial can be so simple that it is filmed exactly as it has always been done, but cut down to the required size. In some cases, there is no other action, art, voice, camera shot or even slide, except for mailing and phone instructions. Many a salesman owning a small company has gone on TV and delivered his own sales talk, cut down to commercial length, with no real production assistance . . . and has been successful. In many cases, the same demonstration commercials are effective for years.

The reason is often that a demonstration "hit" has been translated into TV. And the less tampering with the already successful demonstration, the better chance it has to succeed in TV as well. Many products are extremely well suited to demonstration. The problem is to find a really effective demonstrator. Often this requires manual dexterity plus natural salesmanship and showmanship. An able TV announcer or actor may lack the necessary dexterity. But sometimes a TV actor or announcer who likes a hobby or sport (even if not really good at it) can demonstrate superbly anything connected with it. It is wise to have a real expert check him or her at each point.

Many product salesmen are *not* natural demonstrators. Others are superb. If a salesman is a natural demonstrator, but has never been on TV, often he or she is *not* bothered at all doing the same demonstration on TV. The same is often true of the product inventor. If someone has demonstrated a product for months or years, then it usually is easy and natural, whether on or off camera. Some demonstrators and salesmen have surprising potential for being entertainers as they demonstrate on TV.

We've found natural talent many times in TV demonstrations by fishermen, artists, cooks, beauticians, dance instructors, home repairmen, sewing experts, musicians, teachers, authors and hobby authorities in many fields. We've also found many authorities who knew their subject, yet froze and became awkward on TV. Usually you can determine before filming or videotaping if your candidate is or is not suited to TV demonstration. And if you do find someone who can successfully sell or demonstrate your product, it may give undreamed-of TV success. That someone might even be *you.*

Public TV has brought back how-to instruction programming, as well. The TV shopping networks have multiplied it. This trend will continue, providing homes with more alternatives to movies and serials. The items that often sell most profitably mail order on TV are demonstration items. We've built entire TV programs around demonstrations: art instruction shows, gardening shows, dressmaking shows and so forth. We are seeing a renaissance of demonstration. And remember, a simple demonstration by a superb demonstrator has the least chance of anything going wrong.

The first decision will be the length of your commercial. This in turn will be affected by the changing policies of TV stations. If business continues to improve for TV stations, there may soon be a trend toward limiting mail order commercials to 60 seconds.

Some mail order offers have succeeded with 60 seconds. Most record offers have required 120 seconds to succeed, but Fats Domino albums have been successfully sold with 60 seconds. The reason is that the name was so accepted and the desire to buy almost anything he performed so great that cataloging could be skimped. But in most record album offers, success depended on cataloging 15 to 18 song hits, usually on a revolving scroll listing each hit, the composer and the singing star. An off-screen voice described each as the scroll listing revolved. Doing so required the full 120 seconds.

You may not believe in long commercials. But try this test. Watch mail order commercials on TV . . . on any old movie and some new ones. Tape the voice and sound. When you see a mail order commercial, you can phone the station and get the exact times it will be on next. Play back the tapes and time them. Write down the words on the *right* side of a yellow pad. On the left side, write down a description of each change of scene that happens on the screen and each super and fadeout where words are superimposed on the screen or taken away. Keep watching, taping, and transcribing until you have a collection of TV mail order commercials. Time each and note which are two minutes, which are one, which in between and which less than one minute. These will be your models to paraphrase.

You will find that the big majority are two-minute commercials. Those that are less are usually asking for inquiries only. Now notice which ones are most elaborate, with dramatizations and lavish production, and whether big-name performers are delivering the commercial. Notice which are simplest, with slides and off-screen voice only, or with one person onscreen doing all demonstration and selling and with slides only for support and mailing instructions.

You will find that some of the most repeated TV mail order commercials are the simplest. Now notice how mailing and phone instructions are handled. You will find that many commercials ask for both mail and phone orders. You will find that many album commercials offer a choice of records or tapes. The combination of seeing instructions in print on the screen and hearing them simultaneously helps make them clearer.

You can keep your TV commercial simple . . . and make a profit.

But even if simple, it is usually not practical to make a TV commercial as you go on the air or just before it. Too much can go wrong. The production staff of the station is either not available or so rushed with other duties as to be unable to get into your problem. Even displaying your product on camera demands effective lighting, and effective lighting is often slow trial and error.

Videotape is far easier to work with than film. It can be seen immediately after being taped. Mistakes can be seen. Scenes can be immediately retaped and corrected . . . or eliminated. Videotape can vastly simplify making a good TV commercial. But still, the more elaborate the TV production you attempt, the more opportunities there are to *destroy* its effectiveness. Each added complication that you put into the production of a TV commercial session is pushing your luck a little more.

Next to a demonstration only, a slide commercial interspersed with several simple action shots and all with off-screen voice is the best bet to get what you expect with the fewest accidents. Even then, to make one two-minute commercial using a competent crew takes most of one eight-hour workday. Making *two* two-minute commercials in an eight hour session is not easy. The logistics of preparation to get full value from these eight hours can be considerable.

The camcorder is the TV moonlighter's friend. Generally, you won't produce a broadcast-quality videotape with your own lower-cost equipment, but you can create the TV equivalent of a copywriter's layout. You can tape an expert demonstrator. You can see it instantly, discuss it and together change the demonstration as needed. You can see ways to shorten it, to highlight important parts of it and to emphasize ease and speed of use of the product or the extent of the bargain.

If you have a friend who owns broadcast-quality equipment, you could conceivably create much of the commercial. The use of a Macintosh could give you ideas for supers of wording over picture.

You're best off in all likelihood if you don't attempt to make your own commercial – but if you do, attempt every practical preparation from a dry run to your own rough-draft videotape.

Otherwise, when you get to the TV studio you may be in for a surprise. You need to bring to the studio in ample time each slide and prop and contingency plans for what might not work. Each component part of your TV commercial has a possibility of not coming off properly. A picture you think is great may look poor on the screen, even one of your product in use. Your producer or director may or may not be as effective as you had hoped. When you arrive, you may find nothing in particular happening, no one particularly concerned and your TV commercial hardly getting underway. Soon in the day, you may realize that it's going to be a race to finish the commercial at all. You're aware of your hourly cost for the studio and crew. You feel helpless. You're in the hands of others. Each suggestion you make might *worsen* the overall effect and get you into expensive overtime as well. That's why careful selection of a TV commercial to paraphrase and careful paraphrasing of it is so important.

Being thorough and careful, from the writing of your commercial to the day of production, can greatly lessen chances of anything going wrong. In writing a TV commercial with off-screen voice, the first tendency is to use too many words and too few pictures. A slide that overstays on the screen can slow the commercial considerably. If you have little or no motion on the screen and do not see the announcer face to face, a mostly slide commercial needs fast change of pace. Keep to the action and timing of the model you paraphrase.

Sometimes a very large advertiser with an ample budget for elaborate commercials will use one with nothing but stills. This is because such a commercial is a complete change of pace from a more sophisticated one. But in such a commercial, one slide after another will pop on the screen. This can be very effective.

For this reason, one of our alumni (and one of the most successful mail order operators on TV) sometimes writes his two-minute TV commercials with 20 slides or action shots. He usually allows 25 seconds for mailing instructions, using only three to four slides. He usually avoids telephone orders, preferring cash only. Each slide or action scene averages six seconds. Four to five of these shots will be motion shots, usually quite simple, such as a hand picking up the product or the product in use. He intersperses these throughout. The rest are slides. He will use approximately 200 off-screen words, running from three to 15 or so per shot. He will super words on the screen in about 15 of the 20 shots. He supers one to five words to a shot. In total, he gets 30 to 40 words on the screen throughout the commercial. Several times he will fade out some words and super in others.

We favor slightly fewer pictures, words and supers. Naturally, each product and commercial has its own requirements. Either way it's fast moving . . . and subject to possible mistakes. That's why so much preparation to avoid error is required. Sometimes it's possible to view certain important shots in advance at a cooperative TV station. This is particularly important for a product shot. If such a shot does not come off, the entire commercial could be unproductive. Your art director can be of tremendous help in creating a TV commercial and preparing for it. This can be so even if he or she has previously had no experience in TV. But tell your art director how important it is to paraphrase . . . and do it. Accustom yourself to working with a storyboard sheet or creating your own when you write your TV commercial. It causes you to put TV picture ideas next to words and helps you work with your art director. Use the same number of words with each frame as your model commercial.

It's wise to compare costs of producing a TV commercial by different talent, producers, studios and in different cities. Los Angeles, Chicago and New York are expensive production centers. There are competent crews in lower-cost centers elsewhere. From Long Island, New York, we'll sometimes go to Lancaster, Pennsylvania, or Syracuse, New York, to produce a TV commercial. Costs are modest, production facilities excellent and efficiency good.

There is a risk anywhere of less than competent announcers, actors, cameramen or directors. There can be more risk where experience is less, which can occur in small cities. If you at first associate with others more professional in TV than yourself, at their risk, you will quickly learn where and how they make professional commercials at reasonable cost.

TV can be extremely powerful in using real-life testimonials, if you use them correctly. Just going out with a tape recorder and interviewing *enough* customers at their homes or offices will uncover some so natural and convincing that you could not write anything yourself, or pay anyone to act the part, anywhere near so effectively. Giving the same testimonial on TV is more difficult. None of your customers giving testimonials may come across on TV. Many may even be unwilling to take the time required to go to a studio and make a commercial. In such a case, it may be necessary to dramatize with commercial talent the testimonial for which you have a release. Be sure you identify it as dramatized, in whatever manner the latest rules of the FCC and FTC require. Just ask them.

Featuring the telephone on TV gives urgency and maximum immediacy of action. The toll-free 800 number is particularly effective and simple to present with both audio and video.

If your paraphrase works, your TV projection can make so much money and run so widely that you may become a desired advertising account to the right advertising agency. If you lack money, but do have a successful commercial, you can attract partnership or association from financially responsible experts.

But be discreet. The right experts or consultants can make you rich . . . and the wrong ones steal your item and commercial. Let's discuss finding the right agency or expert.

Chapter 14

THE EXPERTS

The ideal advertising agency . . .
finding . . . winning . . . pleasing . . .
working with one . . . being your
own . . . the same for a consultant

Obtaining the *right* mail order advertising agency can change your mail order life. The right agency can compensate for lack of mail order marketing experience on your part . . . or augment your know-how. The less advertising and promotional background you have, the more important the right advertising agency is to you.

The chances of a mail order moonlighter getting a top mail order advertising agency are almost nil. Large advertising agencies desire large accounts. Getting any competent mail order advertising agency to accept you is difficult. Small to medium advertising agencies are sometimes tempted by smaller accounts they hope will grow. Sometimes they do not have the time for their smaller accounts to cause them to grow. This is sometimes a surprise to those who have the impression that it is possible to get part of the 15% commission back from the agency.

Far from trying to get advertising talent to work for less than full commission, the problem is to get real advertising talent at all, and if you get them . . . to motivate the talent to *work* for you. More incentive, not less, is needed. Some small mail order firms give a partnership to outstanding, creative advertising talent. Some give minimum fees against commission. Some give a bonus on successful ads. I've been paid a royalty on sales by substantial companies, as have others. Of course, you can get part of the commission back from an advertising agency which places the ad for you but does no work other than mailing in the order.

In my book, Mail Order Know-How, I tell the stories of some of the most successful direct marketing advertising agencies in the world, almost all bought by the top general agencies. These have minimum fees no moonlighter can pay.

A new agency is often more willing to speculate its time and talent by taking on a smaller account it has confidence in with no minimum fee. New talent is constantly starting up shop on its own. You may be fortunate enough to select the right young advertising agency at the right time. When starting out, an agency is more willing to use its best efforts to make a success of your business. But a new agency may be tempted and take you on because it wants to *list any accounts to* start. It may not have time to work on your account.

More small advertising agencies can give you excellent media selection help than give top creative help. Less time is required for the first. There are few very small advertising agencies expert in each form of media. You can often get excellent media buying advice on one form of advertising. This is fine if you concentrate on that form to start. Sometimes you can combine selecting a quite small advertising agency, quite strong in media, with offering to pay for freelance copywriting as an advance against future advertising agency commissions. Or you can create the ad yourself and get the agency to help in media.

As soon as you have your first successful test in any form of advertising, you become more interesting as a prospective advertising agency client. As you develop more hits and project each, you become a bit more desirable. Agencies which had no interest in you before may now consider you as a client. The more you grow, the higher up the ladder you can go in getting consideration from desirable advertising agencies.

Even among smaller agencies, the more successful the advertising agency you wish to interest in your account, the higher is their overhead. If your account is small, either be prepared to pay a minimum service fee to a larger agency or seek a smaller advertising agency. That minimum agency fee can be the safest money you'll ever gamble. It may enable you to get top talent instead of mediocrity.

Getting the right agency to accept you is a step toward your success. Winning their interest and confidence that you can be a big client can greatly speed your success.

The difficulties in creating your own advertising are powerful reasons for working with a competent mail order advertising agency. If you are starting off with very little money, this may not be possible. You may have to begin largely doing your own creative work. You will probably start with a quite small advertising agency, if any. Even if a small agency creates advertising for you, you may be disappointed.

A smaller agency is tempted to secure more and more small clients. Each may get less and less time. A retail store can train a copywriter to write very fast. So can a radio station, a printer, or a creative service doing quick jobs for small advertisers. The one common denominator of such work is that there is no time to *think*.

Very small advertising agencies are often a combination of artist and former space salesman, artist and printing salesman for direct mail or announcer-producer and time salesman for TV or radio. Usually the emphasis in such small advertising agencies is on the salesman-account executive. Often there are too many accounts, too little time and limited professional training. The objective can be billing for the agency. It may not know how to get the most from each advertising dollar for the client.

For any size advertising agency, the weakness of being a client is that you cannot be the only client. You share the time and talent with others. If you're a small account, you may get *Junior*, being broken in on YOU! If you get the agency's better talent and your billing is much smaller than other clients, you may get much less attention and thought from them. Advertising agencies must make money. They must make a profit on time and work invested. They must make money now and not gamble on futures to too great an extent. A smaller agency can give more time, but cannot escape the basic economics. Generally, a smaller agency, with lower overhead and lower-cost executives and creative people, can profitably give more time for the same billing. But the most talented mail order advertising people usually earn more. If you get the services of lower-cost mail order advertising talent, it is usually less effective for you. So there are frustrations and drawbacks in dealing with large and small advertising agencies until you're a large enough advertiser to be profitable for top advertising talent to deal with you.

Pleasing the client can produce more short-term billing and agency commission than improved creativity. Sometimes a copywriter, art director or account executive develops an extraordinary ability to "sell" creative work. He or she is a showman, setting off the work to best effect, usually only after a persuasive "pre-sell." Creative ability that might have been improving the advertising has been devoted to selling it.

When your account becomes big enough to interest a leading mail order advertising agency, your real growth opportunity will arrive.

A top mail order advertising agency can be an exciting clearinghouse of mail order opportunities. So many tests are being made so fast that new information of what works is pouring in. Newspaper and magazine salesmen and their bosses are meeting with the agency executives, as are station representatives. Publishers and TV and radio station managers are coming in on periodic trips to touch base with the agency. You, as a client, are getting access to the newest techniques uncovered, the newest exciting media buys. Often opportunities arise for joint ventures, cross mailing inserts, list swaps or whatever with other clients.

Check on any agency you consider. Call several clients and ask if each is satisfied. Call several publications or broadcast stations and talk to the credit manager. Explain that you are considering the agency and have heard good things about them, but that you would appreciate any information on how promptly the agency pays its bills.

If you get to be a larger account and are considering a larger agency, check on them more thoroughly. Be diplomatic, but ask how much percentage they add to production bills . . . the greatest sore point with clients. Ask the agency what functions it charges for and what it gives for its commission. Try to avoid future surprises.

Look over the creative work of the agency. Meet those who will work with you. Be frank about your present size. Don't exaggerate your hopes. But try to impress them with your honesty, competence and sensible plan for your business. Discussing your business with their specialists can be revealing. Judge the common sense of any observations, reactions or suggestions that each gives you.

Ask for financial statements of any advertising agency that you're ready to select. Clear them with your accountant. An underfinanced agency can hurt you. You may be asked to pay an advertising bill twice, once to an agency and, if it goes bankrupt, once again to a publication or broadcasting station if it was never paid by the agency. Check if any of the partners have been involved in a previous bankruptcy in any business. This can be a bad sign. Such a history can repeat itself.

What is the company's policy on competing accounts? Do they handle accounts you feel are competitive? How much information about your business will be passed on by agency personnel? Check their clients for the agency's reputation for discretion in such matters. Ask who would be your account executive. The definition of an effective account executive is that to the account he is the agency, and to the agency he is the account. He may turn out to be a salesman trying to get you to spend more. Or he can be the key to harnessing the maximum abilities of the agency most effectively in your behalf. Of all the agency personnel, he must be the most discreet. For he will learn more about your business than any other. Be sure he does not handle any account in the agency you feel is at all competitive. The chemistry between you and him or her will be the most important.

Don't rule out any agency for a single reason. Consider all factors. The most understaffed agency with a very talented one-man owner enthused over your growth potential may be better than a top agency that looks at your account with a jaundiced eye. Using *any* advertising agency exposes you to the danger of vitally secret information about your business getting out. Some super secret mail order men have a house agency solely for reasons of internal security. More feel that the assets of dealing with the right agency outweigh such liabilities.

Many mail order firms do have their own "house" advertising agencies, owned by them but recognized by all media and receiving their 15% and 2% cash advertising agency commissions. These firms seldom set up their "house" agencies just to save money. Sometimes the principal owner or a partner is an advertising agency man and, if so, is often an egotist. He wants things done quickly his way. He wants creative people to report to him. Sometimes the mail order firm is too small to be interesting to most advertising agencies. Instead of paying a minimum service fee to an agency, the mail order firm sets up its own. Sometimes it's just a self-defense against the choice of an agency inexperienced in mail order or getting Junior in an experienced one.

Few mail order companies I know use a house advertising agency to save money. The main advantage is getting what you want done, when you want it, and getting moment-to-moment control of your advertising. There is a difference in the economics. An advertising agency tries to take the long view, but must make a day-to-day profit on motions made and time spent. But on your own advertising, you are solely interested in profit overall, not commissions earned. In one case, we spent five months of a top copywriter's time to write one ad, but made $100,000 from it in the next 40 days. We'll discuss later how to organize your own advertising agency.

If you are an advertising man gone into mail order, it will be hard for other advertising people to satisfy you. If you are a superb businessman without advertising background, why not team up with equally superb mail order advertising people? Why have a fool for your client? As far as getting a kickback rebate of some of the advertising agency commission, it may appeal to a non-advertising-background businessman, but it takes the heart out of any interest in creative work by the agency. It is usually less profitable for the advertiser. But if you are an advertising man who would like support in some advertising area, it might work. This could be so if you write your own advertising but need the agency's media help. I would personally still recommend giving full commission and pushing them to make up for your writing contribution in other ways. So act according to your own talents and situation.

Start your agency relationship with a test of their advertising for your product. Proceed cautiously with projections. Try to put yourself in the agency's shoes and then be a good partner to them. The proof of the pudding, for both you and the agency, will be in the eating. And once you start a good relationship, keep it. Don't be a "tap dancer," dancing from one agency to another. If you're fortunate enough to find a competent agency, handle it with care.

The right agency has the right team for you. You want to help that team to work for you. But your efforts to contribute creatively to their work could drive them out of their minds. Proceed with care. Try to simplify and not complicate their work.

Any research that you do helps your advertising agency create better ads. It can dramatically increase the percentage of "hits" they create . . . and their total billing from your account. Incidentally, it can *multiply* profit you get from advertising they create.

If your account is small and you are not on a fee basis, they are always trying to determine whether to keep working on the account, probably at a loss but in the hopes of future profit, or to drop it. You could push them over, either way, by personally helping or hindering them.

Don't dominate. A determined client can get advertising that pleases him, but far inferior, creatively, to advertising that the agency could prepare for him.

Working with your advertising agency should be *supportive* and time saving for them. Start with your account executive. Make him realize that you feel you can help him and the agency build billing and profit. Then gradually convince him that this is so. What you innocently propose may be upsetting. Each creative specialist has an ego. An advertising agency, no matter how objective it collectively tries to be, has ego, too. Any offer to contribute creatively can be taken as a reflection on the agency's creative ability, and perhaps the first step to a more partial use of the agency, perhaps even leading to a future request for a partial kickback of agency commissions.

Working creatively with your advertising agency requires spending time in their offices with their specialists. It sometimes upsets the internal procedures they have set up. The more you're in their shop, the more you see their problems that perhaps might embarrass them. The man you're talking to may be getting an angry phone call from another client. Just seeing how much time they devote to other clients, and how little to you, can disturb the illusion all clients and agencies like to preserve of an organization working primarily for one client, *you*. You can be like a guest walking into the bedroom you weren't expected to see . . . with unmade beds, clothes scattered and bathroom in disarray.

So be easy on them and be a good account. The chances are that, initially, your advertising agency can do more for you than you can for them. You want to correct the balance . . . and more. In this way, you can hope to attain a relationship where your account is desired . . . and the loss of it to be regretted. Your account then becomes desirable to other agencies . . . and in turn, more desirable to your present one where you wish to stay.

Just expressing your appreciation of *any* work they do is important. Your account executive, in one way or another, personally benefits from the growth of your account. Your first job is to prove your *competency* to help him and the agency. Let him realize your respect for the agency's ability. Simply *present* him with your own copywriter's layouts and copy as a further step beyond research.

The account executive himself may be quite realistic. He may be quite aware that your present billings are not attractive enough to the agency for him to get much creative time from the agency for your account. He may *appreciate* your contribution. The proof will be in the pudding. Your research material alone may be tempting and provocative to the copywriter assigned. He or she may be a junior writer anxious for a chance to write a "hit." Your research and your rough ads may be more help than that writer is getting from other clients. It may result in a "hit," even if credit should go mainly to *their writer*.

Now there will be *requests* for more research material and more consideration for any rough ads and layouts you contribute. Now you will have a chance to meet the young copywriter who, from your material, scored a "hit." There is mutual appreciation and the beginnings of mutual respect. If the net result of your meeting with the writer is that the next "hit" is written faster, with more projection of advertising billing for the agency, you will find the agency more receptive to more help from you.

Now you can meet the art director and the production manager, and eventually achieve closer cooperation with them. It's a slow, *step-by-step growth of a relationship.* And at each step you must prove competence to additional specialists in order to win respect. Gradually, you'll be invited to sit in at a photo session, to meet with artists, retouchers, engravers and other specialists. Each step will have the same requirement. *If you save them more time and help them make more money, you're welcome.* If you waste time and hinder them, you're endangering your relationship. And you must be a diplomat at all times.

Most advertising agencies are strongest in space and broadcast advertising and weakest in direct mail. Many do not handle it at all. Many mail order firms accept the idea that the agency should make its 15% on space and broadcast advertising but not on direct mail advertising. It's very hard to pay out in direct mail advertising. Adding 17.65% to costs to average out at 15% is not worthwhile to some mail order firms.

Some mail order firms believe that the right direct mail consultant can advise them on all they need to know for a flat fee, and that they can perform all actual functions. And in any form of mail order, a top talent executive who has spent his life developing a new successful technique for big mail order advertisers can, on a part-time basis, sometimes be a gift from heaven to other mail order advertisers.

In my book, Mail Order Know-How, I interview 47 of the world's greatest direct marketing consultants, ranging from computer experts to shipping specialists, telephone marketing experts to creative stars, list consultants to research specialists. The woods are full of mail order consultants. Many are simply between jobs, fired from one and looking for another, maintaining a feeling of dignity by hanging out their shingles. But some mail order consultants can be invaluable, particularly in direct mail.

Selecting the right consultant can be more difficult than picking the right advertising agency. First check his biographical sketch. How long has he been a consultant . . . and for whom? Exactly what functions does he perform? Does he advise only, create copy, make list or media schedule recommendations? Which big companies or agencies has he worked for? Was he on their payroll . . . before he was a consultant? When did he learn his trade from them? How recent or obsolete is his present know-how?

Ask his clients if he has been worth the fees they have paid him, if he has tangibly increased their business . . . and if so, exactly how. Ask if they feel he's familiar with the very latest techniques. Ask exactly what he has done for his fees.

Talk to him about his career and your business. See how you get along . . . and how common sense his reactions are. I know one mail order consultant who has a fantastic background. He is fascinating to talk with. But he's mentally lazy. His first meeting is his best. In successive meetings, he has less to contribute. After a while, he's squeezed out like a damp towel. He's a poor buy for a yearly fee, but a tremendous bargain at a stiff fee for several meetings. Just one suggestion from him has sometimes made tens of thousands of dollars for his client. But it's most apt to come in earliest meetings.

Select your consultant carefully. Go carefully into the relationship. A quick cancellation privilege of any regular retainer fee is desirable. Different factors can change the worth of the relationship. He's only one person. He may be unable to deliver effectively for you. He may become too successful in getting clients to be able to service them. He may contract an illness. He may undergo an upset in his personal life. So try to select the best on the most flexible basis.

If you're starting out without adequate capital, but you succeed in securing the rights to an outstanding product, you might consider proposing a partnership to the right direct mail consultant for direct mail only. You might provide the product, do the fulfillment and take the risk on the actual mailing costs, but give a partnership for direct mail only for the creative work. It might make you rich.

And now, with all this help (or self-help), let's discuss just how good advertising should be.

Chapter 15

THE MONEY-MAKING LABORATORY

*The perfectionist concept . . . post
mortem lessons . . . continuous
testing . . . perpetual improvement*

In this course, I have asked you to master your product and its field, to study and analyze successful mail order advertising closest to your product and field and to apply lessons learned.

Adapting your advertising to a "model advertisement" you select is the method I've successfully used to start young men and women in this field. Most had no prior copy, advertising or mail order experience whatsoever. It's the method by which I taught myself.

Step by step, you will familiarize yourself with more and more successful mail order advertising. More and more, you'll see how to apply it to your own. My hope is to help you to apply *your own* actual experience to originate your ads more and more without formula or model.

My interest is to get you to create a successful mail order ad in the shortest possible time and start making money. I'd like you, as you make money, to make a continuing laboratory study of improved creative techniques . . . simply by analyzing actual mail order sales of each ad you create. I want you to become a perfectionist, not a hack. I want you to make this hobby a mail order university.

A perfectionist can't stand any of his work that is less than perfect in his eyes. A hack is always happy. Time after time, working with talent in radio and TV, I've seen the same reaction. The more top the talent is, the more they worry about each tiny facet of each phase of their work . . . and the more endlessly they go over and over it, again and again, to correct it. The happy faces that come out of the studio after a TV show, radio show, taping or recording are often the hacks. The tense, worried ones are . . . the stars.

I've gone out with a top Viennese photographer to various locations day after day to get desired shots and seen him again and again refuse to pull the lever of his camera! "The only thing that will come out is what I see through the view finder. If it isn't right when I look through the finder, it won't be right when I develop the picture!"*

We've sent a crew of three to take color pictures outside for one of our products every sunny day for seven weeks. They have taken over 2,000 shots and selected only a dozen or so for our advertising material. Great art directors make initial layouts and then, one tissue overlay after another, change parts of the layout endlessly until completely satisfied. And great copywriters working with art directors insist that they do. I've seen bitter fights between the copywriter and art director over two versions ended by testing *each.*

What I'd like to get across is that the way you work creatively is only important in that it should be the way suited to *you.* But accepting mediocre work from yourself, your copywriters (regularly employed or freelance), your consultants or your advertising agency is condemning you to mail order failure or, at best, mediocre success.

How good should an advertisement be, whether publication, direct mail or broadcast? An advertisement must be the best that can be made.

Like a good product, a good advertisement can always be made better. The Model T Ford was a good car, the best that could be made for the money at that time. It went 40 miles an hour. You could have it in any color, provided it was black. Later it was not good enough. Today's Taurus is a great car, the best Ford can make for the money at this time. But soon it will not be good enough. Never give up on improving your advertising.

Every sports record was made to be broken. Your advertising can also be made better. Year after year, products thought to be perfect are radically improved. And advertisements, like *anything* created by the human mind, are capable of constant and infinite improvement. The mind does not have the physical limitations of the body.

Yet improvements in advertising often do not keep pace with improvements in products. This is particularly true in good times. When advertising billing is huge and the advertising agency business is booming, new clients can become more tempting than improved advertisements. When ads make money in mail order, it is tempting for the mail order company to stop worrying about further improvements of the advertising.

Even in good times, mail order advertising often fails in initial tests. In times of business adversity, almost all tests can fail. Fortunately, adversity is the mother of improvement.

We have, for our clients, spent many millions of dollars for hundreds of products under the stress of having to make a profit keyed to the advertising. We have had to work under laboratory conditions where the exact sales produced by each form of advertising and each separate advertisement were measured exactly in dollars and cents. It has taught us the hard way that advertising can constantly be improved. Over many years, we have keyed separate advertisements for over 50,000 individual mail order situations. These tests, in each case, recorded exact sales of a separate advertisement in print or broadcast. They covered most units of advertising space from a one-inch ad to a seventeen-page section with return envelope.

We like to think of ourselves as a money-making laboratory. We try to be a laboratory devoted to the development of new techniques to sell more goods at less advertising cost. We think of all our work as one large, continuing experiment to determine exactly what it is that makes certain advertisements more productive than others, and to insure more effective advertising a bigger share of the time.

Others have more experience, with bigger companies, spending many more millions of dollars. Others are technically far more authoritative in specific fields of business, mail order and advertising. Books have been written in far more detail on each of many aspects of mail order and advertising.

We have worked for large companies. In this course, my concern is the practicalities of making money in mail order for the smallest moonlighting entrepreneur. We have already been through the mill ourselves. Thousands of times, we have observed what happened with a specific advertisement.

We have observed what happened when we changed a headline, layout or copy approach and when we cut or expanded copy. We have observed case after case of seemingly slight changes, slight shifts, slight improvements which had startling sales effects.

We try to keep all factors constant but one. We avoid testing different headlines *and* different prices at the same time. We try to be scientific. Scientists can often measure *exactly* what happens each time they change one element of a chemical formula. You can become a mail order scientist measuring exactly what happens when you change one element in an advertisement.

There have been tremendous improvements in recent years in mail order testing methods. Yet many advertisers and some agencies still do not realize exactly what could happen in sales if they slightly changed certain elements of the mail order advertising.

Test after test for product after product has shown conclusively that the apparent difference between overpoweringly effective advertising and ineffective advertising is far slighter than most people have any inkling of. Again and again, seemingly slight variations have made the difference.

That one extra test could make the money, even for a tiny ad. In an inch ad, just putting in a thick dotted line border will sometimes improve results 20% or more. This simple addition attracts more readers. In a tiny ad, *bigger* type in the headline can make a 35% or more difference. It usually more than pays to make a small ad bigger for this purpose. More white space around the headline helps, too. Often a several-line headline asking a question will stop readers and increase orders.

Of course, it's *what* the headline says that determines readership. Just changing to a stronger, more universal product claim can make the difference. In any size or form of ad, there are many ways to improve results.

Execution of any ad, direct mail piece or radio or TV commercial can sometimes be far from the great expectations of the layout, script or audio-video sequence sheet. Fighting to insure that the final effect equals or surpasses your expectations is an unending battle.

Each specialist concerned must realize how vital a contribution he or she can make to perfecting the presentation. Artist, copywriter, announcer, actor or actress, producer, director, special visual or sound effects man, each can help or hinder the final effect. Utilize the special advantages of each form of advertising you employ . . . whether newspapers, direct mail, radio, magazines, television . . . or whatever.

In any mail order or direct response activity you go into, I urge you not to stray from the straight and narrow path of mail order success once you've found a successful test. Just keep doing what you did the first time successfully, and in the same identical way. Never stop testing improvements, but only change your main advertising when you've proven a new changed advertisement or form of advertising.

Never fall in love with a business, a product or an ad. The day you get your first copy of a publication carrying your latest test is usually a thrill. As you read the ad, mesmerized by your own copy, it seems absurd that the ad should be anything but an overwhelming success.

When an ad fails, it's hard to accept the results. The first reaction is to blame the entire thing on the unconscionable slowness of the post office. The next is to search for any reason for the surprising lack of mail; any reason that is outside of the fact that it has bombed out. Your beautiful ad has collapsed.

Take your time. Give the post office every chance to produce a belated avalanche of mail. But finally, read your ads, both sides of a split, again. You will see them with a new eye. Try to analyze why readers didn't buy. They didn't want it, didn't understand it or didn't believe it.

Try to analyze why they might not have wanted it. Does it seem too expensive, too difficult to assemble, too difficult to use, too impractical with too limited benefits? Does it seem to have too *specialized* an appeal? Is the copy clear? Is part of it confusing? Is it offensive? Does it talk woman language to men, grown up talk to children, or hip talk to adults? Does it offer easy enough terms? How about the photographs and art? Did they do what you hoped for in the ad? Would you now use a different picture idea?

Examine the ad element by element. Then go home and sleep on it. Put it aside for days, weeks or months. But don't necessarily give up on it. Your work may yield future benefits. One of the biggest hits we ever had got 40% of break-even on its first test. A partner (one of the top copywriters in the country) had written it. The next day, he rewrote it. The next week, we retested it. And in the next few months, we made several hundred thousand dollars. It could happen to you.

Let's get a little deeper into the science of testing and projecting.

BOOK IV

SELECTION AND NEGOTIATION

*Tactics of tiniest tests
... strategies of safest
projections in
newspapers,
magazines, direct
mail, radio, TV
advertising*

Chapter 1
PSYCHOLOGY BY THE NUMBERS

*Measuring human behavior
reactions . . . media selection . . .
probing firm and flexible rate cards:
asking . . . analyzing . . . deciding*

Testing in mail order is the art of buying information. You are trying to find the answer . . . whether a certain product, price, approach, or offer can make money. It is based on the surprising science of human behavior reactions. If, out of 1,000 people, three or five or 12 can be induced to take a certain action, the same proposal made the same way to another thousand similar people will usually induce approximately the same percentage of people to take the same action. Without that, we'd all be broke. Because of it, you or anyone who gets the "feel" of this science sufficiently can make a mail order fortune. The secret of testing is the ability to buy information at the least cost. All too often, costs of tests are higher than necessary, especially for newcomers . . . and often because of advice from interested parties.

Tests are unprofitable to advertisers, advertising agencies and services involved. All concerned, if asked advice, try to be objective. Yet a small, struggling advertising agency may advise a somewhat larger test ad for a somewhat larger commission. Space salesmen, asked for advice, have difficulty recommending a smaller rather than larger advertisement or a later rather than earlier one. Coming rate increases, closing dates, the possibility of losing a position become reasons to do something that maybe you shouldn't. List brokers, printers, artists, TV producers, time salesmen all want to help, but are tempted to recommend what's good for them, which means more money.

The business of mail order is based on testing items and then fully projecting the successes. The art of mail order is to test in pennies and project in dollars. Every unnecessary dollar spent in a test is the enemy of that art. Spending any more money on one ad test than needed limits other tests.

Ever lower-cost testing is the answer, as is ever closer to maximum projection of hits. If losses on a number of tests are extremely low and projection of one success is major, the profits of the one success can easily wash out all losses of all losing tests and make a handsome overall profit as well. It's amazing how tiny an effective test can be.

Different forms of advertising such as newspapers, TV, magazines and direct mail are called media. Selecting the right media for *your* advertising and getting the right position and the best advertising rates is also an art.

Doing this has been much of my job almost all my business life. Before I bought advertising, I sold it for newspapers, magazines, bus cards and direct mail. I have bought radio advertising and TV advertising both on individual stations and networks. I have bought advertising in newspapers and Sunday newspaper magazines and in general magazines, specialized and trade magazines. I have bought direct mail lists, printing and paper, billing inserts and package inserts. I have bought the hybrid media of direct mail co-ops in newspapers, magazines, and mailings, packages of loose postcards, bound postcard magazines and who knows what.

In buying advertising in any form, much of the secret is getting all and not just some of the facts needed, analyzing these facts and acting on them in the buying decision.

Every time, the method needed to make the right buy is very much the same. If you carefully research the facts and analyze them correctly to buy even a classified ad, you can gradually apply the same approach to larger and larger media buys, each time to your benefit.

Making the right media decision is a matter of media research. This means asking more questions, insisting on getting *full* answers and judging whether these answers make sense. One of the shrewdest buyers of mail order advertising in the country (an old agency client of ours) has made some of the soundest decisions in media I'm familiar with. He simply insists on getting *more* facts – *all* the facts needed – for a media decision. This can be a lot.

Each form of advertising has its own most important questions to ask. But whatever form of advertising you are buying, the selection procedure is much the same. Pitfalls to check into vary by media, as do the comparison points most important to investigate. The need to dig is the same. For each medium, deeper digging means safer buying.

Patient telephoning to other mail order users of the medium considered can uncover important information. Simply ask: What did they sell? How did it pay out? How did results compare with results advertising the same product elsewhere? Often this way you will get some other good buys to consider, too.

In selecting each form of advertising, skilled professionals can help you buy advantageously. But even in media selection, the small agency's resources will be limited. A larger agency specializing in mail order has specialists in different media. In television alone, a top mail order advertising agency can have a number of knowledgeable buyers. The quite small agency will probably have one buyer for all media. The bigger the agency, the better the deals they are in contact with. Unfortunately, they are usually reserved for bigger clients.

As previously explained, your problem as a moonlighter is that it is not profitable for such agencies to handle your account. You may get a smaller agency excellent at media buying, particularly if you find a good one just starting out. You may simply sell your product to a top mail order firm. You may select just *one* form of advertising to start off in. If so, you may get a small advertising agency specializing in that one field. You can succeed in that field and go on to the next.

But however you proceed, it is wise to familiarize yourself with media selection. If you use an advertising agency strong in media selection, this background will be helpful. If not, it will be necessary.

As a small moonlighter, if you use an advertising agency, you *may* end up with a beginner to work with. He may know little more than you do. Or you may get little time from an experienced media buyer. With possible billing small, your desire for lots of information may seem premature to him or her.

If you deal directly with media, you will probably be assigned the newest, least experienced and least informed salesman. He may know nothing of mail order. He may have no idea whether advertising your product in his medium is sensible for you. The temptation for all concerned, including yourself, may be to make a *quick* decision, particularly for a small buy. The very fact that you are dealing with others almost as inexperienced as yourself makes your questions seem an unnecessary waste of time. The salesman wants to make his sale or go make another sale.

Yet only your dredging up necessary facts from him and others can help in your decision. Your job is to sell each person you work with on yourself. Each media salesman you deal with may be able to help you either directly or indirectly with answers you seek. Just cultivating each person involved can help get you more answers. If you don't have ample money, it's vital to devote ample time to make each dollar spent less risky. Asking questions, getting answers and analyzing them is the way to do it. The decisions are usually just plain common sense, once you have all the necessary facts.

Let's consider what you need to know to make a sound media decision. Advertising costs money and delivers readers, listeners and viewers. The number of readers, listeners, and viewers is calculated in determining how much to charge for advertising. In magazines and newspapers, this is usually on the basis of the total *paid* circulation: subscribers and newsstand buyers. However, research is often done and quoted on numbers of actual readers (rather than buyers), including "pass along" circulation. This is usually for the purpose of justifying rates. Mail order media buyers usually simply calculate the cost per thousand paid circulation.

Radio and TV rates for individual stations are different for different arbitrary time classifications. These rates are usually based on the amount of listeners or viewers averaged out for each time classification. Research surveys to determine the actual tune-in of listeners and viewers are quoted to justify these rates.

The rates are determined by human beings and not always with perfect logic. A small moonlighter making his first test has little chance to negotiate better than quoted rates. He can decide whether to pay it or not advertise. For larger advertisers, the "rate card" is strictly adhered to by some media businesses and less so by others. A magazine publisher will sometimes be more flexible than a newspaper publisher and a broadcaster more so than a magazine publisher. We'll discuss negotiating rates later.

All you have learned so far will help you in making sound media buying decisions. The item you select will be more logical for one form of advertising than another. The advertising presentation that you develop will give it a better chance in one form of advertising than another. The price you sell at will help determine the most logical advertising medium to select. The right price can differ in different media. The price ideal in one medium can be suicide in another. The medium that you advertise in must be suited to the item and price that you sell it at.

The National Enquirer is a "shot gun" mass medium. For total number of people reached, it's a rare bargain. The lower-cost the product you advertise in it, the bigger the percentage of the total circulation that can afford it.

A "solo" piece in direct mail is a super accurate rifle, hopefully aimed at exactly the prospects you're after. It costs far, far more per thousand reached. Usually, higher-priced items ideally suited to the list do better. With each postage and printing price increase, the average price of successful direct mail items goes higher.

Radio and TV require the low-price, common denominator item that the National Enquirer does. The average newspaper and mass circulation magazine is suited to a slightly higher-priced item. Highly specialized magazines sometimes are suited to the same priced items as those successful in direct mail to similar audiences.

Even the same people can best be sold *differently* priced products when reached in different ways.

The American Express credit card has five million members. You can reach members via Travel and Leisure magazine, via inserts in bills sent out monthly or via "solo" direct mail kits mailed out separately to the list. You can reach a thousand members via the magazine for a fraction of the cost to reach the same thousand members via billing inserts. And the use of billing inserts is a fraction of the cost to reach the same thousand with a direct mail "solo" piece.

The most desirable retail price of an article offered in the magazine is lower than via inserts and substantially lower than via the "solo" direct mail piece. This is so true that American Express direct mail specialists in their own mail order division have told me there is very little correlation between what sells successfully in the magazine and what sells successfully via their "solo" pieces.

This means that each mail order article you sell, by its very retail price, is *limited* somewhat as to how and where and to whom it can best be advertised. Trying to sell the *right* article at the *right* price but in the wrong place for that price is like trying to put a square peg in a round mail order hole.

Media testing works hand in hand with product selection, developing price and offer and advertising creation. Here's how.

Chapter 2

SPLIT-RUN UNIVERSITY

The mail order laboratory . . . testing
half circulation one way . . . half the
other . . . keying results . . .
limitations

In mail order, partners need not argue about advertising. It is simpler to test. It is easy to try out either partner's preferred way in regards to copy, price or offer, each tested in a separate ad and keyed separately. Then count the mail.

On television or radio, it's possible to select two different times with about the same viewing or listening audience and try one commercial one way and one another way and compare results. We've done it many times. In publication advertising and in direct mail advertising, it's possible to do so more accurately with a split-run ad. Half the circulation gets ad "A" and half gets ad "B." The best offer or ad wins.

Anything in the ad can be tested this way: two different headlines, two different prices, one giveaway or two different giveaways, two different pictures on top, different items, different body copy, a buried offer of a free booklet deep in copy versus none or whatever. In each case, all other elements but the two being tested should be kept identical. Testing, keyed and measured, has taught us most of what we know. We never stop testing and learning.

Tests teach us how changes in ads can increase profits, often seemingly slight changes and surprisingly big profit jumps.

A first test is sometimes quite a borderline success. Every mail order man can tell you stories of an apparently minor change made in a later test that skyrocketed results in the more successful half of a splitrun test. Many mail order fortunes have been made this way.

For a publishing client, we once created a mail order ad we were proud of. It made quite a modest profit. But it was losing money and here's why. In a split-run, an improved advertisement, telling a more complete story, upped sales 22% and made 56% more profit than the first advertisement. And yet this improved advertisement was still losing money. Here's why. A further improved advertisement with a new approach in a split-run jumped sales exactly 320% and earned

600% more profit than the second advertisement. And yet this further improved advertisement was still losing money. Here's why. A still further improved advertisement, without changing a word of copy, made 82% per dollar more profits than the third advertisement. This was the advertisement used in the final projection of this campaign.

In each test, the offer was the same, with every ad element frozen but those of copy, layout and illustration. In each test, the publication and position were the same. Each ad in each split stayed approximately within the same product claims. But for the ad creating 600% more profit the presentation was in editorial style. It was a complete departure from a book ad, without even a book illustration. For the ad creating a further 82% improvement, the editorial style was also used but changed somewhat. In this split, every word of the copy of each ad tested was identical.

For the second ad, our art director carefully studied the typography and format of the paper selected for the test. In the rearranged ad, the headline and main pictures were actually made smaller. The type was reset to conform even more to the newspaper's own style for its stories. That was all. I have seen this same sort of transformation of profits in other cases as well. Continued improvement of advertising produced continued improvement of profits.

For other editorial-style ads, we've taken special news-type photos of the kind more often used in such a story. For different papers, we have kept headline ad subheads to sizes used in that publication. In each case, we've used the closest equivalent type face permitted to that of the publication. We've split-run the more editorial ads against somewhat less editorial ads. In each split, the version of the ad most authentically identical to a news story in that publication out-pulled the other. This was so even when the changes were not too great. We never stop splitrunning possible improvements for ads. And we never stop being surprised at how dramatic those improvements can sometimes be.

We ran a full tabloid page split-run test to determine the most profitable price to sell an article used by automobile owners. A prior test had been slightly unprofitable. Identical copy and layout was used for *both* sides of the split. Only the price differed. In one half of the split, the price was 50% higher for a slightly more deluxe product. Every other paper carried the alternate advertisement. The unchanged price half of the split broke even. The other half produced one more order and over *50 percent more* revenue. Advertising cost was the same. Product cost was almost the same. The higher-price half of the split made a good profit. It was run elsewhere at an equally good profit. Simply raising the price transformed a formerly unprofitable campaign into a good profit one.

You can only consider selling on any terms but cash if you are financially and logistically equipped to do so. If you are, it's still wise to test alternate terms to determine which will produce the most profit for your product. We often do. We keep price and other factors identical and test alternative items such as:

Cash vs. cash or credit card.

Cash or credit card vs. cash or direct credit one payment.

Cash or direct credit one payment vs. cash or direct credit time payment.

Cash or direct credit time payment vs. direct credit one payment or direct credit time payment.

Let's assume that cash, or cash or credit card, pays out, but cash or charge, or charge or time payment pays out significantly better, assuming reasonable collection and returns. In this case, we immediately start projection of the cash, or cash or credit card offer. Meanwhile, we wait for verification of the hoped-for answer on collections and returns. If collections and returns are each in line in the cash or charge, or charge or time payment offers, we switch to the winning terms.

For direct credit orders it takes considerable time to get the answer on collections and returns, particularly on time payments. Orders may come in at a low selling cost. A good percentage may take a cash option (for a saving or giveaway in return for full cash payment). You may have a satisfactory collection history from similarly priced items sold via similar circulation or lists. If so, it's worth considering projecting before verifying. We, being small and conservative, prefer to wait. We like to verify that we really are collecting the money. We like to be sure that bad credit figures are within our original estimates. We like to know that returns are within our estimate percentage. If all this is so, we can then go ahead.

Factors that are vitally important are these. Does the copy *oversell?* If so, bad credit and returns can be out of line. Does the product *completely satisfy* the customer? Otherwise, bad credit and returns can be catastrophic. Is the collection series used too weak or too strong? If too weak, bad credit can be overly high. If too strong, it can step up returns. That's why we prefer to wait for final test answers. It's slow. Conditions may change radically while we wait. But overall, it's safer.

Simply changing the space size tripled profits per dollar spent in advertising for one client, a thread company. For this client, we tested four space units. One was two inches. One was a 56-line, single-column advertisement. Another was a 200-line ad, a 100-line on two-column advertisement. The last ad was a full tabloid page 1,000-line advertisement.

The basic offer was identical in all advertisements, although more items in the line were featured in the larger space advertisements. The 56-line ad was more profitable per dollar of advertising than the two-inch ad. The 200-line ad was more profitable than the 56-line ad. The full-page tabloid ad was by far the best per dollar. The increased sales per dollar of the biggest versus those of the smallest was about three to one.

For other products and other clients, other size units have sometimes proved most profitable per dollar of advertising spent. Finding the best size advertisement for your product can make a big difference in your mail order life.

We ran a split-run test for an automotive safety product. One of the advertisements featured a problem-and-solution illustration. The difficulty this product guarded against was illustrated, and the product's use was clearly illustrated. The headline was a simple promise. The other advertisement featured an exceptionally dramatic accident photograph. It was a real stopper. The headline was a powerful fear headline. Both appeared in alternate copies of the same newspaper on the same page. The product, offer, publication and body copy were the same.

Fear lost. The non-fear ad pulled 48% more sales than the other. It produced 65% more profit. We've been afraid of fear ever since.

Often a price reduction ad is successful. But never assume so. A price reduction ad yields you *less* gross profit per sale than selling at the higher price. It may give less gross profit from your advertising or even cause a loss. So each price reduction ad must be tested before being projected.

Different elements of ads can be tested in a split run by freezing all other elements. Featuring a giveaway can be tested. The results can surprise you. Often giveaways are selected *without* scientific testing. Time is short. It is assumed that the giveaway *must* help. One is selected arbitrarily and all tests made on other elements.

The benefit of a giveaway should not be taken for granted. Offering a giveaway can actually *reduce* sales or gross profit compared with offering *none*. And if one giveaway is *proven* to increase gross profit, another may do so even more. Each should be tested, with all other key elements of the advertising as identical as possible. One giveaway may take less advertising space or time than another, and no giveaway takes less space than any.

We like to test a giveaway first on its own . . . selling it, itself, as a mail order item. If it won't sell by itself at a price, it's rarely an effective giveaway. If it does sell by itself and we sell it widely enough as a mail order item, then we have established a known retail value. We can then state that it has sold nationally at this price, but is now a *gift* with the purchase.

Often a giveaway, self-liquidator or partial liquidator can also be tested as an add-on at full retail price. An add-on can help considerably or *hurt*. If you get as many basic orders with it as without it, plus some add-ons, you're ahead of the game. But sometimes tests show fewer orders and less total gross profit with the add-on than without it. This can be so if a large size of an item costs far more. The add-on can sometimes cause the prospective customer to decide that he or she *needs* the large size but can't afford it and that the regular size is *insufficient*. The same effect can be caused by an add-on of a deluxe version that is a good deal higher priced than the regular model. The deluxe version may seem to be the good one, but the price may seem more than the prospective customer cares to pay, while the offer of the deluxe may cause the prospective buyer to conclude that the regular model is *inferior* and decide against it. Each add-on must be tested before projection is safe.

A guarantee can be broad and simple or very specific and detailed. How will each affect sales? Testing can tell exactly. Our tests have proved that far more mail order profit is lost by failure to emphasize and repeat the guarantee than by additional returns as a result of a guarantee. Our tests have also proved that a simpler guarantee is good business as well as a builder of good will. But test it yourself.

Compare simplicity with the added protection to you of spelling your guarantee out in maximum detail. Simplicity probably means more sales and customer good will. Spelling out limitations probably means fewer orders, but a smaller refund percentage.

Make a split-run test in publications or direct mail advertising with all elements identical except the guarantee. Run the simpler guarantee in one-half of the test and the more qualified guarantee in the other half. If the simpler guarantee wins, run a confirming test. If it still wins, run it in enough advertising to get over 500 purchasers. Key the guarantee certificates differently thereafter. Watch defective returns under the guarantee. If, after the guarantee period, defective returns are within your estimate, then make the terms of the guarantee your permanent policy. If not, your alternatives are to tighten the guarantee or drop the product. Usually the defective returns are the product's fault, and the simpler and broader guarantee only spotlights them. Otherwise, with the broader and simpler guarantee, any disappointment is rarely great enough to increase returns.

It is practical to make clear and reasonable limitations in your guarantee. It's important to do so for higher-price items.

Department store customers sometimes return purchases . . . more so for more expensive items, still more if bought on credit and most often for items bought on time payments. A person who buys via mail order from an unknown firm may be more tempted to return a purchase. Often the return is only after being billed for months.

No company can risk shipping unlimited amounts of high-ticket items as a perpetual loan to people who constantly postpone their final decision as to whether to buy or return the item and meanwhile don't pay for it. The longer payment is postponed, the greater is the possibility that it will never be paid. In this case, the inertia is against you. The first reaction by such a customer to a strong credit collection follow-up system is to return the item. We have emphasized earlier that only after determining from test orders that the percentage of returns and bad credit is within anticipated estimates is it safe to project.

Because inquiry and conversion selling is more complex, it requires more testing. You can never stop testing ways of lowering lead cost and increasing lead volume. And with each success, you must become suspicious of the effect on lead quality, and test that, too.

Going to four-color can be overwhelmingly more effective or the disappointment of your life. Extra color costs must pull proportionately extra orders.

Some products seem overwhelmingly suited to color. Garden products seem so. Yet for a fertilizer, we arranged an unusual split-run test, half in color and half in black and white. We pulled more orders from the black and white version than from the identical ad in four-color. In black and white, it had an editorial look. In color, it did not.

Color can be a temptress luring us into test costs that we did not originally contemplate and perhaps cannot afford. A product or product use picture can look so stunning in four-color that its black and white advertising seems drab and lifeless. Only a test of full color versus black and white can prove how much of a difference four-color will really make.

The cost of any testing in color escalates. The cost of running a color ad can be substantially more than that of running the same ad in black and white. Even where running in color produces more orders, your color ad can lose money by not producing enough more orders.

For moonlighters, the sound plan in considering color advertising is to crawl before you walk. Test black and white advertising. If successful, project and make profits. If tempted by color then, test in color with part of the black and white profits. If your product seems to require color, and black and white advertising is useless, only test if you have the money to lose or can get around the cost in some way.

Sometimes you can get your four-color test free. A catalog may purchase your item, photograph at its own expense in four-color and run it in four-color as part of a four-color page. Sometimes extra color shots are taken, and the rejects can be obtained for nothing or for very little.

It's sometimes possible to save much of the risk of color tests. You may have available to you at no cost the color separations or engravings, or at least color transparencies, and not realize it.

If you import, your exporter may have them. If you buy from a manufacturer, he may have them. You may have them for another purpose for retail packaging, in trade literature or in a direct mail piece. If so, you may be able to save much of the production cost of testing color in your advertising.

Some publications run mail order shopping section color pages where you can test a small-space color ad with minimum production expense. This is often a safer way to explore the possibilities of color for your product.

When you project a successful test, you may need to make changes to fit different sizes of ads. It is important to avoid changes without testing and to not make any change carelessly. Radical changes can create quite different ads which can have quite different results.

A magazine you are considering may be smaller or larger than the page size your successful ad ran in. You may be offered a bargain in a somewhat different space size. You may have a right-hand coupon and be offered a left-hand page at a bargain. You may be offered a premium position if you will put your coupon *on top* so that it will not be back-to-back with another coupon.

The more radical the change is, the more dangerous it can be to run the changed ad without testing. The bigger the publication, the greater the possibility is that such a change may be needed. You may be trying to meet a closing date deadline. You may not realize the possible effect of a change on your mail pull.

You may be considering a TV Guide-size page vs. your successful Time-size page. If the reduction cuts copy, it may be wise to test the smaller version before running it widely, or you might consider running a TV Guide-size double page in place of a Time-size single page. In a magazine like TV Guide you can test a single page vs. a double page in several small local editions. Both tests can be in the same issue.

Many smart mail order men test even minor changes before projecting them. Be cautious. Go a little slower. Better be safe and test than sorry. But it's time now to discuss some of the practical limitations of testing.

Mail order is an *imperfect* science. Given more time and more money, mail order can be more and more of a perfect science. The problem is more often a slight shortage of the necessary time and money. Time is always short. Tests may not be worth your while if test costs become too excessive. There is always a race to get a "hit," project a "hit," make a season, beat competition or whatever. Testing takes time. Testing more elements takes more time. Test information gained after a competitor has won the race often has little value.

Every test costs money. Production cost for many ads tested is greater than advertising cost. A split-run test of two completely different ads can double test production cost. For elaborate color ads, production cost often runs far ahead of advertising space cost. Small ads usually can't be split-run except in geographical splits.

Testing in newspapers is more difficult than formerly. Fewer newspapers offer split-runs. Many of these newspapers have increased their production charges (aside from advertising cost) for split-runs. Newspaper advertising costs for mail order advertisers have often risen proportionately higher than have magazine advertising costs. Therefore, fewer newspapers now have acceptable costs per thousand for mail order advertisers. Newspaper pages per issue have increased greatly, and proportionately more in advertising than in editorial. Therefore, small ads now have more tendency to become lost in newspapers.

At the same time, newspapers in the biggest cities have more and more been offering remnant space R.O.P., meaning run of paper, which in turn means wherever there's open space. We have found such buys often to be excellent, and we use them regularly. They are usually only available in larger ads in standard sizes of quarter, half and full page.

We avoid geographical splits, where part of the circulation in one geographical area carries one ad and the remaining circulation runs the alternate ad. This is because one part of the circulation might go mainly to lower-income areas and another part mainly to higher-income areas, and the split would teach us nothing. We use "true splits" only, in which special presses print every other copy with the alternate ad. This means that, for a split run ad in a newspaper, every other copy of the paper on each newsstand, wherever sold, will carry the alternate ad. In this case, exactly half the circulation in each geographical area gets each alternate ad.

If, as a moonlighter, you only advertise in small space in newspapers and magazines, you may never get into split runs at all. It is only possible for ads larger than a minimum size, varying by publication.

Production charges are usually higher in relation to space advertising cost for minimum-size split-run ads. Split-run direct mail tests can sometimes be practical in small circulation.

As a moonlighter, your tests will probably be small and sometimes inadequate for a final decision. A successful small test needs to be confirmed by a more adequate bigger test. If, in a split-run test in a newspaper of 50,000 circulation, one ad is 25% better, it's worth a confirming test.

Retest the same split in one or more papers (not the original paper) comprising 150,000 to 250,000 circulation. If the same half is again successful, split-test once more. This time, test still different papers comprising 700,00 to 800,000 circulation. If the last test confirms, project the winner.

In direct mail, follow a similar procedure. Elaborate color mailing kits are far more expensive per thousand in small runs. Therefore, large mailers often jump to a million mailing after the very first test. That's why, for most moonlighters, full-color direct mail is prohibitively expensive.

If a test that you expect to succeed fails, don't be surprised. It happens. But take nothing for granted. Results can occasionally be *tilted* by conditions in that area or at that time.

Houston, Texas, was hardly touched by a major recession when the rest of the country was suffering. A winner in a test in Houston was a *loser* nationally. Conditions were not the same. A very few years later, Texas was hurting badly while business was excellent in much of the rest of the country.

Check conditions at the time and place of your test. Did anything unusual occur? When a President is shot, marches into a far-off country or starts or stops a cold war, mail order results can fall off for a few days or weeks. Check the position in the publication. Check the weather; super hot weather or a snowed-in condition cuts mail orders. Check the competition that day and for weeks before. What looks like the same product at half the price can decimate your mail order results. Was there an error in the coupon? Was there a contradiction in the terms? If in doubt, retest.

Test in *several* sections representative of different parts of the country. Too small a circulation split-run test may not be a sufficient sample. The more expensive an item, the fewer orders you need to pay off. The smaller the number of orders involved, the less adequate is the sample. We run in at least a million circulation to confirm the results of any initial test.

Being overly frugal in test ad production costs may destroy your test. Your ad may look entirely unlike your layout if you resort to publication-set typography. Your pictures and art may be so bad as to keep people from buying. Watch your money, but be professional. One half of the split may be a more professionally *finished* ad than the other and *tilt* your results.

We will test a lower-priced item first in a circulation of several hundred thousand or more. We prefer to test an item selling for $50 or more first in an upscale circulation of 100,000 or more. A less-than-adequate test is better than none. If it fails, not too much is lost. If it pays off, there is little further risk to running a confirming test. The poor results of too small a sample test can cause you to stop further testing. But giving up on testing is more apt to come from poorly made tests or failure to analyze each test properly. The more soundly you select, research and create an ad for your product and the more sensible a media selection you make, the safer your test becomes.

Avoid spending too much on your test. Budget an allowable total for test expenditures. If you're small, you must do so or go broke. This means that you will never have enough money to test all the things you'd like to. Start testing with part of your savings. If successful, project your success and confine future testing to a percentage of actual mail order profits already made. This is realistic. It means each success that you get and project creates a budget for more testing.

Here's what makes mail order an art. First, it's the ability to select most important elements to test. Second, it's to project most safely without unlimited time and money. You should also avoid giving up after an inadequate test or after any test of any ad you have doubts about.

We try never to give up on anything we have faith in, yet not to throw good dollars after bad. We try to put aside an unsuccessful test for a time. Doing so clears the head and gives perspective. A later post mortem going over product, copy, offer and conditions and time of test can sometimes cause us to come up with a new approach. Periodically, we do this. The more faith in the product we have, the more frequently we take another look. Sometimes, months or years later, we come up with a successful test from our earlier failure. Conditions are constantly changing, giving one product less chance and another more. If we observe change and analyze which of our old failures have a new chance because of change, it becomes time to consider a new test.

Ideally, testing should be objective. Your faith in the product is subjective, but it is a most important ingredient. But wishing for success can cause misinterpretation of test results. There is no point to testing if you cannot face the facts of a test. A failure must be faced as a failure. If you test and fail and project anyway, you can lose a lot of money. If you test in too elaborate a fashion because of conviction that it will pay out, you will risk bigger loss than necessary. If you keep testing a proven failure, you will probably keep failing.

Some very successful mail order people drop a product after an unsuccessful test as though with burnt fingers, and never test it again. They have found that, on the average, there is less risk to testing something new and different.

You can get *testitis*, testing anything and everything and falling in love with testing itself. This can be an expensive hobby that can put a moonlighter out of business. Testing is only for the purpose of coming up with a *hit* with the least money and in the fastest time.

A moonlighter starting out may have very little money. Only some of it can be risked on testing. Thereafter, even if you have success, profits may come slowly. Testing will need to be very limited indeed. Each test will need to be kept to smallest cost and risk. Of all the tests you'd like to make, you only make some, and at first maybe only *one*.

Our method is to establish *priorities* for testing. We constantly make "A", "B" and "C" lists for tests of those items, offers and ads we want to test. Those we feel have the best chance we put under "A" and so forth. Changing situations may cause us to move a test candidate from one list to the other or to drop it from all three lists.

By selecting our best "A" list candidate for our first test, we feel we have a better chance and keep testing risk down to a sensible minimum. If we're making more money, we test more, and if less, we test less. If we're losing money, we stop testing, because at this point we would be using *principal* and not income to test.

A mail order moonlighter must keep tests small and occasionally stop testing completely. When you make money again, start testing again with part of the money. It's necessary to *earn* the *right* to test. If an ad unexpectedly makes $1,000, you might take $300 of it to test with.

A sale to a catalog house may make an unexpected modest profit. You can then spend some of it for a long-desired test. We have been able to keep testing without using principal for a number of years, and we hope to keep it that way.

Trying to make it happen can cause test losses. This might break the heart of a determined salesman, but it is so. You may *want* a test to succeed and need it to succeed. But fighting for a test to succeed by a certain date or in a certain way or place can cause a test to become less scientifically and objectively conducted. Christmas items don't sell as well in July. Few people fish in December. Advertising too late or too early for many seasonal products can bring in very little response, despite your desires.

So take it easy when you test. Try not to be too intense. Try to work on another project when your important test is coming up. Watched pots sometimes don't boil. Tests I count on to succeed often fail. Ones I never expected to make it pay off. We don't decide. And what difference does it make which works, as long as one does? The idea is to go with the tide, not to command the waves.

The purpose of testing is to come up with something to project. And when you succeed in a test, the time comes to project. A development engineer sometimes seems never to want to make the product. He seems just to want to keep improving it. The same can be true of a mail order man fallen in love with testing. At some point the airplane must fly. The time comes to run the ads that are succeeding. We try never to stop improving our advertising, but only with part of the profits and only aside from projection of the most profitable advertising we already have. And when a moonlighter succeeds in a test, he needs to *go*. He needs those profits quickly. But he needs to go carefully and thoroughly.

Let's consider the safest ways to start.

Chapter 3

MOONLIGHTER
ADVENTURES IN SPACE

Truths . . . surprises . . . quirks . . .
buying newspaper, magazine ads
from classified to pages . . . favored
positions . . . "remnants

Don't pay for it if you can get it FREE.

The safest way for a moonlighter to start is with free advertising.

In my book, Mail Order Know-How, I tell the story of The Old House Journal, a newsletter which for years got much of its circulation from inquiries about an editorial write-up which offered a free checklist of what to look at when buying an old house.

If you have effective follow-up literature, and if your item sells for over $30, a free write-up asking for inquiries may well be quite profitable. Only do this in a small magazine once, until you see that your inquiries can be closed with your literature in sufficient percentage to be profitable after the cost of mailing. Be particularly cautious of "bingo card" inquiries. These are post cards inserted in the publication and addressed to the publication with numbers printed on it. Each number is also printed at the end of each ad and write-up. The reader circles the numbers of write-ups and ads he or she is interested in. The post card requests more information. The publication's computer service types up labels for each name for as many numbers as circled and forwards them to the proper company. In consumer publications, "bingo" inquiries are sometimes of too poor quality to be worth mailing literature to. But in trade magazines, such inquiries often do convert to sales.

How would you like to make your product a major editorial item?

Years ago, the Curtis Publishing Company sold $1,700,000 of one such mail order editorial item. It was a creative stitchery kit for a grandfather clock. I have seen magazines like American Home sell $70,000 worth of new creative stitchery designs mail order from an editorial feature in a single issue.

Such items are featured by the magazine as an editorial service to readers. A real effort is made to bring an item to the reader as a value and a bargain. It is usually featured in full color, often in full-page space. I've seen a science magazine feature a boat kit with a picture of a one-man speedboat on the front cover and a story on the kit inside, with fabulous results.

The editorial department selects such items. If you're a designer and they like your work, they may give you design ideas to complete. They want you to make a fair return and will offer to work with you again if a promotion succeeds. They're extremely knowledgeable and cooperative and often help you develop a greatly improved product. They use the finest photographers and writers to picture and describe your item. The color separations alone that they invest in for your product might be otherwise beyond your reach. But they are paying for everything, and you are not risking anything.

Warning! Their interest is in *talent*. You must really have a flair for design and an exciting concept in the kinds of items they feature.

Consider starting with a classified ad. A surprising number of small mail order enterprises have started in just this way. My upcoming book, The Mail Order Underground, tells the story of small entrepreneurs, almost all moonlighters, who started in business for the price of dinner and sometimes breakfast . . . with a classified ad. Let's suppose you have an item you've written such a classified ad for.

Go back to the library. Glance again through magazines. This time look for those which carry classified ad sections. Look at Grit, the science magazines, Work Basket and every magazine you can find carrying such ads.

Look at the business opportunities columns of the New York Times and the Wall Street Journal, at outdoor magazines and underground newspapers. Look for those which carry items most similar to yours. You'll find some selling extremely specialized and quite low-cost items. Others seek inquires for exotic or specialized items or catalogs. You'll find it fascinating to read these tiny ads. Just one can launch a new venture.

Reading them is a perpetual course on new items, copy and media. Note which ads repeat regularly in issue after issue. These items are probably profitable. Note each publication that seems logical for your item.

Now phone or write the publication. Ask for rate cards for classified ads and case histories of successes. Ask particularly for the names of the longest running advertisers. These publications usually sell their mail order classified ads by mail order. Therefore, they can send you full information. Of those publications, which seems *most* logical for you, with the strongest success stories? Select the *cheapest.* It will probably be a very small risk.

However, please note that most ads ask for inquiries, not sales. Your chances for success with an inquiry offer are probably several times greater than your chances of selling any item outright.

This possibility is dependent on whether you have such an offer and have created effective direct mail follow-up. A tiny mail order firm selling fisherman fly-tying materials may be able to get qualified inquiries in considerable quantity using classified ads in fishing and outdoor magazines. To succeed, a superior line of fly-tying kits is needed and equally superior follow-up literature for any inquiries secured. One without the other is useless. But the same firm might fail if it attempted to sell the same fly-tying kit in one step in a classified ad.

Tiny classified ads are great for smoking out people genuinely interested in highly specialized activities. If you've come up with a product or service for such an activity, you can get started with a classified ad. Your follow-up and catalog can be the simplest, even photo-set typewriter type with no illustrations. If the interest is there, it will work for a start.

Don't worry how small your beginnings are. A mail order test success can be on a microscopic scale and lead to a big business. If you have very little money, you can only afford a tiny test. Three hundred photo-set, simple letters can pull enough orders to self-liquidate and show a profit. Of course, it's an inadequate test. But who cares if you have no alternative?

A four-line classified ad in one day's insertion can pull $1, $2, $3 or more orders for a booklet you write, type and photocopy yourself. Gamble your time more than your money. Work for months to get the perfect item. Labor over the copy for weeks. Do it yourself or team up on a profit sharing basis with the best mail order copywriter you can find. The more you risk your time, the less you'll risk your money.

And the tiniest display ad that produces a profit for $57 risk or less can be run more places and repeated. The tiniest success can quickly make enough profit to pay cash in advance for your next tiny ad. And as soon as you have provable success in several publications, you can get credit from first one publication, then others . . . and then from a small advertising agency.

Let's consider what to investigate in buying various kinds of display advertising . . . ads bigger than classified ads.

You might expect that any advertising in a newspaper or magazine would cost the same for anybody. It often doesn't. One kind of business may pay one price. Another kind may pay another price. Small users of each kind pay one price and large users another. This varies in application. Sometimes the lower price is for running more total advertising, sometimes for greater frequency of advertising and sometimes a little of each. Each rate card may have its own odd little quirks, charging a higher rate for this classification and a lower rate for that one.

One newspaper in a city may have a lower rate than a competitor in one classification, and a higher rate in another. Various newspapers under the same ownership can have quite different policies on rates for the same classification. When free-standing inserts (usually a postcard thickness brochure) were first put into newspapers for advertisers, one newspaper of one ownership charged over twice as much for each thousand inserts as another paper of the same ownership.

Retailers with substantial lineage contracts usually have far lower rates than one-time mail order advertisers, and often substantially lower than large mail order advertisers. Retail rates in one city may be far lower than national rates and, in another city, far less so. Lowest retail rates in the main section of a newspaper can be far lower than lowest national rates, and in the magazine section of the same newspaper be virtually the same as the lowest rates for national advertising. Retail rates are usually quoted net with no allowance for an advertising agency. National rates are usually quoted *gross*, with 15% commissionable to the agency. And with little trouble, you can organize your advertising agency and receive that 15%.

Newspapers normally will set type for your ads without charge. Magazines will not. This is because newspapers have a staff to set type. Magazines do not, and so must buy the typesetting.

In newspaper or magazine advertising, your first objectives are to create the most effective ad possible and to place your ad in the most perfect publication for it. If so, running the ad once is an adequate test.

Running more times usually gets *worse* results each time, contrary to space salesman talk about the cumulative effect of repeating. There are exceptions. In the last 12 months, we have had a quite successful one-third-page ad for a very successful item. We have run it eight to ten times and more in the same publication. By improving the offer and copy, we actually increased the response of later ads. But this was unusual. More often, the only time you will see cumulative build-up of orders is when you do not key repeat ads separately. Cumulative effect helps store distribution products, but not in bigger mail order ads. The first ad usually pulls best, the second usually worse, the third usually still worse and so on.

I have known some mail order men who have profitably repeated by reducing ad sizes. They ran the biggest ad the first time. They repeated with an ad perhaps 60% of the size of the first. They then repeated again with an ad perhaps 50% of the size of the second. We seldom do this, because it requires more production cost than we care for and we find it difficult to follow widely as a formula with uniform results.

An exception to such drop-off can be a seasonal item. If you run too early, results are worse. If you run two or three months in a row ... in January, February and March for a fishing item, for example ... your March ad will pull best, February second best and January least. This is not cumulative effect. If you skip January, you will do better in February and March. If you skip January and February, you'll do still better in March. A very strong seasonal item will benefit from running each of the three months. But there is no point in testing the same ad more than once in the same publication.

Big ads drop off more than small ads. Very small ads drop off the least and therefore can be repeated the most.

Position can mean profit or loss for an ad. Not asking for any position usually means obtaining the worst position, although sometimes you get a pleasant surprise. One position can produce dramatically more orders than another. A full rate plus premium cost in a premium position can sometimes be more profitable than a cost considerably below rate card for a "back of the book" Siberia position.

Many bigger ads can only pay out in prime position and will not otherwise. A back cover may cost 30% to 40% more than inside space, yet produce 50% to 150% more for it. And some back covers cost only 25% more or even less. Alert small mail order advertisers who pay out in a new, small magazine may have a chance at a back cover just by asking for it. Some publications will give the holder of a premium position the same position for the same month or week, and even the following year – if the advertiser orders enough in advance.

This means that stability and advance planning can pay off for small, new mail order advertisers. New publications constantly appear.

If successful, each is an opportunity for a prime position franchise for years to come. Some mail order advertiser who fails to come up with new winners will relinquish a position. Therefore, while it first seems that large advertisers monopolize most desirable positions, this need not be so. I've seen my products on back covers of huge circulation publications with giant advertisers *inside*, simply because I patiently waited in line but kept *asking* for the position. This has occurred after I anticipated the possibility of a major company cancellation due to a strike, etc.

The smaller an ad is, the greater the response variation can be for good or bad position. Position on the right-hand page is favored. Position on the outside column is preferred, the higher the better. Upper right-hand position is favored. The "gutter", inside left-hand column bottom on a right-hand page or inside right-hand column bottom on a left-hand page, is least effective. It not only is less read, but is more awkward to tear out. However, the editorial matter on the page greatly affects pulling power. Gutter position next to a top editorial feature can be *excellent.*

Favored page positions are back cover, then second cover (back of front cover), then third cover (inside of back cover). After that comes the page facing second cover, which may be page number one. Then come pages three, five and seven. Some favor the page facing third cover ahead of these. After that, it's usually the earliest-right hand page. A bound-in postcard will usually make a magazine flip to that page when opened, thus creating a premium position. If the postcard is with a single page ad, the ad on the left hand page opposite seems to benefit, as does the right-hand page following the bound-in card page.

In a newspaper with many sections, there are wider choices of position and rate. You may run in the New York Times magazine mail order section. Or you might run further forward in the New York Times magazine, outside of the magazine mail order section, but at the same magazine rate. If a boat item, a business item or a stamp item, there are other sections to consider.

We find that products for men often do well in the sports section, and those for women do well in the magazine. We find that smaller ads in the magazine do better in the mail order section of the magazine, and bigger ads do better outside of it. We find that small ads and large ads in the New York Times do well in the most related section. We find that small ads can do well in such a section and in the magazine section as well, even on the same day. The Sunday Times is such a job to read that many tackle just part of it, often resulting in non-duplication between two sections for a good deal of the readership. A book on any how-to subject may do well in the book section. The magazine is *higher* priced, but it is read by more purchasers of the Times than other sections and is worth the higher price. Other big-city papers have similar differences.

The fatter the magazine is, the more likely you are to suffer from a "back of the book" position. This is usually combined with a higher cost per thousand for mail order advertisers than some other magazines. Less successful magazines often give better position and a better mail order rate per thousand. Sometimes, for this reason, they pay out better than the favorite.

Each advertising buy you make must be not only in a publication, on a station or whatever that has produced profitably for others, it must be suitable to *your* kind of product. Some products are suited to a highly specialized hobby publication and do very badly in a general publication. The great opportunity for you is the existence of many specialized places to advertise in. There are magazines for virtually every interest. Direct mail lists are more specialized still. There are items that do well in outdoor magazines, and those appealing to men only, women only, young women only, teenagers, young boys, children, businessmen or covering other special interests.

We have sometimes lost money trying to turn a nice, small, profitable offer, proven successful in special markets, into a more universal mass offer. Some offers will succeed in small space and fail in big ads. Some items sell mainly to rich people, others mostly to low-income groups. It's amazing how comfortably profitable it can be to sell something only in computer magazines or in Ebony or just in Cosmopolitan, just in Work Basket, just Grit or perhaps only projected into the most similar media. Limited objectives can give you limited income year after year, perhaps lifelong. A lot of mail order losses come simply from pushing a good offer into places it shouldn't be. Any mail order moonlighter is best off to limit objectives to start. The empire can come later.

Newspapers are usually firm in their rates. This means they usually get the rates they quote and will not bargain for more reductions. For a newspaper (or magazine), more advertising means more pages, and less advertising, fewer pages. They are not caught with unsold space. Sometimes some paper will quote a "remnant rate" for certain size ads in certain sections. A "remnant rate," sometimes called "standby," is an ad that gets a lower rate if, at the last minute before closing date, it is needed to fill out a section of pages otherwise requiring editorial material. Other than that, newspapers, while keeping their rate card, may wink at some ways of getting around it. A mail order advertiser may pass on a saving to another by having an ad for another run under his contract. He may do this on a reciprocal basis and benefit from someone else's lower rate in another publication. Or he may do so just to help earn a volume rate.

Sometimes, in ways not officially noticed, the smaller mail order advertiser gets a rate that a higher volume would usually earn. Other than this, the attitude is one of shock if the idea of a bargain rate is broached by the advertiser to the newspaper. It's harder to request and get a desired position in newspapers than it used to be, even for bigger space ads. Fewer newspapers are profitable to use for mail order. Those that pay out are less typical of newspapers or magazines than formerly. National ads in newspapers are far less read than local ads.

But remnant, R.O.P. ads at bargain rates are profitable when run where there is space available. We have found that the new magazine sections of bigger-city newspapers, with better paper and excellent color reproduction, do pay out quite well for the right item at the right time. Some have quite major differences between a one-time mail order rate and the volume rate enjoyed by large mail order advertisers.

Many magazines have an absolutely firm rate. Very few offer a "make good" ad "if needed." Some negotiate rates – but usually for big users of space. Still fewer give a guarantee that you will get enough orders to avoid loss on the advertising cost of the ad. In this case, you pay for the ad at the regular rate. Occasionally a publication agrees to run makeup ads without charge until you receive enough orders to avoid loss. Rarely will one offer an outright "P.I." In this case you pay so much per inquiry or per order.

Magazine rate cards vary from the simple to the complex, from one rate for everybody with reductions for total advertising run and for frequency, to different rates for various classifications. In magazines, the rate cards sometimes begin to bend a little. The smaller the magazine and the closer to break-even (or more in the red) it is, the more flexible it becomes regarding rates. Most big newspaper organizations are more stable in their profits earned than most big magazine organizations. There are often more changes of management in magazines. New bosses come in more frequently and are *fired* more frequently.

Attitudes about rates vary with the necessities of the moment. Many magazines sell regional editions in various parts of the country. They sell these at a higher cost per thousand to advertisers who require them. Often a certain page is sold to advertisers in much of the country but not the rest. The remainder of the circulation is sold as a "remnant" or "stand by" at a reduced rate. This is so of national magazine sections appearing in newspapers. The discounts offered vary widely by publication. Originally, they were quite large discounts and big bargains. Often they were actually available for full circulation and sometimes in premium, even back cover (when otherwise unsold) positions. These were the happy days. You may find discounts substantially less, rate card rates far higher and positions worse, with a premium position almost never available.

You need to run in the most appropriate magazine possible. You're looking for a magazine used by mail order advertisers with products similar in price and selling to similar people. Every newsstand you pass is liable to include a magazine for you to consider. Simply going to a library and looking through every magazine that seems logical is a good first step before talking to the publication salesman. From ads in magazines, make a list of the advertisers of mail order products which seem to appeal to the same people your product does. Then call them up.

First, write down on a yellow pad the questions you'd like to ask. Don't call people your product is directly competitive to. Tell others that your product is not competitive, but that you'd appreciate their advice. If they're busy, don't bother them. Years ago, I found that I had to restrict such conversations to my clients. But for a good part of my career, I have been able to spend some time answering such questions. Quite a few people will help with answers. Call only those who repeat their ads in a publication. Explain that you are considering running an ad and how important it is to you. Ask if the publication you are considering has been doing well for the advertiser, whether results are falling off and how it ranks with other magazines used. Try to get the names of the best other magazines used, in the order of effectiveness for the product. Each call you make is teaching you more.

Talk to the salesman for each recommended magazine. Get the rates for each. Calculate the cost of running your ad in that magazine. Divide the cost by the number of thousands of circulation for that magazine. Ask if it is ABC circulation. This means checked by the Audit Bureau of Circulation, an organization subscribed to by leading magazines. It checks and vouches for the honesty of circulation figures quoted by magazines. Compare the cost per thousand circulation for your ad size for magazines considered. Check the rate discounts for running more times and for maximum frequency. Check discounts for dollar volume. You may find that the advertisers you talked to are using their favorite magazine at a far lower rate than you will pay for your first test.

For every magazine, check to see if you're being quoted the regular national rate or the lower mail order rate. If you're selling a book, does the magazine have a special book rate which is sometimes even lower than the magazine rate? If you have a page ad or whatever size required, does this magazine have a remnant rate? If so, what is the reduction or discount from the national rate? Check the position you will get at each rate.

Some magazines have special representatives who act as special mail order salesmen for a number of magazines. Perhaps you will deal with them. They can be particularly helpful. They understand mail order. They're realistic about the rates required in each magazine to give mail order a chance. A few have their own mail order companies. Sometimes you can sell your product to them or get them to advertise your product at their risk. Sometimes they will sit down with you, work out the number of orders you need to break even, gamble themselves up to that point and split profits in some way thereafter. This way you get a risk-free test. If it works, they will then help you to run in other magazines. Once you get to know them, you learn a good deal quite fast about buying magazine space, particularly as you compare what each says.

Chapter 4

BUYING DIRECT MAIL ADVERTISING

From package inserts to "solos" . . .
testing . . . pyramiding . . . selecting
printing . . . envelopes . . . paper . . .
processing sources . . . renting . . .
swapping names

If you use direct mail, the printer you deal with may have no idea whether the cost of his printing is "in the ball park" or not. He may know nothing of mail order. The kind or printing he specializes in may be impractical for you.

Printing costs vary tremendously. Different printing equipment is suited to different purposes. The small-town newspaper printer who can computer-set simple type at a small fraction of the cost of a sophisticated typographer can print a very small run competitively. For a somewhat bigger run, a small, quick, copy photo offset house is usually cheaper. Neither can compete with a bigger, faster photo offset press. There are printers that can give superb quality in color reproduction, but specialize in runs of 20,000 to 150,000. Many such printers do not realize that for most items their costs are so high per thousand as to make it impossible to use direct mail profitably. The use of a high-speed web press that turns out rich four-color pieces with a little less quality can be (in an enormous run) a fraction of the limited run color cost per thousand.

The envelope man you deal with may be a retailer buying from an envelope wholesaler, who in turn buys from an envelope manufacturer. Any printer you deal with may have equipment that's wrong for *your* purpose and not realize it himself. Your art director may be quite unaware of any dollars and cents requirements of mail order, yet help you select your printer. But your dogged asking of questions can provide the answers you need. Just telephoning mail order advertisers who use direct mail can give you priceless information.

If you talk to such a direct mail user who has a mailing piece of similar size and treatment to yours and mailed in similar volume, you

---

can usually find out what his experience has been. If his product is not competitive to yours, he will often answer questions frankly. By calling small, medium and large successful users of direct mail, you soon learn current costs in the mail usual for the kind of mailing you're considering.

You also often get specific names of printers, mailing houses, typesetters, artists, engravers or whatever you need to know, competent, nearby and competitive in mail order. And as you start to deal with suppliers experienced in working with mail order people, each can teach you more. You learn whom to use and what to pay them.

Testing in direct mail is often most practical. Keying is simple. Lists are keyed by computer on the label for very little cost. You can split to your heart's content, not just two ways, but three, four, five or as many ways as desired. You can take the identical list and split it as many ways as you desire for as many tests. You can split price, terms, copy, picture or whatever. All that is required is to use enough names for each split to be a representative sample. Small splits of 1,000 names or so are liable to reverse themselves if you run another 1,000. Usually 1,000 names is not an adequate sample.

The number of names you need to test to get a satisfactory split varies with the price of your offer. The lower the price of your offer, the more orders per thousand you should pull and the smaller the list of names need be for a satisfactory test. The reverse is also true. As direct mail grows more expensive, the average retail price of a successful offer goes higher, too. Fewer orders are then needed per thousand. This means a bigger list is then required for an adequate test.

What you must do is pull enough gross profit from each 1,000 mailed to cover a good deal more than all costs in the mail, including product, printing, postage and allowing for returns – ideally twice as much. Let's assume that for an offer this required a 2% response.

This means 20 orders per thousand. A minimum of 100 orders is needed by most direct mail testers for each segment of a test (and several hundred are desired) to give a representative sample. This means each segment of a test should be 5,000 to 15,000 names as a minimum, depending on the price of the offer.

However, it's better to make a less than adequate test rather than no test at all. It may be necessary to start very small in your direct mail test. If so, test 10,000 to 25,000 names in all. Start with simple black and white tests. Use a friend's word processor to set type for a simple letter, brochure and return card.

At first we usually test one basic mailing piece and separate lists only. We select one to 3,000 names from each different list for the first test. If successful, we go on to 25,000 to 40,000 names, then to 80,000 to 125,000 and then increments of 200,000 to 300,000. If a seasonal product, we may have to go faster. As soon as we begin buying 10,000 or more names of one list at one time, we begin breaking them down into splits. At first we make copy tests of 2,500 to 5,000 names each.

When we buy 20,000 or more names of one list, we make larger splits or more splits of the same list. We begin to test 10,000 names for each segment as a confirming test for an earlier, smaller and less adequate test.

We prefer to start out tests for direct mail as package inserts in our own packages. We usually are not shipping enough units fast enough to provide enough circulation for split-runs, so we test one way. A package insert usually pulls better for us than a direct mailing to outside lists, and sometimes better than a mailing to our own lists.

Assuming you have a low-priced, very related offer, a single package insert might pull 4% to 10%. For a higher-priced, quite related and equally appealing offer, your package insert might pull more in dollars but less in percentage. An item three times as expensive might pull 40% as much and so forth. Unrelated offers would probably pull as little as half or less of these percentages.

If you do ship your 20,000 packages, this means that you might sell 800 to 2,000 low-priced, very related items. An unrelated, higher-priced item might pull 160 to 200 pieces. Other factors will cause this to vary. If your customers are happy with your product, more will buy. If they're unhappy, far fewer will buy. If they know your firm, more will buy. If not, fewer will buy. If you sell a high-priced product, a bigger percentage will buy a higher-priced item from an enclosure.

Consider these points. First, do you have any other products of your own? If you don't, it's probably not worth your time to look for one yet just for the insert. If you do, is your product at all appropriate? Don't waste your time putting an insert for a $10 item into a package of a product selling for $300. Instead, select either a needed accessory selling for $50 to $100, a related item selling for $100 or more or a more expensive unrelated item. The higher-priced the item, the fewer the packages you will ship and the more trivial will be the sales of a very low-priced item. Further, you have a tremendous asset if you have a customer for an expensive item. Don't waste it. He or she is a prospect for higher-priced, higher-quality merchandise. And don't destroy the relationship by offering him or her junk. Offer quality to quality customers. Stay away from junk, anyway. You'll be happier and make more money.

If you're shipping a higher-priced item, particularly if sold on credit and far more so on time payments, a resell insert on the product *already bought* can cut returns and bad credit.

A successful test can be projected to inserts in other firm's packages of related products. We now try to convert our package insert to a billing insert for use in other firms' bills. Both package inserts and billing inserts can be projected widely. They are an ideal method for the moonlighter to get started in direct mail, project gradually and make good money.

Another low-cost test can be a loose postcard or a bound postcard mailing. For a specialized industrial or technical product, this can be an ideal way to start in mail order. It's also a simple translation for a half-column ad. We've found it particularly good for office products and executive gifts. It has had great success with products sold to doctors. It's been very successful in producing specialized inquiries in volume at low cost and closable in profitable percentages. Most such mailings are to credit-checked firms or high-income professions such as to doctors. More expensive products are therefore saleable. And by selling only for cash or through credit cards, it is not necessary to sell on credit. This is a perfect way for a moonlighter to start.

Black and white loose postcards often give a low-cost split-run test. They're ideal to test offer variations, half and half. Or you can splitrun test advertising on one side with a return postcard on the other, versus advertising on both sides with no return postcard.

In running an inquiry ad in a postcard publication, be sure to test the inquiry quality by keying the conversion coupons in your follow-up material to the postcard publication. If disappointed in the percentage of conversions, stop. If satisfied, continue.

In a postcard publication, we have succeeded with a single card on one side with another advertiser on the other side. Each had a coupon. There was no return postcard. We have done well with an ad on one side and a return postcard on the other. We've succeeded with one item on each side. Sometimes we use a coupon on each side, sometimes only on one. We have succeeded with a double card and even a triple card, using both sides for one item and return card.

The next safest and lowest-cost test is in billing inserts. If you go into billing inserts, you can start where you can be the only insert. If this works, try multiple billing inserts. If this works *very well*, try multiple mailings. In this case, you pay substantially more because you are paying a proportionate share of the mailing plus a proportionate share of a profit. You also can anticipate pulling *less* because almost *all* bills are opened and much third-class junk mail is not. And the package of different direct mail brochures will be considered junk mail by many. However, a share of a multiple mailing is still safer and far cheaper than a "solo" mailing where you are the only advertiser. It points up how very safe and attractive billing inserts and package inserts are.

If you have a *proven* and desirable offer, you may not have to gamble the entire test and perhaps not at all. A "syndicator" may take these risks and perhaps even buy your product from you. They are highly computerized and strongly connected with credit card companies, company credit card divisions and other owners of tens of millions of names. Your offer will be made on credit, perhaps on time payments, with the syndicator taking the risk.

You could earn $25,000 to $50,000 yearly with just one insert run widely by syndicators. They are very selective, and yours may never be chosen. It's best to approach them after you have a proven success story.

These kinds of direct mail are very important to the mail order moonlighter. You can get started testing with very small sums of money: $300 to $500. Yet you can project to millions of package and billing inserts if tests are successful. You can expand a little at a time. There's not too much risk after the first successful test. Multiple mailings are bigger volume, and you can get more circulation. Of course, these big projections are only possible for fairly universal appeal products. The more specialized your product, the more limited your potential projection is.

In direct mail, the safest, quickest, lowest-cost testing is to your own lists as soon as you acquire names. If you sell a quality product and not junk, you have satisfied customers. They should be good direct mail names. They need to have bought items in the price range that you can normally profitably sell. For our Sea Eagle inflatable boats, mailings to our house list of customers and inquiries pull an average order of $273. The higher-priced the articles your customers buy from you, the more valuable their names are to you. But to benefit, you need to find or develop other mail order items in the same price range or higher.

If you get inquiries from any form of advertising, what you do with your inquiries once you get them can be important. A single follow up requires you to show a profit after initial advertising cost and follow-up cost. The advertising which secured the inquiry has now been paid for. Your next follow-up mailing can show a profit with a far smaller percentage of response, because now the total advertising cost is printing, art and preparation, mailing and postage.

We follow up inquiries for our Sea Eagle inflatable boats seven or eight times the first year, somewhat less the second year and less still the third. We make a profit on each mailing by offering a variety of different inflatable boats and related products. We mail our owner list more frequently.

With the right follow-up offers and presentations, you can do additional business on each follow-up. If you are actively building a list and have a consistent program of mailing the list with other offers as well, you are further amortizing your original advertising cost of getting the names. If you run an annual or semi-annual sale of offers mailed to them earlier at full price, you may get further benefits.

If you work your customer list first with package enclosures, then (if sold on credit) with billing enclosures and then with mailings of other items, you get another plus. If you ask customers for referral names and get good ones in this way, you get another bonus. If you consistently build your list with customers for the same or similar products, and "clean" the list by mailing it yourself first-class and correcting addresses with the help of the Post Office, you will start to build list rental income. This, too, affects your decision as to how much you can afford to pay for the original inquiry which makes it all possible.

Much of the art of direct mail is getting a core of good names and then mailing the list. Of course, for a small moonlighter to develop a big list of high-ticket items can take a long time. More probably, you will first succeed in space or broadcast with a lower-priced item. This list *might* be responsive to higher-ticket items. It is not safe to use it for another single, low-cost item. It also might respond to a specialized catalog in the same field of products in the same or somewhat higher price range. It also might be responsive to a multiple mailing of different insert brochures for products in the same or somewhat higher-price range.

Ambassador Leather originally succeeded by selling a very low-priced product – to holders of credit cards. But credit card holders could afford higher-priced merchandise and could be safely sold on credit directly and even on time payments. Ambassador sold a tremendous volume to credit card users and built a great business of somewhat more expensive products. It also created a tremendous list rental business – from sellers of a wide variety of products, mostly at considerably higher prices.

The smaller your list, the more vital it is to keep advertising production cost of mailings to it as low as possible. For small lists, this usually rules out any catalog. The multiple mailing is still practical for a list of a few thousand names. Photo offset advertising for your own proprietary product or products and complete your mailing with literature you do not pay for but get from other mail order people. This literature should not have another product company address on it. If you pay nothing for such literature with no one else's address on it, it is well worthwhile to insert it on a very attractive basis to the cooperating company, taking only 25% of sales as your share.

The larger your list gets, the more important it is to use it – always assuming you are securing satisfied customers. As your list gets larger and more profitable to mail, you will prefer, more and more, to photo offset your own literature of other people's products and work on *higher* percentages of sales. You will begin to *combine* this with including inserts of others with their address printed on it but charging them per thousand to insert their literature. This becomes practical when your mailings are big enough to be handled by an automated mailing house. Your costs of inserting will drop sharply for each of a number of brochures. Inserting for others can therefore be quite profitable. Also try to develop more of your own items to mail to your own list. On these you will have better gross profits.

If your list keeps growing still further, you can go in either of two directions. You can convert your multiple mailing into a small catalog. Or you can organize a co-op multiple mailing, selling others per thousand for sharing costs, and retaining your own *proprietary* items with maximum margin. The ideal is to get enough participants to cover your entire cost and even a small profit. Then all gross profit from your own items is free and clear. You can't lose and can only *make* money.

At this point, *exchanging* names with others multiplies your potential. If your names are on computer, the running charge from the computer house is usually very little. On a swap of lists, this cost of running off the equivalent labels of your names for those you receive is your total list cost for renting such names. You can swap just some of your names and *test* those you exchange your names for. If profitable, go ahead with the entire swap. Do this carefully, list by list. Surprisingly quickly, you can multiply a number of times your total list to mail to. Your volume and profits grow, too. Usually your own customer list will remain most profitable to use.

Your own list will usually be the safest to mail to for your first "solo" if your list consists of customers for products selling for $30 or more, and particularly for a very related item. Otherwise, you may be able to swap your list for names of such customers. If so, it's even more important that such a list be quite related to the item you are advertising in your mailing. If you neither have a list nor can obtain a list on an exchange basis, you will need to rent an outside list or lists as a test.

A "solo" direct mailing costs a number of times as much to reach each person as any other form of advertising. For some, it still makes money. Part of the reason is that a "solo" usually contains far more advertising material. But by far, the major reason is the selectivity possible, the rifle approach compared with the shotgun. The "solo" continues to work in direct mail *despite* rising costs. There is an increasing ability of the direct mail user to select more scientifically lists of names better suited to the offer and with the least waste.

But proper selectivity is still a matter of human judgment. Poor judgment or careless selection throws away the advantages available for scientific selection. For beginners, more initial "solo" tests now fail than years ago. But successful "solo" tests project to far bigger volume. As a moonlighter, you may not have previous knowledge. You may not yet have skilled advisors. You may feel quite confused about how to go about making the safest, wisest selection for your first "solo" test. But you do have *time* and *motivation* to make a sound decision.

In considering a list, investigate what items those on the list bought. A list of buyers of a single specific item very related to the product you are selling is preferable. Sometimes a specialized catalog list is excellent. Otherwise be cautious when considering a list of a variety of items. Be sure that all those items are fairly equally related to the item you are selling. Sometimes a list owner mixes different lists into one. It gives a larger total list to rent. Revenue is greater. And list users like big lists. It means that if a test works they have a big volume to project to. But they find year by year that the key to success is selectivity by segmentation – using only the parts of lists most perfectly suited to the offer.

If a list is a *mixture* of lists, the mixture can be an unfortunate one. It may include lists that are good, mediocre and poor. It may include lists of buyers of good products and poor products, of satisfied customers and resentful ones. It may include buyers of products very related to the product you are selling and of products very unrelated to it. On a modest test, you probably can only use one to half a dozen lists, so why not pick only the most perfect for you? Why not play safe and select buyers of a single product most related to yours?

Next investigate how these names were obtained. What kind of advertising was used where? If sold in magazines and newspapers, which were used? If sold on TV or radio, was it secured by telephone or by mail? Was the article sold for cash or on credit? If sold on credit, have the bad payment names been left on the list or deleted? If sold via direct mail, what specific lists were used?

Generally, names of purchasers of higher-priced articles are preferable, but only if the article you are selling would appeal to such people. Names of customers who bought from the Wall Street Journal are sometimes preferable to those who bought from the National Enquirer, if your item appeals to better-income people. Generally, those sold through magazines and newspapers are better names to mail to than those sold through TV and radio. Generally, names of those who bought through TV and radio, via credit card or *mailed* in cash, are safer than those who bought C.O.D. Generally, names of those who bought via radio or TV are less responsive. If sold on credit (direct billing) via radio or TV, those sold via telephone are generally worse. However, if bad credit names have been later *deleted*, the remaining names are usually better than cash names because they are candidates to sell safely on credit.

Names that are very fresh, obtained just in the last few months, are most responsive. These are called "hot line" names and get a premium rental price. However, they are the best buys and safest to use. Their only drawback is that, even if successful, other names on the same list must be carefully retested before any major projection of list use. Names that are one year old generally pull better than those two years old or older. Lists of names must be "cleaned" regularly by the list owner or the list quickly gets hopelessly out of date. Theoretically, a constantly cleaned and renewed list can be kept constantly up to date and productive for all names. The secret of list buying is to buy a small test of any large list and increase in gradual steps, feeling your way at all times. Some list owners mix several years, state that the entire list is constantly recleaned, and refuse to break it down by years for rentals. For your first "solo" test, we recommend that you do not select such a list. Later, if successful, you have ample time to include it in future tests.

The list business is built on trust. Cheating by either party can occur. The list owner can misrepresent the names as being newer than they actually are, can represent TV names as magazine names, can adulterate a desired list by *adding* less desirable names and can even include *duplicate* names (if not caught by a merge-purge computer). The list renter usually gets the labels he rents in his possession, where he can duplicate them and thus *steal* them. Fortunately, most people are honest and you can trust them. But in a business built on trust, it's wise to deal with *trustworthy* people. There *are* others. Lists from bigger companies are more likely to be as represented than lists from temporary promoters.

Rental prices per thousand vary considerably but are usually about the same as *similar* lists based on type of item, price range and recency. In making a test, often the last thing to worry about is the cost per thousand of the list you are testing. It's not a huge sum for a small test.

Some big list owners – Dun & Bradstreet, for example – have a high price per thousand for a small test and a dramatically lower cost per thousand for the full run. Other big list owners have sometimes agreed to a better price per thousand when offered a flat price. If you ever mail in huge volume, you, too, may discover savings.

In renting magazine names, "expires," those who no longer subscribe, are usually considerably less responsive than current subscribers. We have often found magazine subscribers less responsive to related merchandise offers than buyers of related merchandise. "Compiled" names gathered from directories are usually less responsive than buyers. Buyer names are far more responsive than inquiry names. Premium names who mail in boxtops and cash for bargains are usually far less responsive than mail order purchasers of merchandise at more normal prices. Inquiry names secured through "bingo" cards are usually far less responsive than inquiries for the same products obtained in the same magazines through coupons. "Bingo" card inquiries in trade magazines are usually of higher caliber than "bingo" card inquiries in general publications. "Take-one" card inquiries are usually far less productive than inquiries in publications and magazines.

For top professionals, renting names is an extremely sophisticated art. A consultant can be invaluable. For beginners with less money, trial and error can be expensive, but renting names scientifically boils down to common sense. If you sell anything successfully in any magazine and wish to sell it successfully in direct mail, you don't have to look very far for desirable lists. Simply notice what firms advertise mail order similarly priced products or services in the same magazine. Those who repeat are probably successful and probably sell to the same kind of people you sell to for your product. Other publications they advertise in successfully might well work for you. And their customer list is a very logical one for you to consider. Often, too, *your* list is ideal for them, and you have the natural makings of a *swap*. Otherwise you can consider them for *your* test purchase of names.

Another common-sense step to being safe is to investigate which firms repeat their rentals of a list you are considering. If a firm selling a product in the price range of your product to the kind of people you sell to keeps buying one list, that list may be good for you. The fact that a firm repeatedly buys a list, if selling a product quite unlike yours, sometimes has little bearing on your problem. A sex book that succeeds on a list may not indicate success for a stitchery kit.

You may buy your lists through a list broker. There are excellent list brokers available. Often they will work patiently with small mail order entrepreneurs on small tests. If they have faith in you and your product, they will do so. They have seen many big direct mail users start as small ones. The good list brokers are very knowledgeable. They have information about myriads of lists instantly at hand. They can save you lots of time. Most list renting is done through them. They collect their commission from the list owner, but work for you. They usually are also list management firms as well. Any one of many of them usually will manage your list (if large enough) if you desire it. Therefore, a small group of list brokers and managers usually work with and know each other intimately. They can be a big help to you.

You may buy your list through your advertising agency. Here you have the advantage of a firm which is, hopefully, already thoroughly oriented to your product, market and problems. More advertising agencies who specialize in mail order are taking over such responsibilities. But this is more true of larger mail order advertising agencies. If you select an advertising agency, discuss this with them and judge their ability in list selection for yourself. If you set up your own "house" advertising agency for yourself, you may also select your own lists and make your "house" agency your "house" list broker, saving 20% but taking all responsibility on your shoulders.

It's actually easier for a moonlighter to get help from a top list broker than from a top advertising agency. Therefore, if you can't find an advertising agency you like and set up your own "house" advertising agency, it's probably safer and wiser to work with a list broker. A top broker will be teaching you a lot about direct mail each time you work with him or her.

Now let's investigate your use of broadcast advertising.

Chapter 5

THE TIME BAZAAR

*Negotiating "by the book" . . . and
for help . . . deals . . . PI's on AM and
FM radio and on VHF, UHF and
cable TV*

If the rate cards and policies of newspapers and magazines seem at all perplexing, enter the wonderful world of TV and radio. There are almost 10,000 broadcast stations, including VHF, UHF and cable TV and AM and FM radio. Most of these stations actually make money. And some make a lot. But some lose, some break even and some worry that they won't keep making present fat profits.

In good, lush years, I've heard a broadcaster call his license "a license to steal." It seemed so easy to make all that money. But even in a fat conglomerate, a broadcast station which year after year cranks out fabulous profits can start to produce thinner profits, or it might even go into the red. For years, this caused all the flexibility in rate negotiation of an Arabian rug bazaar. If earnings dropped, managers' heads sometimes rolled. Prudence called for an open mind to ward off such an eventuality. Holding *too* firmly to the rate could produce a dead hero.

A radio or TV station is like a hotel, while a newspaper is like an accordion. A newspaper can be expanded or contracted at will. When a newspaper has less advertising it simply uses fewer pages. There's no real reason to gamble. But there are 24 hours in a day, no more and no less, regardless of how much advertising the time salesman brings in. A broadcaster can't add or take away time. Any unsold time from sign-on to signoff is available for use. In publishing, there are out-of-pocket costs for each extra page printed, notably paper. But in broadcasting, once the overhead is covered, it's hard to find what it costs the station to run an extra paid commercial. Extra gross dollars tend to become extra net dollars.

Since broadcasting began, for many less successful stations one solution was to provide direct response advertising without risk and accept as payment a percentage of mail order sales produced. This was the way some new independent stations got into the black. It provided

---

a good share of the first income of cable networks. It created mail order fortunes without risk.

The top management of one station, with whom Huber Hoge and Sons spent over $100,000 a year on a percentage basis for a client, has told me why it has been such a good business for them. "We don't want to be sold out on a rate card basis. It can only mean our rates are too low. We'd rather raise our rates, have 5% to 10% unsold time and make deals with people like you."

The biggest bonanza for TV mail order advertising began years ago when tobacco advertising was banned from TV, leaving a gaping revenue hole. At first, deals were made which differed widely from station to station. Meanwhile, a greater and greater number of the biggest audience stations became owned by a smaller number of more powerful groups. Tighter management from headquarters came in.

The sale of commercial time was tied more to specific audience ratings or specific programs and to seasonal peaks and valleys of advertiser demand. The decision was made to take stand-by orders from mail order advertisers not as a percentage of sales but at a huge discount.

The rates for direct response reminder commercials were fixed at the lowest for the first quarter of the year, which for this purpose began just before Christmas. In the second quarter, the rates became higher. In the third quarter they dropped in between. In the fourth quarter they went to their highest. But week by week, the computer at each station (and management) varied the rates by demand. The computer began to be used in a sort of electronic auction of unsold time.

The reductions were far greater than the discount offer by print media for stand-by space. At the same time, far more TV stations – and bigger ones – accepted two-minute commercials. The result was to multiply the size and number of fortunes made by mail order entrepreneurs who sold via TV – and to attract many more big companies to use direct response advertising on TV.

Under most favorable conditions, it has become possible to buy advertising for mail order on TV at 25% or even less of the cost to general advertisers. But there is complete uncertainty as to how much advertising will be available on this basis or how much more it may suddenly cost. The market decides. There is a constant possibility that the two-minute commercial will become a thing of the past.

And with all these advantages, there are enormous dangers in TV for small firms which are suddenly successful. A known amount of merchandise is made or bought. But an unknown amount of advertising is available. There is the risk it won't pull and the risk it can't be obtained.

A tremendous danger can be the use of the 800 telephone number on TV if C.O.D. orders are accepted. Usually a choice is offered to mail in a check or to phone in an order. Some small TV mail order advertisers only solicit telephone orders by credit card. Many offer a choice of credit cards or C.O.D. But of those who order by telephone, from 50% to 90% try to buy C.O.D. Most offers without C.O.D. for smaller firms fail. As many as 50% of C.O.D. shipments are not accepted. In about 75% of these cases the person shipped to was not at home. Most adults work during the day, and UPS and Post Office personnel only deliver during the day. After they come three times when an addressee is not home, they return the package to the shipper. This causes most bankruptcies of TV mail order firms.

An alternative used by some very big direct marketers on TV who feature an 800 number is to offer open credit. This takes sophisticated controls and the ability to resell enough to those who pay to absorb losses from those who don't. It also requires lots of money. For the small mail order advertiser on TV, to offer open credit can be an invitation to disaster.

For the small mail order operator who successfully sells on TV and suddenly expands, there are sudden new changes. The biggest danger is control of purchases of TV advertising. We are highly computerized and could not otherwise control the buying, cancelling and renewing of TV time in the volume we run. A station reports the actual broadcasts they run against an order after the days of broadcast – often days later, sometimes a week or more later. They report this to the station representative firm they deal with, who in turn reports to the advertising agency. It's done by telephone. There can be delays at each step and occasional mistakes. Bills can come in far higher than expected, yet they must be paid.

So if you start small on TV and succeed, beware. Your best strategy may be to join forces with someone with a bigger organization, more TV know-how and more capital. Take a smaller share of more. Another choice is to do much less business via TV more safely.

Be particularly careful about TV inquiries. TV is the ultimate mass media. It has great immediacy. The telephone featured on radio and TV can zoom inquiries. At once, the mail order man must get a *caution reflex*. Inquiries can even come in from applicants who can't afford or even use the product or service or who completely *misunderstand what* it is. Test such inquiries carefully. Make sure conversions are satisfactory before taking on a big broadcast schedule featuring telephone inquiries.

Run only on stations which will accept a percentage of sales as payment for advertising. This is called PI mail order. Don't take phone orders, or take credit card orders only. Fewer offers will succeed, and on much fewer stations. But you can make a little money and sleep at night. The amount of PI TV mail order will probably be more in bad economic times, less in better times and very little in really good business years.

What stations give such deals? Only when the deal is made do you know for sure. And asking whether such an arrangement can be made can be an insult to one and acceptable to another. But if you're turned down, you're no worse off than you were before.

How do you go about it? The first step is to write or have written a TV and/or radio commercial. Lists of susceptible stations are sold to the unsuspecting for $50, more or less. Ignore such lists. But don't ignore the list of any friend who *currently* is on the air on PI stations. A station can "get religion" at any time and refuse all future offers. Or a rate card station can "go off the wagon" and start taking a PI deal or two. Policy can shift with the manager, the last quarter's financial report or last week's time sales.

Get your hands on the Radio and TV Standard Rate and Data books. Find an advertising agency friend and beg for a several-months-old copy of each. Now look through them. Ignore the TV network stations of the largest cities. They would be slightly surprised at your proposal. On TV, the smallest markets will often pull. Now compile a list or three lists, "A," "B" and "C." Your TV PI prospects will be largely non-network in large cities and any station in quite small markets. You'll gradually notice certain prestige time sales representatives that are the same for a number of the largest stations. They will usually influence stations *against* PI deals, and stations represented by them will be more dubious. Now guess which will be the easiest and put them under "A," next easiest "B," and next "C." Ignore the ones that seem most difficult.

Write a persuasive letter about your offer. Emphasize your product's quality as well as pulling power and your ability to ship *promptly* and answer complaint correspondence quickly. Next, try to follow up by telephone. Don't get discouraged if most turn you down. The first acceptance and you're in business. Now wait for results. If a dismal failure, and on checking you find others have done far better on the same station, *forget your offer.* If successful, telephone every other station on your list and tell them your good news. And congratulations!

It is almost always far faster to buy at your risk an advertising test on one station. It is more conclusive. The cost of television time on a small station for a sample test is low. It is usually only a fraction of the cost of producing a TV commercial. The object is to show a profit after advertising, product cost and all costs of processing orders, handling, packing and shipping (and an allowance for returns).

An adequate test on television can be one to ten broadcasts of a commercial at a good viewing time on a good station. If you are running a schedule on a station for a successful offer, dropping in a test one to three times for a new item can be practical. If you are not running a schedule on a TV station, you may pay a high premium to run your TV commercial only one, two or three times. A schedule of 10 spots may be so much less per spot as to make the ten-spot test more sensible. In TV, there is advantage in some continuity. A viewer may not get the price, address or phone number straight the first time, but get it clearly the next.

To investigate a television buy requires obtaining listener ratings, preferably from more than one audience rating service. Such ratings are based on scientific samples of typical viewers who are asked which station they are watching or did watch, depending on the system used. First it's necessary to get the actual audience for the station and time spot considered for each competing station. On TV, programming is changed seasonally quite considerably. A survey of summer watching has to be further checked for upcoming fall program changes. Therefore, it's necessary to get any information possible on upcoming program changes.

How long does the station plan to run the program in which you plan to run your commercial? If it is substituting another, this is a new ball game. What is that program? Is it a new program? If now on the station at another time, what is its current rating? If it only runs fall through spring, was it on at this time last fall? If so, what were the ratings last fall? If not, where was it on and what was its rating? If on at another time, what was its competition and what did it precede and follow? What will it precede and follow and compete with this fall? If the spot is between shows, what does the spot precede and how long is the spot? What other mail order advertisers have used and repeated spots on this program? And what have they used elsewhere on the schedule of this station?

As TV has grown more successful, time has been sold in smaller and smaller time segments. The segment used most is a 30-second spot. Stations usually have far more 30-second availabilities than one-minute availabilities. Now they offer 15-second spots. Gradually, one-minute spots have been priced less attractively than 30-second spots. Network and independent stations in smaller cities are more willing to run two-minute spots in more desirable times than those in larger cities. UHF stations in all cities are more open to doing so than VHF stations. And cable networks are more willing than UHF stations. Yet only two-minute and occasionally one-minute spots will usually pay off for mail order on TV.

We find that certain offers work better than others in one minute vs. two. We find that one-minute commercials do better after a two-minute schedule has run. One-minute commercials have also been more profitable when run together with two-minute commercials. We usually use a one-minute commercial to ask for phone orders only. But we find that a big one-minute schedule acts as support for the two-minute schedule. Phone response and mail response to the two-minute schedule usually goes up when a big one minute schedule is added. A bigger one-minute schedule pulls better per spot than a smaller one – contrary to our experience with other types of mail order advertising.

Some stations have the equivalent of remnants in weekend schedules. Time for Saturday and Sunday, unsold as of business Friday, is sometimes available at a lower rate to stand-by advertisers. These advertisers provide filmed or videotaped spots to the station in advance, with an authorization to run if the time is obtainable at the special rate.

Station policies vary. Managers are given some autonomy or sometimes take it anyway, but they are sometimes fired if the results of their decisions are bad. A new broom sweeps clean, often setting up a policy veering away from that previously followed. The same station guarantees results and then, under another manager, refuses to do so. The same station may refuse to sell two-minute spots, then sell two-minute spots, then refuse all mail order commercials in any length.

It depends also on the behavior of mail order people. If a mail order firm advertises on a station, ships a defective product months late, then is publicized in local papers as being a fraud pursued by the Post Office, FTC and Better Business Bureau, and caps it all by going bankrupt and not paying the station, the station's eagerness for other mail order advertising can cool.

Attitudes of stations and networks toward mail order constantly change. Some decide they'd rather gamble completely in mail order, but control it completely. They will demand that you supply them with a stock of merchandise that they themselves will ship instantly to any complaint and that you deposit a substantial sum, as much as $5,000 or $50,000. Then they guarantee to produce enough orders to give you a profit at no risk at all. In such cases, the station quickly becomes sophisticated and wants a higher percentage for themselves, with less for you. They also quickly form opinions about which kinds of offers have a chance and which don't. Again, this entire plan might last for a few weeks, months or a year or so and then be abolished completely, usually with the arrival of a new manager.

Essentially, stations are attracted to mail order as extra income and constantly frustrated by disappointments and difficulties working with mail order firms. They are inclined to work with the firms they trust and have found honest and competent in past transactions and stay away from the rest.

They want to deal with the direct marketing advertising agencies representing old, live, solid accounts. If you can become the client of such an agency, a lot of your problems are over. But if you are a small moonlighter with little money, this is not too probable. If you have a good product, you may interest an agency to go into business with you or a mail order firm active on TV to buy from you. If you have a product and an effective TV commercial, you can bargain better with them or, despite problems, you can get started yourself.

If you see mail order commercials on a TV station, try talking to the station. Tell the station your situation. Be frank. Explain that you are not familiar with their rates, that you believe you could succeed, but that you surely can't pay if you pay a higher rate than others. Try to talk to the station manager or sales manager and work your way down. Show your commercial. They may like your product, your commercial and you and help you get started. Even if you are overcharged for your test, it may be wise to make it anyway. When your commercial might have paid off quite well at a bargain rate, it may pay off marginally at the higher rate. If the test does this well, the station may suggest a bigger schedule at a far lower rate for each spot. If they don't, other stations may.

TV can quickly grow from a small test to bigger volume. If a station manager sees an advertiser pay off on his station, he realizes that it can probably increase the schedule and keep running for a while. If the station is making a profit, this added revenue increases that profit with almost no extra cost. An alert salesman, sales manager or station manager usually knows how well a mail order account is doing. It becomes obvious that a bigger schedule is feasible, if at a competitive price per spot.

Generally, the salesman has to go more by the book than the sales manager, and the sales manager more than the manager. But an aggressive, competent and trusted salesman can often sway the sales manager and manager. If a salesman sees that his commission on his account depends on management cooperating with you in some way, he may turn his salesmanship on management to gain cooperation for you. If your offer is paying out exceptionally well, if the availabilities are open for a good schedule and if there is pressure for more business at that time, the chances for cooperation grow.

American business goals are based on beating last year and last month. This means if a business keeps sales for February of this year above February of last year and so on, the business is consistently ahead of last year. Inflation can cause overhead costs of salaries and expenses to be higher by a known percentage. Each business must beat last year by that percentage to come out the same and by more than that percentage to be at all ahead. Along with other duties, station managers are hired to beat last year by more than the inflation increase percentage. If they don't, they risk being replaced. Responsibility is subcontracted by manager to sales manager and by sales manager to individual salesmen. A salesman who produces can usually keep his job, even if the sales manager or manager or both are replaced. Such a salesman is a big asset to the new manager or sales manager.

Your successful schedule of additional spots can help beat last year's figures. It can help safeguard a job and get a bonus. Salesman, sales manager and manager are therefore tempted to be on your side. They want each mail count to be good, just as you do.

Some successful mail order advertisers and accounts capitalize on this situation. They do not bargain, ask for special advantages, guarantees, PI's or whatever. Instead they turn the responsibility of paying out over to the station. They give a budget for one week for a small market for $200. They ask the station to select times and to give whatever spots are reasonable for this sum. They offer to increase this budget to $1,200 the next week if the first week is successful. If successful, the next week's budget is increased to $2,700, and so forth.

They simply tell the station how many orders are needed to be successful. The station can run a schedule at card rates, give a bargain or simply run enough spots to pay out. The mail order man does not attempt to influence the station decision. There is nothing on an order, in a contract or in any correspondence referring to anything but normal station rates. But the temptation exists for the station to give more in order to get a renewal or increase of schedule.

The end result can be that, in weeks, from a tiny test, a small entrepreneur is running a major schedule, yet never gambling more than a single week at a time. If he watches the mail counts carefully, he can cancel the first week the orders slack off. If so, he can usually only lose in the last week part of what he has made to date on that station. In a quite large city, a schedule can quickly get up to over $10,000 a week. The larger the city and the more varied the audience of programs run on, the bigger the schedule can be and the longer it can run.

In the course of one campaign projecting a test to a successful schedule, you can soon become quite professional as a buyer of advertising. Water seeks its own level. Stations want business and, to get it, will do for you what they do for others. You will learn the different varieties of station transactions. Some stations prefer some form of guarantee or PI arrangement, because it is a simple way to have automatic renewal and increase of a schedule as long as results continue. Other stations are shocked at the idea. Some have policies in between. A station manager may make a practice of "helping where necessary" with extra spots, but will never say so in writing. Others will never say so even verbally, but still do. Others will infer they will or might help, yet not really mean it.

There is always the chance of misunderstanding. A salesman might think his station will help, but top management won't. A manager might intend to help, but the very next week be forbidden to do so, generally by ownership, or he might lose his job.

The key is to avoid fuzziness. I remember as an advertising agent attending lunches between station client and station manager. At the end of lunch, client and station manager shook hands and said, "It's a deal." I asked, "What deal?" Each then stated the opposite of the other. The station manager would prefer a schedule with no deviation from rate card. The client would like a 100% protection that he cannot lose. Each talks sympathetically to the other and often avoids a confrontation. The station manager wants business, but not to risk his job. The mail order firm wants orders, but not at a loss.

The careless mail order operator gets into misunderstandings and loses money. The prudent, thorough and careful mail order operator knows where he stands. If he is taking a risk, he knows it. If he thinks he's protected, he has it in writing legally. If you sign a contract with a station and have a verbal understanding that you will get extra broadcasts, this will not stand up legally. You can be billed according to the letter of the contract. You can even write the station manager a letter confirming a previous verbal agreement by him to give you more broadcasts if needed. This still won't hold up legally. You still must pay as billed. Any contract change or addition must be signed by both parties. Otherwise the original written contract stands as the sole written agreement.

Despite this, some new mail order entrepreneurs keep getting in trouble, thinking they are protected when they are not. Be careful. Say what you mean and keep your word. Forcing a station manager to put in writing the protection you want could risk his job and lose the deal. Gambling with him that he will keep his word, has authority and won't be overruled or fired before the transaction is completed is reasonable. But you must realize it is a gamble, and you must be able to afford that gamble. This means that if there is a risk it should be for a limited amount of money that you can afford to risk, preferably a one-week schedule. Then if misunderstandings come up, they should be clarified before further risk. You should not risk a blank check of a continuing schedule.

The ideal is to only order in writing one week at a time. If you do have a written agreement for a continuing schedule, make it subject to cancellation by you. If sufficient orders are not coming in, cancel instantly. But in practice, to keep the time, you have to keep running on a larger contract. Most orders end up being made by telephone. We usually get the right to cancel in three working days.

The logistics of the mail order commercial are complex. Each commercial on each station receives a dubbed-in, off-screen voice and a dubbed-in video slide of a mailing address different for each station. Only a very big phone answering company with hundreds of trained operators and completely computerized equipment can be used. The phone service computer communicates with our computer, and orders they take come to us electronically each day for the previous day. Control is a nightmare.

The young entrepreneur who is intoxicated by seeming success is inclined to let schedules continue. If lazy or careless, he may not be aware of correct mail counts or may not be methodically acting on them. Success on one station does not mean automatic success on another. One manager may do what he says in addition to his written commitment. This does not mean that another manager will. Assume the worst. Be content with less profit, watched more carefully. Limit your objectives. Go a little slower, but more safely. Be thorough. Pay your bills promptly. Clear up misunderstandings as soon as they occur. Do so in a fair manner. If you get bills one way and pay them another, even if you are shaving off small amounts, you are building up to more misunderstandings. It is better to take your losses from a misunderstanding and be more explicit thereafter. The best plan is to call whomever is responsible at the station. Then reach an equitable compromise, if possible, put the compromise in writing, have it signed by the station authority and pay the revised bill.

In business, you can deal with some people on a continuing, mutually satisfactory basis and cannot do so with others. Avoid the latter as fast as you compare their words and actions. Others will judge you similarly. Build your reputation. Be proud of the products you sell, or drop them. Keep your copy honest. Ship on time. Do what you say. Pay your bills. Be competent, and make and protect your needed profit. However small you are to start, on this basis you are desirable to deal with.

As station managers find you trustworthy, they will trust you. Your products will be preferred by them. All this can happen surprisingly quickly. In a few months' time, you can become a larger advertiser than you might have anticipated.

To have a margin for possible sudden losses, the ideal in mail order is to make "a buck for a buck" or better. This means the objective is to make a dollar in profit for each dollar spent in advertising. You should be making at least 50 to 60 cents for each dollar spent. This means after all costs of merchandise, processing, packing, handling, shipping and allowance for returns.

Pyramiding of TV profit can come quickly. A small station with a $200 test can make a $200 profit the first week. Increasing the schedule and running from week to week for even five or six weeks can bring expenditures up to $2,500 to $3,000. Profits may drop percentagewise, but your only real risk was the $200 to start. The increased schedule and renewals had far less risk. A larger station starting with $500 might make $10,000 to $20,000 in the same period. A very big station starting with $1,000 might make $25,000 to $100,000.

Profits on a number of stations can jump much faster, from $2,000 in a week to $7,000 to $19,000 to whatever. Mail order on TV can actually make a new mail order entrepreneur hundreds of thousands of dollars in one season on one item, and sometimes millions. If you operate with prudence, the risks are surprisingly small to accomplish this. Just remember that doing so is a rarity. You may never achieve such success. But others have, and you can too, with the right item, the right commercial and the right approach.

Often a young, new mail order entrepreneur will be carried away by apparent big success. He increases his schedule rapidly. His bills come in. Orders are fair, but he has been promised make-goods (he thinks). He begins to get some bills far out of line with orders received. He's convinced that his friend Bill or Joe will reduce the bill or get more orders for him. He pays a bill or two and puts the other bills in a drawer. He isn't facing the facts. He's losing money, and the stations have no intention of bailing him out. And suddenly he can't pay his bills and can't continue. Don't let this happen to you.

New situations constantly change TV advertising opportunities for mail order. In five years, over 250 new independent TV stations started. Many were in big cities. Almost all carried more mail order commercials. Far more took the 120-second commercials usually necessary for best results. Far more gave more favorable rates. Some gave guarantees and percentage of sales deals. Television Age or Broadcasting Magazine each run mentions of new stations about to start. Usually the phone number is given with the news story and the name of the manager or sales manager. You can contact them.

More and more viewing audience has been moving over from VHF and UHF stations and networks to cable TV. We have been very successful selling by mail order via cable TV. At first cable had little audience and produced very little in sales. As cable mushroomed, so did mail order success via TV. At one time it seemed that cable would offer an infinite variety of high specialized programming, each on a different channel, with extraordinary opportunities for mail order offers in that specialty. MTV showed only rock videos and became a medium to sell rock records by TV mail order. The Lifetime Network emphasized health and fitness and became ideal to sell exercise equipment by TV demonstration and 800 phone numbers. The Financial News Network became a perfect place to direct market investment newsletters and so forth.

But as cable saturated the country, cable networks went for more mass audience. Now there was a mix. ESPN was ideal for a sports item, but also for any item for men. Nashville Network could sell subscriptions to a country music magazine, but also any mail order item successful on general audience TV stations. Suddenly cable could sell in enormous value by mail order.

WTBS was an unsuccessful UHF station. But when it broadcast its programming via satellite to cable systems, it became the super station. Mail order provided huge revenue for WTBS, and the super station made enormous fortunes for mail order entrepreneurs, some of whom started as moonlighters.

Cable grew so huge so fast and proliferated into so many networks that volume for mail order seemed limitless. But the news of mail order success got around. More and more entrepreneurs and big-company direct marketers jumped in. Audience ratings began to be perceptible, then bigger than big. National advertisers rushed in. Rates soared.

Now the traditional TV stations and networks began to hurt. Their rates began to soften a bit. It seemed that soon there would be proportionately less mail order on cable and more than before on VHF and UHF stations everywhere, even on the old line networks.

Suddenly the most talked of phenomena on TV were the home shopping networks. They became the darlings of Wall Street. It was predicted that they would become the fastest growth form of retailing. Twenty-four hours a day they demonstrated. They constantly gave prizes to viewers, in ever bigger amounts. The habit of watching and then telephoning in orders seemed like a combination of hypnotism and addiction. The way to sell was simply to offer goods to the shopping networks. The more demonstrable the item by TV, the more acceptable it was. Soon it was possible to pay a charge for an item to be presented on TV in a way comparable to paying all or part of a co-op or with a department store.

Soon the sales volume of some TV shopping networks became enormous. Some bought TV stations. They fought for positions on space satellites most favorable for relay to most cable systems. They bought hour strips of demonstration programs turned into game shows on TV stations. But some TV shopping networks were folding. Some were merging. Some seemed on the financial ropes. Predictions for the future were mixed.

There began to be an opportunity for the smallest mail order moonlighters to get a TV shopping network to buy and test their items at its risk. The moonlighter's risk was that others might be able to supply the same item at lower cost to the same TV shopping network.

Before you approach a TV shopping network, be sure you have a proprietary item you control solely. Your best opportunity is to supply an item you have already tested successfully on a TV station and which is patented or copyrighted and you control. It could be an import on a sole rights basis. To get the latest list of TV shopping networks, phone Direct Marketing Magazine at (516) 746-6700 or DM News at (212) 741-2095. Then phone the TV shopping networks. Ask for a vendor kit. It will be mailed to you and tell you exactly what to do to submit your product for consideration as a TV demonstration item.

One TV opportunity building fast has been the video catalog. We have shot 70,000 feet of videotape for our Sea Eagle inflatable boat video catalog. Catalogs like this in every field have been proliferating.

In most cases, a moonlighter can't afford to produce a video catalog to start. But you can become a supplier to a video catalog, just as you can to a TV shopping network. Read Catalog Age Magazine and Catalog Business for latest news of the newest video catalogs. Look for one in a field in which you have an exclusive item. The narrower the field and the better suited your item is to it, the better is the chance of acceptance. If you've already pre-tested your item successfully on TV, you're in even better shape.

One much talked of TV development has been narrowcasting. This is broadcasting by very low-powered television stations authorized by the Federal Communications Commission. The FCC keeps TV stations far enough apart and limits their broadcast power enough so that two stations on the same channel do not conflict. This sometimes leaves gaps between two stations which neither station reaches. Narrowcast stations can be put in the middle of such gap areas and power kept so low that there is no conflict on the same channel. It has been questioned whether such stations could get enough audiences in such nooks and crannies to attract advertisers. They became a possible source of percentage of sales advertising for small mail order entrepreneurs. It would take time to determine if they could produce perceptible sales.

Conditions constantly change. It's possible that the two-minute commercial will be harder to place on TV, no longer accepted generally or more prevalent than ever. Successful phenomena such as the TV shopping networks may suddenly disappear or grow bigger and bigger. But constant change will always make some kinds of mail order no longer profitable and open up undreamed-of opportunity for others. Study change and try to act in time to avoid dangers and benefit from opportunities.

There was a time when we used radio very heavily and very successfully for every form of direct response advertising. We pioneered the use of it for our clients. This was before and in the early days of TV. Today we have found direct response opportunities in radio again, but in special ways. The opportunities could grow far greater for far more products and services or could shrink greatly. It will depend on radio stations and network policy, on freer interest in and need for direct response advertising in greater volume than they already enjoy. This will depend on economic conditions, changing formats of successful radio stations and the changing character of mail order and direct marketing.

A big percentage of all the commercials run on radio, whether AM or FM, local or network, ask for direct response. Most radio advertisers can trace and measure the response and accurately judge the pulling power of networks, stations, times and programs. The big changes in radio have been a constantly growing swing from AM to FM and the development of a greater variety of specialized programming formats to appeal to special groups.

Research on radio audiences has been greatly improved. It is possible to determine sex, age groups, incomes and interests of the audiences of specific stations and networks. By selecting offers just right for a specific group, it's possible to be very successful with direct response advertising – but very seldom with mail order offers which ask for orders only.

Radio has become a two-step direct response medium and often a threestep one. Listening is more casual. Radio music is background to driving a car, cooking, clerking in a store, or assembly line work in a factory. People listen everywhere, but usually when doing something else, whether reading a book, eating a meal, playing cards or whatever.

Since broadcasting began, stations and networks have cut up segments of time offered into ever smaller slices. In the early days of radio, advertising sponsored hour programs, then half-hour programs, then quarterhour, then five minutes. The use of spot announcements started gradually and steadily grew. In the old days before TV, we ran five-minute commercials on hundreds of stations. Later we cut down to two-and-a-half-minute commercials followed in a few minutes by a half-minute reminder. When we were cut down to two-minutes, this seemed as far as we could cut a commercial down and still pull enough orders.

But stations found that one-minute commercials could be sold to national advertisers for more than half of what they charged for two minutes. Then they found they could sell 30-second commercials, each for more than half of what they charged for a minute. Finally they sold 15-second and even 10-second commercials.

While all this has been going on, business has been good. Even direct response advertisers have been successful – when inquiries could be successfully followed up. This has been infrequent doing so by direct mail. What has been very successful has been to secure leads for salesmen and appointments at a place of business with the use of an 800 phone number. The commercial only asks that a listener phone in, and a telephone marketer sets up an appointment. A salesman then takes over. It is not mail order, but direct marketing. Few moonlighters can find a way to benefit. Quite small retailers and services often can – and grow big in one area and then branch out, sometimes going national.

But some mail order advertisers do succeed, more with two-step and occasionally with one-step. Great numbers of magazine subscriptions are successfully sold by a radio request to call an 800 phone number and solicitation by phone for a subscription.

If you become a moonlighter with a specialized item or service which appeals strongly and specifically to the audience of a specialized audience radio station, you may find success, particularly if station policy on that station changes. Suppose your item or service appeals particularly to older people. While radio does not produce the mail order response it once did, it can still produce mail orders and inquiries profitably – if used correctly. Specialized radio has held up best.

Some of the old, clear-channel, 50,000-watt AM stations have continued to run more talk shows and kept a following of older listeners. They still pull for offers suited to this group. Records and tapes do not sell as well on radio as on TV. This is partially due to the fact that nostalgia albums appealing to a somewhat older audience have often sold best. Old movies on TV provide this audience better than teenage record shows on radio. However, there are now nostalgia music radio stations which sometimes do successfully sell nostalgia records and tapes by mail order.

If you have a product or service for teenagers, a rock station may be just what you need. If you have one for serious music fans, consider classical music stations. Classical stations like WQXR AM and FM in New York have become more scarce, but they are productive, particularly for specialized offers. We have sold many thousands of opera appreciation books this way. Classical stations may be right for some kinds of books, for stereo accessories, for travel-related offers or for lovers of wine or art prints.

If your product or service is for yuppies, you may want stations which play nostalgic music only going back to the 1960's. Country music stations do well for folk collectable offers. Black radio is a more recent medium, with loyal and intense listenership more comparable in pulling power to the old radio. Offers most suited to it often pull the best.

We have often found that a commercial on news programs was more closely listened to and pulled better than the same commercial on the same station on a music program with the same audience rating. All-news stations have mostly adult audiences and are ideal to use for a broader variety of adult offers than other radio stations. But there are fewer of them now – often with less audience. There is now much less news on radio and more on TV.

Always remember that the programming of each radio station is designed to appeal most to a certain segment of the population. The characteristics of each audience are carefully researched. It's important to suit your offer – and your copy – to the audience. Station representatives are quite knowledgeable about their audience, but they are inclined to recommend a bigger schedule for a longer period than we use for testing. We get an adequate test of a radio station with as few as three spots run on one day.

When you are quoted audience ratings and told of very big audiences tuned in, always consider who is listening. Many radio stations get good audience ratings by appealing to teenagers. Teenagers don't buy much mail order. Constant contests with incentives to listen and to say they are listening when called by telephone can increase audience ratings more than actual audience. Housewife circulation is sometimes casual in listening and less apt to buy mail order. Adult circulation, aside from housewives, is concentrated in the very early morning and in "drive time" (8:00 to 9:00 AM and 5:00 to 6:00 PM). It's harder to order by mail while driving.

Radio stations do not offer the special direct response advertising rates which TV stations do. This is because there is little straight mail order on radio due to the 60-second commercial requirement – and because a big share of all radio advertising is based on some form of direct response. Otherwise radio time is sold on much the same basis as on TV, in that the rates are constantly increased and decreased based on rating and demand.

As on TV, radio, time rates are different for different classifications, called day parts. Any station may choose to charge somewhat differently and have more or fewer classifications. In each classification, the rate for one spot may be a good deal higher than buying a schedule of spots. Ten spots a week is often substantially less per spot. Stations prefer to sell a "package," usually of good, fair and bad time. You're forced to take all together to get a rate per spot. It's usually a "rotater" – by computer – but might not be. If not by computer, you might get more poor and bad times and fewer good ones.

One difference between TV and radio is that TV in smaller markets can be very productive for mail order. Radio in the same smaller markets is far less effective. Successful mail order AM radio is best on a station with a good position on the dial, middle to low; with strong power, 50,000 watts; as close to clear channel as possible, with no competition anywhere on the frequency; and top rating.

In recent years, this has been less possible. Top audience in a metropolitan area is often on a lower-powered station with a worse frequency. This means the signal does not go out as far. Proliferation of stations has cut the huge, scattered, out-of-town audience of the old bigpower stations. FM has taken away a great share of AM audiences, which in turn were already cut tremendously by TV. The audience is fragmented and not as productive for really big-volume mail order purposes.

FM radio started out with almost all classical musical stations, but could not get sufficient audience. Now it has big audiences for a variety of popular music programming and a constantly widening audience. FM has not been remotely as successful as the old AM radio in selling adult products in one-step mail order. FM has hurt AM listening. Still, FM can be used profitably for mail order for *highly specialized offers* suited to the station used.

For most, one-step opportunities to use radio profitably will only open up when two-minute commercials become generally available. If this happens, it will probably start on AM radio as audience and advertising income decline faster. It could happen on all stations if at any time total advertising for radio drops off. If headache remedies were forbidden to advertise (very improbable), suddenly there would be less advertising revenue. Mail order would become more desirable.

It is very probable that certain kinds of catalogs with items just right for a special radio audience will find a way to use radio profitably in big volume with one-minute commercials. A moonlighter could create a very simple catalog in black and white which could conceivably do this although most catalog experts would be most dubious of success. If you do, you can test for very little expense . . . less than $1,000 for radio time, even less than $500. If you succeed on one station, you very likely can find stations with the same format, equally logical to succeed in each major city. But be careful.

Use radio – but selectively. You can test for very little expense. But be cautious. Now let's discuss the "hybrid" media.

Chapter 6

THE HYBRID MEDIA

Publication forms of direct mail . . .
direct mail forms of publications . . .
cable TV catalogs . . . mixed media

The recently developed "hybrid" media has become a big opportunity for big mail order advertisers. They can be for smaller advertisers. First it was return postcards bound in next to advertisements of the same offer. Then it was free-standing inserts (brochures on postcard stock) with an actual return postcard perforated at lower right. More recently have come multiple mailing envelopes in a newspaper section.

At first such advertising seems just for giants, but this is not always so. I've seen our products in a sixteen-page section with return envelope, run as a specialized catalog in a specialized magazine. It was an advertisement bigger than that of any giant company in the issue. Yet I've seen the orders come in to self-liquidate and make a profit.

In some big-city newspapers, free-standing inserts can be run in only a small minority of total circulation – in most desired suburbs, for instance. They can then be expanded city-wide in the future, if warranted. The advertiser supplies the inserts and pays for insertion.

However done, inserting of direct mail material in publications will continue to grow. It simply becomes a logical projection of a successful direct mail brochure and an alternative to list buying (and postage, envelope and mailing costs). It is not a big risk to insert an already successful brochure in a smaller-city newspaper or part of the circulation of a larger-city newspaper. If this is successful, projection can be enormous. But such success rarely comes.

Organizers of co-op multiple direct mail pieces inside an envelope in a newspaper are becoming publishers of alternatives to syndicated Sunday newspaper magazines. It is possible to supply a simple insert for such a multiple envelope and to test it in very limited circulation. This becomes practical even for the small mail order moonlighter. Organizers of co-ops in newspapers or by mail become tempted to go into the mail order business themselves or to take risks and share profits. The smallest moonlighter may secure rights to a product and create an exciting brochure for it that may appeal to such a co-op entrepreneur.

It could become another opportunity for the smallest moonlighter to start without risk.

It's hard to tell *what* some of the new hybrid media actually are. A great book publisher started a bound co-op publication, mailed to its list and sold advertising in it to other mail order firms. Is it a magazine? Whatever it is, it is an opportunity for small mail order firms. You can buy a page in a small run or an even smaller space. All orders come to the publisher in a return envelope bound into the publication. For each customer who orders products advertised by any participating mail order firm, the publisher adds a free gift. The publisher forwards orders and money to participating firms.

Executive Mart is a bound postcard publication going to a big list of executives with premium buyers mixed in. Any moonlighter or anyone else can advertise in small space in Executive Mart for inquiries at no risk. He just pays per inquiry and sends literature for follow-up. Or he may buy a return postcard with advertising on one side selling an item or items. For us, it's worked on item after item. We give a choice of four credit cards or cash. If cash, the card is put in an envelope with a check by the customer. Three postcards are printed on one side of each page. Each card has printed on that side the advertiser's address with a post office permit number so that it may be mailed free and postage paid at the other end. The customer can sign an order and drop it in the mail.

These new forms of advertising, custom created for mail order, have been jumping up faster and faster. In some cases, direct mail uses a publication for its delivery. In others, it *becomes* a magazine itself, a participating catalog in which you can take a small share of the cost and risk. An Executive Mart achieves printing savings which a quite small catalog cannot achieve, and it passes much of them on to participating mail order firms.

The publishers of free-standing insert sections in newspapers designed for users of cents-off coupons also offer remnant rates to mail order advertisers. Entrepreneurs put Dutch Door sections in Parade and U.S.A.-WeekEnd in which advertising is available advantageously to mail order advertisers. These are full width, but a minority of the height of a normal page, and are usually eight pages.

More and more bigger trade magazines are organizing direct mail co-ops of loose postcards, bound postcard publications, or multiple brochure mailings to their lists without the burden of editorial costs. Such co-op mailings can often be safer to advertise in than the equivalent trade publications. Don't close your mind to *any* new form of mail order advertising, however unusual. But investigate each carefully.

Investigating these new media requires the same thorough questioning technique as for any other form of advertising. There is a cost for each that can be calculated per thousand. You quickly see that some bound postcard publications cost far more per thousand than others.

Some are far more expensive per thousand in black and white than others in full color. Some packages of loose postcards have far more postcards sharing readership than other packages. Some packages charge over twice as much per thousand postcards as other packages. The cost of inserting a free-standing insert is different per thousand in different publications. So is the cost of an adsert postcard affixed to the back cover of different magazine sections. And so is the charge for inserting a return postcard next to your ad in magazines. Sometimes it's simply an effort to get a sharply higher rate per thousand for quite similar circulation.

Only thoroughly researching each hybrid medium buy can indicate if its cost is reasonable and probably safe. When mail order advertisers selling products of similar appeal to yours run repeatedly in any of these media buys, it's safer to consider. Telephoning other mail order advertisers can give more answers and make your decision sounder.

Any catalog can secure inquiries from bingo card type ads that describe catalogs. Many of these offers are made by magazines and some by entrepreneurs. If you charge for a catalog, this may be a safe offer. However, be cautious. You may not convert satisfactorily from inquiries to customers. The volume of inquiries can be high, and you pay for names, not sales.

Chapter 7

BARTER ADVERTISING

---

*Direct and indirect . . .
misconceptions . . . benefits . . . risks
. . . broadcasters and publishers . . .
safely buying it . . . barter gamblers.*

Barter in advertising is as old as advertising. The owner and printer of the first newspaper was happy to pay a bill by giving the equivalent in advertising. And it's been happening ever since. For any publisher or broadcaster, barter is an alternative to rate-cutting for last minute unsold space or time. Originally, barter was directly between the owner of a product or service and the publisher or broadcaster.

Later, barter also became indirect. The publisher or broadcaster would receive a product or service from a company which would get space or time in return and then swap or sell it to some other firm. Years ago, in return for acquiring an interest in a broadcasting network, I became part of a group that received over $500,000 of broadcast time. My assignment was to exchange the broadcast time for advertising space in magazines. We then ran mail order ads in the magazine space with cash orders coming to us. At other times I have arranged to purchase big blocks of broadcast time at 50% discount and then swap it for advertising space. We traded card rate for card rate. Thus it became a way to buy advertising space in excellent publications at half price.

Many publishers and broadcasters exchange some space or time for something. Some do not. Some only exchange in very specific situations. Some swap in a wide variety of situations and on a very large scale. Barter or swap is interesting to you only as a means of getting advertising space or time for less cost or risk. Sometimes this is possible.

Today large companies exist which do nothing but barter something for advertising and then resell the advertising at a discount. Naturally, their effort is to purchase something for very little, barter it for advertising which therefore costs them far less than rate card, then sell it at under rate card, keeping as big a profit for themselves as possible.

TV programming is the biggest field of barter. Many TV stations always want and need more programming than their cash budget will normally allow them to buy. Older, weaker and more specialized programs are offered on a barter basis. It is attractive to many stations to pay for them by giving broadcast time. On a series of programs, a station will sometimes give one-third or one-half of the spot availabilities within each program to the program owner. The owner will try to sell these spots to a national advertiser. For strong programs, he will do so at full price. For new and weaker programs, he may sell at a bargain price or gamble on the time he owns.

The biggest and most successful "program packages" will not have to sell at a bargain or gamble. But anyone can become a small "program packager." Any show produced by anyone or any station and videotaped can be offered to other stations on a barter basis. There are many small TV "program packagers" who have time to sell at a bargain or to gamble with if they choose. They usually don't.

A small mail order moonlighter might have a chance to deal with such a small TV "program packager." If the product is related to the program, it can be very successful. It can be the basis of a partnership between packager and product owner, either on a percentage of sales with no risk to the moonlighter or as a separate corporation partially owned by each.

There is little chance of doing business with a large program company. As a moonlighter, you're too small. Most barter companies want to sell large blocks of time for real money to substantial companies. They seldom wish to gamble with the time they have acquired. And if they did, they would probably consider you too small. However, nothing ventured, nothing gained. If venturing is merely making a no-risk proposal, you really can't lose. If you have a product that is extremely related to a specific program, it might pull extremely well, and the big owner of the program just might see the potential. The barter company likes to line up purchasers first and obtain time as needed, thus having no inventory risk. But often the barter company can't avoid program inventory risk, and sometimes its acquisition of space or time is hard to sell. It's always possible that at some point the barter company will gamble with the time. Not being in the mail order business, it may do so on a percentage of sales basis. But this rarely occurs.

A surprising number of firms and individuals have blocks of bartered broadcast time. Far fewer have publication space. Caution! Broadcasters and publishers are not foolish. Naturally, their interest is to obtain good value in what they get and to exchange the least desirable time and space for it. There is a continual battle between those offering anything for space and time and those giving space and time. Barter companies try to barter merchandise at full retail price at published rates for advertising rate card. Publishers and broadcasters try to barter advertising at published rates for lowest wholesale cost. Program packagers have offered programs for a cash price to a broadcaster or for *four times* the cash price for time valued at rate card. The outcome has varied constantly. When a publisher or broadcaster needs cash badly, a broker will sometimes put up a big block of cash prepayment for a very big bargain in space or time and then resell it at a discount, but still at a good profit. With better business, barter is less attractive to media. Yet barter is increasing.

The result is great confusion. Sometimes space or time available through barter for a lower cash price is a bargain. Sometimes it's just about what you'd get if you bought at best rates directly, and sometimes it costs you *more* than if you dealt directly. This is particularly so in broadcasting. There are adventurers, dreamers and frauds in the barter field. Some offer lists of stations on which they do not actually have time. Some did have time but don't now. Some have restrictions on their time which make it impossible for you to get a two-minute TV commercial.

Before you acquire barter time, remember that in general the very shrewd owners of barter time do not use it to sell by mail order. And the very shrewd mail order advertisers usually prefer to buy other than barter time. Barter space in a publication which rarely cuts its price is sometimes more desirable. Barter may not be for you. But don't be concerned. Some new opportunity will turn up.

A given situation may make some way of buying advertising advantageous for a while. Then this situation varies and something quite different becomes the advantageous way to buy. It's ever changing. Fortunately, there's usually some new way to buy advertising advantageously enough to make money in mail order. It can be something you would never expect. The opportunity may be available for a day, a month or for years. It may stop at any time.

Chapter 8

MAIL ORDER WAR

Fighting off "knock-offs" . . . and
winning . . . making competitors say
"uncle"

From the first thrill of a new "hit" in a test result to full projection, the name of the game is speed and secrecy. Because in mail order, it's easy for someone else to steal a good part of your success.

A competitor can apparently duplicate your product. His looks like yours in the advertising. Yours may be top quality and his junk, but the customer doesn't see either until after he's bought it. Customer inertia can cut your competitor's returns, at least to a "profitable nightmare." A patent is a "license to sue." A good percentage of patent claims originally granted are denied in the first lawsuit. It is slow, expensive and dubious.

Later we'll discuss how to beat your competitor to the punch; but why have a competitor unnecessarily? Discretion and secrecy can make the difference much of the time. Every salesman who calls on mail order people, each mutual friend, even your own employees can pass on the vital information that you have a "hit" to "knock off." You, yourself, can mention your first success to your later loss. Until you give the fact away, only you know for sure, so keep it quiet.

In considering any kind of mail order advertising buy, ask what *direct* competitors have used it. Find out how often, and how recently. Ask if any are scheduled to run before or on the date of issue you are considering. If so, it's important to find out what price your competitor sells his product at, what the terms are, if there's a giveaway, what the claims are and what the guarantee is. It's necessary, if at all possible, to see the competitive advertising.

A competitive ad with about the same price, giveaway value, terms and claims will affect your results badly if run before your ad runs. If run more than once, the effect will be worse. If run very recently, the effect is worse. If it runs the day your ad runs, it will be a good deal worse. But if the competitive ad has a lower price, has a more attractive giveaway, gives better terms, a stronger guarantee, has better copy or simply stronger claims, the effect on your ad's results will be the worst, particularly if run close to your ad date, and catastrophic if in the same issue as your ad. You simply *increase* your competitor's orders at your expense.

But if *your* ad offers a low price, etc., *you* may win. But price alone may not be the deciding factor. If you're up against severe price, claim and offer competition, one strategy is to *avoid* the competition. As soon as your tests warrant, race into media your research indicates he has not yet bought. Direct item competition then becomes a race to get there first. It sometimes happens that, without realizing it, you and your competitor *share* the market, almost as partners, one getting first into one publication, one in another, or one racing first into TV and the other jumping into direct mail. Each pushes in the form of advertising he feels safest in using, based on past experience.

Such competition can become mail order war. If you have a fine quality product, you do not care to have profits you're entitled to turned into big losses because someone copies your ad and ships a far inferior product that can only disappoint . . . looking for a profitable nightmare by going way under your price and at your expense. On TV, we were advertising America's finest roses for Jackson and Perkins. A competitor offered seven times as many roses for two-thirds the overall price and ran big schedules on the stations our Jackson and Perkins garden programs were running. We instructed our TV garden personality to give a little lesson on the difference between grades of roses. He held our quality rose plant up for a close-up of size, root structure, thickness and sturdiness. He held up the next more borderline grade and showed how much thinner and weaker it was. He then held up the cheapest bargain grade and showed the measly roots and skinny trunk and weak structure. He called it a "garden cripple" and threw it to the ground. Our offer did better than ever and our competitor had to get off TV stations we were on. But when you're a mail order moonlighter, duck any such mail order competition. It's far too dangerous, and that's why it's important to get a mail order product that does not yet have direct competition. Test it as fast as prudence permits and project it *before* competition arises.

In mail order war, you may have to sue legally. You may be sued legally. We'll take up the selection and use of lawyers as we next discuss the day-to-day operations of a mail order business.

BOOK V

NUTS AND BOLTS

*Recommendations and
warnings . . . what to
do and not to do in
operations from
moonlighting start to
big success*

Chapter 1

ALONE OR TOGETHER

*The pro's and cons . . . selecting a
partner . . . negotiating a partnership*

As you make a hobby of making mail order money, you will find a
quiet satisfaction unlike that in any job.

In your job you are a cog, perhaps quite small in a quite large
wheel. In a mail order partnership, the partners are the wheels. If entirely on your own, you are the big wheel. In either case, the daily round
of your own business can become a pleasure and a joy.

Your part-time business and hobby can become a stepping stone
to a full-time business, either shared or entirely your own. To make it
secure and increasingly profitable, your enjoyment of and interest in
routine activities can be vital. The most brilliant mail order man or
woman can go bankrupt fast, simply by neglecting little things that
seem minor but can be all-important.

Let's discuss the nuts and bolts of daily mail order business
operation. Each moonlighter will start and operate his or her business
somewhat differently. Some will be amply experienced in business.
Some will have had no previous business experience. Many will start
with very little money. Some will become quite successful and may grow
far beyond their moonlighting beginnings. We'll take up various eventualities. If any does not concern you, just skip through.

Some moonlighters will be best suited to being sole owner, more
to partnership and many to either. You may feel equally suited to
partnership or to sole ownership. Your first decision will be whether to
go it alone or to team up with others. Before deciding, consider these
advantages of each choice.

Your solely owned business may give you more satisfaction. You
are sovereign, the sole ruler of your moonlight empire. You are also
alone and may be lonely. But you have no friction, because you need
not please anyone but yourself. You are truly your own boss. You are
flexible. You can act at once without consultation. You can still go into
various forms of joint ventures with others on individual transactions.
It's simpler. It's also more work, strain and risk. And it's slower. You
may have limited time and money.

Advantages of partnership can be greater. A partnership may be far more suited to you personally than going it alone. You may gain partners perfect for you. Even if your partners have shortcomings, you may be far better off with them than without. With partners, you will have more combined money to risk and more man hours available.

Partnership can be a way to get help without risking more overhead. A partner doubles the facilities of the organization. Several partners build a larger organization of just themselves. Partners, between them, may provide equipment first. One may already own a personal computer, another a camcorder, and another a photocopy machine. One partner may even be in business and, as his contribution, allow the partnership to use his facilities. One partner may have storage space, another a little machine shop in his cellar and another a needed skill in advertising or product design. One may be the inventor. One may be a salesman who can get a mail order product going in the stores as well. One may travel to foreign countries and be able to negotiate sole import rights. Or one may already have the rights to an item which he will contribute to a partnership.

You can gain and learn much from your partner or partners. You can move faster and possibly achieve success earlier. Your first success as a moonlighter probably will mean faster success the second time around. Each success then accelerates progress to the next. Your partnership can be your start. If it's a great partnership, you may continue in it lifelong. If not, it may be a more temporary joint venture. And when you part and divide up, you may have a nest-egg starting capital for your solely owned business to help accelerate its growth. Caution! Look before you leap into any partnership.

Even if you and a neighbor take a flyer together on one ad in one paper for one item, it's best to consider the future implications. Thinking and talking things out *before* can go a long way towards a long, happy relationship *after*. Otherwise, misunderstandings can sow seeds of future disputes, bitterness and possible financial loss to you, all started the moment the business began. A partnership is a business marriage with lots of emotion potential in it.

It is also possible in business to marry in haste and repent at leisure. The agreement that you make with a partner can be a mortgage on your entire life. As a potential partner, many of us look better than we do in the realities of partnership. We're often disappointed in each other. And business divorce can be as painful, emotionally tearing and expensive as a broken marriage. Too often, no provision has been made for the terms of splitting up if the partnership should not turn out. It's wise to start a business partnership as a trial marriage, with a clearcut agreement for a severance division of products and assets or a mutual buyout clause. Business divorce can then be amicable, without shock or bitterness, and may never come at all. Mail order usually involves a continual development of new items. A dividing up of items at severance, one to one partner and one to another, is not unreasonable.

When analyzed years later, one might have gotten better items than the other. But more important is going ahead on your own again and ending a bad relationship.

Partnerships sometimes fail when one is far abler than the other, when one is unstable, dishonest, far more financially pressed, lazier or when the objectives of one are far different from those of the other. Good businessmen can be poor partners and simply strip each other's gears. Ego is the greatest enemy of partnerships. Social friends or relatives are often the worst partners. The best partners, who have usually known each other in business or hobbies or interests before, are working individuals, and each contributes his or her share. The ideal business marriage in mail order is between two or more partners, each compensating for the other's weaknesses and benefitting from the other's strengths.

A dreamer and doer partnership can be perfect. The dreamer can develop concepts, and the doer can carry them out. But dreamers and doers often do not have sufficient respect for each other. Are you a dreamer or a doer? At first, in your own business, you'll have to be both. Maybe you'll develop the ability to be both permanently. More likely, you should consider partnership with your opposite.

Before you go ahead with any partnership, talk out with him or her possible future friction points. Each partner going into partnership instead of on his own is surrendering some sovereignty. Each risks losing by the association. Consider these points: Who will do what? If fifty-fifty partners, what will happen when you and your partner disagree? Who will sign checks? If your partner signs checks for more than the bank account, unless incorporated you are personally responsible. If both partners must countersign each check before it is valid, it may be safer. But if so, and you disagree and one won't sign, will it stop the business?

Suppose one of you is financially better off than the other. Should one draw money from profits before the other one? Suppose one has a very demanding job and travels on business as well, while the other has a lowerpressure job with far more time off for moonlighting. If one works far more in the moonlighting business, will he accept the fact that the other doesn't and can't?

Should this be a fifty-fifty partnership? If so, who will row the boat? If not, who will own less than half? And if one will, how can he or she be protected from being taken advantage of by the other? If the business succeeds and one suggests hiring or taking in his unsuccessful brother-in-law, what will be the attitude of the other? If the company succeeds and there's a company car, who will keep it after hours? What happens if one partner gets a job in another state or country?

Money partners putting in limited sums once are one-time contributors, usually resented from the day after the money is paid in. But money partners able to finance future needs can help build a Rock of Gibraltar solidity. If you can contribute more in other ways but lack money, the right money partner can speed your success. Before you start, discuss with your partner future eventualities. Determine your own financial needs. You'll make a better deal if he can loan to the company instead of investing. Discuss what will happen if the partnership makes money and financing needs grow. Will your money partner put up more money, guarantee a bank loan or take a smaller share if more money men are needed? Think out if you will appreciate your partner less if your partnership does so well that it is self-financing.

If you have ample money, would *you* like to be a money partner to a mail order man or woman? If so, be careful. If neither you nor your partner has a "feel" for mail order, your chances are poor indeed. If your working partner has it, your chances are better. If you have it, they're even better. If your partner is frugal and hard working, it helps. My advice is to extend your risk over a number of smaller tests rather than one or two bigger tests.

But what will happen if success comes? Consider this carefully in advance. Will he resent you? Can you get your share of profits out? Will he draw too much? One way to operate that may be good for you is on an arm's length basis. Help him get started and own nothing in his business. But have all orders for each test come directly to a box number controlled by you. Bank all receipts and parcel it out on an agreed basis. Pay first for merchandise costs, then shipping labor and postage or freight costs, then advertising bills, then yourself and the money loaned. Then divide profit on an agreed basis. Nothing goes for overhead or his draw. That comes from his share of profit. Control the projection of successful tests the same way. Only gamble one season at a time. If successful, try again, and perhaps with others as well.

One man I know has backed entrepreneur after entrepreneur in mail order over the years. He's never greedy and usually takes 20% ownership, often for backing someone in a desperate situation. He has helped some mail order men within days of their own disaster to make a new start. He has taken any promising young man who has done well in mail order as an employee, but only when out of a job, and backed him the same way. Gradually he has developed minority interests in dozens of mail order companies and suppliers and service companies to the mail order field. He doesn't breathe down the back of any of them. Usually the actual cash he has put up has been quite small. He has seldom lost on his credit guarantees. Usually he has been able to develop some activities between companies he has an interest in that contribute to profits. He now has such partnerships all over the world. Many only needed a $5,000 to $15,000 investment. Some of these companies now do millions of dollars a year. Gradually, he has pyramided profits and gambled up to $150,000 at a time.

As a money partner in mail order, you can go on as small or as large a basis as you care to. But developing a "feel" for mail order is one key. The other is to be fair to your partner when you start and later on. Put yourself in his position. If the business is turning into a bonanza, ask yourself how you would feel if you were him. Once he's on his feet, he may feel he's creating profits that become capital and that he's a money investor equal to you. Further, he may feel that he is contributing skill and know-how and endless working hours that you are not. Once the company is prospering, if he feels he can make more money in any other way, he may want to unload you.

My suggestion is to only take as a partner someone you feel is a real mail order "star." Then make sure you're right by working with him. And if convinced, *hold onto him* on any basis that makes sense. If from time to time you renegotiate, increasing his percentage and decreasing yours, he may make money for you *all your life* and for your children as well. Or consider bringing in *more strong partners*, contributing for them proportionately more from your share than his.

Any partnership can be adjusted as things change. Partnerships tend to grow and take in more partners. Younger partners tend to increase their roles. Older partners like to taper off. From time to time, ownership adjustments can and sometimes need to be made.

A really good partnership can be perfect for you. The monies gained from participation in good partnerships are overwhelmingly greater than those lost in bad ones. A bad partnership is more often an exception, an accident, but it could happen to *you*. You want the benefits. You want to protect yourself from the dangers. If you select your partners carefully and discuss possible conflicts with them thoroughly, the chances are that you can have a happy, productive partnership.

Usually, the longer you have known the possible partners, the more probable will be the smoothness of your relationship. Check on a potential partner and ask him or her to check on you. If you find any background of instability, over-suspiciousness, a tendency to quarrel or sue others, laziness, selfishness, previous bankruptcy or shoddiness, simply back away from that partnership. Just a little checking on an affable acquaintance may dig up such a background. People rarely change, and partnerships are best avoided when such a background is uncovered. Don't look for perfection. Don't go by one or two bad reactions. We all have faults. But if the concensus of reports is negative, stay away.

Fortunately, there are more potential good partners than bad ones. And most who check out as good will be good. If so, it becomes a matter of chemistry. Will we like each other and work well together? Sometimes, even with no bad reports, one partner goes into business with the other with some misgivings. Usually, if you don't feel right about a partnership before you start, it's better not to start.

Once you have partners, be understanding in working with them. Try not to be jealous when your partner contributes, or bitter when he doesn't. The chances are that you'll contribute more some of the time and less at other times. A renegotiation of partnership interests each time could be a strain. It is impossible to avoid all risk of partner incompetence, instability or dishonesty. Many shrewd businessmen feel that the best plan is to accept the fact that there is risk, and simply get out of a proven bad partnership quickly. If you form a corporation with partners as fellow shareholders, you reduce the personal risk of a partnership. An embittered partner could still sue you personally, but you would not be ruined personally by the bankruptcy caused by an unstable partner.

Try to choose as a partner someone who can contribute as much time as you can, someone who does not have to draw money faster than you do and someone who wants to go at about the same pace and in the same direction as you. Try to make a policy that each partner draw the same in salary and expenses, whether trips, cars or lunches, and that the partnership avoid hiring the relations or friends of either partner. Many smart businessmen feel that, aside from this, mutual trust is the answer. Each should have sole check signing privileges, and each should accept the other as a fifty-fifty equal partner. If so, it is often advisable to divide jurisdiction, giving one the final say on advertising decisions and the other an inventory decision, and so forth.

If there's a will, it's amazing how smooth and comfortable a partnership can be. The right partnership can create synergy, a more total mutual benefit than the sum of partner abilities. Each can stimulate the other.

With an advance agreement, most problems might never occur. That's why getting a lawyer as soon as you decide that you want to go ahead is well worth the cost. If you can't afford a lawyer, it's wise to postpone the partnership. Often it's possible to agree to share income or profit *without* forming a partnership. Your future partner may be just as happy for you to act as sole principal while the test is going on. You and he can agree on a simple deal with a simple letter. You can pay him a percentage of profits after all out-of-pocket costs, charging nothing for overhead, or pay him a royalty. A lawyer would advise that you have a lawyer draw up a legal contract for you. But many make that first test just with a simple letter. If so, the letter should *limit* the sharing to results of the first ad. Then, if the ad succeeds and it seems to be a business, you may feel it important enough to afford a lawyer. Most businessmen would. Or you and your associate may choose to go ahead, ad by ad, according to the terms of the letter of agreement, with you owning the business but sharing as agreed.

To summarize, analyze whether *you* are suited to have partners. Check thoroughly on your future partners *before* they're partners. Work out in your agreement exactly what will happen later if you split up. And then go ahead and make it work.

Chapter 2

SIMPLEST STARTING

Least paperwork beginning steps
. . . survival tips through initial tests

It's quite a thrill to hang out your own shingle and get underway. Most mail order moonlighters start by picking an unincorporated company name and product name (if needed) to use in their first ad. In many states, the law requires that anyone doing business under any name not their own must register it at their county clerk's office. The form to fill out is usually simple and the fee nominal. A proprietorship or partnership can usually be registered in this way. Some moonlighters test first and register later if the test succeeds. Lawyers recommend that you do register and use a lawyer to avoid error by county office personnel.

Most businessmen would advocate incorporating quickly. Any growth from here on in will mean obligations and risks. If you operate as a proprietorship or partnership, you are personally obligated for company debts. If the business goes under, you can go under personally. This could be the result of a business disaster that you could not have reasonably foreseen. If you don't want to risk your family's future as well as your own, it may be wise to consider forming a corporation. Most partnerships are actually in corporate form, with each partner a stockholder.

Some cautious people would not even run their first ad before incorporating. Most mail order moonlighters incorporate later. Take your choice and maybe your lawyer's advice. Lawyers usually recommend that you incorporate right away, guided by a lawyer. Books are available at your library which tell you how to incorporate for little money without a lawyer. We have used a lawyer each time at a cost of several hundred dollars, including the pretty kit consisting of stock book, minute book, stock certificates and corporate seal.

Organizing your business either way is quite simple. You don't need a license to be in the mail order business. Alone or with others, you need to determine whether to organize in unincorporated form or as a corporation. You may prefer to postpone forming a corporation until your test succeeds, unless your lawyer advises it.

When you incorporate, ask your lawyer or accountant about a Chapter T corporation. At the advice of our accountant, the third largest in the world, we have just become one. It's a corporation in which you pay taxes all through a partnership. Your share of profits becomes personal income for tax purposes. You do not pay a corporate tax, just a personal income tax. You need to draw from the corporation enough money to pay the tax. The time to form a Chapter T is probably when your company becomes a money maker big enough to make the extra trouble worth it.

When you run your first tests, there's no assurance that *any* will pay off at a profit. If the tests all fail, you may later regret any expense other than these tests.

The word for any starting business is *survival.* Most that start don't survive. The way to survive is to *limit your objectives.* If you work at too hard a pace, you will endanger your health, upset your marriage, risk your job and take away all the fun that you can have in mail order. Crawl before you walk, walk before you run, and you'll *survive* to run far faster than you may realize. Let's begin in the simplest way possible.

As a moonlighter, you can start without a staff if you do everything yourself or have it done as needed. You don't need to print any stationery, billheads or business cards. That can come later.

First bills can be paid by personal check (unless otherwise advised by your lawyer). First stationery can be plain paper with a rubber stamp for your name, address and telephone number. First merchandise can be ordered on blank, standard purchase order forms from any stationery shop. Just stamp and fill in. If you prefer orders not to come to your home, simply rent a post office box and pick them up.

As soon as checks and money come in, you can deposit them in a new account in the name of your business. If a proprietorship, your bank can tell you the simple procedure. If others are principals with you, it would be wise to get a lawyer and form a corporation before you run your ad. The bank account can be opened accordingly. Whether you use a lawyer or not, if you incorporate and open an account, the bank will require written designation of individuals properly authorized to sign checks and will give you the necessary legal forms to fill out.

Your object is to test, and *avoid* buying anything or hiring anyone for even part-time hours except when absolutely needed–and out of profits. For first tests, you can operate from home, using your telephone, without buying or renting any equipment. Some letters you receive do not need to be answered. Most others can be answered by telephone.

You can word-process your own letters or use a temporary secretary hired by the hour or day to come to your home. You can keep your own books, coached by your accountant. If your business is very small, your only financial statement need be a business tax return prepared with your accountant at the same time as you prepare your personal tax return. Or you can even get the IRS local office to help you without charge, just as it may do with your personal return. A personal computer and tax software program can help.

As soon as you advertise, help can come in the mail. Letters will usually come from a publisher, broadcaster, printer, mailing house, etc., soliciting advertising. But read each letter carefully. You may get a pleasant surprise if you have the sole rights to make or to sell the item in most ways. A catalog house may be intrigued by your ad and write that it is interested in running it. An advertiser may be interested in it as a premium. A mail order firm may want to advertise it on TV or in some other way and buy it from you. A store may want to buy some. A publication may want to do a story on it. Alert follow-through can turn mild interest into a sale with a profit, more than wiping out any loss your ad may have had. Or it may be pure profit on top of the profit of a successful test.

Before you advertise, make sure you have the right product and advertisement. Then worry about shipping it.

Let's assume that you have an item and are scheduling a test. You've packed it carefully in a shipping carton or padded envelope. You've found out it's acceptable for shipping at the post office or by United Parcel Service. You've compared the costs of each.

Before the test, ship one to a friend. Ask him or her to open it up, check for breakage and ship back the same day. If you have breakage at either end, try to determine the cause. The package may be crushed, indicating too weak a package. The item may not be wedged in or cushioned firmly and properly. This may have caused breakage due to the item shaking loosely within a strong container.

In either case, hold up the test. If a crushed package, repack in a stronger carton or a heavier, more thickly cushioned jiffy bag. If loose in a carton, take special care to cushion with tissue, newspaper or plastic material. Now send two packages as corrected to two friends with the same request as before. If each arrives in fine condition, go ahead with your test. If there is still breakage in either package, either way, cancel your test and forget it. However, if you're still sold on the item and convinced that you can correct the shipping problem, you can always go ahead and repackage or repack more carefully or both.

We have occasionally had breakage problems, but almost always have been able to correct them. Sometimes a spring in an action toy will be shaken out of place within the toy, causing it to jam. Sometimes the manufacturer (perhaps you) can correct this. But sometimes you discover that the item you've selected is simply too flimsy for mail order shipping. Let's assume that your breakage problem is solved and that orders do come in. You will need to keep track of them.

Mail order is a science because results from each advertisement in whatever media can be measured. The ability to key addresses and count separately mail addressed to each key makes evaluation of tests possible. It is vital in comparing the results of two or more ads in a split-run test. Whatever form of mail order advertising used can be keyed.

Keying each publication and direct mail advertisement can be done by printing a slight variation in the address. A key can be printed in a coupon and changed for each advertisement. It can be printed in the final mailing instruction at the close of any ad without a coupon. It can be changed in the mailing instructions of each TV commercial or each radio commercial on each station. If telephone orders are taken, different telephone numbers can be arranged with a telephone service and each used as a key.

In direct mail, each label is keyed with the same number series for each list used. If one list is broken into test segments, each is keyed this way. Otherwise, and usually for multiple mailings, billing inserts and package inserts, the key must be printed on the order card, coupon or mailing instructions. The key must be changed for each segment of the run as required (each 5,000 for instance). If a window envelope is used, the original label, key and all, can be placed on the return order used in the right position to be seen through the window. In a mailing or catalog, the customer can be asked to use the special peel-off label used on the original envelope and to reuse it on the order form. In this case, many will not do so, and such orders will be listed on receipt by you as miscellaneous. The ratio of miscellaneous to keyed must then be determined, and the percentage of miscellaneous to the total added to each key when judging results.

On radio or TV, mail is keyed by the station or box numbers. A key might be Bargain Books, 1001 Grand Central Station, with city, state and zip code added. Another key might be "Best Sellers," with all else the same. A different, simple word or phrase can be each key. Large mail order companies usually key each advertisement in whatever form with a special number sequence and enter mail counts for each sequence into their computers. As a moonlighter, you will probably key and enter mail as most smaller mail order firms do. A key will often be simply the initials of a publication and numbers designating the date. A key in the coupon of a Woman's Day ad would be WD-11 plus the last two numbers of the year. This would mean that the order came from the November issue of that year of Woman's Day. A split-run test would usually add the letter "A" to the keyed address of half the circulation with one keyed ad, and the letter "B" to the keyed address of the other test ad in the other half of the split.

The smallest mail order moonlighter must key his mail for specific advertisements. He must count and enter it for each key into some kind of record. There's no thrill in mail order like counting the mail for an important test or big advertising buy. Entering keyed results can be simple and fast.

If each advertisement is properly keyed, every order coming in on a coupon can be quickly separated into the proper keys. The mail count for each key is entered into some sort of mail count sheet, book or books. If ads are unkeyed and results not entered, mail order becomes a lottery ticket. Advertising buying decisions cannot be based on past experience.

One big publisher I know mails book bargain catalogs in huge quantity with 500 or more book titles. For years, he kept his mail count in a very primitive but quite practical manner. He didn't use computers, printed forms or specially trained personnel. He didn't enter detailed information about the orders, but just the number of orders received for each book. His mail opening staff kept records on big blank sheets of white paper, all entered by hand. It was all done fast. There was no mail entry record by days. But it was adequate. You could instantly see how the mail count for each book compared. At a later date, you could multiply total orders received for each book by its price. Different sheets were made up for different mailings and inserts in newspapers. Each was compared with the other.

A very able mail order man I know, who mainly buys TV advertising, entered mail count in almost as simple a way. He taped to the wall a big piece of paper ruled into small squares. For years, even when doing several million dollars a year, he has kept these charts on the wall in his own office. When he made a test, he entered the mail count himself. When he ran a schedule, an assistant helped. Even the squares were marked out by hand. Only the numbers of mail count received were entered. The number of spots weekly, times run and cost were written underneath the TV station call letters.

If you don't have a computer, try to keep mail entering simple and mail records easy to refer to and understand. Mimeograph your own form on 8 1/2 × 11" punched sheets kept in looseleaf binders. Print on top:

PUBLICATION_____DATE_____ KEY_____

OFFER _____COST OF AD_____

Rule out on the page enough vertical and horizontal lines to produce 24 small boxes vertically and 20 horizontally. Each square should have enough room for one entry for one day. To start, use the far left vertical boxes for the date and weekly totals. Enter numbers of pieces of mail only or numbers of orders for each of several offers in the same ad, or both. Use one column for each offer. Put in the dollar volume total each day of orders received for the key or for each item offered, or both. Use each sixth vertical box for a cumulative total before filling in the next daily count.

Use one or more pages for each key. If you have several offers in an ad, keep records for each offer, and then determine the average order in dollars and cents by dividing the total dollars and cents for the key by the total number of orders. Thereafter, only enter the number of orders received each day, and assume each is an average order.

If your ad asks for inquiries for later follow-up by your literature, key each piece of literature mailed as follow-up. Use the same key as for the inquiries. You can do this with a rubber stamp, handwritten initials or a simple code mark in ink. To determine profit or loss for each ad, trace in this way actual sales converted from each ad. The same mail count sheet can record inquiries and conversions in separate columns. If the conversion is for a standard price, show number of conversions only. Otherwise, show conversions in dollars and cents as well as by number.

However you enter your mail count, keep the records where you can quickly and easily refer to them. Looking over your own previous mail counts will help determine future advertising buying decisions.

Before you run your first test, you will have to decide on the form of payment your ad asks for. The simplest way to start is to ask for cash. This will be check or money order. If you ask for C.O.D. orders, get from the post office their C.O.D. labels and tags and fill them out by hand. Later, if you get C.O.D. orders in volume, you can have C.O.D. labels printed. UPS and the Post Office will each provide continuous forms to use on a special machine to prepare C.O.D. labels for each. Your ad may have stated the price and added "plus C.O.D., postage and shipping charges." The shipping charge can cover your labor of making out labels and tags, plus a reserve against refusals.

If you ask for credit card orders, first make your arrangements with each credit card company. Do so if your item sells for over $15. Remember! When using credit cards be sure to ask each customer their credit card expiration date. Master Charge and Bank Americard are by far the two most widely distributed credit cards. Start with them. You'll probably deal with a nearby bank franchised by one of them. Explain that you are not a store. Otherwise an electrician may install electrical equipment needed by stores but which you don't need and which costs you money. Get the pads of little invoices to fill out and exact instructions on how to fill them out and where to forward them. In several weeks, you will start getting checks from the credit card companies for orders which you have shipped to their members.

As soon as you succeed in selling profitably in enough volume, you can get a machine to process these orders for the credit card company. As soon as you get a computer, everything will become easier and faster.

If C.O.D. money orders come in from customers, deposit them in your bank. Soon you will also get C.O.D. refusals back. These are C.O.D. packages which your customers refused to accept or were not home to receive. You may refuse to accept these packages back from the Post Office. In this case, they will be destroyed, and you will lose the merchandise. Otherwise you may pay postage both ways, plus the C.O.D. charges. C.O.D. orders using UPS work differently. Get from the Post Office and UPS their latest regulations and rates.

If you start moonlighting in a small town or village, you could become important to the Post Office. One mail order firm that booms in a tiny village can ship out enough packages and mail with enough increased dollar volume of postage to change the classification of a small post office. If so, the postmaster and in some cases other personnel can get a raise. Often a tiny mail order firm is catapulted by successful tests into big volume shipments. This could happen to you and help them. And they can help you. The personnel of the post office you use may not be familiar with mail order. In most post offices, they are.

Years ago, when Post Office salaries were lower, it was always possible for a mail order firm to hire post office personnel after hours by the hour. It costs more now, but it can still be helpful for a mail order moonlighter.

Ship promptly. If you use a drop-shipper, ask for Post Office or UPS receipts. Only deposit a check after receiving this receipt. On any orders you ship, deposit checks after shipping. This is required by law. If you know the delay is a matter of weeks, write a note of apology on a postcard, rubber stamp your business name and address, and mail. If you get any complaints of non-delivery, even after you have shipped, send a note or a postcard that shipment has been made. For an item of $50 or more, consider insuring for your cost in the mail. Do so at your post office. If a low-cost item is lost in the mail, it is usually cheaper to consider the occasional refund paid as your insurance cost.

Read carefully any customer mail. It may show you how to repack or write new directions for an item or even tell you that you should give it up. Letters of praise can suggest new uses, give new advertising approaches and be invaluable testimonials.

Before using a testimonial in advertising, you need a release signed by the writer. Some lawyers draw up a release so legal as to frighten away testimonials and charge more than you care to pay. A simple short release may not be airtight. We have no standard one. We write and clear one each time with our lawyer. Some moonlighters make up their own. Others get someone else's standard release. The public relations or advertising department of a large company might be willing to show you its standard release for testimonials.

Let's now discuss organizing for safer growth.

Chapter 3

ORGANIZING FOR GROWTH

*First allies . . . selecting your
accountant . . . bookkeeper . . . bank
. . . lawyer . . . forming an
advertising agency*

Of all specialized services, an accountant is most needed.

The right accountant often really costs a small firm nothing at all. Used frugally and properly, the right accountant can frequently save you the cost of his fees again and again.

Today, simply coping with government forms is difficult for the owner of a tiny firm. The accountant can take over for you, filling out much of the necessary paperwork and explaining each piece to you carefully before you sign it. The right accountant can keep you out of financial trouble in many ways. He can warn you, but cannot stop you from unwise, false moves.

He can help you select a temporary bookkeeper by the hour, and often teach you or your spouse how to set up and keep your own books. He can catch bookkeeping errors, calculate all corporate taxes and often advise you on tax benefits you might not otherwise be aware of, and handle your personal taxes as well.

For years, our accountant was like a member of our family. He was with us through good times, boom and adversity, when we were tiny and when we were a good deal bigger (although still small). He helped us select and train personnel, buy accounting equipment (even a computer), approve and get credit. He acted for us in tax audits and checked out order margins. We never concluded royalty agreements, formed a corporation, got into a partnership or made an acquisition without clearing certain financial and tax implications with him. He advised us how best to take advantage of a tax loss, helped us prepare cash flow estimates and assisted in countless other ways. Now he is retired, and we use Coopers & Lybrand, one of the big eight accounting firms, in much the same way.

From moonlight start to selling out or going public, the right accountant can be your right arm. As soon as you start making money, he can help free you to make more money. He may gamble on a young, tiny firm's future and charge very, very little to start. If you have very little money, find the right young accountant just starting out, and be frank. If he likes you and has confidence in you, he may become part of your team for a very modest starting fee.

A good way to select one is to call larger accounting firms and ask for recommendations of smaller ones. Another way is to call the professor of accounting at a good business college. Interview several. Check clients or recent employers for opinions. In talking to each prospective accountant, explain that you can pay little now but will pay more as soon as able. Consider an older, semi-retired accountant. He may be understanding about working for little. But get a good accountant and you won't regret it.

Your accountant can keep your books, but will cost you more an hour than a bookkeeper would. A bookkeeper enters transactions. An accountant starts work with the bookkeeper's figures. With very little help from your accountant, you can keep your own books to start.

But let's hope that your mail order moonlighting business prospers. If so, you may soon prefer to pay a temporary bookkeeper by the hour and use the time saved to make more money. If you have kept your own books, it will help you help the bookkeeper and help you keep a sense of control.

Tiny firms often get behind in their bookkeeping. Often the owner plans to keep his own books but does it irregularly, if at all, and soon gets hopelessly behind. Sometimes the firm gets a bookkeeper for three hours or ten hours a week of work. Often, in either case, records get tangled, papers misplaced, errors are made, and soon there's a bookkeeping mess to clean up. Roughly speaking, at this stage, each hour of work undone or done incorrectly takes three to five hours to catch up. And usually a regular bookkeeper will not attempt it. Only a higher-cost-per-hour specialist in cleaning up such messes may then do so.

If you do your own bookkeeping, do it *correctly*, under your accountant's instruction and supervision, and do it regularly and promptly. Don't get behind. And if you use a temporary bookkeeper, see that books are up to date. If one leaves and you can't get another, fill in yourself or, if necessary, pay your accountant to come in extra hours even at higher costs per hour. Keep up to date and you won't regret it.

When you pay for an accountant and a bookkeeper, much of what you can ever find out about what they do is contained in your financial statement. Preparing a statement is legally necessary. You pay for the statement. You might as well know fully what it's trying to tell you.

A financial statement is the scoreboard of your business. Never can so few words say so much to anyone who understands them as in a financial statement. Your own financial statements can become a continuing course on how to make more money. In each new statement, you can see briefest but most needed do's and don't's, easiest ways to cut overhead, where to get most profitable sales, how best to increase net worth. You get more value from your accountant. You can better understand what he's advising you. You don't have to ask him simple, basic, fundamental questions and get the answer at an accountant's hourly rate. You can now ask him for more advanced help and get it in the same time and at no more cost than when he had to explain beginning principals.

And of course, if you start selling the trade and giving credit, getting financial statements from those asking for credit is more practical if you can understand them. Understanding how experts rate financial statements can also help the firm asking for a business loan. I think that if you are in business you should be able to clearly understand a financial statement. I may be prejudiced. Business Studies, Inc., of which I am president, publishes a course on "The Analysis of Financial Statements." Four-hundred banks and the Small Business Administration used our course to train lending officers.

As soon as mail order brings you money in the mail, make up a bank deposit slip showing cash, money orders or checks. Keep a duplicate for whatever simplest bookkeeping records you set up, take your deposit to your bank and open up a business account. Let's hope that you will keep putting money in the bank and for some time not need to borrow from it or require long-term credit.

Mail order done on a cash basis can bring in cash in time to pay inventory and advertising bills. Each profitable purchase can bring in cash to pay for the next. The safest procedure is to keep original test advertising and inventory costs to what you have in the bank. If you have no money, you must start with free write-ups or risk advertising by someone else. You can only sell what is immediately available and buy inventory as orders come in. In either case, safest projection is to keep future advertising and inventory risk to profits made. You may proceed slowly, but you will pay bills promptly *without* borrowing money.

As you grow and prosper, you can develop good credit. Try to avoid the precedent of paying cash. If you have to pay cash, make the provision that on the next order you get credit. Make your first orders on credit *small.* Refuse any personal guarantee. But pay first credit orders *the day you get the bill.* You'll be surprised how fast you'll be considered good credit. Then begin to specify to your salesman that for bigger orders you want thirty-day credit, and specify this in writing on each order. Pay in *three weeks.* Now for *occasional big orders,* ask suppliers for sixty-day credit. Specify sixty-day payment on the order. Always pay in *50* days. With some suppliers for occasional orders you can go to *90* days. If so, pay in *80* days. Continue to buy smaller orders for normal credit from suppliers, pay ahead of time, and always take cash discounts you are entitled to. On the longer credit orders, you will lose a cash discount, but this is a loan to your business. If at any time any supplier asks for any personal guarantee, explain that it is against your policy.

Officers and directors of corporations are often asked by suppliers and lending institutions to personally guarantee purchases and loans. If you sign your name to any such commitment, you are running a personal risk for your spouse and family. If your business grows and makes bigger purchases and gets bigger loans and you continue to sign such guarantees, you can dramatically increase these personal risks. You are taking away more and more of the personal protection that ownership of a corporation is intended to give stockholders. Don't do it.

When your account at the bank builds up, speak to the highest officer you can. Tell him that you want for your corporation the tiniest loan the bank will make, even $50 for one month. Explain that you cannot guarantee it personally. Explain that you want to build up a record of repayment with small, unguaranteed loans.

Many banks will not make a loan to a business unless guaranteed by assets or by a personal guarantee of officers, or by both. You should be willing to assign business assets such as cash in the bank, inventory or receivables. You should not sign a personal guarantee (although many successful businessmen do). If your bank won't give you a tiny loan on this basis, it's worth looking for another bank that will. Switch your account, however small, to the first good bank that will make your corporation its tiniest loan with *no* personal guarantee signature. This may not be possible. In any case, repay the loan in a few days. Three months later, borrow a little more for 90 days. Pay it back in 40 days. Soon you should be able to borrow your needs seasonally at competitive interest and, perhaps, with no personal guarantee signature.

For years, our company has borrowed fairly big money when necessary with no personal guarantees. More recently, we've been able to self-finance much faster growth from profits–without borrowing. If you have partners, it's wise to insist that all or none sign personal guarantees for your corporation. If you won't sign guarantees and they will, they become your money partners and may soon take over. If they are solely money partners and signing such guarantees is their contribution, that is another matter.

Does a moonlighter need a lawyer?

A lawyer can make an excellent case that you do, from your start as a mail order moonlighter until you retire. Most mail order moonlighters make their first tests without a lawyer. We hope that you will succeed and grow. If so, you will need a lawyer, perhaps two lawyers–one as your business lawyer and one for patents and copyrights.

In each case, you will need an able lawyer whom you can grow with. To start, the cost of a lawyer can be small. Often, in a brief telephone conversation, a lawyer can give a legal answer that can save you a costly mistake. Highly skilled lawyers have played along for modest fees for years with clients whom they had faith in. Sometimes it has paid off for them.

If you get a good lawyer, realize that his time is his money. You must protect it if you wish him to work with you. Usually a lawyer needs facts on paper to give you a sensible opinion. Your work can save his time and reduce your legal bills. The right lawyer will be a realist. He will know your financial limitations and your legal needs. He will realize that, as a tiny entrepreneur, you must walk a tightrope between not taking a step without a lawyer where one is really needed and not using a lawyer for one unnecessary minute. Get the right one, and you can build together.

A successful big businessman uses a lawyer and accountant as a part of his team in on every deal. The right lawyer pays for himself in every negotiation. In any involved negotiation, the quality and caliber of the respective lawyers has much to do with which principal ends up with the best part of the deal.

Lawyers (and law firms) are like doctors. There are specialists and general practitioners. There are great numbers of lawyers greatly varying in training, specialties and competence. There are lawyers who primarily handle real estate, sometimes with little experience in many corporate problems. Young lawyers may be inexperienced. Older lawyers can be, if successful, very expensive, and if unsuccessful, incompetent. Law firms may assign their most junior to guide and counsel you.

You need a lawyer to draw up contracts acquiring sole rights to a product, possibly a partnership with others, help you deal with a government agency, perhaps advise you on procedures from avoiding advertising overclaims to complying with a department of labor regulation. You may not need a lawyer for months or for a year at a time, or you may need him on the telephone only twice a week. You have no need of a patent or copyright lawyer until you are seeking or investigating a patent or a copyright. The more successful you become, the more probable it will be that, from time to time, you will need good legal advice.

Call a top law school. Speak to the dean's office. Ask for recommendations of top-ranking graduates just starting on their own. Ask a big law firm to recommend a small one. Ask a successful businessman friend for his suggestions. His request to *his* lawyer for a recommendation may get you a good one. A semi-retired lawyer formerly with a big-firm background could be a great help if he might be tempted to work with you. He might be, if convenient to him in hours and where you meet. In each case, it will depend on whether, after meeting you, the lawyer or law firm *likes* you and believes in you. In any business, it's worth the time and effort to seek and find the best possible lawyer *for you* that you can possibly get.

A man who is his own lawyer has a fool for a client, but there is a narrow line between what your lawyer can best do and what you can best do in making an agreement. To use your lawyer as a father figure and throw the entire problem in his lap is not fair to him and can be expensive for you. There are lawyers who are superb negotiators and handle entire negotiations for their clients. But they are expensive, and effective only if so familiar with your operation as to almost be a part of it, and practical only for larger transactions. I try to work as part of a little negotiating team with my lawyer. *I* take responsibility for achieving agreement with the other party to all negotiating points I'm after. Only then do I submit the agreement to my lawyer with a memorandum detailing exactly what I'm trying to achieve.

Lawyers are expensive. I try to have the best and use him the least. Essentially, I ask my lawyer to check that each point of agreement I've come to in my negotiation says legally what I think it says. I count on him to avoid traps in any contract submitted to me in a negotiation. I rely on him for suggestions and advice in countless ways. I try to give him the facts on paper–all the facts–and get a fairly fast answer at modest cost. I believe that you can do the same.

What do you do if you don't want to work with an advertising agency? You can buy advertising direct from the publisher or broadcaster. Or, if you start to advertise widely, you may choose to start your own advertising agency.

An advertising agency prepares advertising and buys it for an advertiser (called a client), but is usually paid by the newspaper or other media from which the advertising has been purchased.

Many years ago, an advertising agent (or agency) was a salesman for the media. The agent received a commission of 15% for making the sale. The preparation of advertising copy started as an extra convenience. When advertisers grew larger, an agent began to act for the advertiser as the real boss, but got media to give the 15% commission. The media did so, feeling they were still helped by the agent. The agent became only known as an agency and usually built up an organization with creative and other services. The media then began to employ salesmen (media representatives) to call on the agencies.

So important were the agencies to the media that the media often cooperated with them by refusing to give the 15% agency commission to an advertiser which tried to buy "direct" (without the agency). Different media associations often set up standards to determine whether or not someone stating he or she and associates was an advertising agency should be "recognized" as one and given the 15% advertising agency commission. In particular, it used to be difficult for an advertiser to organize his own advertising agency and receive "recognition" and the 15% commission. In recent years, this has become simpler, but some media, mostly a few newspapers, still require that an advertising agency be "bona fide." Even they usually accept the naming of *two* outside "clients" of the advertising agency as proof that the agency is "bona fide."

Media often have credit recognition rules with minimum net worth requirements for an advertising agency to be given credit. But most media will accept a check with order for the cost, less 15%, from any new advertising agency which fills out a form, and often without the form. Many advertisers, even small mail order firms, have formed their own advertising agencies. Often this has only meant setting up a proprietorship with a different name for the advertising agency than for the mail order firm. Sometimes the entire procedure has been to register the advertising agency name at the county clerk's office (for a nominal fee), to print up some sheets of stationery and open a bank account. Quite a few small mail order firms have done so. Sometimes a mail order man becomes quite proficient at advertising, enjoys it and after opening a "house agency" makes it an active one. He handles outside accounts and enjoys another way of making money.

Some media will grant recognition and give quite limited credit to a small, new advertising agency with almost no "red tape" or stringent credit requirements. If you do decide to set up and own a "house" advertising agency, just talk to the radio station, magazine or whatever medium and ask for credit and recognition. Newspapers often refer you to their association which has minimum net worth and other formal requirements. Some newspapers and many other media will deal with any advertising agency individually. Each one which grants you recognition and credit, even in a tiny way, if paid promptly can be a credit reference for others.

The American Association of Advertising Agencies has set up standard order and other forms for advertising agencies. The use of standard forms for ordering advertising from media and other purposes can be quite helpful.

Who knows . . . maybe you'll like the advertising agency business, too. Or perhaps you'll begin to value more the use of a good advertising agency.

Chapter 4

OVERHEAD

*What it is ... your starting
advantage ... costs to charge to
business ... controlling overhead as
you grow*

A moonlighter can start with almost no overhead.

For first-time tests, out-of-pocket expenses for overhead can be trifling. But some overhead starts with the first phone call, the first letter mailed and the first drive in a car anywhere on moonlighting business.

If you test an ad that succeeds, your business will become more active and your overhead will start to creep in and up. You will make *more* phone calls. You'll use *more* gas and oil, pay *more* tolls, use taxies, buses, subways for your moonlighting business–and all costing money. You may buy someone lunch (and get some free ones too) or take an overnight trip for your moonlighting business. This could go on indefinitely. Make sure that all business expenses are accounted for so that the IRS can see proof of the deductions. Know what you can deduct. Ask your accountant, read the latest book on the newest tax reform or consult with your nearest IRS office.

You will still have very little overhead compared with setting up an outside place of business with any rent, utilities, equipment and staff. But any overhead expense is something to *avoid* whenever possible. Each time you spend one cent for overhead, ask yourself, "Wouldn't it be nicer to keep this cent as profit?" If you're making money, just avoiding spending a dollar can create a dollar profit.

When you perform all functions yourself, your organization is you and can do less than a larger organization. But you can make your organization larger with no employee commitments.

You can have mail keyed to box numbers at your neighborhood post office and pick it up and open it yourself. Or you can use a mailing house with mail addressed to a post office near them, have mail picked up and counted by them with counts to each key forwarded to you, mail opened by them, checks and cash recorded by them (with tallies forwarded to you) and deposited in your bank by them. Computer labels can be typed by them. Orders can be shipped by them from merchandise stored by them. You need only pay for each service per piece as performed.

List brokers can help you select lists to mail to. List managers can help you rent to others names you accumulate as you make mail order sales. Mailing firms, with automated equipment, can mail any number of mailing pieces up to the millions for you. Their machines do everything–insert, seal, stamp, collate by zip code–at far less cost than you would ever employ direct labor for. Your printed material comes to them from the printer, and they take the mailings to the post office. You may not need to store anything.

Advertising agencies can prepare the advertising completely. Or you can employ free-lance copywriters and artists for so much for a specific job and pay for it by setting up your own advertising agency and saving the 15% commission.

You can buy products complete in the U.S. or import them, or you can control manufacture without any factory. If you own molds or dies, you can turn over making the entire product to one supplier or to several, performing separate functions with one final assembler.

One of the biggest money-making mail order men I know (another alumnus) has made millions of dollars in mail order as a Gypsy businessman. There is *no* continuing overhead. Employees only exist month-to-month or week-to-week, paid generously but with *no* commitments. A lease is quickly cancellable. Inventory is bought hand-to-mouth. This is because mail order profits can be *ephemeral . . .* here today and gone tomorrow.

For decades, my friend has every so often made his mail order killing, then folded his tent and vanished, sometimes for several years off on a favorite trip. He goes into mail order as others go into the market. He simply pulls out when the going's tough. And with this method, he's made more money in relation to time and strain and been a better father and husband with more time for his family than any really big earner I know.

You can follow the plan, modified as you prefer, expanding outside your home for a big campaign and back to your home for smaller continuity of volume. Of course, supervising free-lance people and services is work. Depending on others can be disappointing, delaying and frustrating. But for anyone, the safest mail order approach is to start slowly and safely.

Some overhead is necessary. Much overhead, on second thought, is not so necessary. Avoid any overhead as long as you can. Then keep it as low as you can as long as you are in the business.

The biggest overhead expense in any small business is often the salary of the owner or owners. If you have a job, can live within your income and *need* not draw at all from your new mail order venture, you are giving it a far better chance to succeed. Profits made that you don't spend as personal income can start building capital. The more you need to draw money *quickly* and *sizably*, the more risky your moonlighting venture will be.

On the other hand, in operating a small business, the owner sometimes forgets or neglects charging to the business small business expenses he has paid for personally. This is also bad. Whether it's a postage stamp, a phone call, gas money or whatever expense you've paid for, get it back from your business as soon as you lay it out. Your moonlighting business need not tax you or your family. Repaying such expenses is a reminder that your business must make the money to cover such overhead and a reminder to try to *cut* such expenses down.

There's quite a difference between the objectives of a job and business. Many people successful in their jobs get into deep trouble in their business because they don't fully recognize this. And what a difference it is! In a job you want to earn the biggest income possible. In a business you want to build the biggest net worth possible. You are building an estate capital for growth and a cushion against business disaster. In the sudden changes of the economy, the skyrocketing inflation, the need for more inventory investment, the fluctuation currency of recent years, our conservative net worth has saved us at certain times when otherwise we might not have made it.

It's absolutely vital for you not just to make good profits but to build net worth with those profits. A big earner going into business tends to draw big income from that business too fast. Many executives think that in going into their own business they've simply got a new boss, themselves, and draw big money, which keeps their new venture from building capital. Many privately owned businesses, year after year, make nominal profits but provide big salaries to owners. But this is *not* a way to safely operate any business. The more you grow, the more capital you need. The winners in small businesses are those who draw less from their business, perhaps less than they would like, while building capital with *more* than average speed.

Most mergers are submergers, the one in trouble being swallowed without risk and on a bargain basis by the stronger one. And if you build net worth, one day you'll get that desperate phone call from an otherwise able competitor. And you'll grow more in one day than in years, and safely.

So when others drive Porsches and live in super-luxury homes, just point to your financial statements and say, "These are my pearls." And tell your spouse that all else will surely follow, and in this way it will belong to you *permanently*.

Telephone bills can mount up quickly. Charge business calls and minimum service charges to your business pro rata. Longer calls get bigger bills. Make only necessary calls. Call at lowest toll rate hours. Write down what you want to say first. You'll reduce the cost accordingly.

Use the telephone to replace a lengthy letter or to avoid a trip. The telephone can make and save money. Used blindly, it's a blank check on your business. Every unnecessary phone call and phoning minute is destroying money that would otherwise build capital or give income.

Spending money on some kinds of overhead takes *time* as well as money. When you cut it out, you sometimes not only save money but *make* money with the time you also save. Much time as well as money is wasted in business entertaining. It's fun to have lunch as a business expense, but is it doing any good? For years, my wife and I have brought our lunches in paper bags to our office. We very rarely have a business lunch with anyone. The business saves money and, with our time also saved, we are doing some job that would be otherwise undone.

For a mail order moonlighter, time is precious. There is no time to waste on rationalizing business entertaining. Avoid entertaining for business where possible, at least until your business is sound and sizable. Travel can be postponed as well, in most cases. A car may soon be needed just for business or not needed for years or not needed at all. Location will determine this.

The cooperation you get from your local post office may affect this. If you have to mail your customers' packages each afternoon, will the post office pick up for you or will you take packages to the post office? UPS will pick up at your door for a small minimum weekly fee. UPS can be less expensive for certain size and weight packages. It also delivers faster and with less breakage for more breakable packages. Using UPS might save renting or buying a car. If you need a car for business occasionally, rent a car occasionally. If your business grows and you need one continually, buy or lease one. If your accountant approves, your business might buy a car from you, one you find yourself using mainly for business. Caution! Insurance for company-owned cars jumps to far higher rates than for privately owned cars. It may be wiser for your company to contribute so much a mile to maintenance and amortization as well as paying for gas, oil, tolls and repairs while you continue to own your car. Again, check with your accountant.

Next come professional fees for lawyer and accountant. Prudently used as needed, neither should be as high as your phone bill, and yet they are far more necessary. We've already discussed keeping these expenses down.

A mail order moonlighter can start using part of one room in his home for his business. As the business grows, the space used tends to grow. Papers need to be filed. Sometimes things need to be stored. A moonlighting business should pay some kind of rent and share of utilities (heat, light and power). If the business grows, instead of getting a separate place of business it's sometimes wise for the business to contribute a fair share to a somewhat larger home. You may then have a separate room as an office with room for files and perhaps storage space in your garage or elsewhere. It's realistic and fair to your family to pay something for the use of the facilities. It can be a token at first and raised gradually to what your accountant considers reasonable.

Later you may have some expense in going to trade shows. Usually there's no charge to attend, but expenses getting there and for lunches or even staying overnight are involved. When you grow considerably, you'll have more overhead expenses. You may have a secretary come in by the hour as needed, as well as a bookkeeper. If you store considerable inventory, you will probably insure it against fire and possible theft. If you sell to stores, you will need product liability insurance to protect you and those who distribute your product against a possible lawsuit by an unhappy user of your products. You might join a trade association and pay dues. You might exhibit at trade shows. You might subscribe to trade papers, specialized publications, courses and services, like a tax service. Of course, this is in the future.

If you're quite successful, you might rent a place of business or even buy one. If you do, you might have repairs and maintenance. You might rent machinery or office equipment (starting with a typewriter). You might hire some assistants, part or full-time. Now you would have real estate taxes, social security taxes and perhaps other taxes. Your company might be paying health insurance for your staff (including you). Little miscellaneous expenses would creep in from a little Christmas party for staff and suppliers to photocopy paper for a rented photocopy machine (also overhead) and stationery, printing and sundry expenses.

You might start as a moonlighter with a personal computer. You'll soon find it invaluable. You'll also get some software–and then more. And as you grow, you'll never stop updating and trading in computers and software.

We started with a little computer for one function only. We went on to a more general one. Then we got a far more powerful one, a Data General. Then we got an IBM 36. Soon we added terminals all over the office. Then we began to computerize Huber Hoge and Sons. Soon we had a modem in our Long Island plant and one in our Milwaukee warehouse. Then we added two IBM PC ATs and connected them to our IBM 36. Meanwhile, for years, we've had two CPT word processors. At the same time, we've spent more and more on peripherals and software and most of all on programming. But it has all paid off for us as we've grown, and it will for you, too.

I don't calculate overhead exactly the way accountants do. For my purposes, I include depreciation of furniture and office equipment, automobile or building improvements. But advertising I consider in quite a different way, which I will explain later.

To me, overhead is any expense, outside of advertising, that I cannot calculate per-unit as needed specifically to make or to ship a product. Product cost, component cost, product assembly or manufacture, labor cost, cost of running a mold or die, packaging cost and packing cost are not overhead. And any other cost that can be fairly easily calculated per unit and is needed specifically to make or ship the product is not overhead.

Each of these expenses can be calculated at so much per completed unit. You can do the same with an allowance for the cost of handling returns, including refurbishing and repacking them (and cost of replacement packages). In each case, it's fairly simple to get an experience record of what percentage of purchasers don't pay or return the product. You can then apply, as a reserve for the cost of refunds and returns, this percentage to each order. Every businessman needs to know the total of all such direct costs and reserves that can be calculated per order. He needs to make enough gross profit on each order over all such expenses and advertising costs so that, multiplied by total orders received, it can pay all overhead (operating expenses not applied to each order) and still provide a net profit before taxes.

Just looking at the total and the breakdown of overhead and operating costs is usually a shock for a small businessman. A mail order moonlighter starts with as close to no overhead as can be achieved in business. But it is vital for him to look at his financial statement at the end of each year, extract from it all overhead items and total them. Do it once and you will think quite differently about the price you need to charge for anything and the cost you need to get it for. Do it each year, and you will be surprised at how the overhead varies in percentage from year to year. With us, it's varied from 9.5% to 22.5%.

In good years, overhead sneaks in the door without being noticed. After several good years, the "nut" (break-even point) is suddenly substantially higher. A bad year raises the percentage of overhead to sales, that is, sales drop faster than overhead expenditures. A disaster year does so even more. But bad and disaster years force slashing overhead. If sales pick up faster than overhead, the overhead percentage drops.

Once you get a "feel" for testing and projecting, you seldom have overall losses in advertising. If you test small, pyramid carefully and cut quickly when advertising fails, you can be surprisingly safe in your expenditures.

The essence of mail order strategy is to vary advertising risk and volume as results warrant. This means *irregular* volume. All you need is *regular* overhead at too high a level to quickly go out of business. Flexibility in overhead is all-important.

Even after you succeed in a big way, management is best when small and tight. The more you do yourself, the less overhead you take on and the more control you get in every way. You can still do your own buying, check out your advertising claims personally, know your inventory intimately and eliminate most problems I've discussed.

A little restraint in overhead expansion may lose some immediate business but, overall, *save* your mail order business.

Chapter 5

MOONLIGHTER MATH

*Calculating overhead costs and
margins and improving them . . .
setting price . . . determining ad
profit and loss*

The average non-businessman or business employee is often un-aware of the cost structure of any business. Amazingly shrewd businessmen often visualize quite a different cost structure in mail order than in their own non-mail order business.

Since mail order sales are direct to the consumer, it is expected that an article may be sold for less and still make more profit than if sold through the trade. This is seldom possible. Too low a sales price loses money.

The mail order pro will usually rule out selling any product with inadequate mail order margin. Margin is the difference between all it costs you to make, sell and ship your product and the price your cus-tomer pays for it. More factors go into *accurately* figuring costs than often realized.

We do not sell any product by mail order that we lack the margin to sell through the trade. For the trade, we need enough margin to give 50% discount to retailers, or 55% to 60% to wholesalers and above this 5% to 10% to sales representatives. We must also pay for trade and consumer advertising, trade shows, store display and packaging. We have billing costs and collection losses.

It's hard to realize that mail order selling and handling costs can be just as high, particularly when only simpler, lower-cost packaging may be required. But they usually are. Advertising cost alone is usual-ly a number of times the percentage of selling price as in sales to the trade. Individual mail order shipping and handling costs are far more per item than for bulk shipments to jobbers or dealers. Returned goods percentages are far higher, because people buy before they see what they are buying. There are more damaged goods when shipped by mail in small packages. There is some post office or other in-transit mail theft. If sold on credit, there are often more bad credit losses than to the trade. Mail order administrative costs can be higher.

In mail order, the margin is calculated for each mail order and is called the "order margin." The order margin is the amount of dollars and cents left for advertising and profit after the item cost "in the mail" is calculated. Each direct cost to buy or make and ship it is included, as well as allowances for spoilage, refusals, returned goods and, if sold on credit, bad debts.

No one can operate a mail order business safely without understanding all such costs "in the mail" and how to calculate an order margin. Without an order margin, you cannot accurately determine the profit or loss produced by a mail order ad, even after all orders are received. If you calculate an order margin incorrectly or fail to be guided by it, you can go broke. Yet it's easy to grasp and use. All that is necessary is to include *all* costs and allowances and to figure each accurately. Order margins become inaccurate when each such cost or allowance is not calculated or is miscalculated. Sometimes those new to mail order are not aware of, haven't analyzed or prefer not to think about certain of these costs. Here is how we break such costs down for a mail order item.

We first calculate each cost of purchasing in the U.S., and manufacturing 1,000 units. We can then realize more fully the possible savings in dollars achievable in lower competitive quotations.

Because, as a moonlighter, you will probably start manually processing orders without modern equipment or a computer, I am giving you a detailed explanation of how we did this before we were computerized at present labor cost, etc., but merely what classifications of costs you must calculate.

The following is a breakdown of cost on having manufactured for us by a U.S. supplier a plastic fishing lure . Each cost is calculated for 1,000 units.

Item cost per M	$ 467.00
Freight inbound parts	7.50
Component	54.00
Assembly Labor	85.00
UPS inbound for assembled item	9.00
Total unpacked cost	$622.50
Item Cost for 1,000 sets of three is:	1,867.50

Next we calculate the costs and allowances of mail order processing and shipping. Our mail order offer is for a set of three lures. We will not use expensive store packaging but instead use lowest-cost mail order jiffy bags.

To ship each 1,000 packages of three lures, we have the following costs and allowances:

item cost 1000 sets	$ 1,867.50
mail order package 1M	70.00
packing labor	150.00

mail order label	22.00
order entry	250.00
postage	1,320.00
mailing cost	67.00
allowance for returns 1%*	99.50
check cashing	120.00
royalty 5% of selling price**	497.50
Fed excise tax (if payable)***	407.05
Total cost for set of three	**$4,870.55**
M/O selling price 1M	9,950.00
plus coll ship charge 1.32	1,320.00
Total Received	11,270.00
less Total Item Cost	4,870.55
10% of Sales at 7% NY Sls Tax	69.95
Net Cost 1M	4,940.50
GR Profit after Item Cost	6,329.50
GR Profit %	.5616

* **ALLOWANCE for RETURNS:** Selling Price & Ship Chg .... $11.27 = .1127
** **ROYALTY:** 5% of M/O Selling Price .... 9.95 = .4975
*****EXCISE TAX:** 1/11th of Wholesale Price at 50/10/10 Discount = .405 × 9.95 .. 4.03 = .3664

Now we want to convert each per thousand cost to a per item cost. To do so accurately and easily, we need only move each decimal point three digits to the left.

The total cost for one package of three lures in the mail with all allowances becomes $4.87

Selling price is $9.95 plus $1.32 shipping, or $11.27.

We subtract $4.94 from $11.27 and get our order margin of $6.33. It is 56% of $11.27.

We have **not** included advertising costs or overhead.To make a profit before overhead on one ad run, we must receive enough orders from that ad so that $6.33 for each order received from it totals more that its advertising cost . . . including advertising production.

Profits from profitable ads must total more than losses from losing ads. The difference between making and losing ads for one year must be more than all overhead costs for the year. After that, we must pay federal and state taxes before earning a net profit after taxes.

We have not included any state tax in the order margin. In New York State it is 4% plus county sales tax on the retail price. We are responsible for collecting this from each New York State citizen who buys from us and sending on the tax money collected to the State. If we don't collect, we must pay it out of our pocket. If the county tax is 3%, this means 7% of $9.95 = $.6965. New York State orders average 10% of all orders nationally. A New York State business would include 10% of 7% of $9.95, or $.06965, in its order margin. Check your state for its sales tax, if any. Check latest rulings on any liability in other states.

Any cost not included, or shown as less than actual, makes the total of estimated costs less. This causes the order margin to seem larger than it is. To determine the profit or loss for an ad, you multiply the order margin per order times the number of orders received and subtract the ad cost. An apparently larger than actual order margin per order causes the total order margin for the ad to appear larger than it actually is. The result can be a fool's paradise. Break-even or loss ads are assumed to be profitable. Losing advertising can be happily expanded and losses multiplied. An accurately calculated order margin enables a mail order operator to exercise tighter control of advertising purchase decisions. An inaccurate one causes his business to careen out of control.

As explained, we first figure costs per thousand. You may prefer to figure the cost per item from the start. For an item which you buy complete, it's simple. You are usually billed per item. Otherwise, divide the number of items bought into the amount of the bill. If you pay freight cost (trucking, parcel post, UPS or whatever) divide the number of items shipped into the total of the shipping bill. Figuring each other cost is almost that simple.

Postage is. It must be paid to the Post Office per item. An item that you buy complete may not come in a self-mailing carton or cushioned envelope mailer. If it does not, include the cost of one and the labor cost to insert the item. To figure labor cost, pack a hundred cartons or mailing envelopes. Time yourself. Are you clumsy and slow to start? Will you and others be more dexterous later? Or are you speeding through at a rate you could never keep up, much less a goof-off assistant? Be neither overhopeful nor hopeless about future labor speed and cost per item. Make a realistic estimate and include it.

If you buy a finished product, an order margin may be lower (because of the profit of the seller). But you have a *known* cost. You get a bill and pay. When you buy components and assemble it yourself you have more variables, particularly in your labor cost. Your margin for a completed product is usually more accurate and stable than your perhaps higher order margin when you manufacture or assemble yourself.

The more of the manufacturing process you do yourself, the more carefully you must calculate *all* labor costs per unit. If you buy a completed product, you usually get credit for defective merchandise received (if you check it). If a perishable product, you need to calculate the percentage of spoilage. There will be some spoilage of ingredients or components if you manufacture. There will be some overruns of components that do not match other components and, hence, cannot be used.

Add up the dollar value of spoiled or impossible-to-use components or ingredients. Divide into it the dollar value of all such components or ingredients purchased. You now have the percentage of spoilage. Multiply this by the dollar value of such components or ingredients used in one item. Add the figure arrived at to the cost of such components or ingredients used in one item. It may be just 15 or 2% of a component, costing pennies. Calculating *each* cost this carefully gives you an accurate order margin.

As soon as you have any employees, even part-time, you have extra social security costs to contribute. You contribute to unemployment insurance as well. Any employee working regularly gets a regular vacation while paid but not performing. According to law, in the smallest places of business there must be provision for regular break periods of ten minutes while employees are paid but not performing. The bathroom must be visited occasionally by any employee. If an employee works regularly and gets sick, will you pay him or her for hours or days off the job? In a little venture you may do so. And almost every employee is occasionally sick. Even small ventures often get an accident and health insurance plan and often life insurance as well, to which the employer contributes. And what about the cost of a foreman or supervisor who directs, but does not produce?

The cost of packing and any other labor is actually more than the hourly rate paid. Labor cost of packing, assembly or manufacture is easily obtained. Just keep track of hours worked by each worker, multiply the hourly wage cost by hours worked and divide by the total number of items packed, assembled or manufactured. We then add 20% in our estimates for such contingencies.

If a mail order moonlighter performs any labor function himself, he may not consider it a cost. Therefore he may not include the cost of his own time. But labor of any kind is a cost, whether performed by owner, spouse, children or friends for nothing. As soon as you sell your product in volume, you can no longer do all the labor required yourself. And you cannot expect others in your own family or whomever to help you for nothing forever. Even if you do all the work now, you'll hopefully grow and have these costs later, so let's estimate and include them. Calculate your time, or that of anyone helping you for nothing, at the hourly wage it will cost you to hire someone else.

Whenever you increase production and hire assistants and staff, there is a break-in period when labor costs are higher. A somewhat increased labor cost overall can be guestimated to average this out. In importing, be sure to include duty and brokerage, as well as freight and insurance. If your product is subject to an excise tax, figure a 10% excise tax will be one-eleventh of the jobber price which you would sell your product at, not the mail order price to the consumer. Check your accountant on this for latest tax rulings.

If you provide instructions for assembly or use, what was the printing cost per piece? Did the printer pay freight cost, or was there any trucking cost to you (or parcel post or UPS)? Determine the labor cost of putting each sheet or booklet of directions in the mailing box or envelope. Again, do it, time it and calculate it, figuring the probable labor cost per hour.

Now you get the idea. It's very simple but meticulous work. You don't leave anything out. You figure each cost realistically. Do you have a giveaway? If so, what does it cost? What was the trucking cost to you per unit? What is the labor time and estimated cost to pack it into your package or envelope or ship it separately (including cost of its own package and extra postage if needed?)

Is anything else being shipped with this offer? What about advertising literature to ask customers for repeat or other orders? Again, you need to determine the printing cost, trucking cost and labor cost of including it per item.

What does an address label cost you? What is the labor cost of applying it to the package? What is the labor of typing the label? Do it, time it, calculate the rate and cost per hour and, finally, the cost per item with necessary allowances. What does it cost you to open mail and sort it? Follow the same procedure. How about check cashing? The bank will cash a few checks without charge and more and more if your account reaches certain totals. As you get orders in volume, the bank will notice that far more checks are being cashed than normally. It will then charge you for each check it cashes over a minimum allowed free. Bank charges for check cashing vary widely. In Canada, we've paid as high as 25 cents a check. In the U.S., we allow 7 cents a check, although when our bank balances are fairly good we don't have to pay it. Your bank can give you a check-cashing cost. Include it.

How about getting your packages to the post office? Time this and calculate the labor cost per package. Are you paying a royalty? If so, calculate the royalty per item. Just multiply the selling price of one item to your mail order customer by your royalty percentage. Are you getting orders through credit cards? If so, what is the average percentage of sales made through credit cards that you are paying the credit card companies? It will vary by companies depending on their rates and your volume of sales through each. What is your labor cost of filling out the credit card forms, forwarding them to the credit card company and corresponding with them? Again, time the handling of 100 credit card orders, calculate the hourly rate times the number of hours required and divide by the number of credit card orders handled.

What percentage of all orders are by credit card? Take 100 orders (1,000 would be better), count how many are credit card orders and calculate the percentage. Now take the total of the credit card company charge per item and your estimated labor cost of handling paperwork with the credit card company figured per item. Multiply this total by the percentage (of all orders) which you have found credit cards to be. If credit cards are 40% of all orders, then the cost of selling via credit cards per order for all orders must be 40% of the cost of handling one order through a credit card.

It is a discipline. As described in these pages, it seems complicated. Done step by step, it's tedious but really quite simple. Use your good common sense. For a handful of orders in a losing test of an item you're surely giving up, don't lose further money in endless detailed calculations. I simply wish you to be aware of all possible costs involved.

How about returns? What percentage of your items is being sent back for a refund? In this case, you get back the merchandise and give the customer a refund check including the shipping charge the customer originally paid. You have a labor cost in unpacking each return. Sometimes the item is defective or has been damaged beyond repair in shipping. In either case, it's a dead loss. Or the product is as good as new, but needs a new shipping container and repacking. Or the product may need some minor refurbishing to make it saleable again.

Returns are usually low and most returns are usable. As soon as first returns begin, it's vital to estimate fairly exactly the percentage of returns. It's important to get a fairly good guestimate of the percentage of returns that are reusable.

Let's assume that returns are 3%, and 80% of those returns are reusable, but require new labor for packing and new packaging. Let's just assume that the value of the usable inventory equals the labor cost of handling it and the cost of the new packaging. This value will be higher if the return percentages are low. Therefore, simply show a return cost of 3% of the selling price and shipping charges for one item. If, however, returns for an item are above average, costs of handling returns must be calculated quite accurately.

This situation could occur from a defective product or from such poor packing of a delicate item as to cause great breakage. In this case, most returns would be worthless. You would be out the refund, plus most of the labor cost of processing returns. You must time the labor of handling 100 returns and calculate the cost per return. You could then reduce it somewhat arbitrarily for the value of salvaged products. A 24 cent per unit handling cost might come down to 21 cents, for instance. Add this to the refund cost. Then add the labor of writing the refund check and any bank charge for the check. Multiply this figure by the percentage of returns. This gives you the allowance to put in the order margin for returns.

As you make up an order margin, step by step, you will find each step simpler. If you sell C.O.D., figure the cost of handling one C.O.D. refusal. This means someone who turns the postman or UPS man away and refuses to accept the item ordered. When the C.O.D. package comes back to you, you must pay postage or transportation *both ways*, to the customer and back to you, plus the C.O.D. charge. You calculate exactly as for any other return, but include the C.O.D. costs there and back. If your offer has alternatives in model or multiples, make up an order margin for each alternative offer. Then determine the percentage of each 100 orders for each alternative, and average out. If 20% of your customers buy a deluxe model with a bigger order margin, subtract the regular order margin from the bigger deluxe order margin. Take 20% of the difference. Add this to the regular order margin. You now have the average combined order margin.

Usually, the first time a mail order moonlighter calculates his order margin, he leaves some costs out and calculates others at too low a figure. When he is first shown how to include all costs and calculate them correctly, he is usually surprised at how high the total of costs now becomes. And he is even more surprised at how much less order margin he has than he originally counted on.

An allowance for bad debts is a headache to figure for items billed directly by you. As a moonlighter, you will probably not sell on credit except through credit cards. However large you may become, you may never do so. And if you do, you'll be able to get help from a skilled professional, experienced in mail order credit collection. So don't give up mail order after reading the next several paragraphs. I'm taking it up in this course for a simple reason. If you are financially able and logistically organized to do so, selling on a direct billing basis can be quite profitable. And you should understand it.

What do you lose if someone does not pay you? You lose the full retail price and shipping charge which you billed but did not collect. You lose the printing cost, envelope cost and postage cost of each bill, statement and collection letter sent, plus the labor cost of typing and inserting each. Time the labor in typing the average bill, statement and collection letter. Add 20% for incidentals to the average hourly labor cost. Calculate the average time spent in billing and follow-up for collection and the labor cost to do so.

When you grant credit, you tie up money. Either you are losing interest you could earn on this money or you are paying the bank interest to borrow it. Estimate the average time from receipt of order to full payment. Multiply the daily interest rate which you pay or would pay your bank to borrow money, by the average number of days tied up by the retail price plus shipping charge of one item. Include this as a cost per item.

Key the first 500 bills sent. After six months, add up all payments received. Include in payments the net after subtracting collection fees of any payments collected by a collection lawyer or agency. Subtract the total of payments received from the total billed. Divide into this bad debt total the number of customers billed. This is your bad debt percentage. Multiply this by the total of retail price and shipping charge for one item. You have now calculated your allowance for bad debts for one item for a one-payment offer. Include it as a cost per item.

For time payments, your collection costs are often higher. You send more statements and collection letters. You may offer a cash-up or discount for payment in full after one or more time payments. If so, total your cost in the mail to give a single cash-up gift or discount, including postage and mailing labor. Divide the total of those billed into the total of those who accept the cash-up offer. Multiply the percentage by the cost in the mail of one cash-up. Include it as a cost per item. To calculate interest lost on money tied up, estimate the average unpaid balance over the average collection period. Otherwise, calculate interest cost as above.

Key the entire series of the first 500 bills and statements sent as instructed. Add up all full and partial payments received, including the net after fees of those through collection lawyers and agents. Subtract the total of payments from the total billed. Divide into this bad debt total the total number of customers billed. Multiply this by the retail price plus shipping charge of one item. Include this allowance for bad debts for one item for a time payment offer as a cost per item.

One cost included generally by large companies in an order margin is an arbitrary percentage for overhead (often 10%). I did so for years. But one partner I had insisted on *not* including overhead in a margin. He felt that overhead, any overhead, should be fought and avoided where possible and that including it in the order margin made it seem allowable to spend it. We now leave it out as well. For years, we covered all overhead with income from activities other than mail order. We used mail order to create capital and help launch and increase trade businesses. But now our mail order has grown so much this is no longer so.

The optimist happily leaves some costs out and is sure that others will be lower next week or month. The pessimist grimly assumes costs higher than actual as he slashes the order margin to pieces. The realist veers toward the fears of the pessimist, but simultaneously notes down what can and must be done to come closer to the hopes of the optimist. Just writing down the order margin correctly can become a guideline to improving each cost involved. And often the difference between mail order success and failure is implementing these cost improvements.

The shock of seeing each cost of a product "in the mail" can start you reducing that cost and become the first step toward scientific buying and cost control. Let's start.

Anything bought or made in hand-to-mouth quantities is often dramatically lower in cost in any reasonable volume. Bigger volume drives costs lower. Each labor step can usually be simplified and sped up with sharply lowered cost simply by *familiarity, continued work* at the same thing and organization of tasks performed. Hands grow more skillful. New molds or dies or just improved equipment may multiply production volume. Costs usually drop sharply as volume increases sharply. And mail order projection of a "hit" does increase volume sharply. The pessimist's order margin, if he assumes that in volume conditions will not change, may be far from reality. It can actually cause a success to be dropped. But the optimist's hopes need a realist to make them happen.

Reducing costs may increase profits, create a profit from a break-even or even turn a decided failure into a pronounced success. Reduced costs will sometimes make a reduced price possible to the mail order customer and sometimes jump sales far more proportionately.

If we buy for a small test like a small retailer, we're not going to get the price Sears-Roebuck pays. But if we project a successful test in big volume, we can get a volume price. It's a chicken and egg problem. Often only a low price to us makes possible big volume, which is the only way to get a low price. Act small in tests. Think as big as is realistic for projections. Plan ahead what you will need if your test succeeds.

Explain your problem to your manufacturer. Get quotations for the larger quantities. Ask him (or them) to go along with the volume price for the test. Some will. If he won't, ask for a retroactive discount when you hit an agreed-upon volume figure. Make it a figure that you can reasonably attain if you project. Can the manufacturer streamline the item, simplify it in some way for him, yet keep quality and salability for you? Is there a slightly smaller model? Can he give you a lower price in this way? How about painting and decoration? Can this be simplified? How would it look in a solid color dipped, rather than a hand-decorated design? Is the product now shipped fully assembled? Can it be shipped disassembled with assembly directions? How much labor cost will that save?

If you are buying a product packaged for store display, can the manufacturer pack it instead in a corrugated box or cushioned shipping envelope? This can save money for him. Can he pass it along to you? At least if he gives it to you for the same price, you're saving the cost of mail order shipper, its trucking cost to you and the labor of packing the item.

Check the postage or UPS costs. Is the package just over a certain weight classification? If four pounds and three ounces, just saving three ounces might save substantial postage. Again and again, we have slightly modified weights and sizes of shipping packages for substantial savings. Just dropping the store package and shipping in a shipping container can cut weight. Shipping knocked down almost always saves postage. And each simplification can save product cost, shipping cost, labor cost and postage cost.

If an item is small, compact, light and expensive, shipping cost to you may be a factor not worth worrying too much about. But freight costs, whether truck, train, plane, ship, bus, UPS or Parcel Post, never stop going up. In most cases, it is worthwhile trying to make savings. If your item is bulky, not light, and is inexpensive, then shipping cost to you and by you to your mail order customer is quite important.

First determine the freight classification under which your item is shipped. There are many freight classifications. An item shipped under an incorrect but expensive classification can cost considerably more than if classified correctly. For different situations, different shipping methods are lower-priced than others. You may be shipping parcel post and get a comfortable saving shipping UPS. You don't have to become a freight expert to make savings for your small business. You do have to ask questions and take nothing for granted.

When sending freight by truck, train, plane or ship, the smaller the shipment, the greater the penalty. For a small test, you must order in a very small way, and freight cost will be high per unit. But you can determine how much you need to ship at one time to get shipping cost down to a sensible percentage. This is particularly true in imports. On a 25% duty item, duty freight and brokerage can be over 60% on a very small shipment, when on a big shipment it would be 35%. Determine if you have a reasonable chance to bring in later the volume needed for a sensible shipping cost. To do so often means planning ahead. Such planning can save still higher-cost emergency fill-in shipments by air or however.

On some items, drop shipping from your supplier can be quite a help. If you are located on either coast, you can save money two ways by drop shipping from a Midwest supplier if his drop-ship labor charge to you is no more than your own shipping labor cost. For either UPS or the Post Office, shipping costs to most of the country will usually be lower from a Midwest point than from either coast. You save all shipping cost of merchandise coming *to* and from the supplier. You save *some* of the shipping cost to your customers by having your centrally located shipper use UPS. You send him your labels, addressed to your customers. He puts the label on a carton and ships it. But you must know that your supplier really ships promptly and effectively. That's why we almost never have a supplier drop-ship for us.

If you're making your product, can you manufacture it better and faster? Will making one or more molds or dies multiply production? If you have temporary molds, will a permanent one speed things up? Is there a piece of equipment like an ultrasonic sealer or whatever that will do the job faster? Can you use home workers? Regulations vary by state. The law is usually that a piece-worker can be given an incentive to work, but must be guaranteed a minimum wage. If a piece worker doesn't meet a quota, he or she usually isn't given work for the following week. Usually he meets the quota. There is some spoilage of material given out, and some is not returned and no product delivered. Such losses, if watched, are low. Overall labor cost is usually stable.

Sometimes a small supplier supplies a part, does some processing or makes a complete product for you, yet *cannot* do so at a practical price. He may lack facilities, have the wrong equipment or be inexperienced or even incompetent. Sometimes we've found a substantially lower price, higher quality and far more dependable delivery by switching to a more capable supplier.

In the testing phase, supplying the product is a speculation. It is hard to get cooperation. You, yourself, have little time to improve anything. The moment the test succeeds, the entire situation changes.

The order which you place for the demand caused by any projection of advertising is more interesting to the supplier. The prospect of getting still more volume becomes believable. You become more important to the seller. Competition begins its work. Some supplier is hungrier and needs business more at this time. His quotations are below your present supplier, who suddenly discovers that he can quote lower prices too. One supplier discovers a shortcut and can make the item faster. Another comes up with a nice product improvement. You get a quote from another country with a landed price in the U.S. better than you can make it here. You find that you can often be loyal and fair to those that deserve it, but switch in other cases. When you do, you often get your costs lower as your volume goes higher.

You may improve costs by taking over some or all assembly and manufacturing functions yourself. It depends on whether you have room to work in or can get temporary, month-by-month space. You must be suited to performing such functions. If not, it can cost more. Do what you're good at. Get others to do what you're weaker at. If you have partners, perhaps one has a feeling for and likes simple manufacturing. If so, you will probably improve your order margin with efficiencies, and improve your product as well.

Analyze your returns. Are they too high? Overhigh returns sharply reduce an order margin. If the product is the cause, and you can't correct the shortcoming, *drop it.* But is it the product? How about the directions on how to use it? How about the way you pack it? Is there unnecessary breakage? Read the mail. See what those requesting refunds say. After you've sent refund checks, phone those who requested them and find out in more detail why they returned the item. Sometimes just packing the product with more protection will almost eliminate breakage and cut returns. Sometimes rewriting instructions will make a big improvement. Your product may be good, but your advertising copy leads the customer to expect something better. If so, tone down your copy claims to avoid overselling. This may cut returns. Try to improve your copy to keep sales up. A test of revised, more believable copy may get more orders and fewer returns. Your product may be good, but the price too low. In some tests we've gotten as many or more orders at a higher price, while sharply improving the margin. How about an add-on of a deluxe model at a 20% or so higher price? Usually this does not cut total orders and does increase the average order, as well as the average order margin.

If you project a successful test, you can lower credit card costs to you by increasing volume. You may be able to get extra sales by inserting another offer in a package enclosure. Your customer names may be profitable for follow-up mailings and give you extra revenue from list rentals to other mail order firms.

Gradually you develop a "feel" as to whether you can improve margins and particularly how much better a certain increased volume will make them. This in turn helps you make sounder decisions about buying increased advertising. Anyone new to business and to mail order has three quick shocks. The first is how high overhead actually is. The second is how high all direct costs of buying, making and shipping a mail order product are. The third is how high a percentage of sales the advertising cost is.

Some never realize these basic facts until the furniture is being sold at the bankruptcy sale. Facing these simple facts is a big step toward success.

Specialized catalogs that have survived over the last 20 years have had to change their ideas about sales price versus cost for items they handle. Years ago, a supplier could sell to such catalogs at retail, less 50%. Then such catalogs began to push for 55% off, then for 60% off, then for 66 2/3% off. Then they felt that they needed to import directly or buy from contract manufacturers at still better margins.

Their computers pinpointed more accurately what they needed in gross profit to break even for each square inch of catalog space. A strong selling item with far bigger sales from the same square inches of space could still be safely bought at a lower margin. A weaker selling item had to be dropped or bought at a better margin. Some catalogs have some items imported, specially made up for them or manufactured by themselves with margins of four to one, even ten to one. And still their overall profits are tight.

These same catalogs sometimes make a better profit with a lower margin. If sales pour in for one item, advertising cost for it is often lower than average. Some of that saving of advertising cost can be put into paying more than average for your product and still leave a better-than-average profit.

Arbitrary definitions of the margin needed are unwise. I've seen one mail order man work on what I considered totally inadequate margins for a product and make $38,000 in a week. His margins were much lower than average. But his advertising cost percentage of sales was lower still than average.

The pulling power of advertising for any product will always determine the margin required. A hot item pulling its head off can have a less than desired spread or margin. A run-of-the-mill item can often only be modestly successful with lower product cost. Every mail order man dreams of a hot item with enormous margin, ten to one or better. And it sometimes happens. The real answer is to achieve the very best margins possible, create the best ad possible and pray. We test price and let the public decide at which price and with what margin we should sell.

The tiny mail order operator will try to buy something at a jobber discount on an item which he feels can be sold for more than its usual retail price. By raising the price somewhat, he can achieve a three-to-one margin. Or he buys a discontinued remnant at a smaller fraction of retail price and achieves a four-to-one or better margin. Or he creates a product that requires only simple assembly and gets a margin of three-to-one to ten-to-one. We would not attempt to sell an item with less than a three-and-a-half-to-one spread. We try for a four-to-one or better. Others are willing to try a three-to-one or better. Any generalization is a mistake.

You can determine fairly accurately the specific costs of an item in the mail before you advertise.

You know the cost of advertising before you buy it. But you only know the cost of advertising for each sale made from it after you run an ad. Then it's pretty simple to judge an advertisement success or failure.

You count the mail, multiply the order margin by the orders received and compare this total order margin for all orders with the cost of the ad. The difference is profit or loss for sales keyed to the ad.

Look at the results objectively. Do not make excuses for them. Don't assume that you know a way to improve them. Just accept the results. Be neither overly optimistic nor pessimistic, but simply realistic.

If a test, do not include the production cost of the ad or commercial except as an extra percentage to add to the cost of the ad. Production costs are typography, art, layout, engraving, photostats, announcers, studio, film, recording or tape, director, producer or any other preparation cost.

Many firms (including ours) use a figure of 5% of advertising space, time or direct mail costs which they add to any advertising cost in judging results. It seems to average out that way. But the less you run any ad or commercial, the higher the percentage of production cost to advertising cost will be. It's another reason to watch production costs like a hawk when you're small and to project reasonably safe advertising expenditures as widely as possible when you have a successful ad, commercial or direct mail piece.

Don't pass on price increases automatically. Test first. In periods of sharp inflation, when price increases of material and components on completed articles come in frequently, simply passing on the increases may destroy your business. In some cases, split-run tests have proved to us that we are far better off in working with a smaller percentage gross profit. This is because, at the higher price, sales drop dead, while at the lower price the ad keeps pulling. The profit may be smaller, but better than nothing.

How can you test two different prices, each in one half of a split-run, and still be fair to all customers sold at either price? Include an extra free giveaway (not mentioned in the ad) with each shipment of orders at the higher price. This eliminates complaints of customers, or of the publication used, because each customer is getting a fair value at either price.

We determine the gross profit per order before advertising cost for the higher and for the lower price. We do not include any cost for the giveaway used with the lower price. We do not offer it in the advertising and will not give it in the future, if the ad is successful. We now calculate the total number of orders received from each half of the split. We multiply this number by the gross profit per order and compare the totals.

Judge the success or failure of any test by the costs reasonably achievable if you project the test. Will advertising cost be consistently lower if you project? Color advertising cost per thousand for a few thousand mailing can be three times the cost of a million mailing. Because color is often too expensive and complex, it is usually impractical for mail order moonlighters. In a test of color in a small run, assume that test costs are prohibitive to pay out. Judge results on the cost per thousand of a big run.

Look at all costs in a realistic fashion. A test may be unprofitable judged on higher costs per thousand of test advertising, combined with higher costs of product in test quantities. But when the per-thousand cost of advertising and of manufacture in any reasonable volume is calculated, the test can be judged successful.

Reality must rule–not hoped-for savings that are speculative, but known savings easily available in volume. The volume must be realistically achievable as well. Again, it's a chicken and egg situation. Only volume achieves savings that make volume possible. Volume is often achievable that can make an apparent test failure a signal to proceed. But do so with caution.

The ideal profit to make in mail order is a dollar of profit for each dollar of advertising spent. If you had a gross profit margin of 60%, this would mean that advertising cost would have to be 30%. If you had a gross profit margin of 70%, your advertising could cost you 35%. If you had a gross profit margin (order margin) of 80% cent, your advertising, including production costs, would have to cost you 40%.

The safest and most productive, lowest-cost-per-thousand magazines and newspapers are bought first. The most responsive lists are, too. The most effective stations are as well. If successful enough, more borderline advertising is bought. This means that, as an advertising schedule is cautiously extended, the advertising cost tends to rise in proportion to sales. It is good business to extend the schedule as long as reasonably profitable. Even in a successful projection, there are usually some losers. Therefore there is a tendency for a higher percentage profit initially to average out at lower percentage profit overall. A dollar-for-dollar profit in an initial projection is often lucky to become 60 to 70 cents for a dollar profit in the overall projection. It can come down to less.

Most tests fail. Advertising cost for each failed test may be small, but it mounts up. So does advertising production cost for each test. And some test losses are larger. Profit at year's end is after subtracting loss advertising results from profitable advertising results and then subtracting all overhead expense. Anything left is profit before taxes.

This means that you may be lucky if one dollar in profit for one dollar in advertising settles down to 5% of sales as profit after taxes. How do some mail order companies consistently make 20% before taxes? They minimize test losses, project more safely, get extra business without high advertising cost, get list rental income and fight overhead at all times. And you can, too, if you are extra frugal, extra careful and extra ingenious.

Chapter 6

SAFEST GROWTH

*Putting off expenses . . . tax benefits
. . . keeping your biggest advantage
. . . buying equipment . . . buying
inventory*

From the moment it is a gleam in your mail order eye, the product that you develop or find requires a race against time.

You race to test early enough in season to be able to project without waiting for another year. You race against possible competition. You race to get the test behind you and be ready to give the next high priority item your maximum attention. After you succeed in your test comes the most important race of all. You race to get the *fullest projection* of the original ad or commercial before the season is too late. You race to get production at necessary speed and an adequate supply stream of all component parts or of the entire product. You race to translate your success into each logical form of advertising not yet tested. You race into each of *these* tests and, if successful, also projections.

Haste makes much mail order waste. What is required is *meticulous speed.*

When you *start* as a moonlighter, you are *free* from all fixed overhead and have almost no overhead. You don't have factory rent or mortgages or payroll to sweat out for next week. You don't have payments to make for lavish equipment. You're free. This is your advantage. Keep that freedom. Make some money and spend only part of it for overhead. Only add *any* overhead if you're sure it can help make more money. Drop it if it doesn't. Get along without. Work a little longer and a little harder.

If your growth is quite limited, with few orders coming in daily, you may be able to get along indefinitely on your own and virtually without equipment purchases. You're doing some things you would prefer others to do. You're doing each more slowly than if you had even the simplest equipment to help. You're spending most of your time on less creative work than you'd like. But you're making money. Hopefully, you have enough income from your job for your family's needs.

You're building first capital. This is more important than efficiency. I'm often impressed with how efficient the equipment is at bankruptcy sales. From your start as a moonlighter, cut the pattern to the cloth. Keep overhead expenses to part of your profit after advertising, and preferably a small part.

It's easy to walk into a luxury restaurant and order an elaborate meal. In no time, it's all over. The bill and even the tip charged to a credit card doesn't seem quite real. But it doesn't take many times for us to spend more than we earn. In business, it is the same way. I have investigated many small ventures which needed more money. Next to the owner taking out money when it wasn't coming in, the most frequent cause of financial anemia was hiring people or buying equipment not yet needed or warranted.

As your business grows, you may find certain tax advantages. I am not an accountant. The tax laws and regulations of the federal and state governments constantly change. But to a greater or less degree it is probable that some expenses in a moonlighting business will continue to be deductible. You may have to do a certain minimum of business, at a profit. You certainly should get the advice of an accountant or of the IRS before you assume that a certain kind of expenditure will be considered a business expense by the IRS.

But if you use part of your home or apartment for business, you may be able to rent part of it to your business, whether a corporation, partnership or proprietorship. If you need a car for business (and it certainly helps), you may be able rent or buy a car for business charged to business and deduct the cost from your business income for tax purposes. You may be able to some extent to do the same with gasoline, oil, tolls, parking, maintenance, and repairs to keep your business car operating.

You can be neglected by any supplier or service you use. Cultivating each can make the difference. If you're trying to convince a supplier to give a lower price, entertaining may help. The same goes for each specialized service you use. And if, as we do, you use mail order to launch products into store distribution, you soon have trade customers to entertain as well. This might, to some extent, be a justified business expense.

If your wife is in business with you, she might be occasionally forced to entertain out instead of cooking at home at your expense. This might be to some extent a business expense. If you entertain anyone for your business at home, this too might become partially a business expense deductible from taxes on your business. This might include liquor and some other reasonable expenses. In some cases, a business trip with a customer might also be deductible. But remember: the latest tax laws are tougher.

If it's necessary to travel all over the world to look for desirable items, this too might be a business expense to some extent–if you have an active, profitable business. Phone calls made for business would be also a business expense, and so could a portion of your minimum charge monthly telephone bill. Other purchases might well be needed for business. If you sold garden products, you might need to test them in your own garden at business expense. If in the leisure field selling fishing tackle, your business might require a fishing boat, from a $200 dinghy to a $10,000 bass boat. Your business might need a trailer or motor home to travel and test products from or later to sell to retail stores and demonstrate from. Each may or may not be all or partially deductible. But be very careful. Be honest and always consult your accountant first.

You might need to join a somewhat more elaborate club to entertain from or take a summer home as a business think tank. A ski house might help your business brain waves. Your business might need to subscribe to the Wall Street Journal, buy a TV set or radio to view or hear commercials. When your business accumulates capital, it might find it a good investment to take a second mortgage on a home you buy. Certain books, courses (like this one), magazines, recordings, a film may be needed for business and charged to it. But be careful. Much of it may not be allowed.

Before you get carried away by all this, consult your accountant for latest IRS rulings. In the end, it will come down to common sense. If you do virtually no business and charge many expenses to your business, it will probably be considered a form of tax evasion. I know one man who charged his wedding expense to his small business. It seemed a bit far out. If you are actually doing business, making a profit, and expenses are reasonable and logical, your accountant will probably feel that they will be allowed to some degree. He will also want you to write down each such expense with the business justification for it.

There are other quite important tax advantages. If you lose money as a proprietorship or partnership or one kind of corporation, you may deduct it from personal income. If a corporation makes profits, any losses for three years up to these profits can entitle it to a proportionate tax refund. If your corporation loses money in any year, those losses can be deducted for five years against any profits. In other words, the government is your partner. This is so for federal taxes. State tax practice on this matter varies, but often follows the federal practice. Check with your accountant.

Ask your accountant about making your corporation a Subchapter 5 corporation. In this case, corporate profits are taxed as if from a partnership, personally. This eliminates double taxation. It also makes you personally responsible for payment of the corporate tax. You have to draw enough salary or bonuses to pay the tax or, if there are other stockholders, your share of the tax in ratio to your ownership. Remember: if your corporation makes good profits but has used the cash earned for other purposes, you pay anyway. So consult your accountant. Be careful and put the tax money aside.

As an employee, your taxes are taken from you weekly. As a corporation, you pay on estimated profits quarterly. Mail order profits are hard to estimate and sometimes greater than estimates. The difference between the dollars taken weekly from you as an employee by the government and less frequently taken by the government from your corporation is that the latter is really a loan to your corporation by the government. But the government can charge interest. It can fine for deliberate underestimation.

All this may seem like favoritism, but there is a reason for it. When you start any venture, however small, you become a part of this country's motor that makes everything else go. When you grow, you're creating for others as well as yourself. You may have no direct overhead, but you are adding to employment in the services you use. And when you go beyond your home and set up a place of employment, you're giving direct employment. You become a respected force in your community. And the more you succeed for your family and yourself, the more you are succeeding for and contributing to your town, your state, your country and the world. To do all this, you need a little help, and you get it.

If a woman owns a sewing machine and uses it very little, she would be better off if she had not bought it. If used more frequently, it becomes a good value. If used quite frequently, it's a bargain.

In any business, there is an ego satisfaction in owning equipment and seeing it used. But you may not use it enough, or you may not have the expertise needed to use it properly. Often a business proudly makes a part that is *worse* and *higher in cost* than if bought outside. Equipment used sufficiently, frequently and long enough will often pay off. Mail order is irregular and unpredictable. Equipment payments are quite regular and predictable. Avoid buying equipment unless the savings on it can pay for it *quickly.*

Equipment can sometimes help you *avoid* other expenses and once purchased can seem indispensable.

As your bank account begins to grow, getting credit from equipment suppliers will be easier. You can obtain elaborate machinery or equipment on a lease purchase paid for over a five to seven-year period. You can start with a typewriter and end up with a computer. But whenever possible, get along without, with primitive or with used first-class equipment. Start with corrugated files. Steel ones can come later. Don't be afraid of the impression your office makes. Concentrate on the impression your financial statement makes.

Fight each step to more equipment, stationery, business cards, forms or whatever. But let us hope your success gradually makes each step necessary. As you succeed, you can begin to expand from your moonlighting base. You can get some temporary space convenient to you for an office, warehouse, manufacturing plant or all three. It's more important to avoid lease commitment and get space *month-to-month* than to find a perfect situation. With little equipment, it's not a big chore to move out.

You can avoid overhead and operate from home indefinitely. Or you can vary your activities, briefly taking on month-to-month leases and hiring personnel week-to-week or month-to-month for the same periods. Often a mail order venture starting on a moonlighting basis will grow quite rapidly to be part in the home and part out. You need only make specific runs of merchandise. You do not *have* to make anything in your home or have to rent, build or buy a factory building.

Mail order items practical to ship are often small in size, with the minimum of manufacturing labor. Often the product is shipped disassembled. Some molded plastic items, with no painted decoration needed, come straight from mold to shipping box. Many mail order items are almost this simple. Labor is mainly assembly of proper parts, inserting them into a box and mailing. In art prints, records and many items, the entire product is printed, pressed and molded or stamped in one operation.

When such little labor is required, you can do a surprising volume in your garage, where zoning permits. Just keep the cars outside and invite the neighbors in to help assemble and pack, paid by the hour as needed. Often you can go on to simple, unorthodox quarters without a regular lease. In a barn, you can do as much volume as in a small factory. One couple I know took over month-to-month the upstairs of a firehouse and did very well. They used it for a few months, sold their business at a good cash profit plus a perpetual royalty with guaranteed minimum, and gave up their quarters. Others have taken over empty stores month-to-month until rented regularly. With a few tables and chairs, they were in business.

Usually, when your first big mail order profits come in, you're excited and thrilled and overcome by the sheer number of orders, all those beautiful checks in the mail and the rush of activity needed to fulfill orders. It seems absolutely necessary to hire some help and get some labor-saving equipment. It seems wise to rent space and get a car. It seems ridiculous to do tasks yourself when you could get others to do them for very little and free yourself to make even more money. Yet this rationale can build a prison of overhead and tie up needed cash.

Often when a big rush in business seemed to make it necessary to expand, my wife has quietly gone ahead and gotten the orders shipped . . . without increasing overhead at all. And moonlighters have prospered with stripped-down simplicity.

As soon as you do any real business, you can use a temporary bookkeeper, at first for several hours a month as needed. Some moonlighters use a disabled-person school or organization as a shipping or manufacturing staff (and warehouse). They pay so much a unit for simple functions. There is some spoilage from damage, but often surprisingly little. And the cost per unit is usually quite reasonable. Often excellent professional supervisors are on hand, and sometimes a good deal of equipment. They are also quite practical to use for mailings too small for the big automated mailing houses. Caution! Check other users of the organization's service before going ahead. Be careful. Indoctrinate thoroughly and check work carefully, or you may be disappointed.

You can make a transition from your home quite gradually. A good first step is to warehouse goods elsewhere and work there only yourself after hours and weekends. You may hire one part-time, trusted worker to be there some hours when you are not. It's only a step to one good full-time employee while you, yourself, are still moonlighting. And from then on you can add personnel as needed.

Be cautious about hiring. Building a permanent organization is not your objective. Making temporary money with temporary overhead is. You may make money for months, lose some, make none for more months, make a little, lose some and so on. A regular payroll is not what you want. You need flexibility with people, similar to the irregularity of income.

And always remember this: even if your business jumps to a far bigger size, you can still operate from home with more services.

I know one airline employee who built a moonlighting business up to $1,500,000 yearly and still kept his job. Many businesses are operated mail order from home after retirement, particularly from Florida, Arizona, California and other sun states. Advertising and merchandise decisions are sometimes made from the swimming pool. You can use a public warehouse with your inventory insured and bonded warehouse personnel. You can use a timesharing computer service (or install your own mini-computer at home) to computerize your running inventory, automatically subtracting all shipments from inventory totals and adding purchases to them. If you ever sell on credit in volume, you can computerize your accounts receivable. A minicomputer or computer service can automatically type statements and even address them monthly, deduct receipts, add new sales and keep running totals of monies owed you. The computer can break down on a dated basis the amount of overdue money owed you at all times.

You can build a team of sophisticated experts, work with them entirely from your home, and pay them only when you use them. You pay more per hour or job but risk less at all times. However large you get, you can benefit more and more from part-time specialists without risking overhead.

You can distribute a successful mail order product through stores in the same way. You can build a national force of salesmen, each on commission with no commitment from you. You can manage them from home. With little time from you, they can send in orders daily. You can ship these orders from inventory at your mail order shipping house or a public warehouse.

You can build a creative team the same way. However big and successful you become, you can assemble an entire "house" advertising agency owned by you, with part-time, top experts only used when needed. This can include art directors, photographers, artists, retouchers and film studios, each hired by the job only if and as needed.

Sometimes first success and growth can come in a surprising rush. Mail order can grow so fast that the transition from part of one room at home to 15 or 20 people in a separate place of business can be in a few months' time. In a year or two, you can be doing one to several million dollars yearly. If so, you will buy more equipment and hire more personnel. But be careful.

Cautious mail order can pyramid profits with amazing speed. Some in mail order do everything as they should until that big bonanza comes, but depart from the mail order straight and narrow soon thereafter. Only after losing the money they so quickly made do they realize what they have lost and then take years to regain it, if at all. The need for disciplined spending is greatest when success comes. In disaster, the disciplining is done for you. But when you have money, you can spend it, and it's only a step to spending more than you have.

Most who make their first big profits in mail order have no idea how temporary those profits are. When first profits come, many new mail order people count on more future profits than will occur. They assume that the same offer will pull year after year, and that it will be easy to come up with new offers in an ever-increasing, golden flow. Only in adversity is it finally realized how *irregular* mail order income can be.

Don't make this mistake. When you make that first mail order killing, keep the bulk of net profits in the bank as capital. Overnight, it will change your life. From here on in throughout your life, simply by conserving this first block of capital and gradually, if irregularly, adding to it, you are in a position of strength. Immediately your profits start earning more profits in the form of interest. Most people are forever in the weakest of financial positions and can never take advantage of any business opportunity where cash is required. But now you can.

If you grow, you may begin to import in volume. Fluctuating currency can make anything you import a speculation. To protect yourself, try to pay in U.S. money. But most foreign suppliers prefer to be paid in their own currency. If you agree to pay in their currency, the dollar may go up or down before you pay. To avoid becoming a currency speculator as well as a mail order moonlighter, make a currency contract through your bank on the day you place your order. It takes much risk out of the transaction. Buy the needed foreign currency for future delivery on the date you need it. You know what you are paying, regardless of currency fluctuations.

You need not pay for the currency until the day you use it. Caution! Delivery by a foreign supplier can be in part or not at all. If so, you have bought more of the foreign currency than needed. The same thing happens if you *cancel* part of the order. You will have gambled the difference in currency. The bank will execute the contract, convert the unneeded foreign currency back into dollars and credit you or charge you with the profit or loss. But in most cases, the order will be shipped in full and you will have had no risk. FURTHER CAUTION! If your supplier ships *very late*, you need the leeway in your currency contract. For a tiny extra cost in purchasing the currency, you can have up to *one year* from contract date to take delivery. This should give your supplier time to ship.

I know one mail order man who gave his company to his staff after a big campaign. To him it was preferable to keeping the "people overhead." The more you keep the personnel to partners and those on commission, the better off you are. You may give away twice as much money, yet always sleep at night.

Those new to mail order often draw too much money for themselves, buy too much equipment, hire too many people and then put off letting them go. Mail order gave us our capital and launched us into store distribution. Today, store distribution sales carry our overhead. This has allowed us to have a regular staff. You can do the same if you're interested in and have the ability to go after store distribution on products you control. But when you're starting in mail order, buy inventory hand-to-mouth, buy equipment you can self-liquidate in a few months and hire personnel as week-to-week as possible, preferably day-to-day for however few hours a day employed.

If you do so and acquire good items, create or have created effective advertising and test and project carefully, you have an excellent chance of success.

Most frugal housewives can buy frugally for a business. In each case, it's a matter of *shopping* for *value* at a *price*. Every wife knows that sending hubby to the supermarket is often not the lowest-cost way to shop. She knows what each item ordinarily sells for. He doesn't. She can spot a bargain to pick up and a jump in price to stay away from. He can't. It's easier for her to adapt her shopping technique to buying anything for a business than it is for him to buy anything if he doesn't have a buying background. She knows that some stores charge less than others, and that some stores charge less *sometimes* for products. She has a nose for sales and for value as well as price.

In business, anything bought can often vary in price depending on when bought and from whom. And in business, every salesman is itchy to know how his price compares with his competitor. "How does my price look?" he asks with a worried look. Some printers will meet or beat any competitive price and expect to pick up above-average profit on smaller jobs hurriedly given out without getting competitive quotes. When something is important and is needed in a hurry, there's a tendency to order it without questioning price. Ordering in this way is handing out a blank check.

Simply getting competitive quotes from three sources almost always improves costs. We try to be loyal to suppliers and not run from one to the other for slight differences. We try to buy quality and not switch for lower price and still lower quality. We try to be appreciative of cooperation, prompt delivery and good quality. We try not to leave any supplier without good reason.

But differences in costs are often not minor, but very major indeed. There is one very small component for one of our products that my wife got quotes for from all over the world. She only got a good quote from one company in one country, West Germany. For year after year, despite inflation, currency reevaluation, freight and duty, my wife has saved *two thirds* of the cost of the component if otherwise purchased, saving thousands of dollars *each year* on this one transaction.

When a first test is made, it is sometimes too speculative to devote the time and expense necessary to locate the lowest-cost sources. As soon as the *results* of a test justify, it is worth it. Sometimes you can successfully sell a product in a very small way. You don't have volume and can't hope for volume savings. But even in small volume, savings are often possible. Often key parts of a product are laboriously made by hand when molds or dies for a usable equivalent already exist. This is because the part exists somewhere for another purpose. A key part for a music stand turned out to be quite practical to perform the same function for a dress form stand *for us*. It ingeniously replaced *several* parts we had previously needed. The same supplier made it for the music stands and for us.

You may see no opportunity to make savings in your item. But someone with plastics, chemical, die casting or other production background right for your product might instantly see a way to cut the cost in *half* and *improve* it as well. It pays to be loyal to suppliers. Any competitor can quote slightly lower, get the business and raise the price, at which point your original supplier may not welcome you back at as favorable a price.

If you buy anything requiring plates, engravings, dies or molds, determine who owns them. You may think you do–but don't. Or your supplier may dispute ownership and refuse to give them up. This means that, to change suppliers, you must duplicate your original investment and pay whatever increased cost inflation has created. The rationale for the supplier's opinion is that you could not have bought the plates, etc., at the price paid except through him or that he helped in their creation or selection; and his reward is perpetual continued business.

I have not had any supplier refuse a first order where dies, etc., were needed that specified in writing that *we* owned such plates, etc. And where specified in writing, we've never had difficulty removing such plates, etc., at will. Often the fact that we periodically got competitive quotes made it unnecessary to switch.

However, it is also unfair to get periodic quotes from some firm only as a stalking horse, simply to get your supplier to come down in price.

It costs any supplier money to give quotes. If he doesn't get business, he will stop quoting. Therefore, it's fair and wise to alternate suppliers occasionally. Each knows that he has a real chance if competitive. For any supplier who consistently keeps his word, delivers when he says and consistently delivers quality as represented, we are willing to pay slightly more than competitors we know and more so than competitors we don't have experience with.

Last-minute buying costs more and risks surprises in quality as well. You're in the hands of your supplier. Success in mail order selling simplifies mail order item buying. You can order in bigger amounts at one time. You save on product, shipping and handling at your end. But when you buy inventory, be *cautious*.

Conditions *change* rapidly in mail order. A competitor can knock you out of the box in a week with what appears to the public to be the equivalent of your product, but selling at one-third the price. There's nothing more totally depressing than to buy expensive advertising and find such devastating competition on the same page or, if you have a full page, a page or so away. Or a product looking like yours at one-third the price can suddenly appear in every Woolworth display window, or so it seems, and mail order for the item collapses. The art of mail order is to be quick on your feet and pull back fast when trouble comes. You can be caught and badly! The answer is hand-to-mouth inventory purchase or manufacture to the maximum degree feasible.

Often it is not feasible. But to the degree it is, it's usually a matter of mail order life or death. Many mail order men prefer to use dropshippers for all tests possible and then stock *carefully*. One mail order friend of mine who sells millions of dollars a year is able to confine most of his buying to *once-a-week* purchases for the *following week*, like buying groceries.

Inventory overstocking is the cause of most depressions and many bankruptcies, and it can be *particularly disastrous* in mail order.

In any mail order test of a new item, you may be amazed by the almost *total lack of response*. I have seen a full-page ad in a major-city newspaper *pull seven orders* for several dollars each. It's bad enough to lose money on the advertising. You compound the loss if you purchase or make inventory the ad didn't sell and that you haven't the slightest idea in the world how to move in any other way.

Caution in buying or making inventory is necessary in any business, as any recession has proved. But in mail order, it's particularly important. The shrewdest mail order men I know have assumed that all sales of any item could stop instantly at any time, and they have been determined not to be caught with excess inventory at that time.

This means that having the ability to buy or make *more* inventory is all-important. The *stability* of those whom you deal with is important, and their ability and honesty. There are plenty of reliable people, but it takes time to build up a trusted team. Meanwhile, dreamers, paupers or liars who say they can make or ship, and cannot, can harm you. Your ability to make, assemble, package by yourself or via suppliers to *fulfill* promptly and efficiently orders you receive must be constantly checked.

Mail order inventory problems can be insidious. You may be buying fairly conservatively but simply go into a variety of items. A little inventory here and a little inventory there adds up. Total inventory, as it builds up, ties up cash. Soon you're not as liquid as you were. And once loss of liquidity comes, insolvency may not be far behind.

And the more inexperienced in mail order you are, the faster it can happen. On the other hand, properly used mail order can be the means of turning into cash the inventory you might not otherwise be able to sell.

When you are left with inventory, it can sleep quietly for years. Some inventory you may have optimistically bought may never respond to mail order. But other inventory may be just what the doctor ordered for a new approach to a successful ad. Occasionally I have written an ad that moved out inventory that had been gathering dust for years, and the ad actually forced us back into production. And every mail order man has had this experience.

Often the way to move out inventory in mail is *indirectly*. Instead of straining to sell a hard-to-move, "dead" item, sometimes the easiest way to move it is with a "related" hot item, using a mailing insert or an "add-on" item in a mailing piece or ad. Even an unrelated insert can gradually move off inventory. Often it pulls just as well at full retail price as at a mark-down price. Sometimes an item that hasn't sold can be an excellent giveaway item to add value and urgency to one that does sell.

Generally, if you have a major mail order success, judicious package inserts and mailings to your customer list can gradually move off most "mistakes" at a profit. You may never have to sell off distress inventory. It may be possible to move off inventory gradually. It is far better to buy so cautiously that the problem never comes up.

The more Gypsy the mail order operation, the more important it is to buy from others. The more *permanent* and the bigger the volume, and the more interest you have in building a distribution business, the more important it can be to manufacture yourself. But only manufacture yourself to obtain better quality control and lower price. With high equipment costs and low volume, you won't satisfactorily amortize set-up costs. If you have no space to manufacture, you may be better off to buy than to make. If manufacturing is technically complex, it may be beyond you. You can easily spend far *more* per unit, make the product far more imperfectly and tie up a lot of money in equipment and labor as well.

We try to avoid manufacturing. We do not attempt to make component parts unless it is extremely easy to do so. We have owned our own molding plant, but found it didn't pay. Our volume was too irregular. Sometimes it's even more feasible to have a supplier assemble, paint and decorate rather than ourselves. We stick to original products, preferably patented and protected, but extremely simple to assemble.

A supplier can be your creative partner. We have three fishing lures we formerly made ourselves and now have made by one small manufacturer for us. We can still make these lures at lower cost ourselves. But our supplier has *improved* each one. He has become almost a co-inventor as far as his contributions go. An inventor needs the help of a creative, product-development-minded manufacturer, just as an author needs a publisher with a superb editor. We make less on each lure, but we are adding strengths and building a sound, long-life business. On our imported lures, we import them in bulk and simply warehouse and blister-pack.

We get more and more into the design of our Sea Eagle inflatable boats–often originated or modified by my son Cecil. But we have them made by the most efficient firm in the world for the purpose. My suggestion is, again, to be guided by your natural talent, your experience, your present facilities and alternatives now open to you.

Chapter 7

POLICY DECISIONS

Concentrating vs. diversifying . . .
specialized niches vs. unlimited
growth . . . timing . . . discretion

Should you concentrate on one item at a time or sell a variety of items? Assuming that you're not in the catalog business, this is an important choice.

One friend and former partner has sold at considerable profit up to five-million dollars a year, but rarely more than one or two basic items in any one year.

He has no interest in volume, only in the largest profit from each dollar of sales. He's a perfectionist. He says it's not enough for an ad or commercial to be good; it must be superb. His interest is to buy or make an item at *rock bottom cost,* eliminating every unnecessary expense. He has little confidence in others and wants to control every aspect of his business himself. He even prefers to concentrate his selling in one form of advertising such as TV. He will not operate outside the U.S. His personal way of working is perfectly suited to concentrating on just one item. Another former partner has made far more millions of dollars, with far more concentration. For close to 20 years, he has concentrated on just *one* item all that time, to his great profit.

But two other equally wealthy men, each of whom has made all his money in mail order (and with each of whom I've worked closely for many years), have made their money in just the opposite way. Each has sold a myriad of items and has been associated with a myriad of mail order ventures, all at the same time. Each seems to thrive from the interaction of many simultaneous mail order activities and transactions. Each has combined a variety of functions. Each has owned an advertising agency, space representative firm and mass circulation magazine at the same time. And the overall operation of each is dependent on the intermeshing of the many ventures each is involved in.

I've seen many people make big money in mail order in quite different ways. I've observed that each mail order man or woman entrepreneur can best make mail order profits in the way best suited to his or her personality and personal way of thinking and working.

I'm stimulated by diversity; others are driven out of their minds by it. Most mail order creative people go stale trying constantly to come up with new and more effective approaches for the same product or services. Other people work best in a straight line . . . 1-2-3-4 organized manner. So work the way you feel most comfortable and effective, and concentrate or diversify accordingly.

Where should you operate a mail order business? One highly successful mail order business owner told me, "Once I got into the mail order business, I decided I could run it from *anywhere*. I made an objective survey of where to live for the best development of my children and greatest happiness of my wife. I chose Tucson, Arizona, for its year-round climate, schools, cultural activities and nice people. We've been happy ever since, and my business has prospered."

If you use experts, advertising agencies, consultants and specialists in specific media and advertising techniques who are usually located in large cities, this can in some ways permit you to live and work outside big cities.

Handling of incoming orders can be done anywhere. Shipment can, too, at the lowest cost (for heavier and bulkier products) from a mid-American point. Most mail order items are light and compact enough to allow shipping from many different U.S. locations at a profit.

Only if you are out to become a really large mail order firm do you need to consider being near the big centers where the mail order advertising opportunities are most available and soundest. So if you graduate from moonlighting to full-time mail order, live where you and your family are happiest.

Should you consider specialized niche mail order or broad common denominator products? Your reasons for being in mail order at all will usually determine the answer.

Are you out for a simple, secure living or to make a fortune? Some have done both with either method. A specialized niche can often sell by mail order a special kind of service which is not sufficiently available in other forms of distribution. If so, it can be both safer for initial tests and more limited for projection. The more specialized the field, the more limited it usually is. Fewer broad common denominator products succeed, but when they do, volume can be enormous.

A box company has a cardboard magazine case covered in leatherette which it advertises very profitably in a special way by mail order. The magazine case is for back issues of magazines, with the name of the magazine printed on the front cover. Almost all magazines have a hard core of devotees who keep back copies and value a case for it as a neat way of keeping it on file. This one company seems to have the exclusive for most magazines. In some magazines the advertising is on a percentage of sales, no-risk basis. The publications consider it a service to readers. Usually the ads are in every issue. This is a specialized niche situation. It is an extremely simple business to operate. It has considerable continuity. There are 1,001 different situations like this one. Your own background may come up with the need and solution. Sometimes such a specialized niche business is suited to only a very small field, using only a few small-circulation magazines.

Skin diving started as such a specialized field but became very big. Skydiving and hot-air ballooning are two tiny specialized fields that may never grow or surprise us all. If you intimately know such a field and come up with a unique product or even an intriguing specialized catalog for it, you've got a good chance of some limited success. It's ideal for someone in love with that activity. It's great for someone who wants a limited activity in time, work and money.

The mail order firm or man or woman who goes after broad, common denominator product mail order success is usually out for the big money. Tests are more risky. It takes more test failures to come up with one success. It usually takes more work, more time and more risk before coming up with success. But if a test succeeds for any such item, even with cautious projection it's hard not to sell in big volume. It takes more capital to project a successful test. But sales are apt to be in millions of dollars with profits in the hundreds of thousands of dollars.

Broad common-denominator successes attract "knock-offs" faster. Competitors jump in. It's a race to get there first. I've never had a broad common-denominator mail order success without having a number of competitors move in with attempted "knock-offs." It involves fighting commercially and often legally to protect your rights. Conditions change faster in these big campaigns. Weather, economic collapse, currency devaluations, many factors can catch you in midstream. But it's the mail order "big tent." It's where the action is and where the mail order high-rollers congregate. It's quite a thrill to spend $30,000 in one week on TV, get it all back and make $20,000 profit, or spend $70,000 on a weekend in national supplements and make a profit of $40,000. I once made $30,000 profit in a single newspaper in one day. But be careful. You can be wiped out just as fast.

Obey the "laws" of mail order, proceed with caution and pull back the instant the mail order wind changes. Once you've got your original test success, your projection in mass media is usually fairly safe. So if you want to go for the big time in mail order, *do it*, but *obey those traffic lights*.

Should you keep a product's original name?

Let's consider two points. First, do you own this name or do you just have limited rights to the product and name, perhaps just for mail order or just as long as you fulfill a contract, perhaps with a minimum quota of purchases or guaranteed royalty payments? Do you want to build up a name which, under any set of circumstances, you might in the future lose the rights to or only have limited rights to now? The time to decide is when you *can* decide, when you sign the first contract for the rights. Otherwise you must later renegotiate this all-important point.

Let us presume that you take over the sole import of a product known world-wide, but under a name you can never own. You have good relations, but are not sure you can meet the ever-growing minimum yearly quotas of purchases called for under the contract. But if you can just negotiate an agreement with the exporting company, changing the name (vital to you) can be easily done.

Once it's done, all your advertising benefit is to *your* sole benefit. Because if you ever part company from your exporter, you can now import from another supplier an equivalent product or make it in the U.S. under a name *you* built and *you* own. You can even *export* to other countries under that name.

If you do want to change the name, go about it with all possible speed. For a new, struggling mail order product scarcely known under its old name, there's almost nothing lost in simply switching to the new name from the next mail order ad on.

With a well-known name, the change can be gradual. First use the new name as an adjective to precede the old name. The new name can be the minor element and the old name dominate. As time passes, the new name adjective can grow in size while the old name shrinks. The new name can now dominate. Finally, make the new name the only name. Make the adjective a noun. The old name will have completely shriveled away, with no loss of goodwill at any point.

Selling for cash is the simplest mail order and most necessary for individuals starting out in mail order. Fortunately, more and more people are willing to pay cash for mail ordered merchandise. But credit cards have opened the door to mass selling of ever-higher ticket items. Cost of the credit card service to a mail order operator varies by cards, but may start as high as 10% for test volume. After actually receiving major volume from a projection, the credit card company, on its own formula, reduces its percentage in stages. Bank Americard and Master Charge are so widely distributed that cost can come down even faster in big volume to as low as slightly over 2%. Check current rates.

Merchandise sold through credit cards will usually start at $20 or $50 and go up to over $1,000. If you use the magazines read by credit card holders, you will probably sell merchandise closer to the low end; if you use inserts in bills to credit card holders, somewhat higher, and for solo direct mail pieces to the list, you will probably range more from $100 to $1,000.

Credit card selling is particularly helpful for smaller mail order companies. It eliminates selling on a credit risk. The credit card company guarantees payment. It particularly eliminates lengthy time payments. You can even sell your product on time payments through the credit card company and be paid by them in one payment. Payment is quite fast, usually within three weeks after shipping and processing the order to the credit card company for their billing.

If you start selling your product to the trade, need you give up your own mail order sales? Years ago, we were quite concerned as to whether mail order would *harm* our relationship with the trade.

We were afraid that, if we sold our product by mail order, buyers for stores would be offended, feel that we were unfairly competing with them and stop buying from us. At one time, this may have been so. Once I called a few buyers, said we were considering selling mail order and asked for their reaction. The reaction was *negative*. Some buyers said that if we sold mail order they would refuse to buy again. After weighing pros and cons, we decided to go ahead anyway and did. Not one store stopped buying from us. Our sales to stores we already had went up. And for the first time, we really *broadened* our distribution from scattered to more intensive coverage.

We do take particular care to sell mail order at a retail price as high as or higher than our trade customers do. Our trade customers now complain when we *stop* mail order on a given item. They also complain if they are not told in advance when we run a mail order ad in their area for an item they stock. Because they know they'll benefit. Sometimes when we are running a page ad in a national supplement, we'll run a cooperative ad in one city the same day. Results are usually far above average for our department store ad, although we know it hurts sales for our mail order ad. TV mail order can have a tremendous distribution forcing effect. A mail order ad runs once and, if successful, usually repeats quite a long time. On radio and TV, mail order commercials can often successfully run a number of times a week for a number of weeks. The result is longer continuity from an intense medium that drives a succession of customers into the store for the same item.

You can start with mail order ads or commercials, then adapt them to cooperative store ads or commercials for key retailers and then, as key retailers are obtained, convert the ads and commercials to a more general, go-to-your-dealer basis. You then can go after broad distribution, selling wholesalers and retailers. You may then give up mail order and sell through the trade only.

Timing is all-important in going into some mail order items. An item can catch on suddenly. The momentum of the success begins to build. It is then knocked off (copied) in Hong Kong, then Taiwan, then Korea. Prices collapse. The market for it falls apart. This is a risk of any form of retailing. In mail order, it can be far worse. When ads pull well, you're tempted to project your advertising nationally in a big way. Yet your big projection can be at the point of collapse of the entire field. With every new field of items we consider, we ask, "Is it too late?" And you should too!

When mail order success is great, retailers often move in and mail order falls off! Mail order has been the launching pad for many successful store products.

Butcherblock furniture, water soluble fertilizer, inflatable swimming pools, the telephone-style shower head, safari shirts, jackets and suits, creative stitchery, decorative switchplates, many do-it-yourself kits and endless other, entire fields of items have been originated and made known by mail order advertising. So have most new consumer microelectronic products, the home computer and much software.

A new item can be a big mail order success. But we've found that when department stores in every city run co-op ads promoting the product, suddenly the mail order ads stop pulling. And when the item goes into more universal distribution, the department store ads stop pulling. That's why each product we have is a proprietary product, why so many are patented and why we use mail order to help launch the product into distribution. In this way, we get a benefit year after year from former mail order campaigns.

It's also why we like to originate items and stay out of items that already have been knocked off by others in wide store distribution.

Years ago, one of our now great alumni wrote a cosmetic ad that made a good deal of money for us in mail order. We wanted to convert it to store distribution success. Unfortunately, the ad, although profitable, was *ugly*. Department stores simply did not want to run it as a cooperative ad. I called in one of the grand old copywriters of all time, who had started as a very young man working for my father. The old master did a fine job of converting our ugly mail order ad into a beautiful cooperative department store ad retaining all the mail order power.

Within one year, we were a department store success. We did over one million dollars in sales to department stores and made over $200,000 profit. I was happy and grateful. Meanwhile, a top advertising publication wanted to do a major story on my old friend. He asked whether the story could be built around the department store success. I gave him the okay and full facts. The story broke.

Virtually every major cosmetic company in the country duplicated my product, packaging and advertising. My product was universally available in 30,000 outlets under various brand names, with no profit to me. Within six months my cosmetic business shrivelled to virtually nothing. My co-op ads simply did not pull. I was swamped with returns.

I was not discreet. Don't let it happen to you!

Chapter 8

MAIL ORDER
NEGOTIATION

---

*Joint ventures . . . manufacturing
royalty . . . with or without patent or
copyright . . . sole rights import . . .
buy-out . . . mold rental*

Mail order is ideal for joint ventures splitting profits after actual costs. Such agreements can be simple. Mail order often leads to setting up different corporations in different fields, often with different partners. Each agreement can be most important. Mail order leads into trade distribution businesses which can later be sold for capital gains or turned into public corporations. All this requires agreements.

When in mail order is a detailed written understanding worth the time and effort to make it?

For a mail order catalog house, it is not practical or feasible to make a contract for every item featured. Nor is it sensible to make a written agreement in detail for any item needed only for short-term special purposes, as a related package insert for a specialized publication where you have a good rate, or for a one-time mailing to your list. It usually is not necessary when you buy a generic product easily available from other suppliers.

But there are many times when you do need a precise agreement, particularly if it concerns a proprietary and perhaps patented product that you hope to build a business on for years to come and possibly expand in various areas beyond mail order. A contract always seems to be so simple you could best write a one-paragraph letter on it . . . until you write a rough draft. Then it almost always stretches out to several pages. For it is far better to have no contract than a contract that does not refer to points of possible differences most likely to come up. Some of the best relationships I've had and in biggest dollar volume have been in complete mutual trust without a word in writing.

We try to acquire sole rights to a product on a royalty basis or outright, or to originate the product ourselves. Everything we have is proprietary. If we import, it is on a sole-rights basis for the U.S. and

---

usually North America. We usually pay royalties, own molds or dies and have them run outside by a molder or a machine shop and then assembled in our own plant. If so, we either have a worldwide rights, royalty contract to manufacture and sell, or we own the item outright. This takes time-consuming negotiation and usually commitments, guarantees or cash. We feel we must do so to build a permanent business. We feel a royalty is expensive and try to have a buy-out option in each royalty contract. If we're successful later, it's a reasonable gamble to exercise the option and end up royalty free.

A rights contract is most important if you acquire original items. It is not needed if you copy. Many mail order men make no effort to obtain exclusives, just as they have no interest in store distribution. They save the time of negotiation and happily jump in and out of items with no commitments on either side.

So it's your pleasure, but I thought you'd like to know both viewpoints.

How much royalty can you afford to pay? Any royalty is profitable to pay if there's a good profit left over after you pay it.

Long ago, we found the range of royalties we consider practical for us. If we offered less than 3% royalty, most people were offended by our proposing it. If we offered more than 5%, we usually found later that it left us too borderline a profit. Therefore, we try to keep our range of royalties from 3% to 5% of sales. We usually provide for 5% dropping to 3% in volume. If the gross profit on the item is slim, we may make it a flat 3%. If the gross profit is large, we may make it a flat 5%. Even with quite a large gross profit, we find it best for both parties to keep the royalty to 5% and simply spend a bigger percentage than usual, if necessary, in advertising.

Exceptions make the rule. Once we negotiated an agreement to pay a jewelry designer 5%–and a rock group 10% on top of that–on a piece of jewelry designed for the rock group to be worn and promoted by them with tremendous promotional tie-ins.

Any royalty leaves less profit than if there were no royalty and the same sales. On any business with royalty-free items, it's still hard to make money. Before taxes, 10% to 12% would be considered satisfactory. A 5% royalty would subtract 40% to 50% from profits . . . *perpetually.*

From a business standpoint, paying outright in one lump sum for all future rights is preferable. But in mail order each untested item is a pig in a poke. Even the financially strongest mail order operators hesitate to pay for rights in a lump sum *before* testing. The buy-out option is the answer.

Usually an inventor or rights owner walking into your office will expect one sum of money if a flat payment, and a far larger one if on a when, if and as royalty basis. The sum of a buy-out figure on an option basis would be in between.

The psychology of the inventor or rights owner changes rapidly *after your successful test.* Before the test, his morale is dubious and his hopes vague. After the test, his future income is to him a reality, and all the grief and difficulty of creating his product seem worth infinitely more. Thereafter, the more you succeed with his product, the less interested he is in any buy-out agreement, and the higher the royalty, the bigger the guarantees and the more protection he wants. So make your agreement *before* your test, include a buy-out option and make it crystal clear.

Inventing is a business, but few inventors realize it. A successful inventor usually makes a series of inventions, some of which he sells to others. Income on one invention is often small. But the continuation of that small income, when added to the income on the next invention and the next, gives him a living. The same is true of an author. Only a rare invention or publication hits such a jackpot that it alone can support an inventor or author for life, rather like winning a huge lottery prize.

The very compulsion that drives a creative mind to originate, develop and perfect a product or book or whatever without being underwritten seems to convince him of the huge potential it has. The inventor usually has a vague idea he can make a good deal of money from his work, more than maybe actually feasible for the businessman to ever hope to pay. Often the inventor is quite unrealistic asking for a big *cash* payment, a big yearly guarantee of income and then a too-high perpetual royalty.

We try to avoid *cash* payments. We substitute, for a guarantee, cancellation privileges if we don't deliver an agreed royalty minimum. We keep royalties to our limitations. We try to be frank, and if the inventor seems unrealistic, to forget the transaction.

Once you have made a number of royalty contracts with inventors and owners of items, the next agreement seems like a minor variation.

The situation of the inventor or rights owner is often quite different. This one agreement may seem the most important in life. He may feel that never again will he have an opportunity to make so much money. A businessman, by the very discipline he submits his daily operations to, would rarely speculate over months and years to the degree the inventor has done. No wonder the inventor is nervous about the wording of any agreement.

Few inventors are financially strong. Most *need* money *quickly.* Few inventors understand the economics of business. They often believe the businessman can afford a far higher royalty and still make plenty of money. Few are familiar with contracts. All have wives, husbands, fathers or friends to warn them they're probably being cheated. Often their lawyer is a small-town real estate or other specialist lawyer not too familiar with your marketing problems.

Any contract seems threatening when read by anyone without careful explanation. Before submitting any written contract, I get verbal agreement on the business points in a contract, point by point, in business, not legal language. Before going over *any* points of an agreement, I try to explain my concept of an agreement.

A contract may be evaded, broken or cheated on by anyone really trying to be crooked. A contract cannot give perfect protection from crooks. Legal enforcement may be difficult. Most people are honest. But anyone interprets to his advantage situations not provided for in a contract. If a contract is detailed, covering almost any probable eventuality, most people will live up to it. A contract usually becomes obsolete in some way in years or even months. But the more carefully it is spelled out, the more likely there is to be a long and happy mutual adherence to the spirit of the contract.

A contract should *remove fears*. The biggest reason to seriously question a contract is *fear* of some way of being taken advantage of. I do not want to take advantage of anyone. Therefore, if you have any fear, let's remove that fear with a protective clause in the agreement.

I point out that just "stealing" the item and copying it with no royalty would be easier and cheaper than any contract, and that just submitting the contract is evidence of good faith. I try hard to get across my thinking regarding agreements in general. Any royalty contract is a form of partnership between the inventor and businessman. To be a good partner, the businessman must be both honest and competent.

The most favorable seeming contract may be the worst deal if the businessman does not intend to or cannot fulfill it. Royalties may be and sometimes are paid quite fraudulently. A businessman may go bankrupt. I ask that, before signing any agreement, they check carefully our reputation and our Dun & Bradstreet rating.

I try to explain worrisome points to wife, husband, friend and associates before the actual contract is submitted. I try to read each word of each clause of the contract to the other party and explain which are just standard legal clauses and the reasons behind each clause.

Lawyers like to mail each other contracts. A lawyer receiving a contract likes to suggest changes. Back-and-forth correspondence can stretch out interminably. I like to set up a joint meeting of clients and lawyers and then either agree to disagree or stay and modify and *sign.*

At this time, I try to concede any unimportant points, compromise in any reasonable way, but hold firm on anything important and make or break the deal in that one session.

Other types of agreements may be even more important for the mail order man. If you import on a sole rights basis, it's very hard to tie down exactly what you desire. But it is very important to do so. You may be importing from a small manufacturer to whom a lengthy contract is particularly frightening.

In dealing with someone in another country, there are really *four*, not two, languages to cope with: the two actual languages and the two quite different ways of thinking. Mailing a contract is particularly dangerous. Only a trip will do, and *staying* on that trip until the agreement is signed. The foreign exporter must retain the right to increase prices, yet the very act of raising prices too high can in effect be a cancellation privilege. We try for a clause limiting price increases to provable percentage increases of his labor and material costs.

There must be hundreds of thousands of molds and dies in this country that are *not in use*. The original investment in each mold or die can go into a good many thousands of dollars. Often it's possible to get a cash purchase or royalty sole-rights option on a mold or die and buy enough merchandise for a mail order test. A skilled and creative mold or die maker can often *convert* a mold or die into something *quite different* from it's original product. You can create a mail order item together.

Harrison Hoge Industries, Inc., and subsidiaries own hundreds of thousands of dollars of original molds and dies now valued at zero on the books because nothing made with them is currently being sold. In toys and other volatile fields, once an item stops selling, the molds and dies are considered worthless. But to us, a mold or die can at any time *become* more valuable than ever.

All we have to do is come up with a new successful ad and the mold or die has a brand new life. It's often safer and easier to create a new ad for an old item than for a new one. And many items *are* cyclic. We sold dress forms for home sewers for 30 years. And three times, we sold five or six times what we previously sold in an average year. And circumstances cause the wheel of fortune to spin back to an item's success when you least expect it.

A mold or die can be worthless to the owner and unsalable to anyone else. Your new ad can make it suddenly valuable. An option contract signed before you test can often be negotiated very favorably. Later this may not be so.

Negotiate *first*. It can save you an immediate major cash outlay and perhaps avoid higher royalty payments if negotiated later.

Chapter 9

KEEPING CUSTOMERS HAPPY

*Prompt shipping . . . answering
correspondence . . . guarantees . . .
handling complaints . . . living with
the government*

Your handling of customers must be responsible or you will live to regret it. Orders must be shipped and promptly. Going into many items multiplies the chances of customer disappointment, because the more suppliers you rely on, the bigger chance that one or more will let you down. If you're manufacturing, just one component supplier failing to deliver can make it impossible for you to deliver the entire product.

Realistic appraisal of your manufacturing and shipping capacity *before* major purchases of mail order advertising are made is essential. Nothing maddens a customer more than getting his or her cancelled check back from the bank and no delivery of the product. The moment you run out of merchandise, stop cashing checks of those ordering the merchandise. It saves most correspondence on the product. Cashing the check if you have no merchandise is illegal. Even keeping the check more than 30 days after receipt and nondelivery is illegal without taking certain legally required steps. Consult the FTC.

Set up a proper complaint department from the very start. Answer complaints immediately and meticulously. Form replies will do for most situations. Avoid cashing checks when out of merchandise, promptly answer consumer complaints, and above all, instantly mail out refund checks when merchandise is returned. You'll build a good reputation. Just treat customers as you like to be treated when you buy anything.

When small mail order companies grow fast, delivery problems can come too. Small businessmen have an old saying that "if you can make it, you can't sell it . . . and if you can sell it, you can't make it." In boom times, little manufacturers get shortage components last. In bad times the mail order ads often don't pay out. Usually the small mail order firm's difficulties with delivery logistics are caused by poor planning, ordering, expediting, delayed hiring or other disorganization.

When my wife first came into our business, she had only one year's experience in a clerical job in this country. I explained that I would be away from the business every day but one or two every four to six weeks. Our business involved simple manufacturing of various items which in total included hundreds of components. I told my wife that, although she would have to do all buying, as well as hiring and firing of personnel, not to worry. I said that buying supplies for manufacture was the same as buying at the supermarket. If she had an insufficient shopping list, we could have a chicken dinner without chicken. As that had never happened, I felt sure that she would make up a proper business shopping list and get each item in ample time.

My wife took over, made her list, did her shopping and followed through. From that day we have rarely had delivery problems. A housewife looks in her ice box before going to the supermarket. Any businessman has to look in his ice box, too. He has to know his inventory before he buys. A housewife needs to know how many guests are coming to dinner and order accordingly. A mail order man has to keep track of advertising bought, guestimate orders coming in from the advertising and be ready. The problem is to buy hand-to-mouth and still ship on time. It is amazing how cautiously you can buy or make inventory and yet make plans for rapid expansion of production as needed.

Assume that your scheduled ad will break even. Order in advance what you will need if it does so. If it produces *more* orders than assumed, you will need to buy more and get immediate delivery. Before you run your ad, make sure that your supplier has ample inventory. For each 100 units that you buy, ask him to hold 100 units of backup stock for you. Specify that you have the right to buy but are not obligated to take this inventory and that you require that reorders be shipped within 24 hours notice.

Reach a clear understanding. Some suppliers will do exactly what they say. Others will be guarded, infer faster shipping without actually promising it and then ship slower. Others will promise, but not ship, or even lie that they have shipped. Assume the worst until you have a record of performance. Even then, *check* after you order. Ask if your order was received and exactly what day it will be shipped.

Logistical expediting becomes necessary when a "hot" item starts jumping. Careful follow-through can speed delivery and save risk and cash layout of too big opening orders. It's work, but you want to buy carefully and ship promptly. You may get everything from one source. More likely, you will get directions printed, boxes made, labels purchased and products from different sources.

Anything may happen. Your mailed purchase order may never have arrived because of insufficient postage. Your supplier may be ignoring your order pending clearing of your credit. You may have ordered at the wrong price again, holding up processing. Or your supplier may be closed down for vacation or by a strike. Take nothing for granted. If you manufacture, delay on any single component can hold up your production, increase your labor costs by slowing production and prevent you from shipping. Often, if one supplier falls down in delivery and you know, you can get almost immediate delivery from an *alternate* source. Try to keep a supplier file with a card for each of two alternate suppliers to be used.

When you're caught in a hold-up of one part, it can be quite costly. It's usually better to pay sharply more if necessary for immediate shipment of the needed component. The same goes for rush shipment. Courier services (find them in the yellow pages) offer to pick up at one end, rush to the airport, pick up at the airport at this end and rush to you. It's expensive and often slower than expected, but it usually improves delivery of a desperately needed part. If you import a component, it's good to have an alternate, higher-priced source nearby in the U.S. that you can use for emergency fill-in orders. Advance and contingency planning can go a long way to insure prompt shipping without over investment in inventory.

It is possible to make a fortune in mail order without ever owning one cent of inventory. It requires using a drop-shipper. A drop-shipper stocks inventory, allows you to draw on his inventory and will actually ship individual mail orders for you. You simply receive the orders and have labels typed and forwarded to your drop-shipper.

There are many trustworthy drop-shippers. A good friend of mine has sold millions of dollars of indoor plants where he has actually put the drop-shipper's address in the mail order coupon and directed all orders to the drop-shipper. He has trusted the drop-shipper to bank the checks, type the orders, ship and send him his share of money without any verification. Year after year, the relationship has worked and prospered mutually. My friend has confined his activities to creating and speculating on advertising.

You may very well find someone you can trust too. Just be careful! We have used drop-shippers dozens of times to great advantage, but we have been badly hurt several times where our judgment of character was poor.

It's important to be vigilant. One time years ago, we successfully sold over one million dollars of nursery plants in several months time. One nursery supplied us with one nursery item and drop-shipped for us. Another did the same for a different item. We did about $500,000 on each. Our mail order tests were successful and so were our projections. The orders poured in. In several months, we made over $300,000 profit, and we were most content.

We had worked extremely hard on the entire campaign. We particularly thoroughly checked the plants, the growers and their reputations. To the lesser known of the two nurseries, we sent an employee who stayed for three months and personally checked each day that shipments were made, and they were . . . perfectly.

The other grower was, beyond dispute, of high reputation, president of his regional growers association and the third generation of a long-trusted family. We felt it an insult to send an employee to check on him daily. He assured us all would be fine. But he *did not ship.* We took in over $500,000 in cash, paid for all our advertising, sent an advance payment, made a success in every way and faced disaster because of a gentleman's failure to keep his word.

He shipped a fraction of our orders that spring. After that, it was too late. One of our greatest creative star alumni (then my partner) wrote a masterpiece of direct mail follow-up. It got enough customers to accept shipment next fall to save us from being wiped out. We refunded the balance.

Lesson! Assume *nothing* is done unless you check and verify that the action is completed.

Unstable people under disastrous financial emergency conditions will do almost anything. One drop-shipper of a one-dollar item swore he shipped every order he received from us, but claimed the local post office had a series of thefts. We refunded over $15,0000 to angry people who never received their merchandise. We had endless correspondence, we upset our relations with the media advertised in–and we believe the drop-shipper was the thief. We never got our money back. On another occasion, the drop-shipper swore he was shipping promptly. He finally confessed he hadn't and promptly went bankrupt. In this case, we retrieved the actual orders, secured merchandise elsewhere and shipped ourselves. But we lost advances for shipping sent to him with the orders.

My advice is to work with a drop-shipper you know *well* and trust *entirely.* Then check up on him constantly. Get the post office or UPS receipts of shipment. If in big volume, keep someone on his premises. I recommend *against* selling a wide variety of items this way, using a considerable number of drop-shippers. Control is almost impossible. It's too complex. You're almost sure to have some drop-shippers let you down, and it *can close you down.*

If your strength is in mail order promotion, if you lack space and facilities, if you don't want the detail, drop-shipping can be very sound policy. But protect yourself as suggested.

A retail store or famous catalog house has a known guarantee policy. If great emphasis is placed on the guarantee of any one item, the inference is that its *other* items are not equally guaranteed. Therefore, a store or catalog prefers to make its return and refund policy crystal clear and known to apply to all products unless under special circumstances. The possible need of *servicing,* for instance, requires a special guarantee commitment for a specific product. A mail order moonlighter needs to establish a guarantee policy, too. Being unknown, it is important to make that policy clear in advertising and more than live up to it. He needs to emphasize it for each item.

For lower-priced items, we don't question a refusal or a request for refund for *any* reason. The higher the price of the product, the more it becomes necessary to handle each request in conformance to the actual terms of your guarantee.

Guarantees can be written with intent to avoid replacement or refund in practically all cases. Your desire is to be fair and reasonable. Your guarantee must be fair, specific and clear.

For more expensive items, guarantee limitations may be needed. Any product can be *misused.* Any product has a *use life.* Most products need reasonable care. To flagrantly misuse a product or give *not the simplest reasonable* care, contrary to product instruction, and still demand replacement or refund, is not reasonable.

For a higher-ticket items, the trial period should be brief. An item that can be reasonably judged upon seeing it needs a trial period of only five to 10 days. An item that can only be judged after use might require a 15 to 30-day trial period. Returns for reason of the product being defective need to be allowed for replacement or refund after a longer period. For more expensive items, we usually keep the trial period to 10 to 30 days, but we will accept a return of defective merchandise within six months to one year.

Before you determine the terms of your guarantee, write down all the possible situations that may come up. Establish specifically the kind of product damage caused by misuse of the product by the customer and by a defect of material or fault in construction. Then write a description of each of these two sets of circumstances, stating specifically what you will or will not guarantee, clearly enough to be understood by the average person.

Look over the guarantees in the advertising of equivalent competitive products. Call the trade association of the field the product is in. Discuss the guarantee policy of members. Check if the FTC has an industry advertising code covering guarantees. Check the BBB. Does it have any recommendations regarding guarantees in this product field? In particular, consider the length of the free trial after which you do not consider the product returnable except for defects of material or product workmanship. Consider the length of time or amount of use you wish the defective guarantee to cover. Consider whether you wish to limit your guarantee to replacement or to extend it to refund if desired.

If a user has eight months of good use of your product, then finds a defect covered by your guarantee and applies for recourse, will you replace with a new product or an equivalently aged used product? Will you refund the full cash paid or will you refund pro rata, based on the percentage of reasonable use life not attained? Spell it all out, and revise your guarantee accordingly. Clear it with your lawyer. Have at least 10 people read and tell you their understanding of the guarantee. You must live up to what the average person expects after reading your guarantee. You cannot take refuge in tiny type exceptions and qualifications or weasel-worded limitations that most people simply don't understand.

If your product needs servicing, your guarantee will specify it, and you must be equipped to fulfill the repairs and replacement of component parts needed. Here's why moonlighters should avoid such products.

You will need competent, trained personnel, capable of making repairs. You must carry an adequate inventory of all component parts. If you sell mail order only, you can do all servicing from your factory or warehouse. If you sell through the trade as well, you will be expected to set up service stations in various areas. Each must have competent personnel and an adequate stock of components. Some manufacturers turn over all servicing to independent service stations, in order to make their repairs self-liquidating versus service charges to customers and to sell component parts at a normal profit. If you do, you may create a nightmare of customer complaints to you and to your valued dealers, from whom they originally bought. If so, your service stations will quit in disgust.

If a product requires servicing because of occasional defective parts or construction and you guarantee it, be fair. Absorb such servicing costs. This will average out to a certain percentage of *all* unit sales. When your sales are small and scattered and you set up servicing, this percentage will be highest. When your sales are far larger and when your service is better organized, it will be lower. It is feasible for big-volume, nationally distributed products to make money overall in servicing and replacement parts. The profit in parts replacements not guaranteed can be larger than the losses of no-charge guarantee parts replacement. But that comes later.

You are responsible for every word and comma of your advertising. Ignorance of what your product can or cannot do is no excuse. You must know its limitations, dangers and specific benefits accurately enough to write or approve advertising claims safely.

The government reactions, whether national, county or city, are usually based on common sense. You must be able to vouch for the product's safety. Tiny type disclaimers or modifiers of too strong claims are no excuse if the general effect of the overall ad on the average reader is otherwise.

Government (and BBB) people are human. They're paid in the FTC, Post Office Fraud Department, District Attorney's office and other regulatory agencies to find trouble. Catching a malefactor can be a desired accomplishment. For some, it can be good politics. They can prejudge you, form a negative opinion and act accordingly. When any government regulatory authority starts investigating anything about your advertising, they investigate everything. Suddenly their files seem to contain every advertisement you've ever run on any product you've ever sold, even the most obscure test. The most minor infraction of rules you never heard of can affect their attitude in the case against you. Your delaying tactics can only make their investigation more thorough and more urgent. You become a higher priority.

Occasionally the government is wrong. More often, it's right. In any case, it's almost always far more practical to cooperate complete-ly and instantly. Let's assume you want to cooperate, but are nervous as to what you can and cannot safely say in future advertising. If so, the best policy for some time to come is to submit future advertising to such authorities before you run it. They may not even want you to do so. But submit copy. If you're near Washington and you're submitting copy to a federal agency, go there personally. They may refuse to give a written answer, but informally give their reaction. They may say that they reserve the right to change their mind later and if so, your chang-ing copy as they suggest will be no excuse. If you know the revised copy is truthful, run it. And for every verbal suggested change, send a writ-ten answer confirming that you have changed the copy as they have suggested. Build up such a file of correspondence with the government authorities, showing a continuing and conscious desire to cooperate. If you keep your copy clean and cooperate in this way, it's very doubt-ful that you will ever again have governmental problems with your ad-vertising.

But why have trouble in the first place? Check your products and advertising thoroughly. Tell the truth. Familiarize yourself with the law on advertising the kind of products you sell. The BBB and FTC will give you information, guidelines, industry codes and even the transcribed FTC legal cases of violators. All this takes very little time. A little com-mon sense, caution and discretion should let you and your mail order business live with the government very well.

The phony price reduction is the oldest sin in retailing and in mail order. If you do it, you run into two problems: credibility and the law. A price reduction offer must be believed to be effective. If your price reduction is false, you risk prosecution by government agencies.

The accepted requirement for a legitimate price reduction claim is that sales should have taken place widely at the higher price. Adver-tising a price reduction of prepriced items almost never sold at the tick-eted price is considered fraudulent. A set-up of the original price in one or two stores or one or two limited circulation publications for a very brief period or in just part of the country is not justification for a na-tional price reduction campaign.

The Better Business Bureau and Federal Trade Commission have been through the wars in interpretation of legitimate vs. illegitimate price reduction ads. Since their attitudes change to some degree, con-sult them for latest interpretations.

If you sell on credit, and there is any interest charge, you are a lender under the "Truth in Lending Law." You must conform to the full disclosure provisions of the law, or you are violating it. Your lawyer can interpret exactly what words and phrases of disclosure will, in his opinion, conform to the law. We usually avoid charging any interest for credit or time payments when we give credit directly, rather than get into the wording required.

It is quite complex to offer time payments via a choice of credit cards. Not all credit card companies charge interest in the same manner, and state laws differ. The detailed qualifications required for all time payment interest payments seriously slow up readership and pulling power of the advertising. It's more practical to work through a single credit card company in their magazine or in a mailing to their members. The required wording is simpler.

Chapter 10

CREATING THE BUSINESS
YOU DESIRE

*Building into it stability and security
. . . pride and ethics . . . avoiding all
possible risk*

We try to do a fairly even business each month throughout the year. We are able to do so even more by mixing our mail order business with traditional distribution businesses. We have accomplished our product mix over a period of time. It will probably take you effort and time to do the same. But you will find it well worth it.

Stretching the selling season can often be done for a seasonal product. A pre-season sale will often prove profitable. Often, so will a late season sale. A spring item can sometimes do a good winter business in the south. A seasonal item can also be a good Christmas item. Even more stretching can be done when mail order is used as a springboard to get into a conventional business in the trade as well. The trade selling season starts long before the mail order season and ends earlier.

Consider this question: "Is mail order secure?" In mail order, the insecurity is out there in each day's mail.

The fragility of other types of business is less apparent. A fine building, nice offices, continued paychecks and raises over several years give an air and illusion of permanence and to the employees a false feeling of security. Little do they realize how dubious that stability may be and how insecure their future income may be, or even how close they may individually be to losing their jobs. Getting that dismissal slip is always a surprise.

But in mail order, it's all glaringly apparent. Mail order results are seen immediately. They force you to take actions which give the best chance of security later. They force you to resort to *new* items and methods and keep you from drifting to disaster.

In my lifetime, I've seen America become a nation of employees of ever larger, more anonymous corporations. Today's executives seem less secure, more susceptible to sweeping economic change than their

---

341

fathers. Many of today's small businesses seem on the verge of disappearing into the maws of larger ones.

The art and science of mail order means *extra* security for individuals who go into it. And I've found individuals in mail order *more flexible*, less "frozen" by wildly changing conditions, more able to land on their feet at a profit and do so safely. Yes, mail order can be very "secure."

Can you make money in mail order in an honorable way? Mail order simply involves using the United States Government to ship your product or deliver your advertising literature.

Of course, some "mail order" today is really advertised in many ways, not by mail or delivered by United Parcel Service or some other Post Office method. But the Post Office usually still delivers the order, although more and more even the "mail order" comes by telephone. But none of this makes mail order shady. Only the people in mail order and the way they operate can do so. Only you and your associates, by choice of product, writing, authorizing or approval of copy, use of art, layout or TV presentation can make mail order sneaky fraud or the most authentic offer of top quality and presentation.

There have been and are shady people in mail order, and many, many more highly honorable people, in the same proportion as in any other field. Firm after firm sells by mail, with taste and restraint, products they are proud of, making good money. And you can too.

Too often, a newcomer to mail order believes that the right mail order technique can sell anything. And often an enthusiastic mail order advertising man believes this too. This approach does not give enough *respect* for the *product itself*.

A poor quality product can be sold profitably by mail order before the word gets out. But selling it is building on sand. A good product will *satisfy* the customer and create a *repeat* customer for other mail order items from you. Satisfied customers will build a list that will pull so well that list rentals become an important part of your income. A good product can be sold to quality catalogs and syndicated with successful advertising for inserts and solo mailings of top mail order advertisers. A quality product can build a store distribution business launched with the aid of mail order. Such a business can grow year after year, long after your mail order has stopped.

A business or individual with a fine quality mail order product, but no mail order experience, can usually find an expert to help market it profitably. But a mail order expert whose product does not live up to claims can rarely find a way to convert the shoddy product into a quality one.

Work and expense is the same for a good or bad product. *Respect* your product; look for the best product you can live with for life. Anyone who believes that the mail order marketing technique is *all*-important rarely attempts to *improve* the product. We concentrate on businesses where we have a reasonable expectation of constant product improvement. We never regret royalties if the inventor or author can constantly help improve his original work.

Each of our family has had certain pet items in our business. For years–and now–my son's life revolves around our inflatable boats. He drove a Volkswagon camper full of boats to different whitewater locations, up to Maine, down to Pennsylvania, west to Colorado, south to the Rio Grande. In between, he tested our different boats on weekends in the ocean or on Long Island Sound. Now he knows our product as few do, and each year he helps design new changes.

Our inventors keep us up on fishing lures. My wife concentrates on lure quality control. I like our advertising agency business. For whatever we do, we try to hire experts, or equivalent enthusiasts who can become experts, to take in partners who can do this or to get out of the business. We'd rather match our mail order expertise with an advertising client who *is* a specialist in one of these fields and can constantly improve the product.

Would you like to sell your product to mail order people? Perhaps you're a salesman and would like to marry mail order to *your* skills and take no promotional risk at all. Or you may have never sold anything in your life. You may be intrigued by mail order but want to avoid the promotional risk. Perhaps you feel at home in investing a little money in inventory or even quite simple manufacturing, if someone else will promote your product.

If you get a free write-up, or several, for your item and get orders, you want to go further, but without promotional risk. Let's hope you have a "protected" item, preferably patented, and at least not easy to duplicate. Seek out the catalog houses particularly suited to your item.

By selling to any catalog, you are getting a mail order test *free*. You must be able to produce stock as needed, but you're not gambling one cent for promotion. The copy you have prepared for the shopping column and the photo is ample to show them, plus a sample. The catalog house may sharply *improve* your presentation in their catalog. Often they will take entirely new photographs at their expense to better dramatize your product. You're not only benefitting from the test they're giving you, but also from their creative work. If it works for one catalog, it will work for others. However, it may pay to give your first catalog house an exclusive, allowing them to feature it in advertising elsewhere (if the test works).

And if it works in catalogs, submit it to department stores for featuring in *their* catalogs or in cooperative newspaper ads. Your success with the catalog house may influence them favorably. Selling catalog and department stores your own item, you should be able to get a gross profit of 25% or better of your sale price to them.

Next approach the mail order divisions of various magazines. Many magazines have their own mail order departments. Each has specific ideas about the kinds of items desired. And each can give you your mail order start at no risk to you, and often in surprising volume.

If a catalog sells more of your product than its break-even quota of sales for the space used, you may have something. If it sells a lot more, you've got a hit. Now you have a chance to get far bigger sales without any promotional risk. The catalog house *will* probably repeat your item in future catalogs and may wish to promote it in other ways. You may get your item in more catalogs appropriate to your item. Now you can approach mail order firms who can promote your item in media beyond a catalog.

Be realistic and objective. Be sure your item really was successful for the first catalog. Why waste your time trying to persuade another mail order firm to do something it shouldn't do? Put yourself in the mail order man's shoes. Did your product really make a profit for the first catalog, after payment for it to you, carrying its share of catalog printing and mailing costs and allowing for returns?

When you speak to other mail order firms, don't exaggerate–just tell the truth. You can make a one-time sale with misleading information about your product's sales, but then you're through. Tell the truth, and the results for the mail order firm with your product will bear you out. You'll be trusted. And your statement that a new product of yours made a profit for someone will get you a new order from a firm to whom you gave an earlier success.

Master mail order if you want to sell the maximum to mail order people. The more you know about mail order, the more you can sell to mail order firms. Keep your eye out for old molds and dies that you can get rights for. Find out if, before being discontinued, one of these items was sold to mail order firms. If so, try to revive it by getting a free shopping column write-up with orders coming to you. Often it will revive. Find out if your item has had any previous history, however old, of success in any way that would interest a mail order firm. If imported, it could have been a success in demonstration or mail order in another country. Or if domestic, it might have been here. Check to see if any product directly competitive to yours has successfully sold via mail order.

As you develop trust and respect in your dealings with mail order customers, you can submit such suggestions and get a serious hearing. Offer to contribute an attractive extra discount to a mail order customer who tests a new item for you, but check with your lawyer that you can do it legally. Get your business by selling new money-making mail order items to mail order people and *keeping them from buying mail order failures*. It's your responsibility if you want to be welcomed back.

Be discreet. Don't gossip to one mail order customer about another. Keep confidences. If a mail order customer gives you a mail order hit, cooperate to give him first chance to make money from it.

Should you give a mail order exclusive? It can be very simple and profitable to have one exclusive mail order marketer for your product or even for all of them. If you want to concentrate on acquiring and developing products and also creating advertising and promotion for them, it's nice to have a relationship with a mail order firm that will gamble its money to buy and project them. But how do you find the right marketer to marry?

The pioneer who proved you had an item should get first consideration for an exclusive. But the only reason to give anyone an exclusive is if the mail order firm can give you far more volume and profit than selling through a number of firms. Your original customer whose ad worked may have no interest in running it widely, no money to do so or lack of know-how and facilities. Your customer may be a small catalog house running only a small amount of other advertising. Your original customer may advertise very heavily in one form of advertising and scarcely at all in others.

Once his reorders have indicated to you that you have a hit, talk to him, size up the situation and decide what to do. Usually a hit one place will work every equivalent place. Don't rush into an exclusive. Don't upset your original customer by offering your item to those of his competitors he seems most concerned about. Judiciously seek out other mail order firms, not too competitive to your first customer, give each a taste of your success, get to know them and consider which is best for an exclusive relationship.

You want a firm that's aggressive and fast moving to get the business while it's still around, and perhaps before one of *your* competitors gets a smell of your success. You want someone who's honest, with integrity, who will not test your product and expand with his own. You want a firm that's strong financially, so you can sleep nights after getting your new, big (perhaps biggest) customer. You want a firm that you can live with and get along with, so a lot depends on how you *like* each other. Have lunch with the key men of the different firms. Get to know them. Find out who sells to them. Phone their suppliers and ask how each is making out. Finally, listen to and compare the volume discount each mail order firm may ask for. And when you've found the right one, start the courtship.

The more you master mail order, the more you can understand the kind of items your customer can best sell, and the faster you can acquire or develop them.

An exclusive can be for a limited time, for a single or specific item or for a single form of advertising. We have always retained store distribution and foreign rights. You may have a detailed contract or do business on a handshake. I've often found the handshake the best. I recommend an informal exclusive without a commitment beyond several months–but extending as long as mutually desired. There will be a time when the exclusive arrangement will have maximum mutual advantages and a time when the advantage of an exclusive to either party will be less desirable.

You make less money per item but avoid advertising risk. It's far simpler, with lower overhead than your normal trade sales. The heavy advertising of your mail order marketer for your products can often launch you into or increase trade sales. It can often lead to highly profitable *export* business to other mail order marketers in those countries following the lead of your U.S. mail order marketer. And this can lead to more export trade to normal markets, stimulated by the local mail order promotion of your products.

So pick your firm, make your deal and be free to part in friendship at some future time.

Chapter 11

MAIL ORDER MONEY
TROUBLES

*What can cause them . . . how to
avoid them . . . or if the need arises
. . . overcome them*

In a full-page New York Times advertisement of one of the world's largest advertising agencies, whose direct response division is headed by one of our alumni, I once read the phrase, "Direct response is no panacea."

It certainly is not. The slaughter of the mail order innocents never ceases. Large companies have mail order disasters of enormous magnitude. Countless little entrepreneurs lose their shirts every week pursuing the evasive brass ring of mail order profit. Most of those tempted by mail order, even spending good money on mail order tests, are relying on special-interest advisers trying to *sell them* something.

There are many who benefit from the constantly greater goldrush to these new mail order Klondikes. From trade publications, suppliers, advertising agencies, advisers, brokers, promoters and salesmen, the accent is on the positive to a degree that I sometimes fear for the bankroll of the newcomer. This is because in the real mail order world such dangerous misconceptions can quickly destroy you. So at the risk of discouragement, let's discuss what you are really up against before you start.

Psychologists have described the setting and mood of a supermarket as those of a party for the housewife. The housewife is said to be affected by the brightness . . . background music . . . rhythm . . . and fun of moving through . . . rolling the cart . . . almost hypnotically reaching for the packages . . . almost without will . . . and without thought of the cash register to come.

For the would-be mail order entrepreneur, the equivalent can be the endless stories of success . . . the tiny scale of the tests . . . the explosive growth . . . the sheer *speed* of success . . . and the fifty-billion dollar *enormity* of today's estimated direct response market.

The truth is that mail order is almost as fast as betting on a horse and even more risky for many people. Yet it need not be. Tiny tests cannot cause huge losses. Caution and dogged thoroughness can avoid much test risk before taking each.

You can be surprisingly safe if you mentally treat each advertising risk as a *total* loss before you take it. Regard it as a purchase of experience for a hobby. You should be able to keep making tests from time to time with losses no more than expenditure on another hobby. Yet any of these tests, if profitable and projected, could make you money and perhaps rich.

As a moonlighter, you have a tremendous advantage. Hopefully, you can live on your *regular* job income and bank your irregular mail order profits. If you need to draw income from your mail order moonlighting, draw only *part* of profits *after* you make them.

There's no reason for you to fall into any of the pitfalls I've described, now that I've pointed them out. I'm less concerned about failure to start than I am about success too soon, with too great future hopes and too little experience.

It is surprising how consistently a proper business discipline can keep up sales and profits. But surprises can occur in business, particularly in early business years, when experience has not yet prepared you for a variety of disasters that can occur, and before the disaster cushion of a strong capital reserve is built up.

Few people or companies do not have ups and downs. Simply *being* in business involves business risk. Anyone can sue you, for any reason in his head, and only costly litigation can prove him wrong. A currency devaluation can increase the money required to pay for a shipment on a boat by many thousands of dollars. Sudden inflation of product cost can catch anyone. And in these pages, I describe many mail order mishaps that have happened to me and others and it *could happen* to you. Let's hope you never get wiped out in mail order. And with prudence and a little luck, you never will. But if you dare to be in business, it could happen.

Many losses in business are self-caused and often have very little to do with business. When the Good Lord does not give us our share of natural disasters, he gives us the ability to create our own.

Losing money usually comes from ineffective working, carelessness or poor judgment. Poor judgment usually comes from failure to dig up facts, face facts or *act* on facts. Mental laziness can cause any of these situations. Another reason for loss is using business for another purpose than the simple one of making money. Using business as a way to gain love and popularity by hiring people, buying things and paying too much for either is a misuse of your business and quickly gets you out of it. Many executives and business owners I have known have thought money was their main object, but ego really was. Using business to build ego can lose money. Any personal hang-ups usually cause loss. Getting over hang-ups often starts you winning again.

Let's discuss the symptoms of going broke in mail order. When trouble comes, it can be a *combination* of troubles. Divorce, sickness and business collapse can occur almost simultaneously, each helping to cause the other. Your mail order ads don't seem to be working. Your overhead is continuing. You're drawing too much money. Yet you cannot seem to reduce overhead or personal expenses. Each expenditure seems impossible to cut. Your cash is drying up. Creditors are beginning to push. Your stomach tightens up. You're drifting from disaster to disaster and cannot seem to stop.

In mail order, there is an easy way to put off immediate disaster and make the final collapse infinitely worse. Here is what *not* to do.

Simply *buy advertising*, even when your advertisements don't pull quite enough orders to pay out. Let's assume you need 100 orders to pay out but get only 70 orders. Cash is still coming in. You pay for your merchandise and your payroll with your cash and *double* your advertising schedule. More cash comes in. There is enough to pay another payroll, the rent, for some more merchandise and the first advertising. It's the mail order version of a Ponzi operation (the famous Boston Swindler) and can only hurt others and yourself badly. But it's *so easy* to keep increasing the advertising and *hope* that things will get better that many a mail order man going broke resorts to it. Don't be tempted.

In any business, avoid borrowing unnecessary money and avoid personal guarantees like the plague. This means either to the bank or a supplier. You owe it to your spouse and children *not* to do so. Don't put up your house, insurance or any possession as collateral. If your business goes broke, you'll simply *lose* your house or whatever. Don't fail to deposit unemployment and social security trust money. Never use such monies in *any* emergency. Doing so becomes a personal loan from the government. That plus interest will later be remorselessly collected, however desperate your circumstances may be.

Let's presume you're determined to pay off every creditor every cent. To do so, you must preserve from the wreckage every possible asset of your business. You must not mortgage yourself to individual creditors. You must keep free to pay the kindest creditor as well as the roughest. You must take to the lifeboat in time. You must fight to survive against creditors in order to pay creditors.

Few in disaster can fully realize the *strengths* of their situation. Doing so is the first step back. However bad your situation, however tangled your affairs, you have lost the battle but not yet the war. However successful you may ever be, there is no security, and you can be wiped out tomorrow. But only surrender to *perpetual failure* can keep you from rising again.

However discouraged and disheartened you may be, realize that disaster is *temporary*. Good things can and will happen again. Write down the good things about your situation and don't forget them. Do not in any way be concerned with what others may think of your temporary failure. I have been congratulated and envied for my success when I was in my most desperate hours and commiserated with and pitied when my next boom was already in full swing. Others rarely know about your affairs and even less frequently care. Even if your troubles are publicized, they have far less interest to others than you think. And to those who really know you, your rebound from difficulty will gain all the more respect.

Every step in business success tends to increase business inefficiency. The faster the success, the more this is so. And many business disasters have the seeds of far greater future business success. Every drastic slash in expenses lays the groundwork for a tighter, tougher, more efficient operation in the future. I remember in my worst days walking to work in New York City past the newest building activity. I noticed that the *deepest* holes were dug to build the *tallest* buildings. And properly analyzed and acted upon, the greatest difficulty you may be in can lead to your far greater future success.

Don't *drift!* Don't *freeze!* Don't *panic!* Don't *dream!* Tomorrow . . . next week . . . next month . . . the results of your next test, your newest projection, your greatest hopes must be analyzed coldly . . . suspiciously . . . objectively. Make an estimate of the situation. Set deadlines for successive emergency actions if the hoped-for next hit does not occur. Then take the actions. Fire the personnel, cancel the lease, take your children out of private school, do what has to be done. Don't be concerned about status, personally or for your business.

Changes in your personal and business life which you may have considered impossible will simply occur. You may cut down from a floor to a one-room office and from a beautiful home to a furnished room. But when you do so, you're already on the road back. You may lose inventory, equipment, furniture and personal possessions. You may lose your house or the business itself and still be taking your first steps to new success. Accept your situation. Start planning your comeback. You will find that in some way you will eat and feed your family, keep a roof over your family's head and have some effective working time.

If you preserve your business in simplified form, you'll *have* to fire "indispensable" employees. Business will still go on. Employees you felt responsible for and worried about will get a better job. You'll find that the standards you set as a minimum for your family can be cut and cut again. I've seen many fight to preserve a way of life they struggled hard to attain. But I've seen the fastest rebound for those who adjusted to their difficulty, dropped out of clubs, moved away from expensive suburbs and stripped down to their new situation.

Often only business difficulties can make a man of you in business, and lessons learned can be acquired in no other way. Water will seek its own level. You must first live within your reduced business and personal income and then make your new start, rising from the mail order ashes. All you have to remember is that you are starting over.

The degree of your disaster determines the number of rungs you must drop back. You may be able to keep a stripped-down operation and live within its income. You may have to submerge your business within others and become a partner. You may have signed personal guarantees and be so pursued by creditors that you cannot personally own anything without it's being immediately seized. You may have to work on commission, turning your business over to others with a verbal option to convert to an ownership partner for nothing paid. You may lose all and have to work for someone else in another field and make a new start as a mail order moonlighter.

But life will go on. Your main assets will be your know-how, experience and working habits. You will have to seek a money partner on some basis. But remember: You will be able to make the biggest contribution. With your know-how, you can come up with items, copy presentations, media negotiation, and profit creation that perhaps your partner cannot. No matter how hard creditors press you, you will find a way to go on. First monies earned will go for survival, personal and business. Only gradually will you be able to parcel out creditor payments. They will not be able to accept, nor will you, the fundamental fact of life that a business mess takes a long time to clean up. You may have to go personally bankrupt to get relief, but this is highly unlikely. Some creditors won't trouble you at all. Others will gradually give up their efforts. And the worst and toughest will have to accept the fact that unless you go personally bankrupt you must make such minimum payments regardless of the effect on your personal life. But time will pass, and your situation will improve, and can do so at any time with lightning speed.

Because the sum of all your previous experience, sharpened and honed by adversity, is there, ready at any time to apply itself to the new opportunity . . . that opportunity will surely come.

Chapter 12

THE MAIL ORDER
REVOLUTION

*Getting in on it . . . associating with
the best . . . keeping up with change
. . . attaining lifelong benefits*

If it's so tough, how in the world do so many people get rich in it? Because mail order is an art and a science that can be mastered. It's a way to start out with virtually no money and end up with big money. It's a way for the smallest venture to make it in a big-time world.

There is risk in mail order, as in your own business of any kind, and as in life. From the first breath out of the womb to the last expiring one, there is risk in simply living. We try to warn and caution our children and yet not overworry them. In this exploratory trip with you through the mail order world, I've tried to do the same.

In mail order, with a little caution, there is little chance of real disaster. There is great opportunity, a wonderful chance for a better life and a great deal of fun. And in employed lives, there is *more* risk. There is risk of being fired and risk of a slower, lifetime failure of our hopes.

Reasons for failure are often all too simple. In youth, we want to enjoy the moment, and we rob our future. In middle life, we get bogged down in getting through the week, catching up on bills and trying to escape it all. In later life, terrified by the ticking of life's clock, we dream of a last minute coup to change our fortunes, but feel it's too late to make a long-term push in a new direction.

Yet Youth need not wait 20 years to make a fortune.

The man or woman in middle life can escape his or her troubles with a mail order money-making hobby just as effectively as with a tool shop, travel or big wardrobe, and have an easier life thereafter.

Those later in life can be late business bloomers, even in their sixties or thereafter. In tennis, the old players, by control and placement, can make the young and strong run. The young and strong have all the advantages, but they don't use them. If you're older, take it easy. Use the hidden assets you've accumulated. Realize that, regardless of needs and wants and the quick passing of remaining years, you can only correct your situation gradually. You may still make it in mail order.

Anyone successful in anything may well accelerate that success in mail order. Anyone who has failed in anything may get a new start. Right now is a wonderful time to do so.

It is growing. As huge as mail order and direct response is today, everything points to its faster future growth. Computers, cable TV and telephone marketing alone will cause mail order volume to soar even faster. And variations of credit cards and computerized no-cash ways of transferring cash from your bank to seller of product or service without checks can only make mail order grow still more.

Many consider mail order the last frontier for the tiny venture, a frontier as open to anyone as was the frontier that made America. Anyone *could* make it on the old frontier. It was the safety valve for failure elsewhere. Yet many *did fail* to make it, just as many fail to make it on the new frontier of mail order.

Those who failed were generally quite ill prepared for the real frontier or unwilling or unable to work at it. Those who tried to get rich quick with no knowledge of frontier conditions failed most quickly. Those who succeeded most often applied their past experience and know-how effectively to the new conditions. Basque sheepherders headed for Boise, Idaho, and did what *they* were good at–sheepherding. Swedes, Norwegians and Finns took off for the North Woods of Minnesota and did what they were good at–farming. Carpenters, brewery workers, doctors, lawyers, bakers or whoever used past experience in new places and ways. From the days of John Smith, those who failed to use past experience and skills or who had *nothing* to contribute to the frontier, no background or skills, and no willingness to acquire them and work, often did badly.

It's pretty much the same in mail order today. Success will come fastest to those who apply to mail order effective advantages they possess, develop a "feel" for it and work at it.

My mail order moonlighting method can jump income and create capital all your life. I have tried to give you the facts on the real mail order world, a "feel" and sense of strategy for it. With this "feel" and sense of strategy, you can take fuller advantage of the exciting mail order technology on the way. Because while techniques never stop changing, the "feel" and sense of strategy to *use* the new techniques does not change.

Let's recap what my mail order moonlighting method is designed to do. First, to help you analyze your own suitability for and real interest in mail order.

Second, to show you how to use any special background, knowledge or abilities which you now have to give *your* mail order moonlighting method the maximum chance of success.

Third, to aid you to determine whether you are better off on your own or with a partner, and if with a partner, to help you select the right one and make the right deal with him.

Fourth, to give you enough basic know-how in different aspects of mail order and small business to help you start and grow soundly.

Fifth, to help you avoid some dangers I've observed and mistakes I have made in mail order.

Ask yourself these questions once again:

Is mail order *your* cup of tea? Should you go into it at all? Consider the psychology needed for mail order success and the psychology *not* needed.

A salesman *needs* to be cheerful, to feel good, happy, optimistic, hopeful and to spread the good news. In mail order this psychology is often excellent for creating the selling message.

For other phases of mail order a different psychology is required. The happy soul rarely wants to and almost trains himself not to hear or know any bad news. Often he does not care to get into the drab nitty gritty of everyday. How about you? Do you have an average or better I.Q., consider yourself reasonably stable, work reasonably hard and not get discouraged too easily? Anyone with too low an I.Q., too unstable a personality, too much laziness or too little heart is not going to make it in mail order, with or without my method.

Business operators must balance the optimistic with the pessimistic, cheerful hope with dour suspicion of what might be wrong or might be about to be wrong or even could conceivably become wrong. In this way, they can often prevent or correct disaster.

Do you have a money sense? If you pay too much for your items, either to buy or manufacture them, you will lose money. If your overhead is too high or your own draw too great, you will lose money. If you purchase inventory you later don't sell or buy advertising that doesn't produce sufficient money, you will lose money. If you don't have a feeling for money matters, have you a plan to compensate for this lack? Can you capitalize in mail order on your business or professional background or hobbies and interests? It can be a tremendous help.

This is so if you work in business, a profession, an institution or in government. It is so whether you are in white collar or blue collar work, whether you're starting out or retired, whether you're a housewife, in a service trade, in the retail business or whatever. A newcomer to mail order may be a teacher, a salesman, a bank executive or whatever and have some experience and background quite helpful for future mail order success. With no business experience, a housewife, student or anyone may have a special hobby or interest suited to mail order.

A lady math teacher whom I know invented a dice game to help her students master math principles faster and more thoroughly. Her husband, an electronic sales executive, helped her set up and operate a mail order business to sell the game to other math teachers and to schools. Operating frugally and in small volume on a moonlighting basis, the couple made over $20,000 in the next few months. They adapted the mail order ad first to a Brentano Book Store ad and then to an ad in the F.A.O. Schwarz Toy Catalog. They never unduly gambled in overhead or inventory. They did not need to draw their living from the business. They didn't want to build an empire. They simply sold out to a major game company within a year or so of starting up. Now they're off on their next project to *repeat* the pattern. I've seen this sort of thing happen again and again. They limited their objectives to the easily achievable. Can you?

What is your job or profession? Are you good at it? If so, in what ways are you better than others in it? How can your know-how apply to mail order in your present field? Is there any *trend* in your field which you see developing that is still quite new? Do you know of any product or service in your field which is *better* than competitive products or services?

If your job is boring and you've learned to apply it to mail order, let's consider your hobbies and interests. Are you good at any activity, from cooking to working with tools, any sport or game? If you are, can you apply what you know? Do you have any ideas for better backpacking equipment, new recipes, different and original creative stitchery designs or projects to keep children happy?

If you have no hobbies, interests or sports, do you have a natural curiosity? If so, do you notice new and different developments, new products and new ventures? Do you know of one that seems better than others, but is not yet off the ground?

Do you travel? Do you ever notice interesting products or services in another country but not yet here, or in part of the U.S. but not distributed nationally? Do you have any ideas of different and better ways of doing anything? Do you use anything that you find quite superior to any other way of doing the same thing, yet not widely known? Do you feel sure of yourself going into mail order on your own, or will you be better off with partners? If so, whom can you get as a partner? Do you have friends or even casual acquaintances who have talent or ideas in any of these directions? Could you team up with them in a venture?

Some who have asked me about mail order in my lifetime were *not*, by themselves, suited to it and were best persuaded not to go into it, except with the right partner. Do you have a friend with any advantage to contribute to a mail order business? A retail store owner sees which new items sell best. In a large city, a retail store may be able to buy newspaper advertising substantially below the cost to national advertisers, including mail order advertisers. A talented copywriter as a partner can make you rich. A shrewd buyer of advertising can do the same. A printer as a partner may gamble unused press time. A venture that failed may have molds or dies that you can obtain for no cash on a partnership basis. A programmer has a tremendous edge.

A little analysis of your own experience, background and interests can best show you whether you're better off to be on your own or to match *your* expertise with others in any of the many forms of profitable association possible.

I've tried to get across to you the basic know-how you need. I've spelled out the potentials, limitations, dangers and requirements of the real mail order world. What I have described may be more effort than you care to make or seem too risky for your situation. If so, mail order may not be for you.

If you're willing to go ahead, knowing the odds against you and the effort and discipline required, don't worry *too much* about the mail order difficulties and losses which I have described.

In all probability, you will not encounter anything so difficult. But a little worry in time about a possible disaster can be the first step to preventing it. Forewarned *is* forearmed. Let us hope that you may easily avoid any such mishap by recognizing what is coming. In any business, including mail order, each company must have a reason for being: to survive and prosper.

Those who are tempted into the mail order business to make easy money fast, but have no real reason to be in it, will easily lose their money fast. Your background, your previous skills, your way of thinking and working, your common sense, your overall suitability to mail order or that of your associates must justify your being in the business. You simply must have or develop a "feel" for it. You must have special advantages or be able to develop them to survive and succeed. This entire course is an attempt to help you find a place where you feel you "fit in" this fascinating business, your own personal mail order raison d'etre or reason for being. Mail order is growing fast. It can be an aid to your career.

To be in mail order, you should be good at *something* that can contribute to your mail order success. You should not associate with anyone who is not *equally* good or better in any area you feel weak in. I'm a bit of an egotist and like to feel I have acquired top mail order know-how and ability. If I team up with anyone, a sales manager, fashion expert, manufacturing supervisor, agency client, supplier, partner, royalty inventor or author, I like to feel I've got the best.

Dead wood can be a very heavy load. Mediocrity in associates is a constant brake on *your* potential. Patience with a poor supplier, less than competent inventor, goof-off employee, inadequate anybody is a tax on every competent associate and employee you have and on your family. Your family may stand for it. Others will not.

So be careful with any association. Keep an escape hatch open so that no proven poor association becomes a lifetime mortgage on you and your family. Make the best associations you can. Get out of proven bad ones and try again.

As soon as you run your first successful mail order item "once around the track," much of the confusion you may feel about mail order will disappear. Once you get that first mail order success, you'll find ways to repeat the success again and again. You'll be inclined to stick to what is working as much as possible. This will affect the items you select in the future and how you sell them. And now the experience of others will help you apply your first success to your next. New techniques and methods, as fast as you learn them, will multiply your chances of success further.

Once you have confidence, doubts disappear. Your decisions become surer. You work faster. You've had a chance to see what you're good at and *not* good at, the activities you like and *dislike.* You have a much better idea as to whether you can compensate for weakness by acquiring certain, specific know-how, by staying away from certain kinds of mail order businesses or items, by turning over certain activities to suppliers, by hiring employees strong where you are weak or by seeking a partner or partners to supply those extra strengths. You're getting a "feel" for what you should do and how you should operate in each aspect of mail order.

Mastering any hobby often yields benefits all your life. When you make a hobby of making money and master it, benefits can come lifelong, *in cash.* You may find that you can apply your mail order know-how in some way in any business field. Success in mail order can make you more successful in any other business in retail, wholesale, manufacturing and other areas. It can make you a better executive, manager, partner or business owner.

You may choose, as we did, to *use* mail order to build distribution businesses, or sell only by mail. You may choose to sell just by radio, only via credit cards, only for cash, just via direct mail (even to only highly responsive lists). You may be able to set up the kind of special niche operation that can be the safest form of mail order. It may keep you busy profitably for years to come, such as a joint venture with just one big consumer publication, broadcaster or group of trade publications.

Sometimes you can get started in mail order *without* a penny's risk and then make money continuously. All that is required is willingness to *share* mail order profits with others, *patience* with a slower pace of profit for yourself and *understanding* that you are dependent on the cooperation of others.

Keep on the look-out for the right new item. It may be anywhere. My eyes and ears are drawn as by a magnet to any mail order advertising. Any article in any show or store flashes a mail order red or green light at me when I first see it. And it will for you, too, as you get a "feel" for it. Be cautious about testing. Don't be premature about projecting. Take full advantage of each test success.

Remember to be thorough in research and never stop improving your copy and layouts. Be painstaking in your media selection. Remember always to seek a special advantage to help you survive and succeed. Large mail order advertisers get their "edge" from maximum discount contracts for advertising, buying each advertisement for less.

They also get protected back cover and other premium positions in publications or the equivalent in broadcasting. They often "lock-in" these "position franchises" year after year.

A special relationship with a publication, television station, radio station or printer may give lower-cost or less-risk advertising to a large (or small) mail order firm. For giant mailers, one to ten-million-piece mailings slash costs of everything but postage. This gives the giants mail order profits not possible for others. Find yours.

Be a competitor. Don't expect to win the very first time. In any competition, more lose than win. Most winners must first lose before winning regularly. Most stars must start in the bush leagues. Anyone with any aptitude for any activity who concentrates on it gets better at it than those who don't. In mail order, as in anything else, you must train to become a winner.

Don't be afraid of the giants. The very formula for success of giant companies now creates niches of success for small ones. The giants play it safe and concentrate on safe winners and big chances for success. They concentrate on shorter and shorter lines. They copy each other. Even the giant companies that go into mail order tend to go into the same items, run the same types of ads, mail to the same lists and leave vast areas untapped for you.

Beware of mail order quack "expert" advice. Any specific advice to select a certain article, sell it at a certain price, use certain "sure thing" forms of advertising, create advertising in a certain "foolproof" way, almost any *simple and certain* advice to make money almost automatically disappoints a newcomer in mail order.

Avoid simplistic, get-rich-quick mail order courses, books or schemes of any kind. Their trademark is the absence of any difficulty. They take advantage of those least qualified. They *give* even those who would otherwise have a chance advice that can often be a recipe for losing money in mail order. Rather than being professionals in mail order, they are professionals in getting people into mail order the wrong way with the least chance.

But once you know that you are in the mail order business to stay, keep up with mail order change. The most successful mail order men and women never stop learning. Once you start making mail order money, the cost of keeping up with the latest changes is trifling in comparison. Professionals feel that taking time out to keep up to date is a requirement of being professional and can return the small costs involved many times over. They keep on learning from the leaders.

Don't expect mail order to *give* you a fortune on a silver platter with no thought, plan or work on your part. But give mail order a chance. Many, many others succeed in it and are happy in it, with all its limitations. And never stop learning. There's information on help for you of every conceivable variety. In my book, Mail Order Know-How, I list almost 900 help sources.

In my books, I have written as I have personally talked with those who have come to me with no knowledge of mail order. Many have later graduated into their own mail order enterprises. I have always been interested in the later success of each. It's been a pleasure writing this book to you, and I am interested in your success as well. Please write me after you read my book. Tell me whether it has benefitted you or if you have found shortcomings and what you consider them to be.

Good luck to you. The mail order world, for all its big opportunity, is like a village. I welcome you as a neighbor in that village.